Undergraduate Topics in Computer Science

D1518425

Undergraduate Topics in Computer Science (UTiCS) delivers high-quality instructional content for undergraduates studying in all areas of computing and information science. From core foundational and theoretical material to final-year topics and applications, UTiCS books take a fresh, concise, and modern approach and are ideal for self-study or for a one- or two-semester course. The texts are all authored by established experts in their fields, reviewed by an international advisory board, and contain numerous examples and problems. Many include fully worked solutions.

More information about this series at http://www.springer.com/series/7592

Kent D. Lee · Steve Hubbard

Data Structures and Algorithms with Python

 Springer

Kent D. Lee
Steve Hubbard
Luther College
Decorah, IA
USA

Series editor
Ian Mackie

ISSN 1863-7310   ISSN 2197-1781   (electronic)
ISBN 978-3-319-13071-2   ISBN 978-3-319-13072-9   (eBook)
DOI 10.1007/978-3-319-13072-9

Library of Congress Control Number: 2014953918

Springer Cham Heidelberg New York Dordrecht London

Springer is part of Springer Science+Business Media (www.springer.com)

Preface

Thanks for choosing *Data Structures and Algorithms with Python*. This text was written based on classroom notes for two courses, an introductory data structures and algorithms course and an advanced data structures and algorithms course. The material contained in this text can be taught in two semesters. The early chapters in this text are intended as an introductory text for data structures and algorithms, while the later chapters cover advanced topics that are suitable for the second course in data structures and algorithms. The Python language is used throughout the text and some familiarity with Python or some other object-oriented language is assumed. However, the first chapter contains a Python primer for those coming from a different language background.

This text serves well as a follow-on text to *Python Programming Fundamentals* by Kent D. Lee and published by Springer, but does not require you to have read that text. In this text the next steps are taken to teach you how to handle large amounts of data efficiently. A number of algorithms are introduced and the need for them is motivated through examples that bring meaning to the problems we face as computer programmers. An algorithm is a well-defined procedure for accomplishing a task. Algorithms are an important part of Computer Science and this text explores many algorithms to give you the background you need when writing programs of your own. The goal is that having seen some of the sorts of algorithms presented in this text, you will be able to apply these techniques to other programs you write in the future.

Another goal of this text is to introduce you to the idea of computational complexity. While there are many unique and interesting algorithms that we could explore, it is important to understand that some algorithms are more efficient than others. While computers are very good at doing calculations quickly, an inefficient algorithm can make the fastest computer seem very slow or even make it appear to come to a halt. This text will show you what can and cannot be computed efficiently. The text builds this idea of efficiency from the most basic of facts giving you the tools you will need to determine just how efficient any algorithm is so you can make informed judgements about the programs you write.

The text assumes that you have some prior experience in computer programming, probably from an introductory programming course where you learned to break simple problems into steps that could be solved by a computer. The language you used may have been Python, but not necessarily. Python is an excellent language for a text on data structures and algorithms whether you have used it before or not. Python is an object-oriented programming language with operator overloading and dynamic typing. Whether this is your first exposure to Python or you used it in your first course, you will learn more about the language from this text. The first chapter of the text reviews some of the fundamentals of computer programming along with the basic syntax of Python to get you up to speed in the language. Then subsequent chapters dive into more advanced topics and should be read in sequence.

At the beginning of every chapter the goals of the chapter are stated. At the end of every chapter is a set of review questions that reinforce the goals of the chapter. These review questions are followed in each chapter by a few programming problems that relate to the chapter goals by asking you to use the things you learned in the chapter and apply them to a computer program. You can motivate your reading of a chapter by first consulting the review questions and then reading the chapter to answer them. Along the way, there are lots of examples to illustrate the concepts being introduced.

We hope you enjoy the text! If you have any questions or comments please send them to kentdlee@luther.edu.

Kent D. Lee
Steve Hubbard

For Teachers

A typical introductory data structures course covers the first seven chapters of this text. Chapter 1 introduces Python programming and the Tkinter module which is used in various places in the text. Tkinter comes with Python, so no special libraries need be installed for students to use it. Tkinter is used to visualize many of the results in this text.

Chapter 2 introduces complexity analysis and depending on your needs, some of the material in Chap. 2 could be skipped in an introductory data structures course. In particular, the material on Θ notation and amortized complexity can be skipped. Big-Oh notation is enough for the first seven chapters. Typically, Chap. 7 is covered lightly and near the end of a semester course. It seems there is generally not enough time in a semester to cover graph theory in much detail.

Advanced courses in data structures and algorithms should start with Chap. 1 if students are unfamiliar with Python or Tkinter. A brief refresher may not be bad even for those that have programmed using Python before. Chapter 2 should be covered in detail including the material on Θ notation and amortized complexity.

Some review of hashing as it is used in sets and maps in Chap. 5 may be good review earlier in the advanced course along with a brief discussion of binary search trees and tree traversals in Chap. 6. Depending on your needs, Chap. 7 would be a good chapter to cover next including the material on depth first search of a graph.

Chapter 8 is where the advanced material begins with assumptions made that students understand the concepts presented in the earlier chapters. The two introductory chapters along with Chaps. 8–12 make a seven-chapter sequence that will fill a semeseter in an advanced course nicely.

This text is very project oriented. Solutions for all projects are available from Kent D. Lee. You can contact Kent at kentdlee@luther.edu for instructor solutions. You must provide proof (through a website or other reference) that you are an instructor at an educational institution to get access to the instructor materials.

If you have any suggestions or find any errors in the text, please let us know by emailing Kent at kentdlee@luther.edu. Thanks and we hope you enjoy using the text in your course!

Kent D. Lee
Steve Hubbard

Credits

Connect Four is referenced in Chaps. 4, 12 and Appendix H. Connect Four is a trademark of the Milton Bradley Company in the United States and other countries. Chapter 2 references Mac OS X. Mac and Mac OS are registered trademarks of Apple Inc., registered in the U.S. and other countries. Microsoft Windows is also referenced in Chap. 2. Windows is a registered trademark of Microsoft Corporation in the United Stated and other countries.

Contents

Python Programming 101

1

This Computer Science text further develops the skills you learned in your first CS text or course and adds to your bag of tricks by teaching you how to use efficient algorithms for dealing with large amounts of data. Without the proper understanding of efficiency, it is possible to bring even the fastest computers to a grinding halt when working with large data sets. This has happened before, and soon you will understand just how easy it can occur. But first, we'll review some patterns for programming and look at the Python programming language to make sure you understand the basic structure and syntax of the language.

To begin writing programs using Python you need to install Python on your computer. The examples in this text use Python 3. Python 2 is not compatible with Python 3 so you'll want to be sure you have Python 3 or later installed on your computer. When writing programs in any language a good Integrated Development Environment (IDE) is a valuable tool so you'll want to install an IDE, too. Examples within this text will use Wing IDE 101 as pictured in Fig. 1.1, although other acceptable IDEs are available as well. The Wing IDE is well maintained, simple to use, and has a nice debugger which will be useful as you write Python programs. If you want to get Wing IDE 101 then go to http://wingware.com. The website http://cs.luther.edu/~leekent/CS1 has directions for installing both Python 3 and Wing IDE 101. Wing IDE 101 is the free version of Wing for educational use.

There are some general concepts about Python that you should know when reading the text. Python is an interpreted language. That means that you don't have to go through any extra steps after writing Python code before you can run it. You can simply press the debug button in the Wing IDE (it looks like an insect) and it will ask you to save your program if you haven't already done so at least once. Then it will run your program. Python is also dynamically typed. This means that you will not get any type errors before you run your program as you would with some programming languages. It is especially important for you to understand the types of data you are using in your program. More on this in just a bit. Finally, your Python programs are interpreted by the Python interpreter. The shell is another name for the Python interpreter and Wing IDE 101 gives you access to a shell within the IDE

© Springer International Publishing Switzerland 2015
K.D. Lee and S. Hubbard, *Data Structures and Algorithms with Python*,
Undergraduate Topics in Computer Science, DOI 10.1007/978-3-319-13072-9_1

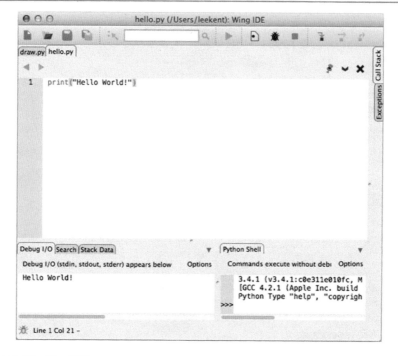

Fig. 1.1 The Wing IDE

itself. You can type Python statements and expressions into the window pane that says *Python Shell* to quickly try out a snippet of code before you put it in a program.

Like most programming languages, there are a couple kinds of errors you can get in your Python programs. Syntax errors are found before your program runs. These are things like missing a colon or forgetting to indent something. An IDE like Wing IDE 101 will highlight these syntax errors so you can correct them. Run-time errors are found when your program runs. Run-time errors come from things like variables with unexpected values and operations on these values. To find a run-time error you can look at the *Stack Data* tab as it appears in Fig. 1.1. When a run-time error occurs the program will stop executing and the *Stack Data* tab will let you examine the run-time stack where you can see the program variables.

In the event that you still don't understand a problem, the Wing IDE 101 (and most other IDEs) lets you step through your code so you can watch as an error is reproduced. The three icons in the upper right corner of Fig. 1.1 let you *Step Into* a function, *Step Over* code, and *Step Out Of* a function, respectively. Stepping over or into your code can be valuable when trying to understand a run-time error and how it occurred.

One other less than obvious tool is provided by the Wing IDE. By clicking on the line number on the left side of the IDE it is possible to set a breakpoint. A breakpoint causes the program to stop execution just before the breakpoint. From there it is possible to begin stepping over your code to determine how an error occurred.

To motivate learning or reviewing Python in this chapter, the text will develop a simple drawing application using turtle graphics and a Graphical User Interface (GUI) framework called Tkinter. Along the way, you'll discover some patterns for programming including the accumulator pattern and the loop and a half pattern for reading records from a file. You'll also see functions in Python and begin to learn how to implement your own datatypes by designing and writing a class definition.

1.1   Chapter Goals

By the end of this chapter, you should be able to answer these questions.

- What two parts are needed for the accumulator pattern?
- When do you need to use the loop and a half pattern for reading from a file?
- What is the purpose of a class definition?
- What is an object and how do we create one?
- What is a mutator method?
- What is an accessor method?
- What is a widget and how does one use widgets in GUI programming?

1.2   Creating Objects

Python is an object-oriented language. All data items in Python are objects. In Python, data items that could be thought of as similar are named by a type or class. The term *type* and *class* in Python are synonymous: they are two names for the same thing. So when you read about *types* in Python you can think of *classes* or vice versa.

There are several built-in types of data in Python including *int, float, str, list*, and *dict* which is short for dictionary. These types of data and their associated operations are included in the appendices at the end of the text so you have a quick reference if you need to refer to it while programming. You can also get help for any type by typing *help(typename)* in the Python shell, where *typename* is a type or class in Python. A very good language reference can be found at http://python.org/doc, the official Python documentation website.

1.2.1   Literal Values

There are two ways to create objects in Python. In a few cases, you can use a literal value to create an object. Literal values are used when we want to set some variable to a specific value within our program. For example, the literal 6 denotes any object with the integer value of 6.

```
x = 6
```

This creates an *int* object containing the value 6. It also points the reference called *x* at this object as pictured in Fig. 1.2. All assignments in Python point references

Fig. 1.2 A Reference and Object

at objects. Any time you see an assignment statement, you should remember that the thing on the left side of the equals sign is a reference and the thing on the right side is either another reference or a newly created object. In this case, writing $x = 6$ makes a new object and then points x at this object.

Other literal values may be written in Python as well. Here are some literal values that are possible in Python.

- *int* literals: 6, 3, 10, −2, etc.
- *float* literals: 6.0, −3.2, 4.5E10
- *str* literals: 'hi there', "how are you"
- *list* literals: [], [6, 'hi there']
- *dict* literals: { }, {'hi there':6, 'how are you':4}

Python lets you specify *float* literals with an exponent.

So, *4.5E10* represents the *float* 45000000000.0. Any number written with a decimal point is a *float*, whether there is a 0 or some other value after the decimal point. If you write a number using the *E* or exponent notation, it is a float as well. Any number without a decimal point is an *int*, unless it is written in *E* notation. String literals are surrounded by either single or double quotes. List literals are surrounded by [and]. The [] literal represents the empty list. The { } literal is the empty dictionary.

You may not have previously used dictionaries. A dictionary is a mapping of keys to values. In the dictionary literal, the key 'hi there' is mapped to the value 6, and the key 'how are you' is mapped to 4. Dictionaries will be covered in some detail in Chap. 5.

1.2.2   Non-literal Object Creation

Most of the time, when an object is created, it is not created from a literal value. Of course, we need literal values in programming languages, but most of the time we have an object already and want to create another object by using one or more existing objects. For instance, if we have a string in Python, like '6' and want to create an *int* object from that string, we can do the following.

```
y = '6'
x = int(y)
print(x)
```

In this short piece of code, *y* is a reference to the *str* object created from the string literal. The variable *x* is a reference to an object that is created by using the object that *y* refers to. In general, when we want to create an object based on other object values we write the following:

```
variable = type(other_object_values)
```

The *type* is any type or class name in Python, like *int*, *float*, *str* or any other type. The *other_object_values* is a comma-separated sequence of references to other objects that are needed by the class or type to create an instance (i.e. an object) of that type. Here are some examples of creating objects from non-literal values.

```
z = float('6.3')
w = str(z)
u = list(w) # this results in the list ['6', '.', '3']
```

1.3 Calling Methods on Objects

Objects are useful because they allow us to collect related information and group them with behavior that act on this data. These behaviors are called *methods* in Python. There are two kinds of methods in any object-oriented language: *mutator* and *accessor* methods. *Accessor* methods access the current state of an object but don't change the object. *Accessor* methods return new object references when called.

```
x = 'how are you'
y = x.upper()
print(y)
```

Here, the method *upper* is called on the object that *x* refers to. The *upper* accessor method returns a new object, a *str* object, that is an upper-cased version of the original string. Note that *x* is not changed by calling the *upper* method on it. The *upper* method is an accessor method. There are many accessor methods available on the *str* type which you can learn about in the appendices.

Some methods are mutator methods. These methods actually change the existing object. One good example of this is the *reverse* method on the *list* type.

```
myList = [1, 2, 3]
myList.reverse()
print(myList) # This prints [3, 2, 1] to the screen
```

The *reverse* method mutates the existing object, in this case the list that *myList* refers to. Once called, a mutator method can't be undone. The change or mutation is permanent until mutated again by some other mutator method.

All classes contain accessor methods. Without accessor methods, the class would be pretty uninteresting. We use accessor methods to retrieve a value that is stored in an object or to retrieve a value that depends on the value stored in an object.

If a class had no accessor methods we could put values in the object but we could never retrieve them.

Some classes have mutator methods and some don't. For instance, the *list* class has mutator methods, including the *reverse* method. There are some classes that don't have any mutator methods. For instance, the *str* class does not have any mutator methods. When a class does not contain any mutator methods, we say that the class is *immutable*. We can form new values from the data in an *immutable* class, but once an immutable object is created, it cannot be changed. Other immutable classes include *int* and *float*.

1.4   Implementing a Class

Programming in an object-oriented language usually means implementing classes that describe objects which hold information that is needed by the program you are writing. Objects contain data and methods operate on that data. A *class* is the definition of the *data* and *methods* for a specific type of *object*.

Every class contains one special method called a constructor. The constructor's job is to create an instance of an object by placing references to data within the object itself. For example, consider a class called Dog. A dog has a name, a birthday, and a sound it makes when it barks. When we create a Dog object, we write code like that appearing in Sect. 1.4.1.

1.4.1   Creating Objects and Calling Methods

```
1   boyDog = Dog("Mesa", 5, 15, 2004, "WOOOF")
2   girlDog = Dog("Sequoia", 5, 6, 2004, "barkbark")
3   print(boyDog.speak())
4   print(girlDog.speak())
5   print(boyDog.birthDate())
6   print(girlDog.birthDate())
7   boyDog.changeBark("woofywoofy")
8   print(boyDog.speak())
```

Once created in the memory of the computer, dog objects looks like those appearing in Fig. 1.3. Each object is referenced by the variable reference assigned to it, either *girlDog* or *boyDog* in this case. The objects themselves are a collection of references that point to the information that is stored in the object. Each object has name, month, day, year, and speakText references that point to the associated data that make up a Dog object.

To be able to create *Dog* objects like these two objects we need a *Dog* class to define these objects. In addition, we'll need to define *speak*, *birthDate*, and *changeBark* methods. We can do this by writing a class as shown in Sect. 1.4.2. Comments about each part of the class appear in the code. The special variable *self* always points at the current object and must be the first parameter to each method in the class.

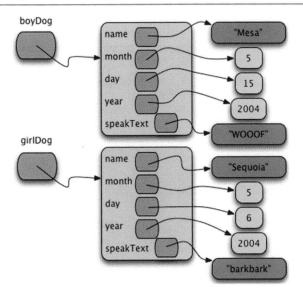

Fig. 1.3 A Couple of Dog Objects

Python takes care of passing the *self* argument to the methods. The other arguments are passed by the programmer when the method is called (see the example of calling each method in Sect. 1.4.1).

1.4.2   The Dog Class

```
1   class Dog:
2       # This is the constructor for the class. It is called whenever a Dog
3       # object is created. The reference called "self" is created by Python
4       # and made to point to the space for the newly created object. Python
5       # does this automatically for us but we have to have "self" as the first
6       # parameter to the __init__ method (i.e. the constructor).
7       def __init__(self, name, month, day, year, speakText):
8           self.name = name
9           self.month = month
10          self.day = day
11          self.year = year
12          self.speakText = speakText
13
14      # This is an accessor method that returns the speakText stored in the
15      # object. Notice that "self" is a parameter. Every method has "self" as its
16      # first parameter. The "self" parameter is a reference to the current
17      # object. The current object appears on the left hand side of the dot (i.e.
18      # the .) when the method is called.
19      def speak(self):
20          return self.speakText
21
22      # Here is an accessor method to get the name
23      def getName(self):
```

```
24          return self.name
25
26      # This is another accessor method that uses the birthday information to
27      # return a string representing the date.
28      def birthDate(self):
29          return str(self.month) + "/" + str(self.day) + "/" + str(self.year)
30
31      # This is a mutator method that changes the speakText of the Dog object.
32      def changeBark(self,bark):
33          self.speakText = bark
```

1.5 Operator Overloading

Python provides operator overloading, which is a nice feature of programming languages because it makes it possible for the programmer to interact with objects in a very natural way. Operator overloading is already implemented for a variety of the built-in classes or types in Python. For instance, integers (i.e. the *int* type) understand how they can be added together to form a new integer object. Addition is implemented by a special method in Python called the *__add__* method. When two integers are added together, this method is called to create a new integer object. If you look in the appendices, you'll see examples of these special methods and how they are called. For example, in Chap. 13 the *__add__* method is called by writing $x + y$ where x is an integer. The methods that begin and end with two underscores are methods that Python associates with a corresponding operator.

When we say that Python supports operator *overloading* we mean that if you define a method for your class with a name that is operator overloaded, your class will support that operator as well. Python figures out which method to call based on the types of the operands involved. For instance, writing $x + y$ calls the *int* class *__add__* method when x is an integer, but it calls the *float* type's *__add__* method when x is a *float*. This is because in the case of the *__add__* method, the object on the left hand side of the + operator corresponds to the object on the left hand side of the dot (i.e. the period) in the equivalent method call $x.\_\_add\_\_(y)$. The object on the left side of the dot determines which add method is called. The + operator is overloaded.

If we wanted to define addition for our *Dog* class, we would include an *__add__* method in the class definition. It might be natural to write $boyDog + girlDog$ to create a new puppy object. If we wished to do that we would extend our Dog class as shown in Sect. 1.5.1.

1.5.1 The Dog Class with Overloaded Addition

```
1  class Dog:
2      # This is the constructor for the class. It is called whenever a Dog
3      # object is created. The reference called "self" is created by Python
4      # and made to point to the space for the newly created object. Python
5      # does this automatically for us but we have to have "self" as the first
6      # parameter to the __init__ method (i.e. the constructor).
```

```
7       def __init__(self, name, month, day, year, speakText):
8           self.name = name
9           self.month = month
10          self.day = day
11          self.year = year
12          self.speakText = speakText
13
14      # This is an accessor method that returns the speakText stored in the
15      # object. Notice that "self" is a parameter. Every method has "self" as its
16      # first parameter. The "self" parameter is a reference to the current
17      # object. The current object appears on the left hand side of the dot (i.e.
18      # the .) when the method is called.
19      def speak(self):
20          return self.speakText
21
22      # Here is an accessor method to get the name
23      def getName(self):
24          return self.name
25
26      # This is another accessor method that uses the birthday information to
27      # return a string representing the date.
28      def birthDate(self):
29          return str(self.month) + "/" + str(self.day) + "/" + str(self.year)
30
31      # This is a mutator method that changes the speakText of the Dog object.
32      def changeBark(self,bark):
33          self.speakText = bark
34
35      # When creating the new puppy we don't know it's birthday. Pick the
36      # first dog's birthday plus one year. The speakText will be the
37      # concatenation of both dog's text. The dog on the left side of the +
38      # operator is the object referenced by the "self" parameter. The
39      # "otherDog" parameter is the dog on the right side of the + operator.
40      def __add__(self,otherDog):
41          return Dog("Puppy of " + self.name + " and " + otherDog.name, \
42                      self.month, self.day, self.year + 1, \
43                      self.speakText + otherDog.speakText)
44
45  def main():
46      boyDog = Dog("Mesa", 5, 15, 2004, "WOOOOF")
47      girlDog = Dog("Sequoia", 5, 6, 2004, "barkbark")
48      print(boyDog.speak())
49      print(girlDog.speak())
50      print(boyDog.birthDate())
51      print(girlDog.birthDate())
52      boyDog.changeBark("woofywoofy")
53      print(boyDog.speak())
54      puppy = boyDog + girlDog
55      print(puppy.speak())
56      print(puppy.getName())
57      print(puppy.birthDate())
58
59  if __name__ == "__main__":
60      main()
```

This text uses operator overloading fairly extensively. There are many operators that are defined in Python. Python programmers often call these operators *Magic Methods* because a method automatically gets called when an operator is used in an expression. Many of the common operators are given in the table in Fig. 1.4 for your

Method Defintion	Operator	Description
__add__(self,y)	x + y	The addition of two objects. The type of x determines which add operator is called.
__contains__(self,y)	y in x	When x is a collection you can test to see if y is in it.
__eq__(self,y)	x == y	Returns *True* or *False* depending on the values of x and y.
__ge__(self,y)	x >= y	Returns *True* or *False* depending on the values of x and y.
__getitem__(self,y)	x[y]	Returns the item at the yth position in x.
__gt__(self,y)	x > y	Returns *True* or *False* depending on the values of x and y.
__hash__(self)	hash(x)	Returns an integral value for x.
__int__(self)	int(x)	Returns an integer representation of x.
__iter__(self)	for v in x	Returns an iterator object for the sequence x.
__le__(self,y)	x <= y	Returns *True* or *False* depending on the values of x and y.
__len__(self)	len(x)	Returns the size of x where x has some length attribute.
__lt__(self,y)	x < y	Returns *True* or *False* depending on the values of x and y.
__mod__(self,y)	x % y	Returns the value of x modulo y. This is the remainder of x/y.
__mul__(self,y)	x * y	Returns the product of x and y.
__ne__(self,y)	x != y	Returns *True* or *False* depending on the values of x and y.
__neg__(self)	-x	Returns the unary negation of x.
__repr__(self)	repr(x)	Returns a string version of x suitable to be evaluated by the *eval* function.
__setitem__(self,i,y)	x[i] = y	Sets the item at the ith position in x to y.
__str__(self)	str(x)	Return a string representation of x suitable for user-level interaction.
__sub__(self,y)	x - y	The difference of two objects.

Fig. 1.4 Python Operator Magic Methods

convenience. For each operator the magic method is given, how to call the operator is given, and a short description of it as well. In the table, *self* and *x* refer to the same object. The type of *x* determines which operator method is called in each case in the table.

The *repr(x)* and the *str(x)* operators deserve a little more explanation. Both operators return a string representation of *x*. The difference is that the *str* operator should return a string that is suitable for human interaction while the *repr* operator is called when a string representation is needed that can be evaluated. For instance, if we wanted to define these two operators on the *Dog* class, the *repr* method would return the string "Dog('Mesa', 5,15,2004, 'WOOOF')" while the *str* operator might return just the dog's name. The *repr* operator, when called, will treat the string as an expression that could later be evaluated by the *eval* function in Python whereas the *str* operator simply returns a string for an object.

1.6 Importing Modules

In Python, programs can be broken up into modules. Typically, when you write a program in Python you are going to use code that someone else wrote. Code that others wrote is usually provided in a module. To use a module, you import it. There are two ways to import a module. For the drawing program we are developing in this chapter, we want to use turtle graphics. Turtle graphics was first developed a long time ago for a programming language called Logo. Logo was created around 1967 so the basis for turtle graphics is pretty ancient in terms of Computer Science. It still remains a useful way of thinking about Computer Graphics. The idea is that a turtle is wandering a beach and as it walks around it drags its tail in the sand leaving a trail behind it. All that you can do with a turtle is discussed in the Chap. 18.

There are two ways to import a module in Python: the *convenient* way and the *safe* way. Which way you choose to import code may be a personal preference, but there are some implications about using the *convenient* method of importing code. The convenient way to import the turtle module would be to write the following.

```
from turtle import *
t = Turtle()
```

This is convenient, because whenever you want to use the *Turtle* class, you can just write *Turtle* which is convenient, but not completely safe because you then have to make sure you never use the identifier *Turtle* for anything else in your code. In fact, there may be other identifiers that the turtle module defines that you are unaware of that would also be identifiers you should not use in your code. The safe way to import the turtle module would be as follows.

```
import turtle
t = turtle.Turtle()
```

While this is not quite as *convenient*, because you must precede *Turtle* with "*turtle.*", it is *safe* because the *namespace* of your module and the turtle module are kept separate. All identifiers in the turtle module are in the *turtle namespace*, while the local identifiers are in the *local namespace*. This idea of *namespaces* is an important feature of most programming languages. It helps programmers keep from stepping on each others' toes. The rest of this text will stick to using the safe method of importing modules.

1.7   Indentation in Python Programs

Indentation plays an important role in Python programs. An indented line belongs to the line it is indented under. The *body* of a function is indented under its function definition line. The *then* part of an *if* statement is indented under the *if*. A *while* loop's body is indented under it. The methods of a class are all indented under the class definition line. All statements that are indented the same amount and grouped together are called a *block*. It is important that all statements within a *block* are indented exactly the same amount. If they are not, then Python will complain about inconsistent indentation.

Because indentation is so important to Python, the Wing IDE 101 lets you select a series of lines and adjust their indentation as a group, as shown in Fig. 1.5. You first select the lines of the block and then press the *tab* key to increase their indentation. To decrease the indentation of a block you select the lines of the block and press *Shift-tab*. As you write Python code this is a common chore and being able to adjust the indentation of a whole block at a time is a real timesaver.

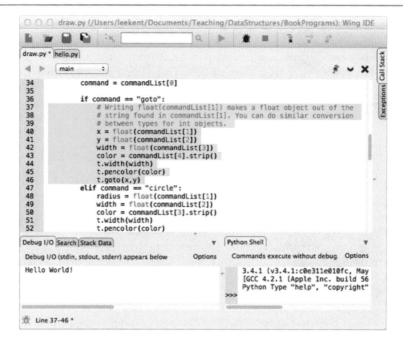

Fig. 1.5 Adjusting Indentation in Wing IDE 101

1.8   The *Main* Function

Programs are typically written with many function definitions and function calls. One function definition is written by convention in Python, usually called the *main* function. This function contains code the program typically executes when it is first started. The general outline of a Python program is given in Sect. 1.8.1.

1.8.1   Python Program Structure

```
1    # Imports at the top.
2    import turtle
3
4    # other function definitions followed by the main function definition
5    def main():
6        # The main code of the program goes here
7        t = turtle.Turtle()
8
9    # this code calls the main function to get everything started. The condition in this
10   # if statement evaluates to True when the module is executed by the interpreter, but
11   # not when it is imported into another module.
12   if __name__ == "__main__":
13       main()
```

The *if* statement at the end of the code in Sect. 1.8.1 is the first code executed after the import statements. The *if* statement's condition evaluates to *True* when the program is run as a stand-alone program. Sometimes we write modules that we may want to import into another module. Writing this *if* statement to call the main function makes the module execute its own main function when it is run as a stand-alone program. When the module is imported into another module it will not execute its main function. Later you will have the opportunity to write a module to be imported into another module so it is a good habit to form to always call the *main* function in this way.

1.9   Reading from a File

To begin our drawing program, let's assume that a picture is stored in a file and we wish to read this file when the program is started. We'll assume that each line of the file contains a drawing command and its associated data. We'll keep it simple and stick to drawing commands that look like this in the input file:

- goto, x, y, width, color
- circle, radius, width, color
- beginfill, color
- endfill
- penup
- pendown

Each line of the file will contain a record with the needed information. We can draw a picture by providing a file with the right sequence of these commands. The file in Sect. 1.9.1 contains records that describe a pickup truck.

1.9.1   A Text File with Single Line Records

```
 1   beginfill, black
 2   circle, 20, 1, black
 3   endfill
 4   penup
 5   goto, 120, 0, 1, black
 6   pendown
 7   beginfill, black
 8   circle, 20, 1, black
 9   endfill
10   penup
11   goto, 150, 40, 1, black
12   pendown
13   beginfill, yellow
14   goto, -30, 40, 1, black
15   goto, -30, 70, 1, black
16   goto, 60, 70, 1, black
17   goto, 60, 100, 1, black
18   goto, 90, 100, 1, black
19   goto, 115, 70, 1, black
20   goto, 150, 70, 1, black
```

```
21    goto, 150, 40, 1, black
22    endfill
```

To process the records in the file in Sect. 1.9.1, we can write a Python program that reads the lines of this file and does the appropriate turtle graphics commands for each record in the file. Since each record (i.e. drawing command) is on its own line in the file format described in Sect. 1.9.1, we can read the file by using a *for* loop to read the lines of the file. The code of Sect. 1.9.2 is a program that reads these commands and processes each record in the file, drawing the picture that it contains.

1.9.2   Reading and Processing Single Line Records

```
1     # This imports the turtle graphics module.
2     import turtle
3
4     # The main function is where the main code of the program is written.
5     def main():
6         # This line reads a line of input from the user.
7         filename = input("Please enter drawing filename: ")
8
9         # Create a Turtle Graphics window to draw in.
10        t = turtle.Turtle()
11        # The screen is used at the end of the program.
12        screen = t.getscreen()
13
14        # The next line opens the file for "r" or reading. "w" would open it for
15        # writing, and "a" would open the file to append to it (i.e. add to the
16        # end). In this program we are only interested in reading the file.
17        file = open(filename, "r")
18
19        # The following for loop reads the lines of the file, one at a time
20        # and executes the body of the loop once for each line of the file.
21        for line in file:
22
23            # The strip method strips off the newline character at the end of the line
24            # and any blanks that might be at the beginning or end of the line.
25            text = line.strip()
26
27            # The following line splits the text variable into its pieces.
28            # For instance, if text contained "goto, 10, 20, 1, black" then
29            # commandList will be equal to ["goto", "10", "20", "1", "black"] after
30            # splitting text.
31            commandList = text.split(",")
32
33            # get the drawing command
34            command = commandList[0]
35
36            if command == "goto":
37                # Writing float(commandList[1]) makes a float object out of the
38                # string found in commandList[1]. You can do similar conversion
39                # between types for int objects.
40                x = float(commandList[1])
41                y = float(commandList[2])
42                width = float(commandList[3])
43                color = commandList[4].strip()
44                t.width(width)
45                t.pencolor(color)
```

```
46              t.goto(x,y)
47          elif command == "circle":
48              radius = float(commandList[1])
49              width = float(commandList[2])
50              color = commandList[3].strip()
51              t.width(width)
52              t.pencolor(color)
53              t.circle(radius)
54          elif command == "beginfill":
55              color = commandList[1].strip()
56              t.fillcolor(color)
57              t.begin_fill()
58          elif command == "endfill":
59              t.end_fill()
60          elif command == "penup":
61              t.penup()
62          elif command == "pendown":
63              t.pendown()
64          else:
65              print("Unknown command found in file:",command)
66
67      #close the file
68      file.close()
69
70      #hide the turtle that we used to draw the picture.
71      t.ht()
72
73      # This causes the program to hold the turtle graphics window open
74      # until the mouse is clicked.
75      screen.exitonclick()
76      print("Program Execution Completed.")
77
78
79  # This code calls the main function to get everything started.
80  if __name__ == "__main__":
81      main()
```

When you have a data file where each line of the file is its own separate record, you can process those records as we did in Sect. 1.9.2. The general pattern is to open the file, use a for loop to iterate through the file, and have the body of the for loop process each record. The pseudo-code in Sect. 1.9.3 is the abstract pattern for reading one-line records from a file.

1.9.3 Pattern for Reading Single Line Records from a File

```
1   # First the file must be opened.
2   file = open(filename,"r")
3
4   # The body of the for loop is executed once for each line in the file.
5   for line in file:
6       # Process each record of the file. Each record must be exactly one line of the
7       # input file. What processing a record means will be determined by the
8       # program you are writing.
9       print(line)
10
11  # Closing the file is always a good idea, but it will be closed when your program
```

```
12   # terminates if you do not close it explicitly.
13   file.close()
```

1.10   Reading Multi-line Records from a File

Sometimes records of a file are not one per line. Records of a file may cross multiple lines. In that case, you can't use a *for* loop to read the file. You need a *while* loop instead. When you use a while loop, you need to be able to check a condition to see if you are done reading the file. But, to check the condition you must first try to read at least a little of a record. This is a kind of chicken and egg problem. Which came first, the chicken or the egg? Computer programmers have a name for this problem as it relates to reading from files. It is called the *Loop and a Half Pattern*. To use a while loop to read from a file, we need a loop and a half. The half comes before the while loop.

Consider the program we are writing in this chapter. Let's assume that the records of the file cross multiple lines. In fact, let's assume that we have variable length records. That is, the records of our file consist of one to five lines. The drawing commands will be exactly as they were before. But, instead of all the data for a record appearing on one line, we'll put each piece of data on its own separate line as shown in Sect. 1.10.1.

1.10.1 A Text File with Multiple Line Records

```
1    beginfill
2    black
3    circle
4    20
5    1
6    black
7    endfill
8    penup
9    goto
10   120
11   0
12   1
13   black
14   pendown
15   beginfill
16   black
17   circle
18   20
19   1
20   black
21   endfill
22   penup
23   goto
24   150
25   40
```

```
26   1
27   black
28   pendown
29   beginfill
30   yellow
31   goto
32   -30
33   40
34   1
35   black
36   goto
37   -30
38   70
39   1
40   black
41   goto
42   60
43   70
44   1
45   black
46   goto
47   60
48   100
49   1
50   black
51   goto
52   90
53   100
54   1
55   black
56   goto
57   115
58   70
59   1
60   black
61   goto
62   150
63   70
64   1
65   black
66   goto
67   150
68   40
69   1
70   black
71   endfill
```

To read a file as shown in Sect. 1.10.1 we write our loop and a half to read the first line of each record and then check that line (i.e. the graphics command) so we know how many more lines to read. The code in Sect. 1.10.2 uses a while loop to read these variable length records.

1.10.2 Reading and Processing Multi-line Records

```python
import turtle

def main():
    filename = input("Please enter drawing filename: ")

    t = turtle.Turtle()
    screen = t.getscreen()

    file = open(filename, "r")

    # Here we have the half a loop to get things started. Reading our first
    # graphics command here lets us determine if the file is empty or not.
    command = file.readline().strip()

    # If the command is empty, then there are no more commands left in the file.
    while command != "":

        # Now we must read the rest of the record and then process it. Because
        # records are variable length, we'll use an if-elif to determine which
        # type of record it is and then we'll read and process the record.

        if command == "goto":
            x = float(file.readline())
            y = float(file.readline())
            width = float(file.readline())
            color = file.readline().strip()
            t.width(width)
            t.pencolor(color)
            t.goto(x,y)
        elif command == "circle":
            radius = float(file.readline())
            width = float(file.readline())
            color = file.readline().strip()
            t.width(width)
            t.pencolor(color)
            t.circle(radius)
        elif command == "beginfill":
            color = file.readline().strip()
            t.fillcolor(color)
            t.begin_fill()
        elif command == "endfill":
            t.end_fill()
        elif command == "penup":
            t.penup()
        elif command == "pendown":
            t.pendown()
        else:
            print("Unknown command found in file:",command)

        # This is still inside the while loop. We must (attempt to) read
        # the next command from the file. If the read succeeds, then command
        # will not be the empty string and the loop will be repeated. If
        # command is empty it is because there were no more commands in the
        # file and the while loop will terminate.
        command = file.readline().strip()
```

```
58        # close the file
59        file.close()
60
61        t.ht()
62        screen.exitonclick()
63        print("Program Execution Completed.")
64
65    if __name__ == "__main__":
66        main()
```

When reading a file with multi-line records, a while loop is needed. Notice that on line 13 the first line of the first record is read prior to the while loop. For the body of the while loop to execute, the condition must be tested prior to executing the loop. Reading a line prior to the while loop is necessary so we can check to see if the file is empty or not. The first line of every other record is read at the end of the while loop on line 55. This is the loop and a half pattern. The first line of the first record is read before the while loop while the first line of every other record is read inside the while loop just before the end. When the condition becomes false, the while loop terminates.

The abstract pattern for reading multi-line records from a file is shown in Sect. 1.10.3. There are certainly other forms of this pattern that can be used, but memorizing this pattern is worth-while since the pattern will work using pretty much any programming language.

1.10.3 Pattern for Reading Multi-line Records from a File

```
1     # First the file must be opened
2     file = open(filename, "r")
3
4     # Read the first line of the first record in the file. Of course, firstLine should be
5     # called something that makes sense in your program.
6     firstLine = file.readline().strip()
7
8     while firstLine != "":
9         # Read the rest of the record
10        secondLine = file.readline().strip()
11        thirdLine = file.readline().strip()
12        # ...
13
14        # Then process the record. This will be determined by the program you are
15        # writing.
16        print(firstLine, secondLine, thirdLine)
17
18        # Finally, finish the loop by reading the first line of the next record to
19        # set up for the next iteration of the loop.
20        firstLine = file.readline().strip()
21
22    # It's a good idea to close the file, but it will be automatically closed when your
23    # program terminates.
24    file.close()
```

1.11   A Container Class

To further enhance our drawing program we will first create a data structure to hold all of our drawing commands. This is our first example of defining our own class in this text so we'll go slow and provide a lot of detail about what is happening and why. To begin let's figure out what we want to do with this container class.

Our program will begin by creating an empty container. To do this, we'll write a line like this.

```
graphicsCommands = PyList()
```

Then, we will want to add graphics commands to our list using an append method like this.

```
command = GotoCommand(x, y, width, color)
graphicsCommands.append(command)
```

We would also like to be able to iterate over the commands in our list.

```
for command in graphicsCommands:
    # draw each command on the screen using the turtle called t.
    command.draw(t)
```

At this point, our container class looks a lot like a list. We are defining our own list class to illustrate a first data structure and to motivate discussion of how lists can be implemented efficiently in this and the next chapter.

1.12   Polymorphism

One important concept in Object-Oriented Programming is called polymorphism. The word *polymorphic* literally means *many forms*. As this concept is applied to computer programming, the idea is that there can be many ways that a particular behavior might be implemented. In relationship to our PyList container class that we are building, the idea is that each type of graphics command will know how to draw itself correctly. For instance, one type of graphics command is the *GoToCommand*. When a *GoToCommand* is drawn it draws a line on the screen from the current point to some new (x,y) coordinate. But, when a *CircleCommand* is drawn, it draws a circle on the screen with a particular radius. This *polymorphic* behavior can be defined by creating a class and draw method for each different type of behavior. The code in Sect. 1.12.1 is a collection of classes that define the polymorphic behavior of the different graphics *draw* methods. There is one class for each drawing command that will be processed by the program.

1.12.1 Graphics Command Classes

```
1   # Each of the command classes below hold information for one of the
2   # types of commands found in a graphics file. For each command there must
3   # be a draw method that is given a turtle and uses the turtle to draw
4   # the object. By having a draw method for each class, we can
5   # polymorphically call the right draw method when traversing a sequence of
6   # these commands. Polymorphism occurs when the "right" draw method gets
7   # called without having to know which graphics command it is being called on.
8   class GoToCommand:
9       # Here the constructor is defined with default values for width and color.
10      # This means we can construct a GoToCommand objects as GoToCommand(10,20),
11      # or GoToCommand(10,20,5), or GoToCommand(10,20,5,"yellow").
12      def __init__(self,x,y,width=1,color="black"):
13          self.x = x
14          self.y = y
15          self.color = color
16          self.width = width
17
18      def draw(self,turtle):
19          turtle.width(self.width)
20          turtle.pencolor(self.color)
21          turtle.goto(self.x,self.y)
22
23  class CircleCommand:
24      def __init__(self,radius, width=1,color="black"):
25          self.radius = radius
26          self.width = width
27          self.color = color
28
29      def draw(self,turtle):
30          turtle.width(self.width)
31          turtle.pencolor(self.color)
32          turtle.circle(self.radius)
33
34  class BeginFillCommand:
35      def __init__(self,color):
36          self.color = color
37
38      def draw(self,turtle):
39          turtle.fillcolor(self.color)
40          turtle.begin_fill()
41
42  class EndFillCommand:
43      def __init__(self):
44          # pass is a statement placeholder and does nothing. We have nothing
45          # to initialize in this class because all we want is the polymorphic
46          # behavior of the draw method.
47          pass
48
49      def draw(self,turtle):
50          turtle.end_fill()
51
52  class PenUpCommand:
53      def __init__(self):
54          pass
55
56      def draw(self,turtle):
57          turtle.penup()
```

```
58
59   class PenDownCommand:
60       def __init__(self):
61           pass
62
63       def draw(self,turtle):
64           turtle.pendown()
```

1.13   The Accumulator Pattern

To use the different command classes that we have just defined, our program will read the variable length records from the file as it did before using the *loop and a half* pattern that we have already seen. Patterns of programming, sometimes called *idioms*, are important in Computer Science. Once we have learned an idiom we can apply it over and over in our programs. This is useful to us because as we solve problems its nice to say, "Oh, yes, I can solve this problem using that idiom". Having idioms at our fingertips frees our minds to deal with the tougher problems we encounter while programming.

One important pattern in programming is the *Accumulator Pattern*. This pattern is used in nearly every program we write. When using this pattern you initialize an accumulator before a loop and then inside the loop you add to the accumulator. For instance, the code in Sect. 1.13.1 uses the accumulator pattern to construct the list of squares from 1 to 10.

1.13.1 List of Squares

```
1   # initialize the accumulator, in this case a list
2   accumulator = []
3
4   # write some kind of for loop or while loop
5   for i in range(1,11):
6       # add to the accumulator, in this case add to the list
7       accumulator = accumulator + [i ** 2]
```

To complete our graphics program, we'll use the loop and a half pattern to read the records from a file and the accumulator pattern to add a command object to our PyList container for each record we find in the file. The code is given in Sect. 1.13.2.

1.13.2 A Graphics Program

```
1   import turtle
2
3   # Command classes would be inserted here but are left out because they
4   # were defined earlier in the chapter.
5
```

```
6     # This is our PyList class. It holds a list of our graphics
7     # commands.
8
9     class PyList:
10        def __init__(self):
11            self.items = []
12
13        def append(self,item):
14            self.items = self.items + [item]
15
16        # if we want to iterate over this sequence, we define the special method
17        # called __iter__(self). Without this we'll get "builtins.TypeError:
18        # 'PyList' object is not iterable" if we try to write
19        # for cmd in seq:
20        # where seq is one of these sequences. The yield below will yield an
21        # element of the sequence and will suspend the execution of the for
22        # loop in the method below until the next element is needed. The ability
23        # to yield each element of the sequence as needed is called "lazy" evaluation
24        # and is very powerful. It means that we only need to provide access to as
25        # many of elements of the sequence as are necessary and no more.
26        def __iter__(self):
27            for c in self.items:
28                yield c
29
30    def main():
31        filename = input("Please enter drawing filename: ")
32
33        t = turtle.Turtle()
34        screen = t.getscreen()
35        file = open(filename, "r")
36
37        # Create a PyList to hold the graphics commands that are
38        # read from the file.
39        graphicsCommands = PyList()
40
41        command = file.readline().strip()
42
43        while command != "":
44
45            # Now we must read the rest of the record and then process it. Because
46            # records are variable length, we'll use an if-elif to determine which
47            # type of record it is and then we'll read and process the record.
48            # In this program, processing the record means creating a command object
49            # using one of the classes above and then adding that object to our
50            # graphicsCommands PyList object.
51
52            if command == "goto":
53                x = float(file.readline())
54                y = float(file.readline())
55                width = float(file.readline())
56                color = file.readline().strip()
57                cmd = GoToCommand(x,y,width,color)
58
59            elif command == "circle":
60                radius = float(file.readline())
61                width = float(file.readline())
62                color = file.readline().strip()
63                cmd = CircleCommand(radius,width,color)
64
65            elif command == "beginfill":
66                color = file.readline().strip()
```

```
67                cmd = BeginFillCommand(color)
68
69        elif command == "endfill":
70                cmd = EndFillCommand()
71
72        elif command == "penup":
73                cmd = PenUpCommand()
74
75        elif command == "pendown":
76                cmd = PenDownCommand()
77        else:
78                # raising an exception will terminate the program immediately
79                # which is what we want to happen if we encounter an unknown
80                # command. The RuntimeError exception is a common exception
81                # to raise. The string will be printed when the exception is
82                # printed.
83                raise RuntimeError("Unknown Command: " + command)
84
85        # Finish processing the record by adding the command to the sequence.
86        graphicsCommands.append(cmd)
87
88        # Read one more line to set up for the next time through the loop.
89        command = file.readline().strip()
90
91    # This code iterates through the commands to do the drawing and
92    # demonstrates the use of the __iter(self)__ method in the
93    # PyList class above.
94    for cmd in graphicsCommands:
95        cmd.draw(t)
96
97    file.close()
98    t.ht()
99    screen.exitonclick()
100    print("Program Execution Completed.")
101
102 if __name__ == "__main__":
103    main()
```

1.14   Implementing a GUI with Tkinter

The word GUI means Graphical User Interface. Implementing a Graphical User Interface in Python is very easy using a module called Tkinter. The Tcl/Tk language and toolkit was designed as a cross-platform method of creating GUI interfaces. Python provides an interface to this toolkit via the Tkinter module.

A GUI is an event-driven program. This means that you write your code to respond to events that occur in the program. The events occur as a result of mouse clicks, dragging the mouse, button presses, and menu items being selected.

To build a GUI you place widgets in a window. Widgets are any element of a GUI like labels, buttons, entry boxes, and sometimes invisible widgets called frames. A frame is a widget that can hold other widgets. The drawing application you see in Fig. 1.6 is one such GUI built with Tkinter. In this section we'll develop this drawing application so you learn how to create your own GUI applications using Tkinter and to improve or refresh your Python programming skills.

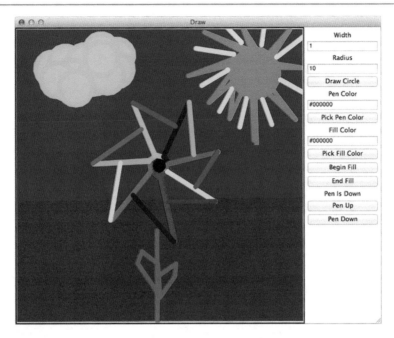

Fig. 1.6 The Draw Program

To construct a GUI you need to create a window. It is really very simple to do this using Tkinter.

```
root = tkinter.Tk()
```

This creates an empty window on the screen, but of course does not put anything in it. We need to place widgets in it so it looks like the window in Fig. 1.6 (without the nice picture that Denise drew for us; thanks Denise!). We also need to create event handlers to handle events in the drawing application.

Putting widgets in a window is called *layout*. Laying out a window relies on a layout manager of some sort. Windowing toolkits support some kind of layout. In Tkinter you either *pack*, *grid*, or *place* widgets within a window. When you *pack* widgets it's like packing a suitcase and each widget is stacked either beside or below the previous widget packed in the GUI. Packing widgets will give you the desired layout in most situations, but at times a *grid* may be useful for laying out a window. The *place* layout manager lets you place widgets at a particular location within a window. We'll use the *pack* layout manager to layout our drawing application.

When packing widgets, to get the proper layout, sometimes you need to create a Frame widget. Frame widgets hold other widgets. In Fig. 1.7 two frame widgets have been created. The DrawingApplication frame is the size of the whole window and holds just two widgets that are placed side by side within it: the canvas and the sideBar frame. A canvas is a widget on which a turtle can draw. The sideBar widget holds all the buttons, entry boxes, and labels.

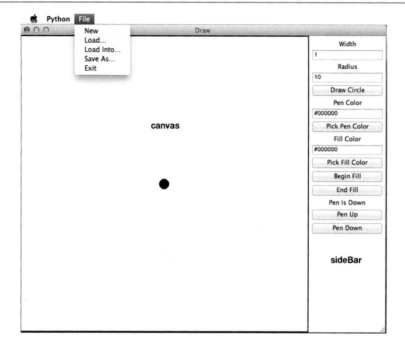

Fig. 1.7 The Draw Program Layout

The DrawingApplication frame *inherits* from Frame. When programming in an object-oriented language, sometimes you want to implement a class, but it is almost like another class. In this case, the *DrawingApplication* is a *Frame*. This means there are two parts to DrawingApplication objects, the Frame part of the DrawingApplication and the rest of it, which in this case is the *PyList* sequence of graphics commands. Our frame will keep track of the graphics commands that are used to draw the picture on the canvas. Portions of the code appear in Sect. 1.14.1. The code in Sect. 1.14.1 shows you all the widgets that are created and how they are packed within the window.

The *canvas* and the *sideBar* widgets are added side by side to the Drawing Application frame. Then all the entry, label, and button widgets are added to the *sideBar* frame.

In addition, there is a menu with the *Draw* application. The menu is another widget that is added to the window (called *self.master* in the code in Sect. 1.14.1). The *fileMenu* is what appears on the menu bar. The menu items "New", "Load...", "Load Into...", "Save As...", and "Exit" are all added to this menu. Each menu item is linked to an event handler that is executed when it is selected.

When *theTurtle* object is created in Sect. 1.14.1, it is created as a *RawTurtle*. A *RawTurtle* is just like a turtle except that a *RawTurtle* can be provided a canvas to draw on. A *Turtle* object creates its own canvas when the first turtle is created. Since we already have a canvas for the turtle, we create a *RawTurtle* object.

In addition to the event handlers for the widgets, there are three other event handlers. The *onclick* event occurs when you click the mouse button on the canvas. The *ondrag* event handler occurs when the turtle is dragged around the canvas. Finally, the *undoHandler* is called when the *u* key is pressed on the keyboard.

1.14.1 A GUI Drawing Application

```
1    # This class defines the drawing application. The following line says that
2    # the DrawingApplication class inherits from the Frame class. This means
3    # that a DrawingApplication is like a Frame object except for the code
4    # written here which redefines/extends the behavior of a Frame.
5    class DrawingApplication(tkinter.Frame):
6        def __init__(self, master=None):
7            super().__init__(master)
8            self.pack()
9            self.buildWindow()
10           self.graphicsCommands = PyList()
11
12       # This method is called to create all the widgets, place them in the GUI,
13       # and define the event handlers for the application.
14       def buildWindow(self):
15
16           # The master is the root window. The title is set as below.
17           self.master.title("Draw")
18
19           # Here is how to create a menu bar. The tearoff=0 means that menus
20           # can't be separated from the window which is a feature of tkinter.
21           bar = tkinter.Menu(self.master)
22           fileMenu = tkinter.Menu(bar,tearoff=0)
23
24           # This code is called by the "New" menu item below when it is selected.
25           # The same applies for loadFile, addToFile, and saveFile below. The
26           # "Exit" menu item below calls quit on the "master" or root window.
27           def newWindow():
28               # This sets up the turtle to be ready for a new picture to be
29               # drawn. It also sets the sequence back to empty. It is necessary
30               # for the graphicsCommands sequence to be in the object (i.e.
31               # self.graphicsCommands) because otherwise the statement:
32               # graphicsCommands = PyList()
33               # would make this variable a local variable in the newWindow
34               # method. If it were local, it would not be set anymore once the
35               # newWindow method returned.
36               theTurtle.clear()
37               theTurtle.penup()
38               theTurtle.goto(0,0)
39               theTurtle.pendown()
40               screen.update()
41               screen.listen()
42               self.graphicsCommands = PyList()
43
44           fileMenu.add_command(label="New",command=newWindow)
45
46           # The parse function adds the contents of an XML file to the sequence.
47           def parse(filename):
48               xmldoc = xml.dom.minidom.parse(filename)
49
50               graphicsCommandsElement = xmldoc.getElementsByTagName("GraphicsCommands")[0]
51
52               graphicsCommands = graphicsCommandsElement.getElementsByTagName("Command")
53
54               for commandElement in graphicsCommands:
55                   print(type(commandElement))
56                   command = commandElement.firstChild.data.strip()
57                   attr = commandElement.attributes
58                   if command == "GoTo":
```

```
59                         x = float(attr["x"].value)
60                         y = float(attr["y"].value)
61                         width = float(attr["width"].value)
62                         color = attr["color"].value.strip()
63                         cmd = GoToCommand(x,y,width,color)
64
65                     elif command == "Circle":
66                         radius = float(attr["radius"].value)
67                         width = float(attr["width"].value)
68                         color = attr["color"].value.strip()
69                         cmd = CircleCommand(radius,width,color)
70
71                     elif command == "BeginFill":
72                         color = attr["color"].value.strip()
73                         cmd = BeginFillCommand(color)
74
75                     elif command == "EndFill":
76                         cmd = EndFillCommand()
77
78                     elif command == "PenUp":
79                         cmd = PenUpCommand()
80
81                     elif command == "PenDown":
82                         cmd = PenDownCommand()
83                     else:
84                         raise RuntimeError("Unknown Command: " + command)
85
86                     self.graphicsCommands.append(cmd)
87
88             def loadFile():
89
90                 filename = tkinter.filedialog.askopenfilename(title="Select a Graphics File")
91
92                 newWindow()
93
94                 # This re-initializes the sequence for the new picture.
95                 self.graphicsCommands = PyList()
96
97                 # calling parse will read the graphics commands from the file.
98                 parse(filename)
99
100                for cmd in self.graphicsCommands:
101                    cmd.draw(theTurtle)
102
103                # This line is necessary to update the window after the picture is drawn.
104                screen.update()
105
106
107            fileMenu.add_command(label="Load...",command=loadFile)
108
109            def addToFile():
110                filename = tkinter.filedialog.askopenfilename(title="Select a Graphics File")
111
112                theTurtle.penup()
113                theTurtle.goto(0,0)
114                theTurtle.pendown()
115                theTurtle.pencolor("#000000")
116                theTurtle.fillcolor("#000000")
117                cmd = PenUpCommand()
118                self.graphicsCommands.append(cmd)
119                cmd = GoToCommand(0,0,1,"#000000")
120                self.graphicsCommands.append(cmd)
121                cmd = PenDownCommand()
122                self.graphicsCommands.append(cmd)
123                screen.update()
124                parse(filename)
125
126                for cmd in self.graphicsCommands:
127                    cmd.draw(theTurtle)
```

```
128
129              screen.update()
130
131      fileMenu.add_command(label="Load Into...",command=addToFile)
132
133      # The write function writes an XML file to the given filename
134      def write(filename):
135          file = open(filename, "w")
136          file.write('<?xml version="1.0" encoding="UTF-8" standalone="no" ?>\n')
137          file.write('<GraphicsCommands>\n')
138          for cmd in self.graphicsCommands:
139              file.write('    '+str(cmd)+"\n")
140
141          file.write('</GraphicsCommands>\n')
142
143          file.close()
144
145      def saveFile():
146          filename = tkinter.filedialog.asksaveasfilename(title="Save Picture As...")
147          write(filename)
148
149      fileMenu.add_command(label="Save As...",command=saveFile)
150
151
152      fileMenu.add_command(label="Exit",command=self.master.quit)
153
154      bar.add_cascade(label="File",menu=fileMenu)
155
156      # This tells the root window to display the newly created menu bar.
157      self.master.config(menu=bar)
158
159      # Here several widgets are created. The canvas is the drawing area on
160      # the left side of the window.
161      canvas = tkinter.Canvas(self,width=600,height=600)
162      canvas.pack(side=tkinter.LEFT)
163
164      # By creating a RawTurtle, we can have the turtle draw on this canvas.
165      # Otherwise, a RawTurtle and a Turtle are exactly the same.
166      theTurtle = turtle.RawTurtle(canvas)
167
168      # This makes the shape of the turtle a circle.
169      theTurtle.shape("circle")
170      screen = theTurtle.getscreen()
171
172      # This causes the application to not update the screen unless
173      # screen.update() is called. This is necessary for the ondrag event
174      # handler below. Without it, the program bombs after dragging the
175      # turtle around for a while.
176      screen.tracer(0)
177
178      # This is the area on the right side of the window where all the
179      # buttons, labels, and entry boxes are located. The pad creates some empty
180      # space around the side. The side puts the sideBar on the right side of the
181      # this frame. The fill tells it to fill in all space available on the right
182      # side.
183      sideBar = tkinter.Frame(self,padx=5,pady=5)
184      sideBar.pack(side=tkinter.RIGHT, fill=tkinter.BOTH)
185
186      # This is a label widget. Packing it puts it at the top of the sidebar.
187      pointLabel = tkinter.Label(sideBar,text="Width")
188      pointLabel.pack()
189
190      # This entry widget allows the user to pick a width for their lines.
191      # With the widthSize variable below you can write widthSize.get() to get
192      # the contents of the entry widget and widthSize.set(val) to set the value
193      # of the entry widget to val. Initially the widthSize is set to 1. str(1) is
194      # needed because the entry widget must be given a string.
195      widthSize = tkinter.StringVar()
196      widthEntry = tkinter.Entry(sideBar,textvariable=widthSize)
```

```
197        widthEntry.pack()
198        widthSize.set(str(1))
199
200        radiusLabel = tkinter.Label(sideBar,text="Radius")
201        radiusLabel.pack()
202        radiusSize = tkinter.StringVar()
203        radiusEntry = tkinter.Entry(sideBar,textvariable=radiusSize)
204        radiusSize.set(str(10))
205        radiusEntry.pack()
206
207        # A button widget calls an event handler when it is pressed. The circleHandler
208        # function below is the event handler when the Draw Circle button is pressed.
209        def circleHandler():
210            # When drawing, a command is created and then the command is drawn by calling
211            # the draw method. Adding the command to the graphicsCommands sequence means the
212            # application will remember the picture.
213            cmd = CircleCommand(float(radiusSize.get()), float(widthSize.get()), penColor.get())
214            cmd.draw(theTurtle)
215            self.graphicsCommands.append(cmd)
216
217            # These two lines are needed to update the screen and to put the focus back
218            # in the drawing canvas. This is necessary because when pressing "u" to undo,
219            # the screen must have focus to receive the key press.
220            screen.update()
221            screen.listen()
222
223        # This creates the button widget in the sideBar. The fill=tkinter.BOTH causes the button
224        # to expand to fill the entire width of the sideBar.
225        circleButton = tkinter.Button(sideBar, text = "Draw Circle", command=circleHandler)
226        circleButton.pack(fill=tkinter.BOTH)
227
228        # The color mode 255 below allows colors to be specified in RGB form (i.e. Red/
229        # Green/Blue). The mode allows the Red value to be set by a two digit hexadecimal
230        # number ranging from 00-FF. The same applies for Blue and Green values. The
231        # color choosers below return a string representing the selected color and a slice
232        # is taken to extract the #RRGGBB hexadecimal string that the color choosers return.
233        screen.colormode(255)
234        penLabel = tkinter.Label(sideBar,text="Pen Color")
235        penLabel.pack()
236        penColor = tkinter.StringVar()
237        penEntry = tkinter.Entry(sideBar,textvariable=penColor)
238        penEntry.pack()
239        # This is the color black.
240        penColor.set("#000000")
241
242        def getPenColor():
243            color = tkinter.colorchooser.askcolor()
244            if color != None:
245                penColor.set(str(color)[-9:-2])
246
247        penColorButton = tkinter.Button(sideBar, text = "Pick Pen Color", command=getPenColor)
248        penColorButton.pack(fill=tkinter.BOTH)
249
250        fillLabel = tkinter.Label(sideBar,text="Fill Color")
251        fillLabel.pack()
252        fillColor = tkinter.StringVar()
253        fillEntry = tkinter.Entry(sideBar,textvariable=fillColor)
254        fillEntry.pack()
255        fillColor.set("#000000")
256
257        def getFillColor():
258            color = tkinter.colorchooser.askcolor()
259            if color != None:
260                fillColor.set(str(color)[-9:-2])
261
262        fillColorButton = \
263            tkinter.Button(sideBar, text = "Pick Fill Color", command=getFillColor)
264        fillColorButton.pack(fill=tkinter.BOTH)
265
```

```
266
267        def beginFillHandler():
268            cmd = BeginFillCommand(fillColor.get())
269            cmd.draw(theTurtle)
270            self.graphicsCommands.append(cmd)
271
272        beginFillButton = tkinter.Button(sideBar, text = "Begin Fill", command=beginFillHandler)
273        beginFillButton.pack(fill=tkinter.BOTH)
274
275        def endFillHandler():
276            cmd = EndFillCommand()
277            cmd.draw(theTurtle)
278            self.graphicsCommands.append(cmd)
279
280        endFillButton = tkinter.Button(sideBar, text = "End Fill", command=endFillHandler)
281        endFillButton.pack(fill=tkinter.BOTH)
282
283        penLabel = tkinter.Label(sideBar,text="Pen Is Down")
284        penLabel.pack()
285
286        def penUpHandler():
287            cmd = PenUpCommand()
288            cmd.draw(theTurtle)
289            penLabel.configure(text="Pen Is Up")
290            self.graphicsCommands.append(cmd)
291
292        penUpButton = tkinter.Button(sideBar, text = "Pen Up", command=penUpHandler)
293        penUpButton.pack(fill=tkinter.BOTH)
294
295        def penDownHandler():
296            cmd = PenDownCommand()
297            cmd.draw(theTurtle)
298            penLabel.configure(text="Pen Is Down")
299            self.graphicsCommands.append(cmd)
300
301        penDownButton = tkinter.Button(sideBar, text = "Pen Down", command=penDownHandler)
302        penDownButton.pack(fill=tkinter.BOTH)
303
304        # Here is another event handler. This one handles mouse clicks on the screen.
305        def clickHandler(x,y):
306            # When a mouse click occurs, get the widthSize entry value and set the width of the
307            # pen to the widthSize value. The float(widthSize.get()) is needed because
308            # the width is a float, but the entry widget stores it as a string.
309            cmd = GoToCommand(x,y,float(widthSize.get()),penColor.get())
310            cmd.draw(theTurtle)
311            self.graphicsCommands.append(cmd)
312            screen.update()
313            screen.listen()
314
315        # Here is how we tie the clickHandler to mouse clicks.
316        screen.onclick(clickHandler)
317
318        def dragHandler(x,y):
319            cmd = GoToCommand(x,y,float(widthSize.get()),penColor.get())
320            cmd.draw(theTurtle)
321            self.graphicsCommands.append(cmd)
322            screen.update()
323            screen.listen()
324
325        theTurtle.ondrag(dragHandler)
326
327        # the undoHandler undoes the last command by removing it from the
328        # sequence and then redrawing the entire picture.
329        def undoHandler():
330            if len(self.graphicsCommands) > 0:
331                self.graphicsCommands.removeLast()
332                theTurtle.clear()
333                theTurtle.penup()
334                theTurtle.goto(0,0)
```

```
335                    theTurtle.pendown()
336                    for cmd in self.graphicsCommands:
337                        cmd.draw(theTurtle)
338                    screen.update()
339                    screen.listen()
340
341            screen.onkeypress(undoHandler, "u")
342            screen.listen()
343
344    # The main function in our GUI program is very simple. It creates the
345    # root window. Then it creates the DrawingApplication frame which creates
346    # all the widgets and has the logic for the event handlers. Calling mainloop
347    # on the frames makes it start listening for events. The mainloop function will
348    # return when the application is exited.
349    def main():
350        root = tkinter.Tk()
351        drawingApp = DrawingApplication(root)
352
353        drawingApp.mainloop()
354        print("Program Execution Completed.")
355
356    if __name__ == "__main__":
357        main()
```

1.15   XML Files

Reading a standard text file, like the graphics commands file we read using the loop and a half pattern in Sect. 1.13.2, is a common task in computer programs. The only problem is that the program must be written to read the specific format of the input file. If we later wish to change the format of the input file to include, for example, a new option like fill color for a circle, then we are stuck updating the program and updating all the files it once read. The input file format and the program must always be synchronized. This means that all old formatted input files must be converted to the new format or they must be thrown away. That is simply not acceptable to most businesses because data is valuable.

To deal with this problem, computer programmers designed a language for describing data input files called XML which stands for eXtensible Markup Language. XML is a meta-language for data description. A meta-language is a language for describing other languages. The XML meta-language is universally accepted. In fact, the XML format is governed by a standards committee, which means that we can count on the XML format remaining very stable and backwards compatible forever. Any additions to XML will have to be compatible with what has already been defined.

An XML document begins with a special line to identify it as an XML file. This line looks like this.

```
<?xml version="1.0" encoding="UTF-8" standalone="no" ?>
```

The rest of an XML file consists of elements or nodes. Each node is identified by a tag or a pair of beginning and ending tags. Each tag is delimited (i.e. surrounded) by angle brackets. For instance, here is one such tag.

```
<GraphicsCommands>
```

Most XML elements are delimited by a opening tag and a closing tag. The tag above is an opening tag. Its matching closing tag looks like this.

```
</GraphicsCommands>
```

The slash just before the tag name means that it is a closing tag. An opening and closing tag may have text or other XML elements in between the two tags so XML documents may contain XML elements nested as deeply as necessary depending on the data you are trying to encode.

Each XML element may have attributes associated with it. For instance, consider an XML element that encapsulates the information needed to do a *GoTo* graphics command. To complete a *GoTo* command we need the x and y coordinates, the *width* of the line, and the pen *color*. Here is an example of encoding that information in XML format.

```
<Command x="1.0" y="1.0" width="1.0" color="#000000">GoTo</Command>
```

In this example the attributes are x, y, *width*, and *color*. Each attribute is mapped to its value as shown above. The *GoTo* text is the text that appears between the opening and closing tags. That text is sometimes called the child data.

By encoding an entire graphics commands input file in XML format we eliminate some of the dependence between the Draw *program* and its *data*. Except for the XML format (i.e. the grammar) the contents of the XML file are completely up to the programmer or programmers using the data. The file in Sect. 1.15.1 is an example of the truck picture's XML input file.

1.15.1 The Truck XML File

```
1   <?xml version="1.0" encoding="UTF-8" standalone="no" ?>
2   <GraphicsCommands>
3       <Command color="black">BeginFill</Command>
4       <Command radius="20.0" width="1" color="black">Circle</Command>
5       <Command>EndFill</Command>
6       <Command>PenUp</Command>
7       <Command x="120.0" y="0.0" width="1.0" color="black">GoTo</Command>
8       <Command>PenDown</Command>
9       <Command color="black">BeginFill</Command>
10      <Command radius="20.0" width="1" color="black">Circle</Command>
11      <Command>EndFill</Command>
12      <Command>PenUp</Command>
13      <Command x="150.0" y="40.0" width="1.0" color="black">GoTo</Command>
14      <Command>PenDown</Command>
15      <Command color="yellow">BeginFill</Command>
16      <Command x="-30.0" y="40.0" width="1.0" color="black">GoTo</Command>
17      <Command x="-30.0" y="70.0" width="1.0" color="black">GoTo</Command>
18      <Command x="60.0" y="70.0" width="1.0" color="black">GoTo</Command>
19      <Command x="60.0" y="100.0" width="1.0" color="black">GoTo</Command>
20      <Command x="90.0" y="100.0" width="1.0" color="black">GoTo</Command>
```

```
21    <Command x="115.0" y="70.0" width="1.0" color="black">GoTo</Command>
22    <Command x="150.0" y="70.0" width="1.0" color="black">GoTo</Command>
23    <Command x="150.0" y="40.0" width="1.0" color="black">GoTo</Command>
24    <Command>EndFill</Command>
25 </GraphicsCommands>
```

XML files are text files. They just contain extra XML formatted data to help standardize how XML files are read. Writing an XML file is as simple as writing a text file. While indentation is not necessary in XML files, it is often used to highlight the format of the file. In Sect. 1.15.1 the *GraphicsCommands* element contains one *Command* element for each drawing command in the picture. Each drawing command contains the command type as its text. The command types are *GoTo*, *Circle*, *BeginFill*, *EndFill*, *PenUp*, and *PenDown*. The attributes of a command are data like *x, y, width, radius,* and *color* that are used by the various types of commands.

To write the commands to a file, each of the Command classes can be modified to produce an XML element when converted to a string using the special __str__ method. For instance, Sect. 1.15.2 contains the modified GoToCommand class supporting the creation of an XML element.

1.15.2 The GoToCommand with XML Creation Code

```
1  # The following classes define the different commands that
2  # are supported by the drawing application.
3  class GoToCommand:
4      def __init__(self,x,y,width=1,color="black"):
5          self.x = x
6          self.y = y
7          self.width = width
8          self.color = color
9
10     # The draw method for each command draws the command
11     # using the given turtle
12     def draw(self,turtle):
13         turtle.width(self.width)
14         turtle.pencolor(self.color)
15         turtle.goto(self.x,self.y)
16
17     # The __str__ method is a special method that is called
18     # when a command is converted to a string. The string
19     # version of the command is how it appears in the graphics
20     # file format.
21     def __str__(self):
22         return '<Command x="' + str(self.x) + '" y="' + str(self.y) + '" width="' + \
23                 str(self.width) + '" color="' + self.color + '">GoTo</Command>'
```

By returning a string like this from each of the command objects, the code to write the draw program's data to a file is very simple. All that is needed is some code that writes the *xml* line as the first line, followed by the *<GraphicsCommands>* tag and the command elements. Finally, the *<GraphicsCommands>* tag must be written. The code in Sect. 1.15.3 accomplishes this.

1.15.3 Writing Graphics Commands to an XML File

```
1   file = open(filename, "w")
2   file.write('<?xml version="1.0" encoding="UTF-8" standalone="no" ?>\n')
3   file.write('<GraphicsCommands>\n')
4   for cmd in self.graphicsCommands:
5       file.write('     '+str(cmd)+"\n")
6
7   file.write('</GraphicsCommands>\n')
8   file.close()
```

Writing an XML file is like writing any text file except that the text file must conform to the XML grammar specification. There are certainly ways to create XML files that differ from how it was presented in Sect. 1.15.3. In the next section we'll learn about XML parsers and a very simple way to read XML documents. It turns out there are at least some XML frameworks that make writing an XML document just as simple.

1.16   Reading XML Files

XML files would be difficult to read if we had to read them like we read a regular text file. This is especially true because XML files are not line-oriented. They conform to the XML grammar, but the grammar does not specify anything about the lines in the file. Instead of reading an XML file by reading lines of the file, we use a special tool called a *parser*. A *parser* is written according to the rules of a *grammar*, in this case the XML grammar. There are many XML parsers that have been written and different parsers have different features. The one we will use in this text is one of the simpler parsers called *minidom*. The *minidom* parser reads an entire XML file by calling the *parse* method on it. It places the entire contents of an XML file into an sequence of *Element* objects. An *Element* object contains the child data and attributes of an XML element along with any other elements that might be defined inside this element.

To use the minidom parser, you must first import the module where the minidom parser is defined.

```
import xml.dom.minidom
```

Then, you can read an entire XML file by calling the *parse* method on an XML document as follows.

```
xmldoc = xml.dom.minidom.parse(filename)
```

Once you have done that, you can read a specific type of element from the XML file by calling the method *getElementsByTagName* on it. For instance, to get the *GraphicsCommands* element from the graphics commands XML file, you would write this.

```
graphicsCommands = xmldoc.getElementsByTagName("GraphicsCommands")[0]
```

The XML document contains the GraphicsCommands element. Calling *getElementsByTagName* on *GraphicsCommands* returns a list of all elements that match this tag name. Since we know there is only one of these tags in the file, we can write [0] to get the first element from the list. Then, the *graphicsCommands* element contains just the one element from the file and all the *Command* elements of the file are located within it. If we want to go through all these elements we can use a for loop as in the code in Sect. 1.16.1.

1.16.1 Using an XML Parser

```
1   for commandElement in graphicsCommands:
2       print(type(commandElement))
3       command = commandElement.firstChild.data.strip()
4       attr = commandElement.attributes
5       if command == "GoTo":
6           x = float(attr["x"].value)
7           y = float(attr["y"].value)
8           width = float(attr["width"].value)
9           color = attr["color"].value.strip()
10          cmd = GoToCommand(x,y,width,color)
11
12      elif command == "Circle":
13          radius = float(attr["radius"].value)
14          width = float(attr["width"].value)
15          color = attr["color"].value.strip()
16          cmd = CircleCommand(radius,width,color)
17
18      elif command == "BeginFill":
19          color = attr["color"].value.strip()
20          cmd = BeginFillCommand(color)
21
22      elif command == "EndFill":
23          cmd = EndFillCommand()
24
25      elif command == "PenUp":
26          cmd = PenUpCommand()
27
28      elif command == "PenDown":
29          cmd = PenDownCommand()
30      else:
31          raise RuntimeError("Unknown Command: " + command)
32
33      self.append(cmd)
```

In the code in Sect. 1.16.1 the *attr* variable is a dictionary mapping the attribute *names* (i.e. keys) to their associated *values*. The child data of a *Command* node can be found by looking at the *firstChild.data* for the node. The *strip* method is used to strip away any unwanted blanks, tabs, or newline characters that might appear in the string.

1.17 Chapter Summary

In this first chapter we have covered a large amount of material which should be mostly review but probably covered some things that are new to you as well. Don't be too overwhelmed by it all. The purpose of this chapter is to get you asking questions about the things you don't understand. If you don't understand something, you should ask your teacher or someone who knows more about programming in Python. They can likely help you. Asking questions is a great way to learn and Computer Science is all about a lifetime of learning.

Here is a list of the important concepts you should have learned in this chapter. You should:

- know how to create an *object*, both from a literal value and by calling the object's constructor explicitly.
- understand the concept of a *reference* pointing at a value (i.e. an object) in Python.
- know how to call a *method* on an object.
- know how to *import* a module.
- understand the importance of *indentation* in Python programs.
- know why you write a *main* function in Python programs and how to call the main function.
- know how to read records from a file whether they be multi-line, single line, fixed length, or variable length records.
- know how to define a *container* class like PyList defined in this chapter.
- understand the concept of *polymorphism* and how that means an object will do the right thing when a method is called.
- understand the *Accumulator* pattern and how to use it in a program.
- know how to implement a simple GUI using Tkinter in Python. Entry boxes, labels, buttons, frames, and event handlers should all be concepts that are understood and can be programmed by looking back at the examples in this chapter.
- and finally you should know how to read and write XML files in your programs.

There is a lot of example code in this chapter and the final version of the *Draw* program is provided on the text's website or in Sect. 20.1. While it is doubtful you will be able to memorize each line of the code you found in this chapter, you should make sure you know how things work when you look at it and you should remember that you can use this chapter as a resource. Come back to it often when you need to see how to do something in later chapters. Using this example code as a reference will help to answer a lot of your questions in future chapters.

1.18   Review Questions

Answer these short answer, multiple choice, and true/false questions to test your mastery of the chapter.

1. What does IDE stand for and why is it a good idea to use an IDE?
2. What code would you write to create a string containing the words *Happy Birthday!*? Write some code to point a reference called *text* at that newly created object.
3. What code would you write to take the string you created in the last question and split it into a list containing two strings? Point the reference *lst* at this newly created list.
4. What code would you write to upper-case the string created in the second question. Point the reference named *bDayWish* at this upper-cased string.
5. If you were to execute the code you wrote for answering the last three questions, what would the string referenced by *text* contain after executing these three lines of code?
6. How would you create a dictionary that maps "Kent" to "Denise" and maps "Steve" to "Lindy"? In these two cases "Kent" and "Steve" are the keys and "Denise" and "Lindy" are the values.
7. Consult Chap. 17. How would you map a key to a value as in the previous problem when the dictionary was first created as an empty dictionary? HINT: This would be called setting an item in the documentation in the appendix. Write a short piece of code to create an empty dictionary and then map "Kent" to "Denise" and "Steve" to "Lindy".
8. What method is called when $x < y$ is written? In which class is the method a member? In other words, if you were presented with $x < y$ in a program, how would you figure out which class you needed to examine to understand exactly what $x < y$ meant?
9. What method is called when $x \ll y$ is written?
10. What is the loop and a half problem and how is it solved?
11. Do you need to use the solution to the loop and a half problem to read an XML file? Why or why not?
12. Polymorphism and Operator Overloading are closely related concepts. Can you briefly explain how the two concepts are similar and how Python supports them? HINT: No is not a valid answer.
13. What would you write so that a program asks the user to enter an integer and then adds up all the even integers from 2 to the integer entered by the user. HINT: You might want to review how to use the *range* function to accomplish this and decide on what pattern of programming you might use.
14. How do you create a window using Tkinter?
15. What is the purpose of a Frame object in a Tkinter program?
16. What are three types of widgets in the Tkinter framework?
17. When reading an XML file, how many lines of code does it take to read the file?
18. How do you get a single element from an XML document? What line(s) of code do you have to write? Provide an example.

19. When traversing an XML document, how do you get a list of elements from it? What line(s) of code do you have to write? Provide an example.
20. What is an attribute in an XML document and how do you access an attribute's value? Provide an example from the text or from another example you find online.

1.19 Programming Problems

1. Starting with the version of the *Draw* program that reads an input file with variable length records, add a new graphics command of your choice to the program. Consider how it would be written to a file, create a test file, write your code, and test it. You must design two files: a sample test file, and the program itself. Some examples might be a graphics command to draw a star with some number of points, a rectangle with a height and width, etc.
2. Starting with the *Draw* program provided in Sect. 20.1, extend the program to include a new button to draw a new shape for the *Draw* program. For instance, have the draw program draw a star on the screen or a smiley face or something of your choosing. HINT: If you use the forward and back methods to draw your shape, you can scale it by multiplying each forward and back amount by a scale value. Then, you can let the user pick a scale for it (or use the radius amount as your scale) and draw your shape in whatever size you like. To complete this exercise you must extend your XML format to include a new graphics command to store the relevant information for drawing your new shape. You must also define a new graphicsCommand class for your new shape.
3. Add the ability to draw a text string on a *Draw* picture. You'll need to let the user pick a point size. For a real challenge, let the user pick the font type from a drop-down list of font types. Draw a string that you have the user enter in an entry box.
4. Find an XML document of your choice on the internet, write code to parse through the data and plot something from that data whether it be some value over time or something else. Use turtle graphics to plot the data that you find.
5. Add a new button to the drawing program presented in Sect. 20.1 that draws a rainbow centered above the current location of the turtle. This can be done quite easily by using *sin* and *cos* (i.e. sine and cosine). The *sin* and *cos* functions take radians as a parameter. To draw a rainbow, the radians would range from 0 to *math.pi* from the math module. You must import the *math* module to get access to *math.cos* and *math.sin* as well as *math.pi*. To draw values in an arc, you can use a *for loop* and let a variable, *i*, range from 0 to 100. Then *radius* * *math.cos(i/100.0* * *math.pi)*, *radius* * *math.sin(i/100.0* * *math.pi)* is the next *x,y* coordinate of the rainbow's arc. By varying the radius you will get several stripes for your rainbow.

Each stripe should have a different color. To vary the color, you might convert a 24-bit number to hex. To convert a number to hexadecimal in Python you can use the *hex* function. You must make sure that your color string is 6 digits long and starts with a pound sign (i.e. #) for it to be a valid color string in Python.

Computational Complexity

2

In the last chapter we developed a drawing program. To hold the drawing commands we built the *PyList* container class which is a lot like the built-in Python list class, but helps illustrate our first data structure. When we added a drawing command to the sequence we called the append method. It turns out that this method is called a lot. In fact, the flower picture in the first chapter took around 700 commands to draw. You can imagine that a complex picture with lots of free-hand drawing could contain thousands of drawing commands. When creating a free-hand drawing we want to append the next drawing command to the sequence quickly because there are so many commands being appended. How long does it take to append a drawing command to the sequence? Can we make a guess? Should we care about the exact amount of time?

In this chapter you'll learn how to answer these questions and you'll learn what questions are important for you as a computer programmer. First you'll read about some principles of computer architecture to understand something about how long it takes a computer to do some simple operations. With that knowledge you'll have the tools you'll need to make informed decisions about how much time it might take to execute some code you have written.

2.1 Chapter Goals

By the end of this chapter you should be able to answer these questions.

- What are some of the primitive operations that a computer can perform?
- How much time does it take to perform these primitive operations?
- What does the term *computational complexity* mean?
- Why do we care about *computational complexity*?
- When do we need to be concerned about the complexity of a piece of code?
- What can we do to improve the efficiency of a piece of code?
- What is the definition of Big-Oh notation?

© Springer International Publishing Switzerland 2015
K.D. Lee and S. Hubbard, *Data Structures and Algorithms with Python*,
Undergraduate Topics in Computer Science, DOI 10.1007/978-3-319-13072-9_2

- What is the definition of Theta notation?
- What is *amortized complexity* and what is its importance?
- How can we apply what we learned to make the *PyList* container class better?

2.2   Computer Architecture

A computer consists of a *Central Processing Unit* (i.e. the *CPU*) that interacts with *Input/Output* (i.e. *I/O*) devices like a keyboard, mouse, display, and network interface. When you run a program it is first read from a storage device like a hard drive into the *Random Access Memory*, or RAM, of the computer. RAM loses its contents when the power is shut off, so copies of programs are only stored in RAM while they are running. The permanent copy of a program is stored on the hard drive or some other permanent storage device.

The RAM of a computer holds a program as it is executing and also holds data that the program is manipulating. While a program is running, the CPU reads input from the input devices and stores data values in the RAM. The CPU also contains a very limited amount of memory, usually called *registers*. When an operation is performed by the CPU, such as adding two numbers together, the operands must be in registers in the CPU. Typical operations that are performed by the CPU are addition, subtraction, multiplication, division, and storing and retrieving values from the RAM.

2.2.1   Running a Program

When a user runs a program on a computer, the following actions occur:

1. The program is read from the disk or other storage device into RAM.
2. The operating system (typically Mac OS X, Microsoft Windows, or Linux) sets up two more areas of RAM called the run-time stack and the heap for use by the program.
3. The operating system starts the program executing by telling the CPU to start executing the first instruction of the computer.
4. The program reads data from the keyboard, mouse, disk, and other input sources.
5. Each instruction of the program retrieves small pieces of data from RAM, acts on them, and writes new data back to RAM.
6. Once the data is processed the result is provided as output on the screen or some other output device.

Because there is so little memory in the CPU, the normal mode of operation is to store values in the RAM until they are needed for a CPU operation. The RAM is a much bigger storage space than the CPU. But, because it is bigger, it is also slower than the CPU. Storing a value in RAM or retrieving a value from RAM can take as much time as several CPU operations. When needed, the values are copied from the

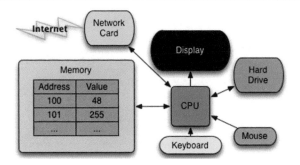

Fig. 2.1   Conceptual View of a Computer

RAM into the CPU, the operation is performed, and the result is then typically written back into the RAM. The RAM of a computer is accessed frequently as a program runs, so it is important that we understand what happens when it is accessed (Fig. 2.1).

One analogy that is often used is that of a post office. The RAM of a computer is like a collection of post office boxes. Each box has an address and can hold a value. The values you can put in RAM are called bytes (i.e. eight bits grouped together). With eight bits, 256 different values can be stored. Usually bytes are interpreted as integers, so a byte can hold values from 0 to 255. If we want to store bigger values, we can group bytes together into words. The word size of a computer is either 32 bits (i.e. four bytes) or 64 bits, depending on the architecture of the computer's hardware. All modern computer hardware is capable of retrieving or storing a word at a time.

The post office box analogy helps us to visualize how the RAM of a computer is organized, but the analogy does not serve well to show us how the RAM of a computer *behaves*. If we were going to get something from a post office box, or store something in a post office box, there would have to be some kind of search done to find the post office box first. Then the letter or letters could be placed in it or taken from it. The more post office boxes in the post office, the longer that search would take. This helps us understand the fundamental problem we study in this text. As the size of a problem space grows, how does a program or algorithm behave? In terms of this analogy, as the number of post office boxes grows, how much longer does it take to store or retrieve a value?

The RAM of a computer does not *behave* like a post office. The computer does not need to find the right RAM location before the it can retrieve or store a value. A much better analogy is a group of people, each person representing a memory location within the RAM of the computer. Each person is assigned an address or name. To store a value in a location, you call out the name of the person and then tell them what value to remember. It does not take any time to find the right person because all the people are listening, just in case their name is called. To retrieve a value, you call the name of the person and they tell you the value they were told to remember. In this way it takes exactly the same amount of time to retrieve any value from any memory location. This is how the RAM of a computer works. It takes exactly the same amount of time to store a value in any location within the RAM. Likewise, retrieving a value takes the same amount of time whether it is in the first RAM location or the last.

2.3   Accessing Elements in a Python List

With experimentation we can verify that all locations within the RAM of a computer can be accessed in the same amount of time. A Python list is a collection of contiguous memory locations. The word *contiguous* means that the memory locations of a list are grouped together consecutively in RAM. If we want to verify that the RAM of a computer behaves like a group of people all remembering their names and their values, we can run some tests with Python lists of different sizes to find the average time to retrieve from or store a value into a random element of the list.

To test the behavior of Python lists we can write a program that randomly stores and retrieves values in a list. We can test two different theories in this program.

1. The size of a list does not affect the average access time in the list.
2. The average access time at any location within a list is the same, regardless of its location within the list.

To test these two theories, we'll need to time retrieval and storing of values within a list. Thankfully, Python includes a datetime module that can be used to record the current time. By subtracting two datetime objects we can compute the number of microseconds (i.e. millionths of a second) for any operation within a program. The program in Sect. 2.3.1 was written to test list access and record the access time for retrieving values and storing values in a Python list.

2.3.1   List Access Timing

```
1    import datetime
2    import random
3    import time
4
5    def main():
6
7        # Write an XML file with the results
8        file = open("ListAccessTiming.xml","w")
9
10       file.write('<?xml version="1.0" encoding="UTF-8" standalone="no" ?>\n')
11
12       file.write('<Plot title="Average List Element Access Time">\n')
13
14       # Test lists of size 1000 to 200000.
15       xmin = 1000
16       xmax = 200000
17
18       # Record the list sizes in xList and the average access time within
19       # a list that size in yList for 1000 retrievals.
20       xList = []
21       yList = []
22
23       for x in range(xmin, xmax+1, 1000):
24
25           xList.append(x)
26
27           prod = 0
28
```

```
29          # Creates a list of size x with all 0's
30          lst = [0] * x
31
32          # let any garbage collection/memory allocation complete or at least
33          # settle down
34          time.sleep(1)
35
36          # Time before the 1000 test retrievals
37          starttime = datetime.datetime.now()
38
39          for v in range(1000):
40              # Find a random location within the list
41              # and retrieve a value. Do a dummy operation
42              # with that value to ensure it is really retrieved.
43              index = random.randint(0,x-1)
44              val = lst[index]
45              prod = prod * val
46          # Time after the 1000 test retrievals
47          endtime = datetime.datetime.now()
48
49          # The difference in time between start and end.
50          deltaT = endtime - starttime
51
52          # Divide by 1000 for the average access time
53          # But also multiply by 1000000 for microseconds.
54          accessTime = deltaT.total_seconds() * 1000
55
56          yList.append(accessTime)
57
58      file.write('   <Axes>\n')
59      file.write('      <XAxis min="'+str(xmin)+'" max="'+str(xmax)+'">List Size</XAxis>\n')
60      file.write('      <YAxis min="'+str(min(yList))+'" max="'+str(60)+'">Microseconds</YAxis>\n')
61      file.write('   </Axes>\n')
62
63      file.write('   <Sequence title="Average Access Time vs List Size" color="red">\n')
64
65      for i in range(len(xList)):
66          file.write('      <DataPoint x="'+str(xList[i])+'" y="'+str(yList[i])+'"/>\n')
67
68      file.write('   </Sequence>\n')
69
70      # This part of the program tests access at 100 random locations within a list
71      # of 200,000 elements to see that all the locations can be accessed in
72      # about the same amount of time.
73      xList = lst
74      yList = [0] * 200000
75
76      time.sleep(2)
77
78      for i in range(100):
79          starttime = datetime.datetime.now()
80          index = random.randint(0,200000-1)
81          xList[index] = xList[index] + 1
82          endtime = datetime.datetime.now()
83          deltaT = endtime - starttime
84          yList[index] = yList[index] + deltaT.total_seconds() * 1000000
85
86      file.write('   <Sequence title="Access Time Distribution" color="blue">\n')
87
88      for i in range(len(xList)):
89          if xList[i] > 0:
90              file.write('      <DataPoint x="'+str(i)+'" y="'+str(yList[i]/xList[i])+'"/>\n')
91
92      file.write('   </Sequence>\n')
93      file.write('</Plot>\n')
94      file.close()

1   if __name__ == "__main__":
2       main()
```

When running a program like this the times that you get will depend not only on the actual operations being performed, but the times will also depend on what other activity is occurring on the computer where the test is being run. All modern operating systems, like Mac OS X, Linux, or Microsoft Windows, are multi-tasking. This means the operating system can switch between tasks so that we can get email while writing a computer program, for instance. When we time something we will not only see the effects of our own program running, but all programs that are currently running on the computer. It is nearly impossible to completely isolate one program in a multi-tasking system. However, most of the time a short program will run without too much interruption.

The program in Sect. 2.3.1 writes an XML file with its results. The XML file format supports the description of experimentally collected data for a two dimensional plot of one or more sequences of data. One sample of the data that this program generates looks like Sect. 2.3.2. The data is abbreviated, but the format is as shown in Sect. 2.3.2.

2.3.2   A Plot XML Sample

```
 1  <?xml version="1.0" encoding="UTF-8" standalone="no" ?>
 2  <Plot title="Average List Element Access Time">
 3    <Axes>
 4      <XAxis min="1000" max="200000">List Size</XAxis>
 5      <YAxis min="20.244" max="60">Microseconds</YAxis>
 6    </Axes>
 7    <Sequence title="Average Access Time vs List Size" color="red">
 8      <DataPoint x="1000" y="33.069"/>
 9      <DataPoint x="2000" y="27.842"/>
10      <DataPoint x="3000" y="23.908"/>
11      <DataPoint x="4000" y="26.349"/>
12      <DataPoint x="5000" y="23.212"/>
13      <DataPoint x="6000" y="23.765"/>
14      <DataPoint x="7000" y="21.251"/>
15      <DataPoint x="8000" y="21.321"/>
16      <DataPoint x="9000" y="23.197"/>
17      <DataPoint x="10000" y="21.527"/>
18      <DataPoint x="11000" y="35.799"/>
19      <DataPoint x="12000" y="22.173"/>
20      ...
21      <DataPoint x="197000" y="26.245"/>
22      <DataPoint x="198000" y="30.013"/>
23      <DataPoint x="199000" y="25.888"/>
24      <DataPoint x="200000" y="23.578"/>
25    </Sequence>
26    <Sequence title="Access Time Distribution" color="blue">
27      <DataPoint x="219" y="41.0"/>
28      <DataPoint x="2839" y="38.0"/>
29      <DataPoint x="5902" y="38.0"/>
30      <DataPoint x="8531" y="58.0"/>
31      <DataPoint x="11491" y="38.0"/>
32      <DataPoint x="15415" y="38.0"/>
33      <DataPoint x="17645" y="31.0"/>
34      <DataPoint x="18658" y="38.0"/>
35      <DataPoint x="20266" y="40.0"/>
36      <DataPoint x="21854" y="31.0"/>
```

```
37        ...
38        <DataPoint x="197159" y="37.0"/>
39        <DataPoint x="199601" y="40.0"/>
40      </Sequence>
41    </Plot>
```

Since we'll be taking a look at quite a bit of experimental data in this text, we have written a Tkinter program that will read an XML file with the format given in Sect. 2.3.2 and plot the sequences to the screen. The PlotData.py program is given in Chap. 20.4.

If we use the program to plot the data gathered by the list access experiment, we see a graph like the one in Fig. 2.2. This graph provides the experimental data to back up the two statements we made earlier about lists in Python. The red line shows the average element access time of 1,000 element accesses on a list of the given size. The average access time (computed from a sample of 1,000 random list accesses) is no longer on a list of 10,000 than it is on a list of 160,000. While the exact values are not printed in the graph, the exact values are not important. What we would be interested in seeing is any trend toward longer or shorter average access times. Clearly the only trend is that the size of the list does not affect the average access time. There are some ups and downs in the experimental data, but this is caused by the system being

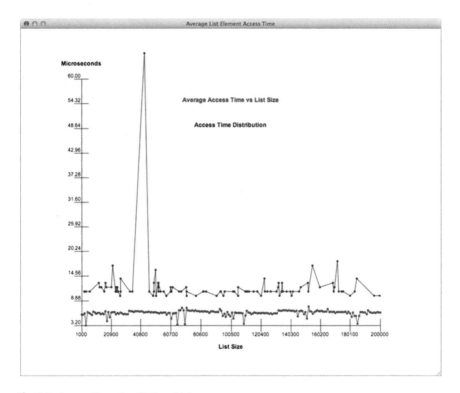

Fig. 2.2 Access Times in a Python List

a multi-tasking system. Another factor is likely the caching of memory locations. A cache is a way of speeding up access to memory in some situations and it is likely that the really low access times benefited from the existence of a cache for the RAM of the computer. The experimental data backs up the claim that *the size of a list does not affect the average access time in the list.*

The blue line in the plot is the result of doing 100 list retrieval and store operations on one list of 200,000 elements. The reason the blue line is higher than the red line is likely the result of doing both a retrieval from and a store operation into the element of the list. In addition, the further apart the values in memory, the less likely a cache will help reduce the access time. Whatever the reason for the blue line being higher the important thing to notice is that accessing the element at index 0 takes no more time than accessing any other element of the sequence. All locations within the list are treated equally. This backs up the claim that *the average access time at any location within a list is the same, regardless of its location within the list.*

2.4   Big-Oh Notation

Whichever line we look at in the experimental data, the access time never exceeds $100\,\mu s$ for any of the memory accesses, even with the other things the computer might be doing. We are safe concluding that accessing memory takes less than $100\,\mu s$. In fact, $100\,\mu s$ is much more time than is needed to access or store a value in a memory location. Our experimental data backs up the two claims we made earlier. However, technically, it does not prove our claim that accessing memory takes a constant amount of time. The architecture of the RAM in a computer could be examined to prove that accessing any memory location takes a constant amount of time. Accessing memory is just like calling out a name in a group of people and having that person respond with the value they were assigned. It doesn't matter which person's name is called out. The response time will be the same, or nearly the same. The actual time to access the RAM of a computer may vary a little bit if a cache is available, but at least we can say that there is an upper bound to how much time accessing a memory location will take.

This idea of an upper bound can be stated more formally. The formal statement of an upper bound is called Big-Oh notation. The Big-Oh refers to the Greek letter Omicron which is typically used when talking about upper bounds. As computer programmers, our number one concern is how our programs will perform when we have large amounts of data. In terms of the memory of a computer, we wanted to know how our program would perform if we have a very large list of elements. We found that all elements of a list are accessed in the same amount of time independent of how big this list is. Let's represent the size of the list by a variable called n. Let the average access time for accessing an element of a list of size n be given by $f(n)$. Now we can state the following.

$$O(g(n)) = \{f \mid \exists d > 0, n_0 \in Z^+ \ni 0 \le f(n) \le d\ g(n), \forall n \ge n_0\}$$

In English this reads as follows: The class of functions designated by $O(g(n))$ consists of all functions f, where there exists a d greater than 0 and an n_0 (a positive integer) such that 0 is less than or equal to $f(n)$ is less than or equal to d times $g(n)$ for all n greater than or equal to n_0.

If f is an element of $O(g(n))$, we say that f(n) is $O(g(n))$. The function g is called an asymptotic upper bound for f in this case. You may not be comfortable with the mathematical description above. Stated in English the set named $O(g(n))$ consists of the set of all functions, f(n), that have an upper bound of $d * g(n)$, as n approaches infinity. This is the meaning of the word *asymptotic*. The idea of an asymptotic bound means that for some small values of n the value of f(n) might be bigger than the value of $d * g(n)$, but once n gets big enough (i.e. bigger than n_0), then for all bigger n it will always be true that f(n) is less than $d * g(n)$. This idea of an asymptotic upper bound is pictured in Fig. 2.3. For some smaller values the function's performance, shown in green, may be worse than the blue upper bound line, but eventually the upper bound is bigger for all larger values of n.

We have seen that the average time to access an element in a list is constant and does not depend on the list size. In the example in Fig. 2.2, the list size is the n in the definition and the average time to access an element in a list of size n is the f(n).

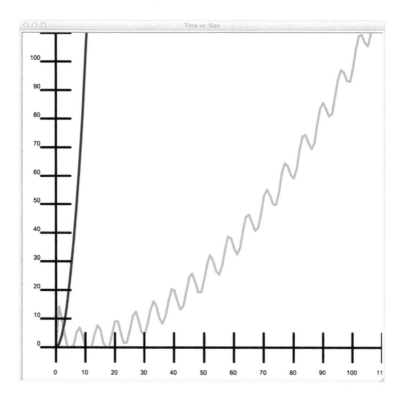

Fig. 2.3 An Upper Bound

Because the time to access an element does not depend on n, we can pick $g(n) = 1$. So, we say that the average time to access an element in a list of size n is O(1). If we assume it never takes longer than $100\,\mu s$ to access an element of a list in Python, then a good choice for d would be 100. According to the definition above then it must be the case that f(n) is less than or equal to 100 once n gets big enough.

The choice of $g(n) = 1$ is arbitrary in computing the complexity of accessing an element of a list. We could have chosen $g(n) = 2$. If $g(n) = 2$ were chosen, d might be chosen to be 50 instead of 100. But, since we are only concerned with the overall growth in the function g, the choice of 1 or 2 is irrelevant and the simplest function is chosen, in this case O(1). In English, when an operation or program is O(1), we say it is a *constant time* operation or program. This means the operation does not depend on the size of n.

It turns out that most operations that a computer can perform are O(1). For instance, adding two numbers together is a O(1) operation. So is multiplication of two numbers. While both operations require several cycles in a computer, the total number of cycles does not depend on the size of the integers or floating point numbers being added or multiplied. A cycle is simply a unit of time in a computer. Comparing two values is also a constant time operation. When computing complexity, any arithmetic calculation or comparison can be considered a constant time operation.

This idea of computational complexity is especially important when the complexity of a piece of code depends on n. In the next section we'll see some code that depends on the size of the list it is working with and how important it is that we understand the implications of how we write even a small piece of code.

2.5   The PyList Append Operation

We have established that accessing a memory location or storing a value in a memory location is a O(1), or constant time, operation. The same goes for accessing an element of a list or storing a value in a list. The size of the list does not change the time needed to access or store an element and there is a fixed upper bound for the amount of time needed to access or store a value in memory or in a list.

With this knowledge, let's look at the drawing program again and specifically at the piece of code that appends graphics commands to the PyList. This code is used a lot in the program. Every time a new graphics command is created, it is appended to the sequence. When the user is doing some free-hand drawing, hundreds of graphics commands are getting appended every minute or so. Since free-hand drawing is somewhat compute intensive, we want this code to be as efficient as possible.

2.5.1   Inefficient Append

```
1   class PyList:
2       def __init__(self):
3           self.items = []
4
5           # The append method is used to add commands to the sequence.
6       def append(self,item):
7           self.items = self.items + [item]
8
9           ...
```

The code in Sect. 2.5.1 appends a new item to the list as follows:

1. The item is made into a list by putting [and] around it. We should be careful about how we say this. The item itself is not changed. A new list is constructed from the item.
2. The two lists are concatenated together using the + operator. The + operator is an accessor method that does not change either original list. The concatenation creates a new list from the elements in the two lists.
3. The assignment of *self.items* to this new list updates the PyList object so it now refers to the new list.

The question we want to ask is, how does this append method perform as the size of the PyList grows? Let's consider the first time that the append method is called. How many elements are in the list that is referenced by self.items? Zero, right? And there is always one element in [item]. So the append method must access one element of a list to form the new list, which also has one element in it.

What happens the second time the append method is called? This time, there is one element in the list referenced by *self.items* and again one element in [*item*]. Now, two elements must be accessed to form the new list. The next time append is called three elements must be accessed to form the new list. Of course, this pattern continues for each new element that is appended to the PyList. When the nth element is appended to the sequence there will have to be *n* elements copied to form the new list. Overall, how many elements must be accessed to append *n* elements?

2.6   A Proof by Induction

We have already established that accessing each element of a list takes a constant amount of time. So, if we want to calculate the amount of time it takes to append *n* elements to the PyList we would have to add up all the list accesses and multiply by the amount of time it takes to access a list element plus the time it takes to store a list element. To count the total number of access and store operations we must start with the number of access and store operations for copying the list the first time an element is appended. That's one element copied. The second append requires two copy operations. The third append requires three copy operations. So, we have the following number of list elements being copied.

$$1 + 2 + 3 + 4 + \cdots + n = \sum_{i=1}^{n} i$$

In mathematics we can express this sum with a summation symbol (i.e. $\sum$). This is the mathematical way of expressing the sum of the first n integers. But, what is this equal to? It turns out with a little work, we can find that the following is true.

$$\sum_{i=1}^{n} i = \frac{n(n + 1)}{2}$$

We can prove this is true using a proof technique from Mathematics called mathematical induction. There are a couple of variations of mathematical induction. We'll use what is called weak induction to prove this. When proving something using induction you are really constructing a meta-proof. A meta-proof is a set of steps that you can repeat over and over again to find your desired result. The power of induction is that once we have constructed the meta-proof, we have proved that the result is true for all possible values of n.

We want to prove that the formula given above is valid for all n. To do this we first show it is true for a simple value of n. In our case we'll pick 1 as our value of n. In that case we have the following.

$$\sum_{i=1}^{1} i = 1 = \frac{1(1 + 1)}{2}$$

This is surely true. This step is called the *base case* of the inductive proof. Every *proof by induction* must have a base case and it is usually trivial.

The next step is to create the meta-proof. This meta-proof is called the *inductive case*. When forming the inductive case we get to assume that the formula holds for all values, m, where m is less than n. This is called *strong induction*. In *weak induction* we get to assume that the formula is valid for $n - 1$ and we want to show that it is valid for n. We'll use weak induction in this problem to finish our proof. Again, this step helps us form a set of steps that we can apply over and over again to get from our base case to whatever value of n we need to find. To begin we will make note of the following.

$$\sum_{i=1}^{n} i = \left(\sum_{i=1}^{n-1} i\right) + n$$

This is true by the definition of summation. But now we have a sum that goes to $n - 1$ and weak induction says that we know the equation is valid for $n - 1$. This is called the *inductive hypothesis*. Since it holds for $n - 1$ we know the following is true. We get this by substituting $n - 1$ everyplace that we see an n in the original formula.

$$\sum_{i=1}^{n-1} i = \frac{(n - 1)n}{2}$$

Now we can use this fact in proving the equality of our original formula. Here we go!

$$\sum_{i=1}^{n} i = \left(\sum_{i=1}^{n-1} i\right) + n = \frac{n(n-1)}{2} + n = \frac{n(n-1)}{2} + \frac{2n}{2} = \frac{n^2 - n + 2n}{2} = \frac{n^2 + n}{2} = \frac{n(n+1)}{2}$$

If you look at the left side and all the way over at the right side of this formula you can see the two things that we set out to prove were equal are indeed equal. This concludes our proof by induction. The meta-proof is in the formula above. It is a template that we could use to prove that the equality holds for $n = 2$. To prove the equality holds for $n = 2$ we needed to use the fact that the equality holds for $n = 1$. This was our base case. Once we have proved that it holds for $n = 2$ we could use that same formula to prove that the equality holds for $n = 3$. Mathematical induction doesn't require us to go through all the steps. As long as we've created this meta-proof we have proved that the equality holds for all n. That's the power of induction.

2.7   Making the PyList Append Efficient

Now, going back to our original problem, we wanted to find out how much time it takes to append n items to a PyList. It turns out, using the append method in Sect. 2.5.1, it will perform in $O(n^2)$ time. This is because the first time we called append we had to copy one element of the list. The second time we needed to copy two elements. The third time append was called we needed to copy three elements. Our proof in Sect. 2.6 is that $1 + 2 + 3 + \cdots + n$ equals n*(n + 1)/2. The highest powered term in this formula is the n^2 term. Therefore, the append method in Sect. 2.5.1 exhibits $O(n^2)$ complexity. This is not really a good result. The red curve in the graph of Fig. 2.4 shows the actual results of how much time it takes to append 200,000 elements to a *PyList*. The line looks somewhat like the graph of $f(n) = n^2$. What this tells us is that if we were to draw a complex program with say 100,000 graphics commands in it, to add one more command to the sequence it would take around 27 s. This is unacceptable! We may never draw anything that complex, but a computer should be able to add one more graphic command quicker than that!

In terms of big-Oh notation we say that the *append* method is $O(n^2)$. When n gets large, programs or functions with $O(n^2)$ complexity are not very good. You typically want to stay away from writing code that has this kind of computational complexity associated with it unless you are absolutely sure it will never be called on large data sizes.

One real-world example of this occurred a few years ago. A tester was testing some code and placed a CD in a CD drive. On this computer all the directories and file names on the CD were read into memory and sorted alphabetically. The sorting algorithm that was used in that case had $O(n^2)$ complexity. This was OK because most CDs put in this computer had a relatively small number of directories and files on them. However, along came one CD with literally hundreds of thousands of files on it. The computer did nothing but sort those file names alphabetically for around 12 h. When this was discovered, the programmer rewrote the sorting code to be more efficient and reduced the sorting time to around 15 s. That's a BIG difference! It also illustrates just how important this idea of computational complexity is.

If we take another look at our PyList append method we might be able to make it more efficient if we didn't have to access each element of the first list when concatenating the two lists. The use of the + operator is what causes Python to access each element of that first list. When + is used a new list is created with space for one more element. Then all the elements from the old list must be copied to the new list and the new element is added at the end of this list.

Using the *append* method on lists changes the code to use a mutator method to alter the list by adding just one more element. It turns out that adding one more element to an already existing list is very efficient in Python. In fact, appending an item to a list is a O(1) operation as we'll see later in this chapter. This means to append *n* items to a list we have gone from O(n^2) to O(n). Later in this chapter we'll learn just how Python can insure that we get O(1) complexity for the append operation. The blue line in Fig. 2.4 shows how the PyList append method works when the + operator is replaced by calling the list append method instead. At 100,000 elements

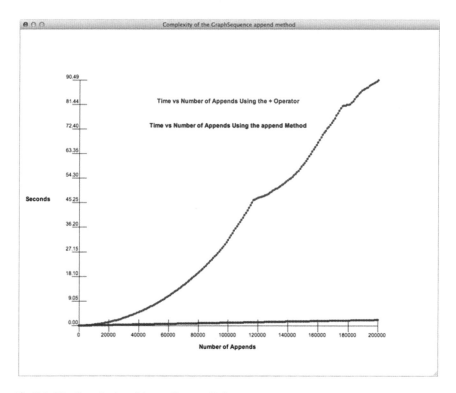

Fig. 2.4 The Complexity of Appending to a Pylist

in the PyList we go from 27 s to add another element to maybe a second, but probably less than that. That's a nice speedup in our program. After making this change, the PyList append method is given in Sect. 2.7.1.

2.7.1   Efficient Append

```
class PyList:
    def __init__(self):
        self.items = []

    # The append method is used to add commands to the sequence.
    def append(self,item):
        self.items.append(item)

    ...
```

2.8   Commonly Occurring Computational Complexities

The algorithms we will study in this text will be of one of the complexities of $O(1)$, $O(\log n)$, $O(n \log n)$, $O(n^2)$, or $O(c^n)$. A graph of the shapes of these functions appears in Fig. 2.5. Most algorithms have one of these complexities corresponding to some factor of n. Constant values added or multiplied to the terms in a formula for measuring the time needed to complete a computation do not affect the overall complexity of that operation. Computational complexity is only affected by the highest power term of the equation. The complexities graphed in Fig. 2.5 are of some power n or the log of n, except for the really awful exponential complexity of $O(c^n)$, where c is some constant value.

As you are reading the text and encounter algorithms with differing complexities, they will be one of the complexities shown in Fig. 2.5. As always, the variable n represents the size of the data provided as input to the algorithm. The time taken to process that data is the vertical axis in the graph. While we don't care about the exact numbers in this graph, we do care about the overall shape of these functions. The flatter the line, the lower the slope, the better the algorithm performs. Clearly an algorithm that has exponential complexity (i.e. $O(c^n)$) or n-squared complexity (i.e. $O(n^2)$) complexity will not perform very well except for very small values of n. If you know your algorithm will never be called for large values of n then an inefficient algorithm might be acceptable, but you would have to be really sure that you knew that your data size would always be small. Typically we want to design algorithms that are as efficient as possible.

In subsequent chapters you will encounter sorting algorithms that are $O(n^2)$ and then you'll learn that we can do better and achieve $O(n \log n)$ complexity. You'll see search algorithms that are $O(n)$ and then learn how to achieve $O(\log n)$ complexity. You'll also learn a technique called hashing that will search in $O(1)$ time. The techniques you learn will help you deal with large amounts of data as efficiently

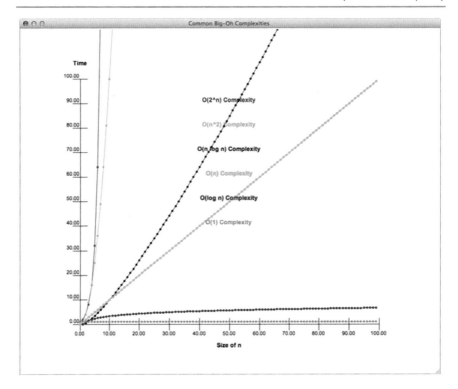

Fig. 2.5 Common Big-Oh Complexities

as possible. As each of these techniques are explored, you'll also have the opportunity to write some fun programs and you'll learn a good deal about object-oriented programming.

2.9   More Asymptotic Notation

Earlier in this chapter we developed Big-Oh notation for describing an upper bound on the complexity of an algorithm. There we began with an intuitive understanding of the idea of efficiency saying that a function exhibits a complexity if it is bounded above by a function of n where n represents the size of the data given to the algorithm. In this section we further develop these concepts to bound the efficiency of an algorithm from both above and below.

We begin with an in-depth discussion of efficiency and the measurement of it in Computer Science. When concerning ourselves with algorithm efficiency there are two issues that must be considered.

- The amount of time an algorithm takes to run
- and, related to that, the amount of space an algorithm uses while running.

Typically, computer scientists will talk about a space/time tradeoff in algorithms. Sometimes we can achieve a faster running time by using more memory. But, if we use too much memory we can slow down the computer and other running programs. The *space* that is referred to is the amount of *RAM* needed to solve a problem. The *time* we are concerned with is a measure of how the number of operations grow as the size of the data grows.

Consider a function $T(n)$ that is a description of the running time of an algorithm, where n is the size of the data given to the algorithm. As computer scientists we want to study the *asymptotic behavior* of this function. In other words, we want to study how $T(n)$ increases as $n \to \infty$. The value of n is a Natural number representing possible sizes of input data. The natural numbers are the set of non-negative integers. The definition in Sect. 2.9.1 is a re-statement of the Big-Oh notation definition presented earlier in this chapter.

2.9.1   Big-Oh Asymptotic Upper Bound

$$O(g(n)) = \{f(n) \mid \exists d > 0 \text{ and } n_0 > 0 \ni 0 \le f(n) \le dg(n) \ \forall n \ge n_0\}$$

We write that

$$f(n) \overset{is}{=} O(g(n)) \Leftrightarrow f \in O((g(n)))$$

and we say that f is big-oh g of n. The definition of Big-Oh says that we can find an upper bound for the time it will take for an algorithm to run. Consider the plot of time versus data size given in Fig. 2.3. Data size, or n is the x axis, while time is the y axis.

Imagine that the green line represents the observed behavior of some algorithm. The blue line clearly is an upper bound to the green line after about n = 4. This is what the definition of big-Oh means. For a while, the upper bounding function may not be an upper bound, but eventually it becomes an upper bound and stays that way all the way to the limit as n approaches infinity.

But, does the blue line represent a tight bound on the complexity of the algorithm whose running time is depicted by the green line? We'd like to know that when we describe the complexity of an algorithm it is truly representational of the actual running time. Saying that the algorithm runs in $O(n^2)$ is accurate even if the algorithm runs in time proportional to n because Big-Oh notation only describes an upper bound. If we truly want to say what the algorithm's running time is proportional to, then we need a little more power. This leads us to our next definition in Sect. 2.9.2.

2.9.2 Asymptotic Lower Bound

$$\Omega(g(n)) = \{f(n) \mid \exists c > 0 \text{ and } n_0 > 0 \ni 0 \le cg(n) \le f(n) \; \forall n \ge n_0\}$$

Omega notation serves as a way to describe a lower bound of a function. In this case the lower bound definition says for a while it might be greater, but eventually there is some n_0 where $T(n)$ dominates $g(n)$ for all bigger values of n. In that case, we can write that the algorithm is $\Omega(g(n))$. Considering our graph once again, we see that the purple line is dominated by the observed behavior sometime after $n = 75$. As with the upper bound, for a while the lower bound may be greater than the observed behavior, but after a while, the lower bound stays below the observed behavior for all bigger values of n.

With both a lower bound and and upper bound definition, we now have the notation to define an asymptotically tight bound. This is called *Theta* notation.

2.9.3 Theta Asymptotic Tight Bound

$$\Theta(g(n)) = \{f(n) \mid \exists c > 0, d > 0 \text{ and } n_0 > 0 \ni 0 \le cg(n) \le f(n) \le dg(n) \; \forall n \ge n_0\}$$

If we can find such a function g, then we can declare that $\Theta(g(n))$ is an asymptotically tight bound for $T(n)$, the observed behavior of an algorithm. In Fig. 2.6 the upper bound blue line is $g(n) = n^2$ and the lower bound purple line is a plot of $g(n)/110$. If we let $c = 1$ and $d = 1/110$, we have the asymptotically tight bound of $T(n)$ at $\Theta(n^2)$. Now, instead of saying that n-squared is an upper bound on the algorithm's behavior, we can proclaim that the algorithm truly runs in time proportional to n-squared. The behavior is bounded above and below by functions of n-squared proving the claim that the algorithm is an n-squared algorithm.

2.10 Amortized Complexity

Sometimes it is not possible to find a tight upper bound on an algorithm. For instance, most operations may be bounded by some function $c*g(n)$ but every once in a while there may be an operation that takes longer. In these cases it may be helpful to employ something called *Amortized Complexity*. Amortization is a term used by accountants when spreading the cost of some business transaction over a number of years rather than applying the whole expense to the books in one fiscal year. This same idea is employed in Computer Science when the cost of an operation is averaged. The key idea behind all amortization methods is to get as tight an upper bound as we can for the worst case running time of any sequence of n operations on a data structure (which usually starts out empty). By dividing by n we get the average or *amortized* running time of each operation in the sequence.

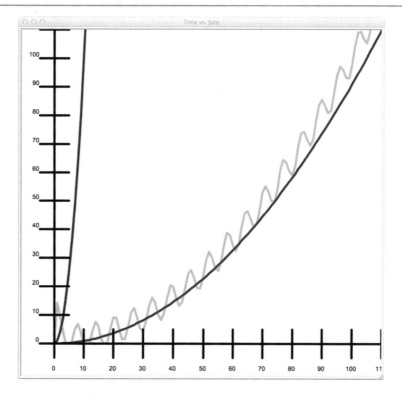

Fig. 2.6 A Lower and Upper Bound

Consider the PyList append operation discussed earlier in this chapter. The latest version of the PyList append method simply calls the Python append operation on lists. Python is implemented in C. It turns out that while Python supports an append operation for lists, lists are implemented as arrays in C and it is not possible to add to an array in C. An array can be allocated with a fixed size, but cannot have its size increased once created.

Pretend for a moment that Python lists, like C arrays, did not support the *append* method on lists and that the only way to create a list was to write something like *[None]*n* where *n* was a fixed value. Writing *[None]*n* creates a fixed size list of *n* elements each referencing the value *None*. This is the way C and C++ arrays are allocated. In our example, since we are pretending that Python does not support append we must implement our PyList append method differently. We can't use the *append* method and earlier in this chapter we saw that that adding on item at a time with the + operator was a bad idea. We'll do something a little different. Our PyList append operation, when it runs out of space in the fixed size list, will double the size of the list copying all items from the old list to the new list as shown in the code in Sect. 2.10.1.

2.10.1 A PyList Class

```
1   class PyList:
2       # The size below is an initial number of locations for the list object. The
3       # numItems instance variable keeps track of how many elements are currently stored
4       # in the list since self.items may have empty locations at the end.
5       def __init__(self,size=1):
6           self.items = [None] * size
7           self.numItems = 0
8
9       def append(self,item):
10          if self.numItems == len(self.items):
11              # We must make the list bigger by allocating a new list and copying
12              # all the elements over to the new list.
13              newlst = [None] * self.numItems * 2
14              for k in range(len(self.items)):
15                  newlst[k] = self.items[k]
16
17              self.items = newlst
18
19          self.items[self.numItems] = item
20          self.numItems += 1
21
22  def main():
23      p = PyList()
24
25      for k in range(100):
26          p.append(k)
27
28      print(p.items)
29      print(p.numItems)
30      print(len(p.items))
31
32  if __name__ == "__main__":
33      main()
```

The claim is that, using this new PyList append method, a sequence of *n* append operations on a PyList object, starting with an empty list, takes O(n) time meaning that individual operations must not take longer than O(1) time. How can this be true? Whenever the list runs out of space a new list is allocated and all the old elements are copied to the new list. Clearly, copying *n* elements from one list to another takes longer than O(1) time. Understanding how append could exhibit O(1) complexity relies on computing the *amortized complexity* of the *append* operation. Technically, when the list size is doubled the complexity of *append* is O(n). But how often does that happen? The answer is *not that often*.

2.10.2 Proof of Append Complexity

The proof that the append method has O(1) complexity uses what is called the accounting method to find the amortized complexity of append. The accounting method stores up cyber dollars to pay for expensive operations later. The idea is that there must be *enough* cyber dollars to pay for any operation that is more expensive than the desired complexity.

Consider a sequence of n append operations on an initially empty list. Appending the first element to the list is done in $O(1)$ time since there is space for the first item added to the list because one slot was initially allocated in the list. Storing a value in an already allocated slot takes $O(1)$ time. However, according to the accounting method, we'll claim that the cost of doing the append operation requires an additional two cyber dollars. This is still $O(1)$ complexity. Each time we run out of space we'll double the number of slots in the fixed size list. Allocating a fixed size list is a $O(1)$ operation regardless of the list size. The extra work comes when copying the elements from the old list to the new list.

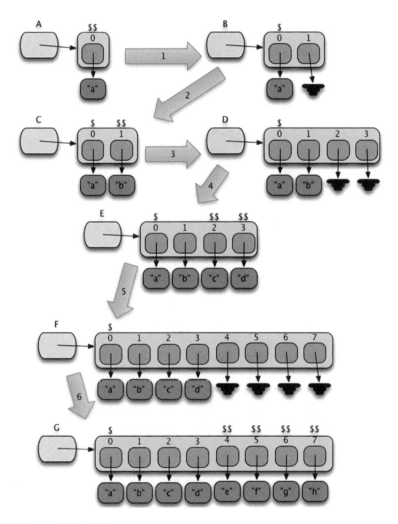

Fig. 2.7 Append Cyber Dollars

The first time we need to double the size is when the second append is called. There are two cyber dollars stored up at this point in time. One of them is needed when copying the one element stored in the old list to the new fixed size list capable of holding two elements. Transition one in Fig. 2.7 shows the two stored cyber dollars and the result after copying to the new list when moving from step A to step B.

When append is called on version B of the list the result is version C. At this point, three cyber dollars are stored to be used when doubling the list size to four locations. The first two are filled with the old contents of the list. Two of the three stored cyber dollars are used while copying these values to the new list. When the list of size four fills, two additional append operations have occurred, storing five cyber dollars. Four of these cyber dollars are used in the copy from step E to step F. Again, when the list of size eight fills in step G there are nine stored cyber dollars to be used in doubling the list size and copying the elements over.

But, what if we didn't double the size of the list each time. If we increased the list size by one half its previous size each time, we could still make this argument work if we stored four cyber dollars for each append operation. In fact, as long as the size of the list grows proportionally to its current size each time it is expanded this argument still works to prove that appending to a list is a $O(1)$ operation when lists must be allocated with a fixed size.

As mentioned earlier, the Python list object is implemented in C. While Python provides an append operation, the C language can only allocate fixed size lists, called arrays in C. And yet, Python list objects can append objects in $O(1)$ time as can be observed by experimentation or by analyzing the C code that implements Python list objects. The Python list *append* implementation achieves this by increasing the list size as described in this section when the fixed size array runs out of space to achieve an amortized complexity of $O(1)$.

2.11   Chapter Summary

This chapter covered some important topics related to the efficiency of algorithms. Efficiency is an important topic because even the fastest computers will not be able to solve problems in a reasonable amount of time if the programs that are written for them are inefficient. In fact, some problems can't be solved in a reasonable amount of time no matter how the program is written. Nevertheless, it is important that we understand these issues of efficiency. Finding the complexity of a piece of code is an important skill that you will get better at the more you practice. Here are some of the things you should have learned in this chapter. You should:

- know the complexity of storing or retrieving a value from a list or the memory of the computer.
- know how memory is like a post office.
- know how memory is NOT like a post office.

- know how to use the datetime module to get information about the time it takes to complete an operation in a program.
- know how to write an XML file that can be used by the plotting program to plot information about the performance of an algorithm or piece of code.
- understand the definition of big-Oh notation and how it establishes an upper bound on the performance of a piece of code.
- understand why the list + operation is not as efficient as the *append* operation.
- understand the difference between $O(n)$, $O(n^2)$, and other computational complexities and why those differences are important to us as computer programmers.
- Understand Theta notation and what an asymptotically tight bound says about an algorithm.
- Understand Amortized complexity and how to apply it in some simple situations.

2.12   Review Questions

Answer these short answer, multiple choice, and true/false questions to test your mastery of the chapter.

1. How is a list like a bunch of post office boxes?
2. How is accessing an element of a list NOT like retrieving the contents of a post office box?
3. How can you compute the amount of time it takes to complete an operation in a computer using Python?
4. In terms of computational complexity, which is better, an algorithm that is $O(n^2)$ or an algorithm that is $O(2^n)$?
5. Describe, in English, what it means for an algorithm to be $O(n^2)$.
6. When doing a proof by induction, what two parts are there to the proof?
7. If you had an algorithm with a loop that executed n steps the first time through, then $n - 2$ the second time, $n - 4$ the next time, and kept repeating until the last time through the loop it executed 2 steps, what would be the complexity measure of this loop? Justify your answer with what you learned in this chapter.
8. Assume you had a data set of size n and two algorithms that processed that data set in the same way. Algorithm A took 10 steps to process each item in the data set. Algorithm B processed each item in 100 steps. What would the complexity be of these two algorithms?
9. Explain why the *append* operation on a list is more efficient than the + operator.
10. Describe an algorithm for finding a particular value in a list. Then give the computational complexity of this algorithm. You may make any assumptions you want, but you should state your assumptions along with your algorithm.

2.13   Programming Problems

1. Devise an experiment to discover the complexity of comparing strings in Python.
   Does the size of the string affect the efficiency of the string comparison and if so,
   what is the complexity of the comparison? In this experiment you might want to
   consider a best case, worst case, and average case complexity. Write a program
   that produces an XML file with your results in the format specified in this chapter.
   Then use the PlotData.py program to visualize those results.
2. Conduct an experiment to prove that the product of two numbers does not depend
   on the size of the two numbers being multiplied. Write a program that plots the
   results of multiplying numbers of various sizes together. HINT: To get a good
   reading you may want to do more than one of these multiplications and time
   them as a group since a multiplication happens pretty quickly in a computer.
   Verify that it truly is a O(1) operation. Do you see any anomalies? It might be
   explained by Python's support of large integers. What is the cutoff point for
   handling multiplications in constant time? Why? Write a program that produces
   an XML file with your results in the format given in this chapter. Then visualize
   your results with the PlotData.py program provided in this chapter.
3. Write a program to gather experimental data about comparing integers. Compare
   integers of different sizes and plot the amount of time it takes to do those comparisons. Plot your results by writing an XML file in the Ploy.py format. Is the
   comparison operation always O(1)? If not, can you theorize why? HINT: You
   may want to read about Python's support for large integers.
4. Write a short function that searches for a particular value in a list and returns the
   position of that value in the list (i.e. its index). Then write a program that times
   how long it takes to search for an item in lists of different sizes. The size of the
   list is your *n*. Gather results from this experiment and write them to an XML file
   in the PlotData.py format. What is the complexity of this algorithm? Answer this
   question in a comment in your program and verify that the experimental results
   match your prediction. Then, compare this with the *index* method on a list. Which
   is more efficient in terms of computational complexity? HINT: You need to be
   careful to consider the average case for this problem, not just a trivial case.
5. Write a short function that given a list, adds together all the values in the list and
   returns the sum. Write your program so it does this operation with varying sizes
   of lists. Record the time it takes to find the sum for various list sizes. Record this
   information in an XML file in the PlotData.py format. What complexity is this
   algorithm? Answer this in a comment at the top of your program and verify it
   with your experimental data. Compare this data with the built-in *sum* function in
   Python that does the same thing. Which is more efficient in terms of computational
   complexity? HINT: You need to be careful to consider the average case for this
   problem, not just a trivial case.
6. Assume that you have a datatype called the Clearable type. This data type has a
   fixed size list inside it when it is created. So Clearable(10) would create a clearable
   list of size 10. Objects of the Clearable type should support an append operation
   and a lookup operation. The lookup operation is called __getitem__(item). If *cl* is

a Clearable list, then writing *cl*[*item*] will return the item if it is in the list and return *None* otherwise. Writing *cl*[*item*] results in a method call of cl.__getitem__(item). Unlike the append operation described in Sect. 2.10.1, when the Clearable object fills up the list is automatically cleared or emptied on the next call to append by setting all elements of the list back to *None*. The Clearable object should always keep track of the number of values currently stored in the object. Form a theory about the complexity of the append operation on this datatype. Then write a test program to test the Clearable object on different initial sizes and numbers of append operations. Create one sequence for each different initial size of the Clearable datatype and write your results in the plot format described in this chapter. Then comment on how your theory holds up or does not hold up given your experimentation results.

Recursion

3

Don't think too hard! That's one of the central themes of this chapter. It's not often that you tell computer programmers not to think too hard, but this is one time when it is appropriate. You need to read this chapter if you have not written recursive functions before. Most computer science students start by learning to program in a style called *imperative* programming. This simply means that you are likely used to thinking about creating variables, storing values, and updating those values as a program proceeds. In this chapter you are going to begin learning a different style of programming called *functional* programming. When you program in the functional style, you think much more about the definition of *what* you are programming than *how* you are going to program it. Some say that writing recursive functions is a *declarative* approach rather than an *imperative* approach. You'll start to learn what that means for you very soon. When you start to get good at writing recursive functions you'll be surprised how easy it can be!

Python programs are executed by an interpreter. An interpreter is a program that reads another program as its input and does what it says. The Python interpreter, usually called *python*, was written in a language called C. That C program reads a Python program and does what the Python program says to do in its statements. An interpreter interprets a program by running or executing what is written within it. The interpreter interacts with the operating system of the computer to use the network, the keyboard, the mouse, the monitor, the hard drive, and any other I/O device that it needs to complete the work that is described in the program it is interpreting. The picture in Fig. 3.1 shows you how all these pieces fit together.

In this chapter we'll introduce you to scope, the run-time stack, and the heap so you understand how the interpreter calls functions and where local variables are stored. Then we'll provide several examples of recursive functions so you can begin to see how they are written. There will be a number of recursive functions for you to practice writing and we'll apply recursion to drawing pictures as well.

One thing you will not do in the homework for this chapter is write code that uses a *for* loop or a *while* loop. If you find yourself trying to write code that uses either kind of loop you are trying to write a function imperatively rather than functionally.

© Springer International Publishing Switzerland 2015
K.D. Lee and S. Hubbard, *Data Structures and Algorithms with Python*,
Undergraduate Topics in Computer Science, DOI 10.1007/978-3-319-13072-9_3

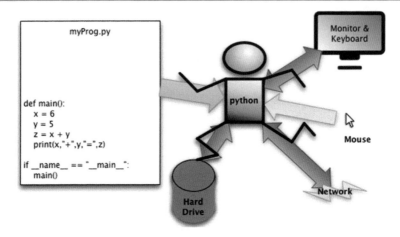

Fig. 3.1 The Python Interpreter

Recursion is the way we will repeat code in this chapter. A recursive function has no need for a *for* or *while* loop.

3.1   Chapter Goals

By the end of this chapter, you should be able to answer these questions.

- How does Python determine the meaning of an identifier in a program?
- What happens to the run-time stack when a function is called?
- What happens to the run-time stack when a function returns from a call?
- What are the two important parts to a recursive function and which part comes first?
- Exactly what happens when a return statement is executed?
- Why should we write recursive functions?
- What are the computational complexities of various recursive functions?

   You should also be able to write some simple recursive functions yourself without thinking too hard about how they work. In addition, you should be able to use a debugger to examine the contents of the run-time stack for a recursive function.

3.2   Scope

To form a complete mental picture of how your programs work we should further
explore just how the Python interpreter executes a Python program. In the first chapter
we explored how references are the things which we name and that references point
to objects, which are unnamed. However, we sometimes call an object by the name
of the reference that is pointing at it. For instance, if we write:

```
x = 6
```

it means that x is a reference that points to an object with a 6 inside it. But
sometimes we are careless and just say that x *equals 6*. It is important that you
understand that even when we say things like x *equals 6* what we really mean is
that x *is a reference that points to an object that contains 6*. You can see why we
are careless sometimes. It takes too many words to say what we really mean and
as long as everyone understands that references have names and objects are pointed
to by references, then we can save the words. The rest of this text will make this
assumption at times. When it is really important, we'll make sure we distinguish
between references and objects.

Part of our mental picture must include *Scope* in a Python program. Scope refers
to a part of a program where a collection of identifiers are visible. Let's look at a
simple example program.

3.2.1   Local Scope

Consider the code in Fig. 3.2. In this program there are several scopes. Every colored
region of the figure delimits one of those scopes. While executing line 23 of the
program in Fig. 3.2 the light green region is called the *Local* scope. The local scope
is the scope of the function that the computer is currently executing. When your
program is executing a line of code, the scope that surrounds that line of code is called
the local scope. When you reference an identifier in a statement in your program,
Python first examines the local scope to see if the identifier is defined there, within
the local scope. An identifier, *id*, is defined under one of three conditions.

- A statement like $id = \dots$ appears somewhere within the current scope. In this case
  id would be a reference to an object in the local scope.
- *id* appears as a parameter name of the function in the current scope. In this case
  id would be a reference to an object that was passed to the current function as an
  argument.
- *id* appears as a name of a function or class through the use of a function *def* or
  class definition within the current scope.

While Python is executing line 23 in Fig. 3.2, the reference *val* is defined within
its local scope. If Python finds *id* in the local scope, it looks up the corresponding
value and retrieves it. This is what happens when *val* is encountered on line 23. The
object that is referenced by *val* is retrieved and returned.

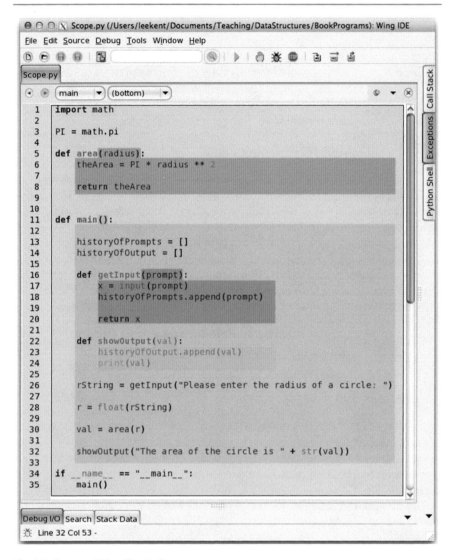

Fig. 3.2 Scopes within a Simple Program

3.2.2   Enclosing Scope

If Python does not find the reference *id* within the local scope, it will examine the *Enclosing* scope to see if it can find *id* there. In the program in Fig. 3.2, while Python is executing the statement on line 23, the enclosing scope is the purple region of the program. The identifiers defined in this enclosing scope include *historyOfPrompts*, *historyOfOutput*, *rString*, *r*, *val*, *getInput*, and *showInput*. Notice that function names are included as identifiers. Again, Python looks for the identifier using the same conditions as defined in Sect. 3.2.1 for the local scope. The identifier must be defined using *id = …*, it must be a parameter to the enclosing function, or it must be an identifier for a class or function definition in the enclosing scope's function. On line 23, when Python encounters the identifier *historyOfOutput* it finds that identifier defined in the enclosing scope and retrieves it for use in the call to the append method.

Which scope is local depends on where your program is currently executing. When executing line 23, the light green region is the local scope. When executing line 18 the brown region is the local scope. When executing line 14 or line 26 the purple region is the local scope. When executing line 6 the darker green region is the local scope. Finally, when executing line 1 or 3 the blue region is the local scope. The local scope is determined by where your program is currently executing.

Scopes are nested. This means that each scope is nested inside another scope. The final enclosing scope of a module is the module itself. Each module has its own scope. The blue region of Fig. 3.2 corresponds to the module scope. Identifiers that are defined outside of any other functions, but inside the module, are at the module level. The reference *PI* in Fig. 3.2 is defined at the module level. The functions *area* and *main* are also defined at the module level scope.

While executing line 23 of the program in Fig. 3.2 the identifier *val* is defined in the local scope. But, *val* is also defined in the enclosing scope. This is acceptable and often happens in Python programs. Each scope has its own copy of identifiers. The choice of which *val* is visible is made by always selecting the innermost scope that defines the identifier. While executing line 23 of the program in Fig. 3.2 the *val* in the local scope is visible and the *val* in the enclosing scope is hidden. This is why it is important that we choose our variable names and identifiers carefully in our programs. If we use an identifier that is already defined in an outer scope, we will no longer be able to access it from an inner scope where the same identifier is defined.

It is relatively easy to determine all the nested scopes within a module. Every function definition (including the definition of methods) within a module defines a different scope. The scope never includes the function name itself, but includes its parameters and the body of the function. You can follow this pattern to mentally draw boxes around any scope so you know where it begins and ends in your code.

3.2.3   Global Scope

Using Python it is possible to define variables at the *Global* level. Generally this is a bad programming practice and we will not do this in this text. If interested you can read more about global variables in Python online. But, using too many global variables will generally lead to name conflicts and will likely lead to unwanted side effects. Poor use of global variables contributes to spaghetti code which is named for the big mess you would have trying to untangle it to figure out what it does.

3.2.4   Built-In Scope

The final scope in Python is the *Built-In* scope. If an identifier is not found within any of the nested scopes within a module and it is not defined in the global scope, then Python will examine the built-in identifiers to see if it is defined there. For instance, consider the identifier *int*. If you were to write the following:

```
x = int("6")
```

Python would first look in the local scope to see if *int* were defined as a function or variable within that local scope. If *int* is not found within the local scope, Python would look in all the enclosing scopes starting with the next inner-most local scope and working outwards from there. If not found in any of the enclosing scopes, Python would then look in the global scope for the *int* identifier. If not found there, then Python would consult the *Built-In* scope, where it would find the *int* class or type.

With this explanation, it should now be clear why you should not use identifiers that already exist in the built-in scope. If you use *int* as an identifier you will not be able to use the *int* from the built-in scope because Python will find *int* in a local or enclosing scope first.

3.2.5   LEGB

Mark Lutz, in his book *Learning Python* [6], described the rules of scope in Python programs using the LEGB acronym. This acronym, standing for *Local, Enclosing, Global*, and *Built-In* can help you memorize the rules of scope in Python. The order of the letters in the acronym is important. When the Python interpreter encounters an identifier in a program, it searches the local scope first, followed by all the enclosing scopes from the inside outward, followed by the global scope, and finally the built-in scope.

3.3   The Run-Time Stack and the Heap

As we learned in the last section, the parameters and body of each function define a scope within a Python program. The parameters and variables defined within the local scope of a function must be stored someplace within the RAM of a computer. Python splits the RAM up into two parts called the *Run-time Stack* and the *Heap*.

The run-time stack is like a stack of trays in a cafeteria. Most cafeterias have a device that holds these trays. When the stack of trays gets short enough a spring below the trays pops the trays up so they are at a nice height. As more trays are added to the stack, the spring in this device compresses and the stack pushes down. A *Stack* in Computer Science is similar in many ways to this kind of device. The run-time stack is a stack of *Activation Records*. The Python interpreter *pushes* an activation record onto the run-time stack when a function is called. When a function returns the Python interpreter *pops* the corresponding activation record off the run-time stack.

Python stores the identifiers defined in the local scope in an activation record. When a function is called, a new scope becomes the local scope. At the same time a new activation record is pushed onto the run-time stack. This new activation record holds all the variables that are defined within the new local scope. When a function returns its corresponding activation record is popped from the run-time stack.

The *Heap* is the area of RAM where all objects are stored. When an object is created it resides in the heap. The run-time stack never contains objects. References to objects are stored within the run-time stack and those references point to objects in the heap.

Consider the program in Fig. 3.2. When the Python interpreter is executing lines 23 and 24 of the program, the run-time stack looks as it does in Fig. 3.3. There are three activation records on the run-time stack. The first activation record pushed onto the run-time stack was for the *module*. When the module first began executing, the Python interpreter went through the module from top to bottom and put any variable definitions in the module scope into the activation record for the module. In this program that consisted of the reference *PI* to the value 3.14159.

Then, at the end of the module the *if* statement called the *main* function. This caused the Python interpreter to push the activation record for the main function. The variables defined within the main function include *historyOfPrompts*, *history-OfOutput*, *rString*, *r*, and *val*. Each of these appear within the activation record for the main function.

As the main function began executing it called the *getInput* function. When that call occurred there was an activation record pushed for the function call. That activation record contained the *prompt* and *x* variables. This activation record does not appear in the figure because by the time we execute line 23 and 24 of the program the Python interpreter has already returned from the *getInput* function. When the interpreter returned from the function call the corresponding activation record was popped from the run-time stack.

Finally, the program calls the *showOutput* function on line 26 and execution of the function begins. An activation record for the *showOutpout* function call was pushed onto the run-time stack when *showOutput* was called. The references local to that scope, which includes just the *val* variable, were stored the activation record for this function call.

You can run this example program using Wing or some other IDE. The code for it appears in Sect. 20.2. When you use the Wing IDE to run this program you can stop the program at any point and examine the run-time stack. For instance, Fig. 3.4 shows Wing in the midst of running this program. A breakpoint has been set on line 24 to stop the program. The tab at the bottom of the Wing IDE window shows the *Stack Data*. This is the run-time stack.

Right below the *Stack Data* tab there is a combination box that currently displays *showOutput(): Scope.py, line 24*. This combo box lets you pick from the activation record that is currently being displayed. If you pick a different activation record, its contents will be displayed directly below it in the Wing IDE.

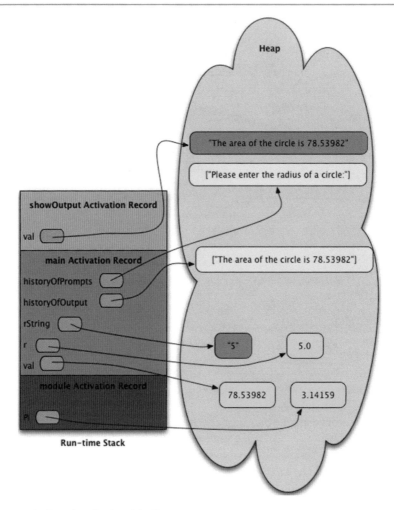

Fig. 3.3 The Run-time Stack and the Heap

One important note should be made here. Figure 3.4 shows *historyOfOutput* as a local variable in the *showOutput* function. This is not really the case, because the *historyOfOutput* reference is not defined within the local scope of the *showOutput* function. However, due to the way Python is implemented the reference for this variable shows up in the activation record for *showOutput* because it is being referenced from this scope. But, the reference to *historyOfOutput* in the activation record for *showOutput* and the reference called *historyOfOutput* in the *main* activation record point at the same object so no real harm is done. The important thing to note is that the Wing IDE is correct in showing the *historyOfOutput* variable as a local variable in this activation record since this is a reflection of Python's implementation and not due to a bug in Wing IDE 101.

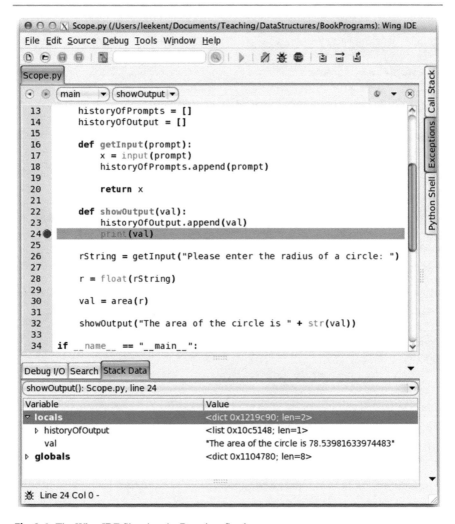

Fig. 3.4 The Wing IDE Showing the Run-time Stack

3.4 Writing a Recursive Function

A recursive function is simply a function that calls itself. It's really very simple to write a recursive function, but of course you want to write recursive functions that actually do something interesting. In addition, if a function just kept calling itself it would never finish. Actually, it would finish when run on a computer because we just learned that every time you call a function, an activation record is pushed on the run-time stack. If a recursive function continues to call itself over and over it will eventually fill up the run-time stack and you will get a stack overflow error when running such a program.

To prevent a recursive function from running forever, or overflowing the run-time stack, every recursive function must have a base case, just like an inductive proof must have a base case. There are many similarities between inductive proofs and recursive functions. The base case in a recursive function must be written first, before the function is called recursively.

Now, wrapping your head around just how a recursive function works is a little difficult at first. Actually, understanding *how* a recursive function works isn't all that important. When writing recursive functions we want to think more about *what* it does than *how* it works. It doesn't pay to think too hard about *how* recursive functions work, but in fact even that will get much easier with some practice.

When writing a recursive function there are four rules that you adhere to. These rules are not negotiable and will ensure that your recursive function will eventually finish. If you memorize and learn to follow these rules you will be writing recursive functions in no time. The rules are:

1. Decide on the name of your function and the arguments that must be passed to it to complete its work as well as what value the function should return.
2. Write the base case for your recursive function first. The base case is an *if* statement that handles a very simple case in the recursive function by returning a value.
3. Finally, you must call the function recursively with an argument or arguments that are smaller in some way than the parameters that were passed to the function when the last call was made. The argument or arguments that get smaller are the same argument or arguments you examined in your base case.
4. Look at a concrete example. Pick some values to try out with your recursive function. Trust that the recursive call you made in the last step works. Take the result from that recursive call and use it to form the result you want your function to return. Use the concrete example to help you see how to form that result.

We'll do a very simple example to begin with. In the last chapter we proved the following.

$$\sum_{i=1}^{n} i = \frac{n(n+1)}{2}$$

So, if we wanted to compute the sum of the first n integers, we could write a Python program as shown in Sect. 3.4.1.

3.4.1 Sum of Integers

```
1  def sumFirstN(n):
2      return n * (n+1) // 2
3
4  def main():
```

```
5        x = int(input("Please enter a non-negative integer: "))
6
7        s = sumFirstN(x)
8
9        print("The sum of the first", x, "integers is", str(s)+".")
10
11   if __name__ == "__main__":
12        main()
```

In this case, this would be the best function we could write because the complexity of the *sumFirstN* function is O(1). This means the time it takes to execute this function is not dependent on the size of the data, *n*. However, to illustrate a recursive function, let's go back to the definition of summation. The definition for summation has two parts. First, the base case of the definition.

$$\sum_{i=1}^{0} i = 0$$

The recursive part of the definition is as follows. This is what we call a recursive definition because it is defined in terms of itself. Notice that the recursive definition is defined in terms of a smaller *n*, in this case *n* − 1. The summation to *n* − 1 is our recursive call and it will work. If we want to compute the sum of the first 5 integers, then the recursive call computes 1 + 2 + 3 + 4 to give us 10. Adding *n* will give use 15, the result we want.

$$\sum_{i=1}^{n} i = \left(\sum_{i=1}^{n-1} i \right) + n$$

The two parts of this recursive definition can be translated directly into a recursive function in Python. The recursive definition is given in Sect. 3.4.2.

3.4.2   Recursive Sum of Integers

```
1    def recSumFirstN(n):
2         if n == 0:
3              return 0
4         else:
5              return recSumFirstN(n-1) + n
6
7    def main():
8         x = int(input("Please enter a non-negative integer: "))
9
10        s = recSumFirstN(x)
11
12        print("The sum of the first", x, "integers is", str(s)+".")
13
14   if __name__ == "__main__":
15        main()
```

The *recSumFirstN* function in the code of Sect. 3.4.2 is recursive. It calls itself with a smaller value and it has a base case that comes first, so it is well-formed. There is one thing that we might point out in this recursive function. The *else* is not necessary. When the Python interpreter encounters a **return** statement, the interpreter returns immediately and does not execute the rest of the function. So, in Sect. 3.4.2, if the function returns 0 in the *then* part of the *if* statement, the rest of the function is not executed. If *n* is not zero, then we want to execute the code on the *else* statement. This means we could rewrite this function as shown in Sect. 3.4.3.

3.4.3   No Else Needed

```
1   def recSumFirstN(n):
2       if n == 0:
3           return 0
4
5       return recSumFirstN(n-1) + n
```

The format of the code in Sect. 3.4.3 is a common way to write recursive functions. Sometimes a recursive function has more than one base case. Each base case can be handled by an *if* statement with a return in it. The recursive case does not need to be in an else when all base cases result in a return. The recursive case comes last in the recursive function definition.

3.5   Tracing the Execution of a Recursive Function

Early in this chapter you were given the mandate "Don't think too hard" when writing a recursive function. Understanding exactly *how* a recursive function works may be a bit difficult when you are first learning about them. It may help to follow the execution of a recursive function in an example. Consider the program in the previous section. Let's assume that the user entered the integer 4 at the keyboard. When this program begins running it will have an activation record on the run-time stack for the *module* and the *main* function.

When the program gets to line 10 in the code of Sect. 3.4.2, where the *recSumFirstN* function is first called, a new activation record will be pushed for the function call, resulting in three activation records on the run-time stack. The Python interpreter then jumps to line 2 with *n* pointing at the number 4 as shown in the picture of Fig. 3.5. Execution of the function proceeds. The value of *n* is not zero, so Python executes line 5 where there is another function call to *recSumFirstN*. This causes the Python interpreter to push another activation record on the run-time stack and the interpreter jumps to line 2 again. This time the value of *n* is 3. But again, this is not zero, so line 5 is executed and another activation record is pushed with a new value of 2 for *n*. This repeats two more times for values of 1 and 0 for *n*.

The important thing to note in this program execution is that there is one copy of the variable *n* for each recursive function call. An activation record holds the local variables and parameters of all variables that are in the local scope of the function.

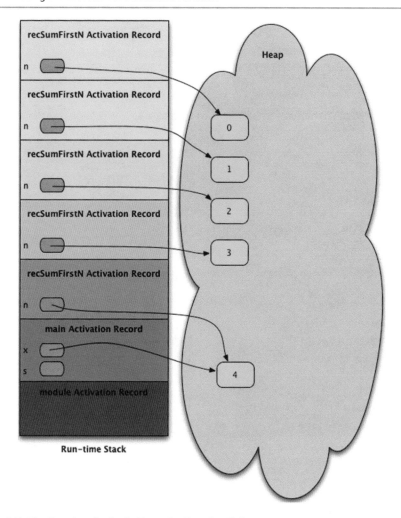

Fig. 3.5 The Run-time Stack of a Recursive Function Call

Each time the function is called a new activation record is pushed and a new copy of the local variables is stored within the activation record. The picture in Fig. 3.5 depicts the run-time stack at its deepest point.

When execution of the function gets to the point when n equals 0, the Python interpreter finds that n equals 0 on line 2 of the code. It is at this point that the *sumFirstN* function returns its first value. It returns 0 to the previous function call where n was 1. The return occurs on line 5 of the code. The activation record for the function call when n was 0 is popped from the run-time stack. This is depicted in Fig. 3.6 by the shading of the activation record in the figure. When the function returns the space for the activation record is reclaimed for use later. The shaded

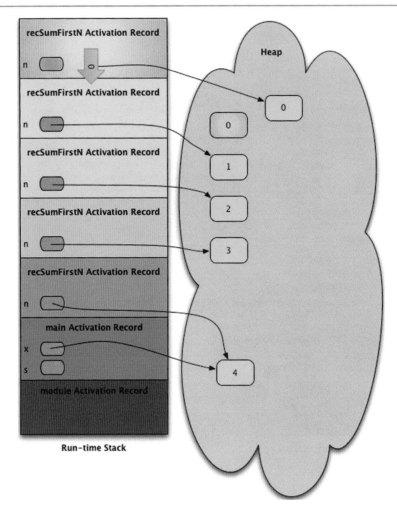

Fig. 3.6 The First Return from recSumFirstN

object containing 0 on the heap is also reclaimed by the garbage collector because there are no references pointing at it anymore.

After the first return of the *RecSumFirstN*, the Python interpreter returns to line 5 in the previous function call. But, this statement contains a return statement as well. So, the function returns again. Again, it returns to line 5, but this time with a value of 1. The function returns again, but with a value of 3 this time. Again, since it returned to line 5, the function returns again with a value of 6. Finally, once again the function returns, this time with a value of 10. But this time the *recSumFirstN* function returns to line 10 of the main function where *s* is made to point to the value of 10. This is depicted in Fig. 3.7.

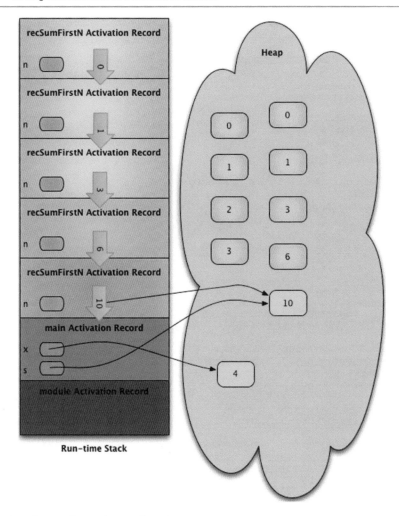

Fig. 3.7 The Last Return from recSumFirstN

The program terminates after printing the 10 to the screen and returning from the *main* function after line 12 and from the *module* after line 15. The importance of this example is to illustrate that each recursive call to *recSumFirstN* has its own copy of the variable *n* because it is local to the scope of the *recSumFirstN* function. Each time the function is called, the local variables and parameters are copied into the corresponding activation record. When a function call returns, the corresponding activation record is popped off the run-time stack. This is how a recursive function is executed.

3.6   Recursion in Computer Graphics

Recursion can be applied to lots of different problems including sorting, searching, drawing pictures, etc. The program given in Sect. 3.6.1 draws a spiral on the screen as shown in Fig. 3.8.

3.6.1   Recursive Spiral

```python
import turtle

def drawSpiral(t, length, color, colorBase):
    #color is a 24 bit value that is changing a bit
    #each time for a nice color effect
    if length == 0:
        return

    # add 2^10 to the old color modulo 2^24
    # the modulo 2^24 prevents the color from
    # getting too big.
    newcolor = (int(color[1:],16) + 2**10)%(2**24)

    # find the color base integer value
    base = int(colorBase[1:],16)

    # now if the new color is less than the base
    # add the base modulo 2^24.
    if newcolor < base:
        newcolor = (newcolor + base)%(2**24)

    # let newcolor be the hex string after conversion.
    newcolor = hex(newcolor)[2:]

    # add a pound sign and zeroes to the front so it
    # is 6 characters long plus the pound sign for a
    # proper color string.
    newcolor = "#"+("0"*(6-len(newcolor)))+newcolor

    t.color(newcolor)
    t.forward(length)
    t.left(90)

    drawSpiral(t, length-1, newcolor, colorBase)

def main():
    t = turtle.Turtle()
    screen = t.getscreen()
    t.speed(100)
    t.penup()
    t.goto(-100,-100)
    t.pendown()

    drawSpiral(t, 200, "#000000", "#ff00ff")

    screen.exitonclick()
```

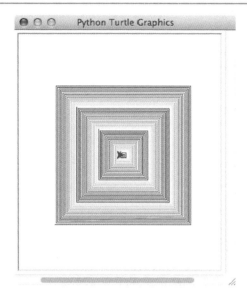

Fig. 3.8 A Spiral Image

```
48   if __name__ == "__main__":
49       main()
```

In this program the *drawSpiral* function is recursive. It has a base case that is written first: when the length of the side is zero it exits. It calls itself on something smaller: the new length passed to it is the old length minus one. The newcolor formula is perhaps the most complex part of the code. There is some slicing going on there to convert the color string from a hexadecimal string to an integer so 1024 can be added, modulo 2 to the 24th. Then it must be converted back to a hexadecimal color string with the "#ffffff" format. The program draws a spiral like the one pictured in Fig. 3.8.

Notice that this recursive function does not return anything. Most recursive functions do return a value. This one does not because the purpose of the function is to draw a spiral. It has a side-effect instead of returning a value.

3.7   Recursion on Lists and Strings

Recursive functions can be written for many different purposes. Many problems can be solved by solving a simpler problem and then applying that simpler solution recursively. For instance, consider trying to write a function that returns the reverse of a list. If we wrote this non-recursively, we might write it as follows.

3.7.1   List Recursion

```
1   def revList(lst):
2       accumulator = []
```

```
3
4      for x in lst:
5          accumulator = [x] + accumulator
6
7      return accumulator
8
9  def main():
10     print(revList([1,2,3,4]))
11
12 if __name__ == "__main__":
13     main()
```

When run, this program prints [4, 3, 2, 1] to the screen. The code in Sect. 3.7.1 uses the *accumulator pattern* to solve the problem of reversing a list. This is a pattern you have probably used before if you first learned to program imperatively. If we think about the problem recursively, we would first consider how to reverse a very simple list, say the empty list. The reverse of the empty list is just the empty list.

Once we have solved the problem for a very simple list, we can assume that if we call a recursive reverse function on something smaller (i.e. a shorter list), it will work. So, then to complete a recursive solution, we have only to piece our solution together. A recursive solution to reversing a list is found in Sect. 3.7.2.

3.7.2   Reversing a List

```
1  def revList(lst):
2      # Here is the base case
3      if lst == []:
4          return []
5
6      # The rest of this function is the recursive case.
7      # This works because we called it on something smaller.
8      # The lst[1:] is a slice of all but the first item in lst.
9      restrev = revList(lst[1:])
10     first = lst[0:1]
11
12     # Now put the pieces together.
13     result = restrev + first
14
15     return result
16
17
18 def main():
19     print(revList([1,2,3,4]))
20
21 if __name__ == "__main__":
22     main()
```

You can write recursive functions that work with strings too. Strings and lists are both sequences. In the code of Sect. 3.7.2 we made sure we recursively called our function on something smaller. The same is true when working with strings. A string reverse function is given in Sect. 3.7.3.

3.7.3   Reversing a String

```
1    def revString(s):
2        if s == "":
3            return ""
4
5        restrev = revString(s[1:])
6        first = s[0:1]
7        # Now put the pieces together.
8        result = restrev + first
9
10       return result
11
12
13   def main():
14       print(revString("hello"))
15
16   if __name__ == "__main__":
17       main()
```

Notice the similarity of these two functions. The functions are nearly identical. That's because the recursive definition of reverse did not change. The only change is that we must use the string concatenation operator instead of the list concatenation operator and the empty string instead of the empty list.

3.7.4   Another Version of Reverse

```
1    def revList2(lst):
2
3        def revListHelper(index):
4            if index == -1:
5                return []
6
7            restrev = revListHelper(index-1)
8            first = [lst[index]]
9
10           # Now put the pieces together.
11           result = first + restrev
12
13           return result
14
15       # this is the one line of code for the
16       # revList2 function.
17       return revListHelper(len(lst)-1)
18
19
20   def main():
21       print(revList2([1,2,3,4]))
22
23   if __name__ == "__main__":
24       main()
```

The examples in Sects. 3.7.2 and 3.7.3 used slicing to make the list or string smaller on each recursive call. It is possible to make a list or string *smaller* without actually making it physically smaller. Using an index to keep track of your position within a list can serve to make the list or string smaller. In that case it may be helpful to write a function that calls a *helper* function to do the recursion. Consider the program in Sect. 3.7.4. This code uses a nested helper function called *revListHelper* to do the actual recursion. The list itself does not get smaller in the helper function. Instead, the *index* argument gets smaller, counting down to −1 when the empty list is returned. The *revList2* function contains only one line of code to call the *revListHelper* function.

Because the *revListHelper* function is nested inside *revList2* the helper function is not visible to anything but the *revList2* function since we don't want other programmers to call the helper function except by calling the *revList2* function first.

It is important to note that you don't have to physically make a list or string smaller to use it in a recursive function. As long as indexing is available to you, a recursive function can make use of an index into a list or string and the index can get smaller on each recursive call.

One other thing to note. In this example the index gets smaller by approaching zero on each recursive call. There are other ways for the argument to the recursive function to get *smaller*. For instance, this example could be rewritten so the index grows toward the length of the list. In that case the *distance* between the index and the length of the list is the value that would get smaller on each recursive call.

3.8   Using Type Reflection

Many of the similarities in the two functions of Sects. 3.7.3 and 3.7.2 are due to operator overloading in Python. Python has another very nice feature called *reflection*. Reflection refers to the ability for code to be able to examine attributes about objects that might be passed as parameters to a function. One interesting aspect of reflection is the ability to see what the *type* of an object is. If we write *type(obj)* then Python will return an object which represents the *type* of *obj*. For instance, if *obj* is a reference to a string, then Python will return the *str type* object. Further, if we write *str()* we get a string which is the empty string. In other words, writing *str()* is the same thing as writing "". Likewise, writing *list()* is the same thing as writing []. Using reflection, we can write one recursive reverse function that will work for strings, lists, and any other sequence that supports slicing and concatenation. A recursive version of reverse that will reverse both strings and lists is provided in Sect. 3.8.1.

3.8.1   Reflection Reverse

```
1   def reverse(seq):
2       SeqType = type(seq)
3       emptySeq = SeqType()
4
```

```
5    if seq == emptySeq:
6        return emptySeq
7
8    restrev = reverse(seq[1:])
9    first = seq[0:1]
10
11   # Now put the pieces together.
12   result = restrev + first
13
14   return result
15
16
17 def main():
18     print(reverse([1,2,3,4]))
19     print(reverse("hello"))
20 if __name__ == "__main__":
21     main()
```

After writing the code in Sect. 3.8.1 we have a polymorphic reverse function that will work to reverse any sequence. It is polymorphic due to reflection and operator overloading. Pretty neat stuff!

3.9 Chapter Summary

In this chapter, you were introduced to some concepts that are important to your understanding of algorithms to be presented later in this text. Understanding how the run-time stack and the heap work to make it possible to call functions in our programs will make you a better programmer. Forming a mental model of how our code works makes it possible to predict what our code will do. Writing recursive functions is also a skill that is important to computer programmers. Here is what you should have learned in this chapter. You should:

- be able to identify the various scopes within a program.
- be able to identify which scope a variable reference belongs to: the local, enclosing, global, or built-in scope. Remember the LEGB rule.
- be able to trace the execution of a program by drawing a picture of the run-time stack and the heap for a program as it executes.
- bc able to write a simple recursive function by writing a base case and a recursive case where the function is called with a smaller value.
- be able to trace the execution of a recursive function, showing the run-time stack and heap as it executes.
- understand a little about reflection as it relates to examining *types* in Python code.

3.10   Review Questions

Answer these short answer, multiple choice, and true/false questions to test your mastery of the chapter.

1. What is an interpreter?
2. What is the Python interpreter called?
3. When the Python interpreter sees an identifier, in which scope does it look for the identifier first?
4. What order are the various scopes inspected to see where or if a variable is defined?
5. Pick a sample program from among the programs you have written, preferably a short one, and identify three scopes within it by drawing a box around the scopes.
6. When is an activation record pushed onto the run-time stack?
7. When is an activation record popped from the run-time stack?
8. What goes in the Heap in a computer?
9. What goes in an activation record on the run-time stack?
10. When writing a recursive function, what are the two cases for which you must write code?
11. If a recursive function did not have a base case, what would happen when it was called?
12. What must be true of the recursive call in a recursive function? In other words, what must you ensure when making this recursive call?
13. What does the *type* function return in Python? If you call the *type* function in a program, what aspect of Python are you using?

3.11   Programming Problems

1. Write a recursive function called intpow that given a number, x, and an integer, n, will compute x ^ n. You must write this function recursively to get full credit. Be sure to put it in a program with several test cases to test that your function works correctly.
2. Write a recursive function to compute the factorial of an integer. The factorial of 0 is 1. The factorial of any integer, n, greater than zero is n times the factorial of n−1. Write a program that tests your factorial function by asking the user to enter an integer and printing the factorial of that integer. Be sure your program has a main function. Comment your code with the base case and recursive case in your recursive function.
3. Write a recursive function that computes the length of a string. You cannot use the *len* function while computing the length of the string. You must rely on the function you are writing. Put this function in a program that prompts the user to enter a string and then prints the length of that string.

Fig. 3.9 A Tree

4. Write a recursive function that takes a string like "abcdefgh" and returns "bad-cfehg". Call this function *swap* since it swaps every two elements of the original string. Put this function in a program and call it with at least a few test cases.
5. Write a recursive function that draws a tree. Call your function *drawBranch*. Pass it a turtle to draw with, an angle, and the number of littler branches to draw like the tree that appears in Fig. 3.9. Each time you recursively call this function you can decrease the number of branches and the angle. Each littler branch is drawn at some angle from the current branch so your function can change the angle of the turtle by turning left or right. When your number of branches gets to zero, you can draw a leaf as a little green square. If you make the width of the turtle line thicker for bigger branches and smaller for littler branches, you'll get a nice tree. You might write one more function called drawTree that will set up everything (except the turtle) to draw a nice tree. Put this function in a program that draws at least one tree. **HINT**: In your drawBranch function, after you have drawn the branch (and all sub-branches) you will want to return the turtle to the original position and direction you started at. This is necessary so after calling drawBranch you will know where the turtle is located. If you don't return it to its original position, the turtle will end up stranded out at a leaf somewhere.
6. Write a recursive function that draws a circular spiral. To do this, you'll need to use polar coordinates. Polar coordinates are a way of specifying any point in the plane with an angle and a radius. Zero degrees goes to the right and the angles go counter-clockwise in a circle. With an angle and a radius, any point in the plane can be described. To convert an angle, a, and radius, r, from polar coordinates to Cartesian coordinates you would use sine and cosine. You must import the math module. Then $x = r * math.cos(a)$ and $y = r * math.sin(a)$.

The *drawSpiral* function will be given a radius for the sprial. To get a circular spiral, every recursive call to the drawSpiral function must decrease the radius just a bit and increase the angle. You convert the angle and the radius to its (x, y) coordinate equivalent and then draw a line to that location. You must also pass an (x, y) coordinate to the *drawSpiral* function for the center point of your spiral. Then, any coordinates you compute will be added to the center (x, y). You can follow the square spiral example in the text. Put this code in a program that draws a spiral to the screen.

7. Write a program to gather performance data for the *reverse* function found in this chapter. Write an XML file in the plot format found in this text to visualize that performance data. Because this function is recursive, keep your data size small and just gather data for string sizes of 1–10. This will help you visualize your result. What is the complexity of this reverse function? Put a comment at the top of your program stating the complexity of reverse in big-Oh notation. Justify your answer by analyzing the code found in the reverse function.

8. Rewrite the program in Sect. 3.7.4 to use an index that approaches the length of the list instead of an index that approaches zero. Then write a main function that thoroughly tests your new reverse function on lists. You must test it on both simple and more complex examples of lists to test it thoroughly.

Sequences

4

Computers are really good at dealing with large amounts of information. They can repeat a task over and over again without getting bored. When they repeat a task they are generally doing the same thing to similar data or objects. It is natural to want to organize those objects into some kind of structure so that our program can easily switch from one object to the next. How objects are added to a sequence or collection and how we move from one item to the next has some impact on how we might want to organize the collection of data in a program.

In this chapter we look at different ways of organizing data into a sequence. We'll also examine how to use Python to make working with sequences convenient. Operator overloading in Python lets us build sequences that we can manipulate with intuitive operations. Finally, we'll also examine how the organization of a sequence affects the computation complexity of operations on it.

An *Abstract Data Type* is a term that is used to describe a way of organizing data. Lists are one way of organizing a sequence of data, but in this chapter we'll discover other ways of organizing sequences as well. Ascending and descending sequences, linked lists, stacks, and queues are all abstract data types that we'll explore in this chapter.

4.1 Chapter Goals

In this chapter you will read about different ways of organizing data within a program. By the end of the chapter you should be able to answer these questions.

- When presented with an algorithm that requires you to maintain a sequence of data, which organizational scheme fits best?
- What are the trade-offs of selecting one type of sequence as opposed to another?
- What are some interesting algorithms that use lists, linked lists, stacks, or queues?
- What sorting algorithm is most commonly used when sorting a sequence of ordered values?
- What search algorithms are possible in a sequence?

© Springer International Publishing Switzerland 2015
K.D. Lee and S. Hubbard, *Data Structures and Algorithms with Python*,
Undergraduate Topics in Computer Science, DOI 10.1007/978-3-319-13072-9_4

- What is the complexity of many of the common operations on sequences and how is that complexity affected by the underlying organization of the data.

You will also be presented with a few interesting programming problems that will help you learn to select and use appropriate data structures to solve some interesting problems.

4.2   Lists

In the first and second chapter we developed a sequence called *PyList*. The *PyList* class is really just a repackaging of the Python *list* class. The example sequence demonstrates some of the operators that are supported by Python. In this section we want to look more deeply into how lists are implemented. There are many operations supported on lists. Chapter 16 contains the full list. The table in Fig. 4.1 is a subset of the operations supported by lists.

Each of the operations in the table has an associated complexity. The performance of an algorithm depends on the complexity of the operations used in implementing that algorithm. In the following sections we'll further develop our own list datatype, called *PyList*, using the built-in list only for setting and getting elements in a list. The *indexed get* and *indexed set* operations can be observed to have $O(1)$ complexity. This complexity is achieved because the memory of a computer is randomly accessible, which is why it is called *Random Access Memory*. In Chap. 2 we spent some time demonstrating that each location within a list is accessible in the same amount of time regardless of list size and location being retrieved. In the following sections we'll enhance the PyList datatype to support the operations given in this table.

Operation	Complexity	Usage	Method
List creation	$O(n)$ or $O(1)$	x = list(y)	calls __init__(y)
indexed get	$O(1)$	a = x[i]	x.__getitem__(i)
indexed set	$O(1)$	x[i] = a	x.__setitem__(i,a)
concatenate	$O(n)$	z = x + y	z = x.__add__(y)
append	$O(1)$	x.append(a)	x.append(a)
insert	$O(n)$	x.insert(i,e)	x.insert(i,e))
delete	$O(n)$	del x[i]	x.__delitem__(i)
equality	$O(n)$	x == y	x.__eq__(y)
iterate	$O(n)$	for a in x:	x.__iter__()
length	$O(1)$	len(x)	x.__len__()
membership	$O(n)$	a in x	x.__contains__(a)
sort	$O(n \log n)$	x.sort()	x.sort()

Fig. 4.1 Complexity of List Operations

4.2.1 The PyList Datatype

In the first couple of chapters we began developing our PyList data structure. To support the O(1) complexity of the *append* operation, the PyList contains empty locations that can be filled when *append* is called as first described in Sect. 2.10. We'll keep track of the number of locations being used and the actual size of the internal list in our *PyList* objects. So, we'll need three pieces of information: the list itself called *items*, the size of the internal list called *size*, and the number of locations in the internal list that are currently being used called *numItems*. While we wouldn't have to keep track of the size of the list, because we could call the *len* function, we'll store the size in the object to avoid the overhead of calling *len* in multiple places in the code.

All the used locations in the internal list will occur at the beginning of the list. In other words, there will be no holes in the middle of a list that we will have to worry about. We'll call this assumption an *invariant* on our data structure. An *invariant* is something that is true before and after any method call on the data structure. The *invariant* for this list is that the internal list will have the first *numItems* filled with no holes. The code in Sect. 4.2.3 provides a constructor that can also be passed a list for its initial contents.

Storing all the items at the beginning of the list, without holes, also means that we can randomly access elements of the list in O(1) time. We don't have to search for the proper location of an element. Indexing into the PyList will simply index into the internal *items* list to find the proper element as seen in the next sections.

4.2.2 The PyList Constructor

```
1    class PyList:
2        def __init__(self,contents=[], size=10):
3            # The contents allows the programmer to construct a list with
4            # the initial contents of this value. The initial_size
5            # lets the programmer pick a size for the internal size of the
6            # list. This is useful if the programmer knows he/she is going
7            # to add a specific number of items right away to the list.
8            self.items = [None] * size
9            self.numItems = 0
10           self.size = size
11
12           for e in contents:
13               self.append(e)
```

The code in Sect. 4.2.3 builds a *PyList* object by creating a list of 10 *None* values. *None* is the special value in Python for references that point at nothing. Figure 4.2 shows a sample list after it was created and three items were appended to it. The special *None* value is indicated in the figure by the three horizontal lines where the empty slots in the list point. The initial size of the internal *items* list is 10 by default, but a user could pass a larger size initially if they wanted to. This is only the initial size. The list will still grow when it needs to. The *contents* parameter lets

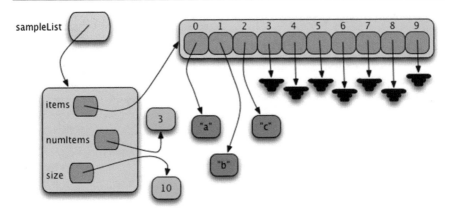

Fig. 4.2 A Sample Pylist Object

the programmer pass in a list or sequence to put in the list initially. For instance, the object in Fig. 4.2 could have been created by writing the following.

```
sampleList = PyList(["a", "b", "c"])
```

Each element of the sequence is added as a separate list item. The complexity of creating a *PyList* object is *O(1)* if no value is passed to the constructor and *O(n)* if a sequence is passed to the constructor, where *n* is the number of elements in the sequence.

4.2.3   PyList Get and Set

```
1  def __getitem__(self,index):
2      if index >= 0 and index < self.numItems:
3          return self.items[index]
4
5      raise IndexError("PyList index out of range")
6
7  def __setitem__(self,index,val):
8      if index >= 0 and index < self.numItems:
9          self.items[index] = val
10         return
11
12     raise IndexError("PyList assignment index out of range")
```

Our PyList class is a wrapper for the built-in list class. So, to implement the get item and set item operations on PyList, we'll use the get and set operations on the built-in list class. The code is given here. The complexity of both operations is O(1). In both cases, we want to make sure the index is in the range of acceptable indices. If it is not, we'll raise an IndexError exception just as the built-in list class does.

4.2.4 PyList Concatenate

```
1   def __add__(self,other):
2       result = PyList(size=self.numItems+other.numItems)
3
4       for i in range(self.numItems):
5           result.append(self.items[i])
6
7       for i in range(other.numItems):
8           result.append(other.items[i])
9
10      return result
```

To concatenate two lists we must build a new list that contains the contents of both. This is an accessor method because it does not mutate either list. Instead, it builds a new list. We can do this operation in $O(n)$ time where n is the sum of the lengths of the two lists. Here is some code to accomplish this.

In Sect. 4.2.5 the size is set to the needed size for the result of concatenating the two lists. The complexity of the *__add__* method is O(n) where n is the length of the two lists. The initial size of the list does not *have* to be set because append has O(1) complexity as we saw in Sect. 2.10. However, since we know the size of the resulting list, setting the initial size should speed up the concatenation operation slightly.

4.2.5 PyList Append

```
1   # This method is hidden since it starts with two underscores.
2   # It is only available to the class to use.
3   def __makeroom(self):
4       # increase list size by 1/4 to make more room.
5       # add one in case for some reason self.size is 0.
6       newlen = (self.size // 4) + self.size + 1
7       newlst = [None] * newlen
8       for i in range(self.numItems):
9           newlst[i] = self.items[i]
10
11      self.items = newlst
12      self.size = newlen
13
14  def append(self,item):
15      if self.numItems == self.size:
16          self.__makeroom()
17
18      self.items[self.numItems] = item
19      self.numItems += 1 # Same as writing self.numItems = self.numItems + 1
```

In Sect. 2.10 we learned that the append method has O(1) amortized complexity. When appending, we will just add one more item to the end of the *self.items* list if there is room. In the description of the constructor we decided the *PyList* objects would contain a list that had room for more elements. When appending we can make use of that extra space. Once in a while (i.e. after appending some number of items), the internal *self.items* list will fill up. At that time we must increase the size of the *items* list to make room for the new item we are appending by a size proportional to the current length of *self.items*.

As we learned in Chap. 2, to make the *append* operation run in $O(1)$ time we can't just add one more location each time we need more space. It turns out that adding 25 % more space each time is enough to guarantee $O(1)$ complexity. The choice of 25 % is not significant. If we added even 10 % more space each time we would get $O(1)$ complexity. At the other extreme we could double the internal list size each time we needed more room as we did in Sect. 2.10. However, 25 % seems like a reasonable amount to expand the list without gobbling up too much memory in the computer. We just need a few more cyber dollars stored up for each append operation to pay for expanding the list when we run out of room. The code in Sect. 4.2.6 implements the *append* operation with an amortized complexity of $O(1)$. Integer division by 4 is very quick in a computer because it can be implemented by shifting the bits of the integer to the right, so computing our new length, when needed, is relatively quick.

The Python interpreter implements append in a similar way. The Python interpreter is implemented in C, so the interpreter uses C code. Python also chooses to increase the list size by other values. In Python list sizes increase by 4, 8, 16, 25, and so on. The additional space to add to the internal list is calculated from the newly needed size of the list and grows by 4, 8, 16, 25, 35, 46, 58, 72, 88, and so on. You can see that the amount to add grows as the list grows and that leads to an amortized complexity of O(1) for the append operation in the Python interpreter.

4.2.6   PyList Insert

```
1   def insert(self,i,e):
2       if self.numItems == self.size:
3           self.__makeroom()
4
5       if i < self.numItems:
6           for j in range(self.numItems-1,i-1,-1):
7               self.items[j+1] = self.items[j]
8
9           self.items[i] = e
10          self.numItems += 1
11      else:
12          self.append(e)
```

To insert into this sequential list we must make room for the new element. Given the way the list is organized, there is no choice but to copy each element after the point where we want to insert the new value to the next location in the list. This works best if we start from the right end of the list and work our way back to the point where the new value will be inserted. The complexity of this operation is O(n) where *n* is the number of elements in the list after the insertion point.

The index *i* is the location where the new value *e* is to be inserted. If the index provided is larger than the size of the list the new item, *e*, is appended to the end of the list.

4.2.7 PyList Delete

```
1  def __delitem__(self,index):
2      for i in range(index, self.numItems-1):
3          self.items[i] = self.items[i+1]
4      self.numItems -= 1 # same as writing self.numItems = self.numItems - 1
```

When deleting an item at a specific *index* in the list, we must move everything after the item down to preserve our invariant that there are no holes in the internal list. This results in a *O(n)* implementation in the average and worst case where *n* is the number of items after the *index* in the list. Here is code that accomplishes deletion.

In the Python interpreter, to conserve space, if a list reaches a point after deletion where less than half of the locations within the internal list are being used, then the size of the available space is reduced by one half.

4.2.8 PyList Equality Test

```
1  def __eq__(self,other):
2      if type(other) != type(self):
3          return False
4
5      if self.numItems != other.numItems:
6          return False
7
8      for i in range(self.numItems):
9          if self.items[i] != other.items[i]:
10             return False
11
12     return True
```

Checking for equality of two lists requires the two lists be of the same type. If they are of different types, then we'll say they are not equal. In addition, the two lists must have the same length. If they are not the same length, they cannot be equal. If these two preconditions are met, then the lists are equal if all the elements in the two lists are equal. Here is code that implements equality testing of two *PyList* objects. Equality testing is a O(n) operation.

4.2.9 PyList Iteration

```
1  def __iter__(self):
2      for i in range(self.numItems):
3          yield self.items[i]
```

The ability to iterate over a sequence is certainly a requirement. Sequences hold a collection of similar data items and we frequently want to do something with each item in a sequence. Of course, the complexity of iterating over any sequence is *O(n)* where *n* is the size of the sequence. Here is code that accomplishes this for the *PyList* sequence. The *yield* call in Python suspends the execution of the *__iter__* method and returns the yielded item to the iterator.

4.2.10 PyList Length

```
1  def __len__(self):
2      return self.numItems
```

If the number of items were not kept track of within the *PyList* object, then counting the number of items in the list would be a *O(n)* operation. Instead, if we keep track of the number of items in the list as items are appended or deleted from the list, then we need only return the value of *numItems* from the object, resulting in *O(1)* complexity.

4.2.11 PyList Membership

```
1  def __contains__(self,item):
2      for i in range(self.numItems):
3          if self.items[i] == item:
4              return True
5
6      return False
```

Testing for membership in a list means checking to see if an *item* is one of the items in the list. The only way to do this is to examine each item in sequence in the list. If the *item* is found then *True* is returned, otherwise *False* is returned. This results in *O(n)* complexity.

This idea of searching for an item in a sequence is so common that computer scientists have named it. This is called *linear search*. It is named this because of its *O(n)* complexity.

4.2.12 PyList String Conversion

```
1  def __str__(self):
2      s = "["
3      for i in range(self.numItems):
4          s = s + repr(self.items[i])
5          if i < self.numItems - 1:
6              s = s + ", "
7      s = s + "]"
8      return s
```

It is convenient to be able to convert a list to a string so it can be printed. Python includes two methods that can be used for converting to a string. The first you are probably already familiar with. The *str* function calls the __str__ method on an object to create a string representation of itself suitable for printing. Here is code that implements the __str__ method for the *PyList* class.

4.2.13 PyList String Representation

```
1  def __repr__(self):
2      s = "PyList(["
3      for i in range(self.numItems):
4          s = s + repr(self.items[i])
5          if i < self.numItems - 1:
6              s = s + ", "
7      s = s + "])"
8      return s
```

The other method for converting an object to a string has a different purpose. Python includes a function called *eval* that will take a string containing an expression and evaluate the expression in the string. For instance, *eval*("*6+5*") results in 11 and *eval*("*[1,2,3]*") results in the list *[1,2,3]*. The *repr* function in Python calls the *__repr__* method on a class. This method, if defined, should return a string representation of an object that is suitable to be given to the *eval* function. In the case of the *PyList* class, the *repr* form of the string would be something like "PyList([1,2,3])" for the *PyList* sequence containing these items. Here is the code that accomplishes this. It is nearly identical to the *__str__* code, except that *PyList* prefixes the sequence.

Notice that in both Sects. 4.2.13 and 4.2.14 that *repr* is called on the elements of the list. Calling *repr* is necessary because otherwise a list containing strings like ["hi","there"] would be converted to [hi,there] in its *str* or *repr* representation.

4.3   Cloning Objects

It is interesting to note that we now have a method of making a copy of an object. If *x* is a *PyList* object, then eval(repr(x)) is a copy or *clone* of this object. Since all the items in the *PyList* object are also cloned by evaluating the representation of the object, cloning an object like this is called a *deep clone* or *deep copy* of the object *x*.

It is also possible to make what is called a *shallow copy* of an object. A shallow copy occurs when the object is copied, but items in the object are shared with the clone. If we wish to create a shallow copy of a *PyList* object called *x*, we would write the following.

```
x = PyList([1,2,3])
y = PyList(x)
```

Here, *y* is a shallow copy of *x* because both x and y share the items 1, 2, and 3. In most cases whether some items are shared or not probably doesn't matter. In this case it doesn't matter if items are shared because 1, 2, and 3 are integers and integers are immutable. However, if the shared items are mutable, then you may care about shallow or deep clones of objects. When working with a shallow clone of an object that contains mutable items the programmer must be aware that the items in the collection might change values without any call to a method on the object. This won't happen to a deep clone of an object.

Which is better, *shallow cloning* or *deep cloning*, depends on the application being written. One is not necessarily better than the other. There is an additional performance and memory hit for making deep clones but they are safer. The type of application being developed will probably help determine which type of cloning is chosen should clones of objects be useful in the application.

4.4 Item Ordering

Now let us turn our attention to implementing the *sort* method on our *PyList* data type. To sort a sequence of items, the items in the sequence must be ordered in some way. For instance, consider a class that is used to represent Cartesian coordinates on a plane. We'll call the class *Point* and it will contain an (x,y) pair. We'll *order* the point objects by their directed distance from the x axis. In other words, they will be ordered by their y-coordinates. Here is our *Point* class. For reasons that will be obvious soon, our Point class will inherit from RawTurtle.

4.4.1 The Point Class

```
1    class Point(turtle.RawTurtle):
2        def __init__(self, canvas, x, y):
3            super().__init__(canvas)
4            canvas.register_shape("dot",((3,0),(2,2),(0,3),(-2,2),(-3,0),(-2,-2),(0,-3),
5            (2,-2)))
6            self.shape("dot")
7            self.speed(200)
8            self.penup()
9            self.goto(x,y)
10
11       def __str__(self):
12           return "("+str(self.xcor())+","+str(self.ycor())+")"
13
14       def __lt__(self, other):
15           return self.ycor() < other.ycor()
```

Objects of the *Point* class have an ordering because we have defined the less than operator (i.e. <) by writing an *__lt__* method in the class. Once defined, this less than operator orders all the elements of the class. Most of the built-in classes or types in Python already have an implementation for the *__lt__* method so we don't have to define this method for types like *int*, *float*, and *str*. Strings are compared lexicographically in Python as they are in pretty much every language that supports string comparison. Lexicographic ordering means that strings are compared from left to right until one character is found to be different than the character at the corresponding position in the other string. In other words, sorting a sequence of strings means they will end up alphabetized like you would see in a dictionary. Under some conditions lists are orderable, too. For lists to have an ordering, the elements at corresponding indices within the lists must be orderable. Consider these sample comparisons.

```
1    Python 3.2 (r32:88452, Feb 20 2011, 10:19:59)
2    [GCC 4.0.1 (Apple Inc. build 5493)]
3    Type "help", "copyright", "credits" or "license" for more information.
4    [evaluate untitled-3.py]
5    lst = [1,2,3]
6    lst2 = list("abc")
7    lst2
8    ['a', 'b', 'c']
9    lst < lst2
10   Traceback (most recent call last):
11     File "<string>", line 1, in <fragment>
12   builtins.TypeError: unorderable types: int() < str()
13   lst3 = [4,5,6]
14   lst < lst3
15   True
16   lst4 = [1,3,2]
17   lst < lst4
18   True
19   lst5 = [1,2,2]
20   lst5 < lst
21   True
22   lst6 = [1,1,'a']
23   lst6 < lst
24   True
```

Comparing *lst* and *lst2* did not work because the items in the two lists are not orderable. You can't compare an integer and a string. However, two lists with similar elements can be compared. List comparison is performed lexicographically like strings. Note the last example. The two lists [1,2,3] and [1,1,'a'] can be compared because the lexicographical ordering does not require that 3 and 'a' be compared.

There are some types in Python which have no natural ordering. For instance, there is no natural ordering for dictionaries in Python. You cannot sort a list of dictionaries. Of course, its unclear why you would want to as well. Since there is no natural ordering there doesn't seem to be a reason to sort them. However, if there were a way to create an ordering on a set of dictionaries you could define it yourself by writing your own class that inherited from the *dict* class and defining its own __lt__ method just as we did for the *Point* class.

Once we have an ordering of elements in a list, we can sort the elements according to that ordering. Lists have a sort method that will sort the items of a list according to their ordering. The code in Sect. 4.4.2 illustrates how the items of a list can be sorted.

4.4.2   Calling the Sort Method

```
1    def main():
2        t = turtle.Turtle()
3        t.ht()
4        screen = t.getscreen()
5        lst = []
6
7        for i in range(10):
```

```
 8          for j in range(10):
 9              pair = Point(screen,i,j)
10              lst.append(pair)
11
12      lst.sort()
13
14      for p in lst:
15          print(p)
```

When the code in Sect. 4.4.2 is called it prints the points in order of their distance from the x-axis as follows.

```
(0,0)
(1,0)
(2,0)
(3,0)
(4,0)
(5,0)
(6,0)
(7,0)
(8,0)
(9,0)
(0,1)
(1,1)
(2,1)
(3,1)
(4,1)
(5,1)
(6,1)
(7,1)
...
```

But, just how does this *sort* method work and what is its cost? In other words, what kind of sorting algorithm does Python use and what is its computational complexity? We explore these questions in the next sections.

4.5   Selection Sort

In the last section we learned that we can call a method called *sort* on a list to sort the items in the list in ascending order. Ascending order is determined by the *less than* operator as defined on the items. So how does the sorting algorithm work. One of the early sorting algorithms was called *Selection Sort* and it serves as a good starting place to understand sorting algorithms. However, this is not the sorting algorithm used by Python. We'll find out why soon.

The selection sort algorithm is pretty simple to describe. The algorithm begins by finding the smallest value to place in the first position in the list. It does this by doing a linear search through the list and along the way remembering the index of the smallest item it finds. The algorithm uses the *guess and check* pattern by first guessing that the smallest item is the first item in the list and then checking the subsequent items to see if it made an incorrect guess. This part of the algorithm is the *selection* part. The *select* function does this selection.

4.5.1 Selection Sort's Select Function

```
1    def select(seq, start):
2        minIndex = start
3
4        for j in range(start+1, len(seq)):
5            if seq[minIndex] > seq[j]:
6                minIndex = j
7
8        return minIndex
```

The start argument tells the select function where to start looking for the smallest item. It searches from start to the end of the sequence for the smallest item.

The selection sort algorithm works by finding the smallest item using the *select* function and placing that item into the first position of the sequence. Now the value in the first position must be put someplace else. It is simply swapped with the location of the value that is being moved. The algorithm proceeds by next looking for the second smallest value in the sequence. Since the smallest value is now in the first location in the sequence, the selection sort algorithm starts looking from the second position in the list for the smallest value. When the smallest value is found (which is really the second smallest value for the list) the value in the second position and this value are swapped. Then the selection sort algorithm looks for the smallest item starting at the third location in the sequence. This pattern repeats until all the items in the sequence have been sorted. The *selSort* function does the actual sorting for the algorithm.

4.5.2 The Selection Sort Code

```
1    def selSort(seq):
2        for i in range(len(seq)-1):
3            minIndex = select(seq, i)
4            tmp = seq[i]
5            seq[i] = seq[minIndex]
6            seq[minIndex] = tmp
```

We can visualize the selection sort algorithm by running an animation of it sorting. The animation is pictured in Fig. 4.3 having sorted more than half the values in a sequence. The green dots represent items that are now in their proper location in the sequence. The height of the dot from the x-axis (i.e. the y-value) is its value. The x-axis is the position in the list. In this animation all the values between 0 and 199 are being sorted into ascending order. The upper-right corner represents those values that have not yet been sorted. The algorithm starts looking for the next smallest value just to the right of the green diagonal line. It finds the minimum value (i.e. closest to the x-axis) by going through all the remaining unsorted dots. Once it finds the small, shortest dot, it swaps it with the left-most dot to put it into is sorted position in the list. The complete code for this animation is given in Sect. 20.3 and can be downloaded from the website accompanying this text. Try it out!

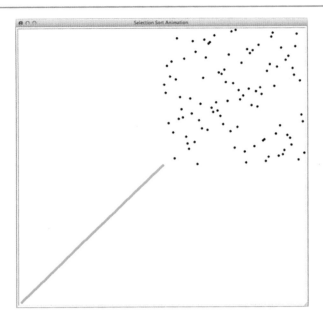

Fig. 4.3 Selection Sort Snapshot

Consider sorting the list [*5 8 2 6 9 1 0 7*] as depicted in Fig. 4.4. After each call
of the *select* function from the *selSort* function the next element of the list is placed
in its final location. Sorting the list leads to the intermediate steps as shown. Each
time the *select* function is called the new smallest element is swapped with the first
location in the rest of the list to move the next smallest element into its location
within the sorted list.

To find each new smallest element we call *select* which must run through the rest
of the list looking for the minimum element. After each pass the list in Fig. 4.4 is one
item closer to sorting the whole list. It turns out that this early attempt at writing a
sorting algorithm is not that great. The complexity of this algorithm is $O(n^2)$ because
each time through the for loop in the *selSort* function we call the *select* function
which has its own for loop. The *for i* loop is executed n times and each time it is
executed the *for j* loop must go through one less item looking for the smallest value
that is left to be sorted. So, the first time we execute the body of the *for j* loop $n - 1$
times, then $n - 2$ times the second time select is called, then $n - 3$ times and so on.
We have seen this pattern before. The sum of the first n integers has an n^2 term in its
formula. Therefore, selection sort is $O(n^2)$. This means as we try to sort some larger
lists the algorithm will really start to slow down. You should never use this algorithm
for sorting. Even on small lists we can do much better.

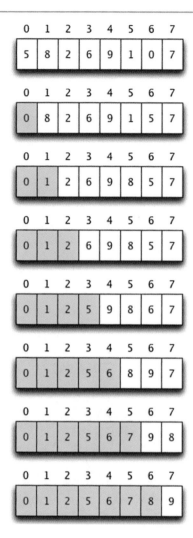

Fig. 4.4 Selection Sort of a List

4.6   Merge Sort

Divide and conquer, as the ancient Romans might have said, is an effective battle strategy. It turns out this concept is very important when writing algorithms. The *Merge Sort* algorithm is one instance of a divide and conquer algorithm. Divide and conquer algorithms are usually written recursively, but don't necessarily have to be. The basic premise is that we divide a problem into two pieces. Each of the two pieces is easier to solve than trying to tackle the whole problem at once because the two pieces are each smaller.

4.6.1 The Merge Sort Code

```
1   def merge(seq, start, mid, stop):
2       lst = []
3       i = start
4       j = mid
5
6       # Merge the two lists while each has more elements
7       while i < mid and j < stop:
8           if seq[i] < seq[j]:
9               lst.append(seq[i])
10              i+=1
11          else:
12              lst.append(seq[j])
13              j+=1
14
15      # Copy in the rest of the start to mid sequence
16      while i < mid:
17          lst.append(seq[i])
18          i+=1
19      # Many merge sort implementations copy the rest
20      # of the sequence from j to stop at this point.
21      # This is not necessary since in the next part
22      # of the code the same part of the sequence would
23      # be copied right back to the same place.
24      # while j < stop:
25      #     lst.append(seq[j])
26      #     j+=1
27      # Copy the elements back to the original sequence
28      for i in range(len(lst)):
29          seq[start+i]=lst[i]
30
31  def mergeSortRecursively(seq, start, stop):
32      # We must use >= here only when the sequence we are sorting
33      # is empty. Otherwise start == stop-1 in the base case.
34      if start >= stop-1:
35          return
36
37      mid = (start + stop) // 2
38
39      mergeSortRecursively(seq, start, mid)
40      mergeSortRecursively(seq, mid, stop)
41      merge(seq, start, mid, stop)
42
43  def mergeSort(seq):
44      mergeSortRecursively(seq, 0, len(seq))
```

The merge sort algorithm takes this divide and conquer strategy to the extreme. It divides the list, then divides it again and again, until we are left with lists of size 1. A sublist of length 1 is already sorted. Two sorted sublists can be merged into one sorted list in O(n) time. A list can be divided into lists of size 1 by repeatedly splitting in O(log n) time. Each of the split lists are then merged together in O(n) time. This results in a complexity of O(n log n) for merge sort. The merge sort code appears in Sect. 4.6.1.

The *merge* function takes care of merging two adjacent sublists. The first sublist runs from start to mid-1. The second sublist runs from mid to stop-1. The elements of the two sorted sublists are copied, in O(n) time, to a new list. Then the sorted list is copied back into the original sequence, again in O(n) time. In the *merge* function, the first while loop takes care of merging the two sublists until one or the other sublist is empty. The second and third while loops take care of finishing up whichever sublist had the left-over elements. Only one sublist will have left-over elements so only one condition on the second and third while loops will ever be true.

Notice that the third while loop in the code is commented out. Copying elements from *j* to *stop* in the third while loop is not necessary since they would only be copied right back to the same place when the contents of *lst* are copied back to the *seq* sequence. This optimization speeds up merge sort a little bit. One other optimization is to pre-allocate one more list in which to copy values and then alternate between merging in the original and the pre-allocated copy. In this way the overhead of creating and appending to lists is avoided. Coding either of these two optimizations does not improve the computational complexity of the algorithm, but can improve its overall performance slightly. One criticism of the merge sort algorithm is that the elements of the two sublists cannot be merged without copying to a new list and then back again. Other sorting methods, like Quicksort, have the same O(n log n) complexity as merge sort and do not require an extra list.

The *mergeSort* function calls a helper function to get everything started. It calls *mergeSortRecursively* function with the sequence and the start and stop values which indicate the entire list should be sorted. The start and stop parameters are used when splitting the list. The list is not physically split when calling *mergeSortRecursively*. Instead, the start and stop values are used to compute the mid point between them and then the two halves are recursively sorted. Since each sublist is smaller, we can rest assured that the recursive call does its job and sorts the two sublists. Then we are left to merge the two sorted sublists by calling the *merge* function. The base case for the recursive function is when the sublist size is 1. At that point we have a sorted sublist.

In Fig. 4.5 the entire left half of the list has been sorted. In addition, three sublists in the right half have been sorted and the third and fourth sublist are in the process of being merged together. The green dots represent the portions of the sequence that are sorted and the black dots indicate the unsorted portion of the original sequence. The red lines at the bottom reflect the recursive calls that are currently on the run-time stack. The length of the red line shows the portion of the sequence that is being sorted by its corresponding recursive call. The blue line underscores the two sublists currently being merged together.

The argument that merge sort runs in O(n log n) time needs just a bit of explanation. The repetitive splitting of the list results in O(log n) splits. In the end we have lists of size 1. If we were to count every merge that occurs there would be n/2 merges at the bottom, followed by n/4 merges at the next level, and so on leading to this sum.

$$\text{The number of merges} \geq \sum_{i=0}^{\lfloor log_2 n \rfloor} 2^i = 2^{\lfloor log_2 n \rfloor} - 1 \approx n$$

This analysis would seem to suggest that the complexity of the merge sort algorithm is O(n²) since there are roughly *n* merges each of which is O(n) itself. However, the

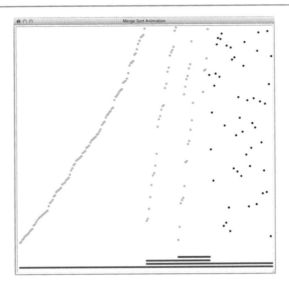

Fig. 4.5 Merge Sort Snapshot

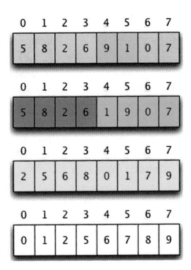

Fig. 4.6 Merge Sort Merges

algorithm is not O(n²). To see why, consider sorting the list [5 8 2 6 9 1 0 7]. After repeatedly splitting the lists we get down to lists of size one as depicted in the first list of Fig. 4.6. The individual items are merged two at a time to form sorted lists of two, shown in the second list of items. While there are four merges that take place at the lowest level of the merge sort, the four merges are each for lists of two elements (i.e. one from each list) and together they form a list of *n* items. So we can group all these four merges together to find that all the merges at that deepest level take O(n) time. Not each, but all of the merges at the deepest level when combined are O(n).

In the second version of the list, two merges are done for the lists of length two. However, each merge is done on one half the list. The purple half is one merge, the green half includes the items that are in the second merge. Together, these two merges include all *n* items again. So, at the second deepest level again at most *n* items are merged in O(n) time.

Finally, the last merge is of all the items in yellow from the two sorted sublists. This merge also takes O(n) time since it merges all the items in the list, resulting in the sorted list seen in the last version of the list.

So, while merging is a O(n) operation, the merges take place on sublists of the *n* items in the list which means that we can count the merging at each level as O(n) and don't have to count each individual merge operation as O(n). Since there are *log n* levels to the merge sort algorithm and each level takes O(n) to merge, the algorithm is O(n log n).

4.7   Quicksort

In a sense, the quicksort algorithm is the exact opposite of the merge sort algorithm. It is also the most widely used and one of the most efficient sorting algorithms known. Quicksort is again a divide and conquer algorithm and is usually written recursively. But, where merge sort splits the list until we reach a size of 1 and then merges sorted lists, the quicksort algorithm does the *merging* first and then splits the list. We can't merge an unsorted list. Instead, we *partition* it into two lists. What we want is to prepare the list so quicksort can be called recursively. But, if we are to be successful, the two sublists must somehow be easier to sort than the original. This preparation for splitting is called *partitioning*. To partition a list we pick a pivot element. Think of quicksort partitioning a list into all the items bigger than the pivot and all the elements smaller than the pivot. We put all the bigger items to the right of the pivot and all the littler items to the left of the pivot. Once we have done this, two things are true:

- The pivot is in its final location in the list.
- The two sublists are now smaller and can therefore be quicksorted. Once the two sublists are sorted this will cause the entire list to be in sorted order, because the left will be the values ascending up to the pivot, the pivot is in the right spot, and the values greater than the pivot will all be in their correct locations, too.

Quicksort is a divide and conquer algorithm. To get the best performance, we would like to divide the sequence right down the middle into two equal sized sequences. This would mean that we would have to pick the value exactly in the middle to be the pivot since the pivot is used to divide the two lists. Unfortunately this isn't possible if we are to do it efficiently. For quicksort to have O(n log n) complexity, like merge sort, it must partition the list in O(n) time. We must choose a pivot quickly and we must choose it well. If we don't choose a pivot close to the middle, we will not get the O(n log n) complexity we hope for. It turns out that choosing a random pivot from the list is good enough. One way to guarantee a random choice of the pivot is to have the quicksort algorithm start by randomizing the sequence. The quicksort algorithm is given in Sect. 4.7.1.

4.7.1   The Quicksort Code

```
1   import random
2
3   def partition(seq, start, stop):
4       # pivotIndex comes from the start location in the list.
5       pivotIndex = start
6       pivot = seq[pivotIndex]
7       i = start+1
8       j = stop-1
9
10      while i <= j:
11          #while i <= j and seq[i] <= pivot:
12          while i <= j and not pivot < seq[i]:
13              i+=1
14          #while i <= j and seq[j] > pivot:
15          while i <= j and pivot < seq[j]:
16              j-=1
17
18          if i < j:
19              tmp = seq[i]
20              seq[i] = seq[j]
21              seq[j] = tmp
22              i+=1
23              j-=1
24
25      seq[pivotIndex] = seq[j]
26      seq[j] = pivot
27
28      return j
29
30  def quicksortRecursively(seq, start, stop):
31      if start >= stop-1:
32          return
33
34      # pivotIndex ends up in between the two halves
35      # where the pivot value is in its final location.
36      pivotIndex = partition(seq, start, stop)
37
38      quicksortRecursively(seq, start, pivotIndex)
39      quicksortRecursively(seq, pivotIndex+1, stop)
40
41  def quicksort(seq):
42      # randomize the sequence first
43      for i in range(len(seq)):
44          j = random.randint(0,len(seq)-1)
45          tmp = seq[i]
46          seq[i] = seq[j]
47          seq[j] = tmp
48
49      quicksortRecursively(seq, 0, len(seq))
```

Once the list is randomized, picking a random pivot becomes easier. The partition function picks the first item in the sequence as the pivot. The partitioning starts from both ends and works it way to the middle. Essentially every time a value bigger than the pivot is found on the left side and a value smaller than the pivot is found on the right side, the two values are swapped. Once we reach the middle from both sides, the pivot is swapped into place. Once the sequence is partitioned, the quicksort algorithm is called recursively on the two halves. Variables i and j are the indices of the left and right values, respectively, during the partitioning process.

If you look at the partition code, the two commented while loop conditions are probably easier to understand than the uncommented code. However, the uncommented code only uses the less than operator. Quicksort is the sorting algorithm used by the sort method on lists. It only requires that the less than operator be defined between items in the sequence. By writing the two while loops as we have, the only required ordering is defined by the less than operator just as Python requires.

The snapshot in Fig. 4.7 shows the effect of partitioning on a sequence. In this figure, the sequence has been partitioned twice already. The first partitioning picked a pivot that was almost dead center. However, the second partitioning picked a pivot that was not so good. The red line indicates the part of the sequence that is currently being partitioned. See how the left-most value in that sub-sequence is the pivot value. The two green dots are the pivot values that are already in their correct locations. All values above the pivot will end up in the partition to the right of the pivot and all values to the left of the pivot are less than the pivot. This is the nature of quicksort. Again, by amortized complexity we can find that the quicksort algorithm runs in O(n log n) time.

Consider sorting the list [5 8 2 6 9 1 0 7] using quicksort. Figure 4.8 depicts the list after each call to the partition function. The pivot in each call is identified by the orange colored item. The partition function partitions the list extending to the right of its pivot. After partitioning, the pivot is moved to its final location by swapping

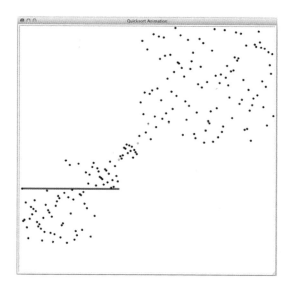

Fig. 4.7 Quicksort Snapshot

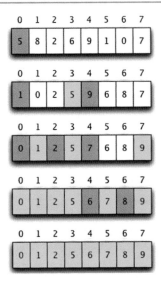

Fig. 4.8 Quicksorting a List

it with the last item that is less than the pivot. Then partitioning is performed on the resulting two sublists.

The randomization done in the first step of quicksort helps to pick a more random pivot value. This has real consequences in the quicksort algorithm, especially when the sequence passed to quicksort has a chance of being sorted already. If the sequence given to quicksort is sorted, or almost sorted, in either ascending or descending order, then quicksort will not achieve $O(n \log n)$ complexity. In fact, the worst case complexity of the algorithm is $O(n^2)$. If the pivot chosen is the next least or greatest value, then the partitioning will not divide the problem into to smaller sublists as occurred when 9 was chosen as a pivot for a sublist in Fig. 4.8. The algorithm will simply put one value in place and end up with one big partition of all the rest of the values. If this happened each time a pivot was chosen it would lead to $O(n^2)$ complexity. Randomizing the list prior to quicksorting it will help to ensure that this does not happen.

Merge sort is not affected by the choice of a pivot, since no choice is necessary. Therefore, merge sort does not have a worst case or best case to consider. It will always achieve $O(n \log n)$ complexity. Even so, quicksort performs better in practice than merge sort because the quicksort algorithm does not need to copy to a new list and then back again. The quicksort algorithm is the de facto standard of sorting algorithms.

4.8   Two-Dimensional Sequences

Sometimes programmers need to represent two-dimensional sequences in a program. This can be done quite easily by creating a list of lists. The main list can represent either the columns or the rows of the matrix. If the main list contains references to

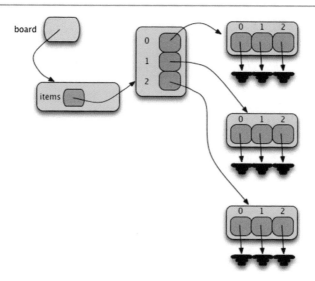

Fig. 4.9 A 2-Dimensional Matrix

the rows, then the matrix is said to be in row major form. If the main list contains references to the columns of the matrix, then it is in column major form. Most of the time, matrices are constructed in row major form. In Fig. 4.9 a matrix is drawn with a row major orientation, but the matrix could represent either row major or column major form. The actual organization of the data is the same either way. The *items* reference points at the main list. The *items* list contains references to each of the rows of the matrix.

For example, consider a program that plays tic tac toe against a human opponent. We would need to represent the board that tic tac toe is played on. To do so, we'll create a Board class that mimics our PyList class in the previous section. The organization of our board class is shown graphically in Fig. 4.9. The outline for the Board class is given in Sect. 4.8.1.

4.8.1   The Board Class

```
1   class Board:
2       # When a board is constructed, you may want to make a copy of the board.
3       # This can be a shallow copy of the board because Turtle objects are
4       # Immutable from the perspective of a board object.
5       def __init__(self,board=None):
6           self.items = []
7           for i in range(3):
8               rowlst = []
9               for j in range(3):
10                  if board==None:
11                      rowlst.append(Dummy())
12                  else:
```

```
13                      rowlst.append(board[i][j])
14
15              self.items.append(rowlst)
16
17      # The getitem method is used to index into the board. It should
18      # return a row of the board. That row itself is indexable (it is just
19      # a list) so accessing a row and column in the board can be written
20      # board[row][column] because of this method.
21      def __getitem__(self,index):
22          return self.items[index]
23
24      # This method should return true if the two boards, self and other,
25      # represent exactly the same state.
26      def __eq__(self,other):
27          pass
28
29      # This method will mutate this board to contain all dummy
30      # turtles. This way the board can be reset when a new game
31      # is selected. It should NOT be used except when starting
32      # a new game.
33      def reset(self):
34          screen.tracer(1)
35          for i in range(3):
36              for j in range(3):
37                  self.items[i][j].goto(-100,-100)
38                  self.items[i][j] = Dummy()
39
40          screen.tracer(0)
41
42      # This method should return an integer representing the
43      # state of the board. If the computer has won, return 1.
44      # If the human has won, return -1. Otherwise, return 0.
45      def eval(self):
46          pass
47
48      # This method should return True if the board
49      # is completely filled up (no dummy turtles).
50      # Otherwise, it should return false.
51      def full(self):
52          pass
53
54      # This method should draw the X's and O's
55      # Of this board on the screen.
56      def drawXOs(self):
57          for row in range(3):
58              for col in range(3):
59                  if self[row][col].eval() != 0:
60                      self[row][col].st()
61                      self[row][col].goto(col*100+50,row*100+50)
62
63          screen.update()
```

Because each row is itself a list in the Board class, we can just use the built-in *list* class for the rows of the matrix. Each location in each row of the matrix can hold either an X, an O, or a Dummy object. The Dummy objects are there for convenience and represent an open location in the board. The equal, eval, and full methods are left as an exercise for the student. The purpose of each will be described in the next section.

Many games, both animated and otherwise, are easy to implement using Tkinter and turtle graphics. Animated characters or tokens in a game can be implemented as a turtle that moves around on the screen as necessary. For the tic tac toe game the X's and O's can be implemented as RawTurtles. A RawTurtle is just like a Turtle object except that we must provide the canvas where a RawTurtle moves around. The code in Sect. 4.8.2 contains the three classes that define the X's, the O's, and the special Dummy class that is a placeholder for open locations in the board.

4.8.2   The X, O, and Dummy Classes

```
1    Human = -1
2    Computer = 1
3
4    # This class is just for placeholder objects when no move has been made
5    # yet at a position in the board. Having eval() return 0 is convenient when no
6    # move has been made.
7    class Dummy:
8        def __init__(self):
9            pass
10
11       def eval(self):
12           return 0
13
14       def goto(self,x,y):
15           pass
16
17   # In the X and O classes below the constructor begins by initializing the
18   # RawTurtle part of the object with the call to super().__init__(canvas). The
19   # super() call returns the class of the superclass (the class above the X or O
20   # in the class hierarchy). In this case, the superclass is RawTurtle. Then,
21   # calling __init__ on the superclass initializes the part of the object that is
22   # a RawTurtle.
23   class X(RawTurtle):
24       def __init__(self, canvas):
25           super().__init__(canvas)
26           self.ht()
27           self.getscreen().register_shape("X",((-40,-36),(-40,-44),(0,-4),(40,-44),\
28               (40,-36), (4,0),(40,36),(40,44),(0,4),(-40,44),(-40,36),(-4,0),(-40,-36)))
29           self.shape("X")
30           self.penup()
31           self.speed(5)
32           self.goto(-100,-100)
33
34       def eval(self):
35           return Computer
36
37   class O(RawTurtle):
38       def __init__(self, canvas):
39           super().__init__(canvas)
40           self.ht()
41           self.shape("circle")
42           self.penup()
43           self.speed(5)
44           self.goto(-100,-100)
45
46       def eval(self):
47           return Human
```

4.9   The Minimax Algorithm

The Dummy, X, and O classes all have an *eval* method that returns either a 1 for a Computer move, a −1 for a Human move, or a 0 for no move yet. The values for these moves are used in an algorithm called *minimax*. The minimax algorithm is a recursive algorithm that is used in two person game playing where one player is the computer and each player has a choice of some number of moves that can be made while taking turns. The minimax algorithm is simple. The idea is that when it is the computer's turn it should pick the move that will be best for the computer. Each possible move is analyzed to find the value that would be best for the computer. We'll let a 1 represent the best move for the computer. The worst move the computer could make will be represented by a −1. Move values can range between 1 and −1. When it is the computer's turn it will pick the move that results in the maximum move value. That's the *max* portion of minimax.

To find the best move, the computer will play out the game, alternating between the best move it could make and the best move the human could make. A best move for a human would be a −1. When it is the human's turn, the computer will assume that the human will make the best move he/she can make. This is the *min* part of minimax.

The minimax function is given two arguments, the player (either a −1 for human or a 1 for computer) and the board for the game. The base case for this recursive function checks to see if one of three things has occurred.

1. The current board is a win for the computer. In that case minimax returns a 1 for a computer win.
2. The current board is a win for the human. In that case minimax returns a −1 for a human win.
3. The current board is full. In that case, since neither human or computer won, minimax returns a 0.

The recursive part of the minimax function examines the player argument. If the player is the computer, then the function tries each possible move in the board by making a computer move. It places a computer move in that spot in a copy of the board and calls minimax with the human as the next player on that board. The algorithm uses the guess and check pattern to find the *maximum* of all possible values that come back from the recursive calls to minimax. The minimax function then returns that maximum value.

When minimax is called with the human as the next player to make a move, it does the same thing as when the computer is called as the player. It makes a human move in a copy of the board and recursively calls minimax on the copy of the board with the computer as the next player to play. The algorithm uses the guess and check pattern to find the *minimum* of all possible values that come back from calling minimax recursively.

There is one little tricky part to minimax. The minimax algorithm is called with a board and the next player to make a move. It returns a number somewhere between −1 and 1 indicating how likely it is that the computer or the human will win given that board. However, it *does not* tell you which move is the best to make. To deal with this we can have the code that executes the computer's turn do a little of the work. For the computer turn code to find the best *move* it makes a move in a copy of the board, calls minimax with the human as the next player to make a move, and then records the value that comes back from the call to minimax. The computer turn code uses the guess and check pattern to find the maximum value for all possible moves and the associated move which resulted in that value. After finding the best move, the computer's turn ends by the computer making that move in the board and returning so the human can make their next move. The tic tac toe code, which can be found on the text's accompanying website or in Sect. 20.5, contains the outline for the game. The *minimax* function and the *computerTurn* code are left as an exercise for the reader.

Minimax can be used in many two person games of perfect information such as checkers and connect four. The term *perfect information* means that both players can see the whole state of the game [3]. Poker is a game of *imperfect information* so would not be suitable for the minimax algorithm. It should be noted that tic tac toe has a small enough search space that the computer can solve the game. That means it will never lose. Most games however are not solvable, at least with the average computer. For instance, connect four has a much larger search space and can't be completely solved. Heuristics are applied to games like connect four to estimate how good or bad a board is after the minimax algorithm has searched as deep as it can given its time constraints. Games like these are often studied in the field of Artificial Intelligence [3]. Artificial Intelligence includes the study of search algorithms that may be used even when the search space is too large to use an exhaustive search. In this text, Chap. 12 covers a few heuristic search algorithms along with a heuristic applied to the minimax algorithm for the game of connect four.

4.10   Linked Lists

Sequences can be organized in several different ways. The *PyList* sequence was a randomly accessible list. This means that we can access any element of the list in O(1) time to either store or retrieve a value. Appending an item was possible in O(1) time using *amortized* complexity analysis, but inserting an item took O(n) time where *n* was the number of items after the location where the new item was being inserted.

If a programmer wants to insert a large number of items towards the beginning of a list, a different organization for a sequence might be better suited to their needs. A linked list is an organization of a list where each item in the list is in a separate node. Linked lists look like the links in a chain. Each link is *attached* to the next link by a reference that points to the next link in the chain. When working with a linked list, each link in the chain is called a *Node*. Each node consists of two pieces of information, an *item*, which is the data associated with the node, and a link to the next node in the linked list, often called *next*. The code in Sect. 4.10.1 defines the Node class that can be used to create the nodes in a linked list.

4.10.1 The Node Class

```
1   class Node:
2       def __init__(self,item,next=None):
3           self.item = item
4           self.next = next
5
6       def getItem(self):
7           return self.item
8
9       def getNext(self):
10          return self.next
11
12      def setItem(self, item):
13          self.item = item
14
15      def setNext(self,next):
16          self.next = next
```

In the Node class there are two pieces of information: the *item* is a reference to a value in the list, and the *next* reference which points to the next node in the sequence. Figure 4.10 is a linked list with three elements added to it. There are four nodes in this figure. The first node is a dummy node. Having one extra dummy node at the beginning of the sequence eliminates a lot of special cases that must be considered when working with the linked list. An empty sequence still has a dummy node. Nodes in linked lists are represented as a rounded rectangle with two halves. The left half of a node is a reference to the item or value for that node in the sequence. The right half is a reference to the next node in the sequence or to the special value *None* if it is the last node in the sequence.

Figure 4.10 depicts a linked list consisting of three pieces of information. We keep a reference to the first node in the sequence so we can traverse the nodes when necessary. The reference to the last node in the list makes it possible to append an item to the list in O(1) time. We also keep track of the number of items so we don't have to count when someone wants to retrieve the list size.

The table of operations in Fig. 4.11 contains the computational complexity of various list operations on the LinkedList datatype presented in this section. Many

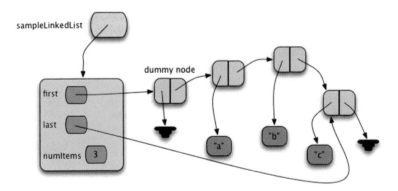

Fig. 4.10 A Sample LinkedList Object

Operation	Complexity	Usage	Method
List creation	O(len(y))	x = LinkedList(y)	calls __init__(y)
indexed get	O(n)	a = x[i]	x.__getitem__(i)
indexed set	O(n)	x[i] = a	x.__setitem__(i,a)
concatenate	O(n)	z = x + y	z = x.__add__(y)
append	O(1)	x.append(a)	x.append(a)
insert	O(n)	x.insert(i,e)	x.insert(i,e))
delete	O(n)	del x[i]	x.__delitem__(i)
equality	O(n)	x == y	x.__eq__(y)
iterate	O(n)	for a in x:	x.__iter__()
length	O(1)	len(x)	x.__len__()
membership	O(n)	a in x	x.__contains__(a)
sort	N/A	N/A	N/A

Fig. 4.11 Complexity of LinkedList Operations

of the operations appear to have the same complexity as the *list* datatype operations presented in Fig. 4.11. There are some important differences though. The following sections will provide the implementations for some of these operations and point out the differences as compared to the *list* datatype operations given in Fig. 4.11.

4.10.2 The LinkedList Constructor

```python
class LinkedList:

    # This class is used internally by the LinkedList class. It is
    # invisible from outside this class due to the two underscores
    # that precede the class name. Python mangles names so that they
    # are not recognizable outside the class when two underscores
    # precede a name but aren't followed by two underscores at the
    # end of the name (i.e. an operator name).
    class __Node:
        def __init__(self,item,next=None):
            self.item = item
            self.next = next

        def getItem(self):
            return self.item

        def getNext(self):
            return self.next

        def setItem(self, item):
            self.item = item

        def setNext(self,next):
            self.next = next

    def __init__(self,contents=[]):
        # Here we keep a reference to the first node in the linked list
```

```
28        # and the last item in the linked list. They both point to a
29        # dummy node to begin with. This dummy node will always be in
30        # the first position in the list and will never contain an item.
31        # Its purpose is to eliminate special cases in the code below.
32        self.first = LinkedList.__Node(None,None)
33        self.last = self.first
34        self.numItems = 0
35
36        for e in contents:
37            self.append(e)
```

Creating a *LinkedList* object has exactly the same complexity has constructing a *list* object. If an empty list is created, then the time taken is O(1) and if a list is copied, then it is a O(n) operation. A *LinkedList* object has references to both ends of the linked list. The reference to the head of the list points to a dummy node. Having a dummy node at the beginning eliminates many special cases that would exist when the list was empty if no dummy node were used.

Declaring the *Node* class within the *LinkedList* class, and preceding the name with two underscores, hides the *__Node* class from any code outside the LinkedList class. The idea here is that only the LinkedList class needs to know about the *__Node* class. Initially, both the *first* and the *last* references point to the dummy node. The *append* method is used to add elements to the LinkedList should a list be passed to the constructor.

4.10.3 LinkedList Get and Set

```
1   def __getitem__(self,index):
2       if index >= 0 and index < self.numItems:
3           cursor = self.first.getNext()
4           for i in range(index):
5               cursor = cursor.getNext()
6
7           return cursor.getItem()
8
9       raise IndexError("LinkedList index out of range")
10
11  def __setitem__(self,index,val):
12      if index >= 0 and index < self.numItems:
13          cursor = self.first.getNext()
14          for i in range(index):
15              cursor = cursor.getNext()
16
17          cursor.setItem(val)
18          return
19
20      raise IndexError("LinkedList assignment index out of range")
```

Implementations for the indexed get and set operations are included in Sect. 4.10.4 largely as an example of traversing a linked list. They are of little practical value. If random access to a list is desired, then the *list* class should be used. Linked lists are not randomly accessible. They require linear search through the datatype to access a particular location in the list. Each of these operations is O(n) where n is the value of the index.

4.10.4 LinkedList Concatenate

```
1   def __add__(self,other):
2       if type(self) != type(other):
3           raise TypeError("Concatenate undefined for " + \
4               str(type(self)) + " + " + str(type(other)))
5
6       result = LinkedList()
7
8       cursor = self.first.getNext()
9
10      while cursor != None:
11          result.append(cursor.getItem())
12          cursor = cursor.getNext()
13
14      cursor = other.first.getNext()
15
16      while cursor != None:
17          result.append(cursor.getItem())
18          cursor = cursor.getNext()
19
20      return result
```

Concatenation is an accessor method that returns a new list comprised of the two original lists. The operation is once again O(n) for linked lists as it was for the PyList datatype presented in Fig. 4.1. In this concatenation code a variable called *cursor* is used to step through the nodes of the two lists. This is the common method of stepping through a linked list. Set the cursor to the first element of the linked list. Then use a while loop that terminates when the cursor reaches the end (i.e. the special value *None*). Each time through the while loop the cursor is advanced by setting it to the next node in the sequence.

Notice in the code that the dummy node from both lists (i.e. *self* and *other*) is skipped when concatenating the two lists. The dummy node in the new list was created when the constructor was called.

4.10.5 LinkedList Append

```
1   def append(self,item):
2       node = LinkedList.__Node(item)
3       self.last.setNext(node)
4       self.last = node
5       self.numItems += 1
```

The code in Sect. 4.10.6 is the first time we see a small advantage of a LinkedList over a list. The *append* operation has a complexity of O(1) for LinkedLists where with lists the complexity was an amortized O(1) complexity. Each append will always take the same amount of time with a LinkedList. A LinkedList is also never bigger than it has to be. However, LinkedLists take up about twice the space of a randomly accessible list since there has to be room for both the reference to the item and the reference to the next node in the list.

The code for the append method is quite simple. Since the *self.last* reference points at the node immediately preceding the place where we want to put the new node, we just create a new node and make the last one point at it. Then we make the new node the new *self.last* node and increment the number of items by 1.

4.10.6 LinkedList Insert

```
1   def insert(self,index,item):
2       cursor = self.first
3
4       if index < self.numItems:
5           for i in range(index):
6               cursor = cursor.getNext()
7
8           node = LinkedList.__Node(item, cursor.getNext())
9           cursor.setNext(node)
10          self.numItems += 1
11      else:
12          self.append(item)
```

The *insert* operation, while it has the same complexity as *insert* on a list, is quite a bit different for linked lists. Inserting into a list is a O(n) operation where *n* is the number of elements that are in the list *after* the insertion point since they must all be moved down to make room for the new item. When working with a *LinkedList* the *n* is the number of elements that appear *before* the insertion point because we must search for the correct insertion point.

This means that while inserting at the beginning of a *list* is a O(n) operation, inserting at the beginning of a *LinkedList* is a O(1) operation. If you will have to do many inserts near the beginning of a list, then a linked list may be better to use than a randomly accessible list.

4.10.7 Other Linked List Operations

The other linked list operations are left as an exercise for the reader. In many cases, the key to working with a linked list is to get a reference to the node that preceds the location you want to work with. For instance, to delete a node from a linked list you merely want to make the *next* field of the preceeding node point to the node following the node you wish to delete. Consider the sample linked list in Fig. 4.10. To delete the second item (i.e. the "b") from this list we want to remove the node that contains the reference to the "b". To do this we can use a *cursor* to find the node preceding the one that references the "b". Once found, the next field of the cursor can be made to point to the node **after** the "b" as shown in Fig. 4.12.

Changing the next pointer of the cursor's node to point to the node after the "b" results in the node containing the "b" dropping out of the list. Since there are no other references to the node containing the "b", and actually to the "b" itself, the two objects are garbage collected.

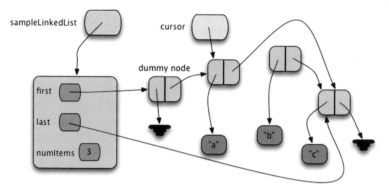

Fig. 4.12 Deleting a Node from a Linked List

Finally, the *sort* operation is not applicable on linked lists. Efficient sorting algorithms require random access to a list. Insertion sort, a $O(n^2)$ algorithm, would work, but it would be highly inefficient. If sorting were required, it would be much more efficient to copy the linked list to a randomly accessible list, sort it, and then build a new sorted linked list from the sorted list.

4.11   Stacks and Queues

There are two other sequential data structures that are very common in computer programming. A stack is a data structure where access is only at one end of the sequence. New values are *pushed* onto the stack to add them to the sequence and *popped* off the stack to remove them from the sequence. The run-time stack, described in Chap. 3, was one such instance of a stack. Stacks are used in many algorithms in computer science. Stacks can be used to evaluate numeric expressions. They are useful when *parsing* information. They can be used to match parenthesis in programs and expressions. The operations on a stack are given in Fig. 4.13.

Stacks are called *Last In/First Out* or *LIFO* data structures. The last item pushed is the first item popped. A *Stack* class can be implemented in at least a couple different

Operation	Complexity	Usage	Description
Stack Creation	O(1)	s=Stack()	calls the constructor
pop	O(1)	a=s.pop()	returns the last item pushed and removes it from s
push	O(1)	s.push(a)	pushes the item, a, on the stack, s
top	O(1)	a=s.top()	returns the top item without popping s
isEmpty	O(1)	s.isEmpty()	returns True if s has no pushed items

Fig. 4.13 Complexity of Stack Operations

ways to achieve the computation complexities outlined in this table. Either a list or a linked list will suffice. The code in Sect. 4.11.2 is an implementation of a stack with a list. The implementation is pretty straight-forward. The main program in Sect. 4.11.2 tests the stack datatype with a couple tests to make sure the code operates correctly.

4.11.1 The Stack Class Code

```
1    class Stack:
2        def __init__(self):
3            self.items = []
4
5        def pop(self):
6            if self.isEmpty():
7                raise RuntimeError("Attempt to pop an empty stack")
8
9            topIdx = len(self.items)-1
10           item = self.items[topIdx]
11           del self.items[topIdx]
12           return item
13
14       def push(self,item):
15           self.items.append(item)
16
17       def top(self):
18           if self.isEmpty():
19               raise RuntimeError("Attempt to get top of empty stack")
20
21           topIdx = len(self.items)-1
22           return self.items[topIdx]
23
24       def isEmpty(self):
25           return len(self.items) == 0
26
27   def main():
28       s = Stack()
29       lst = list(range(10))
30       lst2 = []
31
32       for k in lst:
33           s.push(k)
34
35       if s.top() == 9:
36           print("Test 1 Passed")
37       else:
38           print("Test 1 Failed")
39
40       while not s.isEmpty():
41           lst2.append(s.pop())
42
43       lst2.reverse()
44
45       if lst2 != lst:
46           print("Test 2 Failed")
47       else:
48           print("Test 2 Passed")
49
```

```
50       try:
51           s.pop()
52           print("Test 3 Failed")
53
54       except RuntimeError:
55           print("Test 3 Passed")
56       except:
57           print("Test 3 Failed")
58
59       try:
60           s.top()
61           print("Test 4 Failed")
62
63       except RuntimeError:
64           print("Test 4 Passed")
65       except:
66           print("Test 4 Failed")
67
68   if __name__=="__main__":
69       main()
```

This code, if saved in a file called *stack.py* can be imported into other modules. When this module is run by itself, the test main function will execute. When this module is imported into another program, the main function will not execute because the *__name__* variable will not be equal to "__main__".

A queue is like a stack in many ways except that instead of being a *LIFO* data structure, queues are *FIFO* or *First In/First Out* data structures. The first item pushed, is the first item popped. When we are working with a queue we talk of *enqueueing* an item, instead of *pushing* it. When removing an item from the queue we talk of *dequeueing* the item instead of *popping* it as we did from a stack. The table in Fig. 4.14 provides details of the queue operations and their complexities.

Implementing a queue with the complexities given in this table is a bit trickier than implementing the stack. To implement a queue with these complexities we need to be able to add to one end of a sequence and remove from the other end of the sequence in O(1) time. This suggests the use of a linked list. Certainly, a linked list would work to get the desired complexities. However, we can still use a list if we are willing to accept an amortized complexity of O(1) for the dequeue operation. This Queue class code implements a queue with a list and achieves an amortized complexity of O(1) for the dequeue operation.

Operation	Complexity	Usage	Description
Queue Creation	O(1)	q=Queue()	calls the constructor
dequeue	O(1)	a=q.dequeue()	returns the first item enqueued and removes it from q
enqueue	O(1)	q.enqueue(a)	enqueues the item, a, on the queue, q
front	O(1)	a=q.front()	returns the front item without dequeueing the item
isEmpty	O(1)	q.isEmpty()	returns True if q has not enqueued items

Fig. 4.14 Complexity of Queue Operations

```
1   class Queue:
2       def __init__(self):
3           self.items = []
4           self.frontIdx = 0
5
6       def __compress(self):
7           newlst = []
8           for i in range(self.frontIdx,len(self.items)):
9               newlst.append(self.items[i])
10
11          self.items = newlst
12          self.frontIdx = 0
13
14      def dequeue(self):
15          if self.isEmpty():
16              raise RuntimeError("Attempt to dequeue an empty queue")
17
18          # When queue is half full, compress it. This
19          # achieves an amortized complexity of O(1) while
20          # not letting the list continue to grow unchecked.
21          if self.frontIdx * 2 > len(self.items):
22              self.__compress()
23
24          item = self.items[self.frontIdx]
25          self.frontIdx += 1
26          return item
27
28      def enqueue(self,item):
29          self.items.append(item)
30
31      def front(self):
32          if self.isEmpty():
33              raise RuntimeError("Attempt to access front of empty queue")
34
35          return self.items[self.frontIdx]
36
37      def isEmpty(self):
38          return self.frontIdx == len(self.items)
39
40  def main():
41      q = Queue()
42      lst = list(range(10))
43      lst2 = []
44
45      for k in lst:
46          q.enqueue(k)
47
48      if q.front() == 0:
49          print("Test 1 Passed")
50      else:
51          print("Test 1 Failed")
52
53      while not q.isEmpty():
54          lst2.append(q.dequeue())
55
56      if lst2 != lst:
57          print("Test 2 Failed")
58      else:
59          print("Test 2 Passed")
```

```
60
61      for k in lst:
62          q.enqueue(k)
63
64      lst2 = []
65
66      while not q.isEmpty():
67          lst2.append(q.dequeue())
68
69      if lst2 != lst:
70          print("Test 3 Failed")
71      else:
72          print("Test 3 Passed")
73
74      try:
75          q.dequeue()
76          print("Test 4 Failed")
77
78      except RuntimeError:
79          print("Test 4 Passed")
80      except:
81          print("Test 4 Failed")
82
83      try:
84          q.front()
85          print("Test 5 Failed")
86
87      except RuntimeError:
88          print("Test 5 Passed")
89      except:
90          print("Test 5 Failed")
91
92  if __name__=="__main__":
93      main()
```

4.11.2 Infix Expression Evaluation

An infix expression is an expression where operators appear in between their operands. For example, $(6 + 5) * 4$ is an infix expression because $+$ appears between the 6 and 5 and $*$ appears between its operands. Python, being a programming language, can evaluate infix expressions. However, let's say we would like to write a program that would evaluate expressions entered by the user. Can we do this in a Python program? It turns out we can, and very easily. Python includes a function that will treat a string like an expression to be evaluated and will return the result of that evaluation. The function is called *eval*. Here is a program that uses the *eval* function.

```
1   def main():
2       expr = input("Please enter an infix expression: ")
3       result = eval(expr)
4       print("The result of",expr,"is",result)
5
6   if __name__ == "__main__":
7       main()
```

This is certainly a very interesting, albeit short, program. The *eval* function does an awful lot of work for us. But, how does it work? It turns out we can write our own *eval* function using a couple of stacks. In this section we describe an infix expression evaluator. To make our job a bit easier, we'll insist that the user enter spaces between all operators (including parens) and operands. So for instance, the user might interact as follows.

```
Please enter an infix expression: ( 6 + 5 ) * 4 - 9
The result of ( 6 + 5 ) * 4 - 9 = 35.0
```

The infix evaluator algorithm uses two stacks, an operator stack and an operand stack. The operator stack will hold operators and left parens. The operand stack holds numbers.

The algorithm proceeds by scanning the tokens of the infix expression from left to right. You can do this quite easily in Python by splitting the input string and then iterating over the list of strings from the input. The tokens are operators (including parens) and numbers.

Each operator has a precedence associated with it. Multiplication and division operators have the highest precedence while addition and subtraction are next. Finally the left paren and right paren precedence are the lowest. A function called *precedence* can be written so that given an operator, the *precedence* function returns the proper precedence value. You can decide on your precedence values given the prescribed restrictions.

To begin the operand stack and the operator stack are initialized to empty stacks and a left paren is pushed on the operator stack.

For each token in the input we do the following:

1. If the token is an operator then we need to *operate* on the two stacks with the given operator. *Operating* is described in Sect. 4.11.2.1.
2. If the token is a number then we push it on the number stack.

After scanning all the input and operating when required we *operate* on the stacks one more time with an extra right paren operator. After operating the final time the operator stack should be empty and the operand stack should have one number on it which is the result. You pop the operand stack and print the number as your result.

4.11.2.1 The Operate Procedure

The operate procedure should be a separate function. The operate procedure is given an operator, the operator stack, and operand stack as arguments. To operate we do the following:

- If the given operator is a left paren we push it on the operator stack and return.
- Otherwise, while the precedence of the given operator is less than or equal to the precedence of the top operator on the operator stack proceed as follows:

1. Pop the top operator from the operator stack. Call this the *topOp*.
2. if *topOp* is a +, −, *, or / then operate on the number stack by popping the operands, doing the operation, and pushing the result.
3. if *topOp* is a left paren then the given operator should be a right paren. If so, we are done operating and we return immediately.

When the precedence of the given operator is greater than the precedence of *topOp* we terminate the loop and push the given operator on the operator stack before returning from operating.

4.11.2.2 Example

To see how this algorithm works it will help to look at an example. In the figures the right-most underlined token is the token currently being processed and all tokens to the left have already be processed. The operand stack and the operator stack are labeled in the diagrams. The *topOp* operator and the current *operator* are given as well.

In Fig. 4.15 the tokens (6 + 5 have been processed and pushed onto their respective stacks. The right paren is now being processed and operate was called to process this operator. In the operate procedure the *topOp* is a "+" and "+" has higher precedence than ")" so the right paren cannot be pushed on top of the addition operator. So, we pop the operator stack and operate. Since we popped a "+" we then pop the two numbers from the operand stack, add them together, and push the result as shown in Fig. 4.16.

After pushing the 11 on the stack we found that the top operator was a left paren. In that case we popped the left paren and returned immediately leaving just the single left paren on the operator stack. Then the evaluator proceeded by finding the "*" operator and pushing it and then finding the 4 and pushing it on the operand stack. Next, the "−" operator cannot be pushed onto the operator stack because its precedence is lower then "*". Operate is called and the *topOp* dictates that we pop two numbers, multiply them, and push the result as shown in Fig. 4.17. The "−" operator has higher precedence than the "(" so it is just pushed onto the operator stack. The 9 is processed and pushed onto the operand stack as shown in Fig. 4.17.

To finish up the evaluation of the infix expression, operate is called one more time with ")" as the operator. This forces the 9 to be subtracted from the 44 leaving 35 on the operand stack and the operator stack empty. The final result is 35 and the evaluator pops the result from the operand stack and returns it as the result and that is how the Python *eval* function works. It turns out that the Python *eval* function is a bit more sophisticated than this example. However, the effect of evaluating simple infix expressions is the same.

4.11.3 Radix Sort

The radix sort algorithm sorts a sequence of strings lexicographically, as they would appear in a phonebook or dictionary. To implement this algorithm the strings are

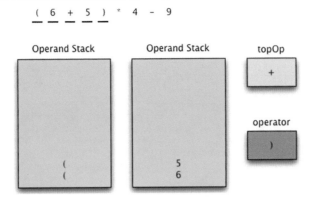

Fig. 4.15 Infix Evaluation Step 1

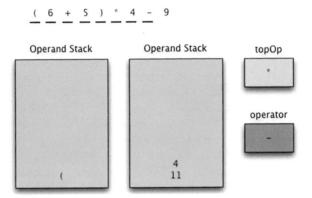

Fig. 4.16 Infix Evaluation Step 2

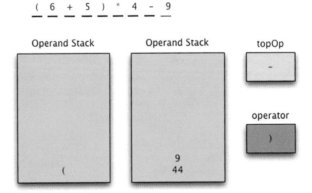

Fig. 4.17 Infix Evaluation Step 3

read from the source (e.g. a file or the internet) and they are placed in a queue called the *mainQueue*. As the strings are read and placed in the queue the algorithm keeps track of the length of the longest string that will be sorted. We'll call this length *longest*.

For the radix sort algorithm to work correctly, all the strings in the mainQueue need to be the same length, which is not likely of course. If a string is shorter than the longest string it can be padded with blanks. To assist, it is handy to have a function that returns a character of a string like the *charAt* function in Sect. 4.11.6.

4.11.4 The CharAt Function

```
1    def charAt(s,i):
2        if len(s) - 1 < i:
3            return " "
4
5        return s[i]
```

The *charAt* function returns the ith character of the string *s* and a blank if *i* is greater than or equal to the length of *s*. With the use of this function the strings in the mainQueue can be different lengths and the *charAt* function will make them look like they are the same length.

In addition to the mainQueue, there are 256 queues created and placed into a list of queues, called *queueList*. There are 256 different possible ASCII values and one queue is created for each ASCII letter. Since most ASCII characters are in the range of 0–127 the algorithm probably won't use the queues at indices 128–255.

The sorting algorithm works by removing a string from mainQueue. It looks at the last character, starting at *longest*-1, in each string and placing the string on a queue that corresponds to the character's ASCII value. So, all strings ending with 'a' go on the 'a' queue and so on. To find the index into *queueList* the *ord* function is used. For instance, writing *ord("a")* would return a 65 which is the index to use into the queueList for the character "a".

Then, starting with the first queue in the queueList, all strings are dequeued from each queue and placed on the main queue. We empty each queue first before proceeding to the next queue in the queueList. This is repeated until all letter queues are empty.

Then, we go back to removing all elements from the main queue again, this time looking at the second to the last letter of each word. Each string is placed on a queue in the queueList depending on its second to last letter. The process is repeated until we get to the first letter of each string. When we are done, all strings are on the main queue in sorted order. To complete the algorithm all strings are removed from the mainQueue one more time in sorted order.

4.11.4.1 Radix Sort Example

To see how radix sort works we'll consider an example where the words bat, farm, barn, car, hat, and cat are sorted alphabetically. In the figures in this section each queue is drawn vertically with the front of the queue being at the bottom of the box and the rear of the queue being at the top of each box. While there are 256 queues plus a mainQueue created by radix sort, the example will show just the queues that are used while sorting these words. The first queue in the list is the queue for spaces in a string. Figure 4.18 depicts the strings on the mainQueue after they have been read from their source.

The first step of the algorithm processes the mainQueue by emptying it and placing each string in the queue that corresponds to its fourth letter (the maximum string length). This results in farm and barn being placed on the m and n queues. The other strings are placed on the space queue as shown in Fig. 4.19.

Then, all the strings are dequeued from the three non-empty queues and placed back on the mainQueue in the order that they were dequeued as shown in Fig. 4.20.

Once again, the process is repeated for the third letter in each string. This results in using the r and t queues as shown in Fig. 4.21.

Again, the strings are brought back to the mainQueue in the order they were dequeued as depicted in Fig. 4.22.

And the process is repeated again for the second letter in each string. All strings have an a as their second character so they all end up on the a queue (Fig. 4.23).

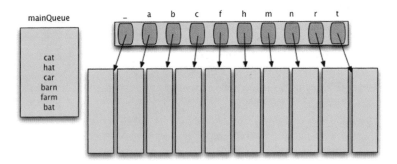

Fig. 4.18 Radix Sort Step 1

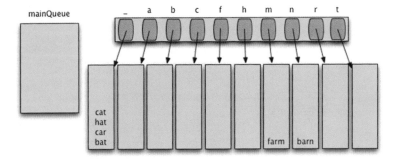

Fig. 4.19 Radix Sort Step 2—4th letter

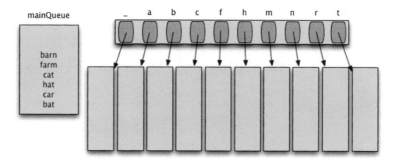

Fig. 4.20 Radix Sort Step 3

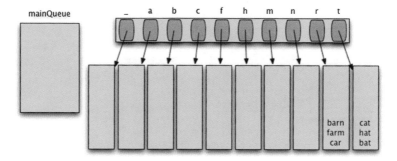

Fig. 4.21 Radix Sort Step 4—3rd letter

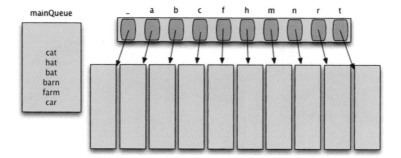

Fig. 4.22 Radix Sort Step 5

And they all go back to the mainQueue as shown in Fig. 4.24. No change from step 5 in this case.

Finally, we look at the first letter in each string and the sort is almost complete as shown in Fig. 4.25.

Bringing all the strings back to the mainQueue results in the mainQueue containing all the strings in sorted order. The mainQueue can be emptied at this point and the strings can be processed in sorted order as depicted in Fig. 4.26.

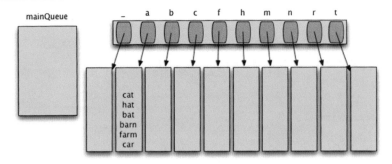

Fig. 4.23 Radix Sort Step 6—2nd letter

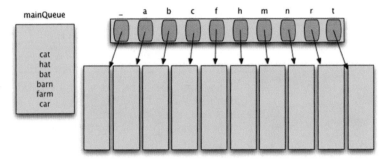

Fig. 4.24 Radix Sort Step 7

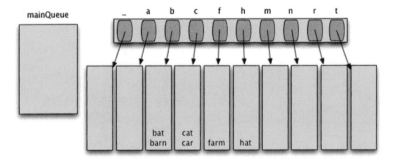

Fig. 4.25 Radix Sort Step 8—1st letter

Radix sort is pretty simple. It is called radix sort because a radix is like a decimal point moving backwards through the string. We move the decimal point one character at a time until we get to the first character in each string.

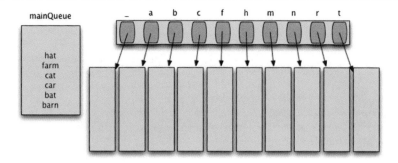

Fig. 4.26 Radix Sort Step 9

4.12   Chapter Summary

This chapter explored the use of linear sequences in computer programming. These sequences come in many forms including randomly accessible lists, matrices, linked lists, stacks, and queues. We also saw that a two-dimensional matrix is just a list of lists. The chapter also explored operations as related to these datatypes and the complexity of these operations.

Algorithms were also an important part of chapter four. The selection sort, merge sort, and quicksort algorithms were studied along with their computational complexities. Minimax was presented as an interesting case study on using two-dimensional matrices and recursion in a program. The infix evaluator and radix sort algorithms were also presented as examples of using stacks and queues.

Having read this chapter you should have an understanding of abstract data types like lists, stacks, and queues. You should understand how an abstract data type is implemented, how the implementation can affect the complexity of its operations, and at least a few algorithms that use these data types in their implementations.

4.13   Review Questions

Answer these short answer, multiple choice, and true/false questions to test your mastery of the chapter.

1. What is the best case, worst case, and average case complexity of selection sort, merge sort, and the quicksort algorithms?
2. How can the append operation achieve O(1) complexity when it sometimes runs out of space to append another item?
3. What is the complexity of the concatenation operator, the + operator, for lists?
4. What is the complexity of the deletion operator for lists?

5. When sorting items in a list, what method must be defined for those elements? Why?
6. Why does quicksort perform better than merge sort?
7. Under what conditions would it be possible for merge sort to perform better than quicksort?
8. Summarize what happens when a list is partitioned.
9. Summarize what happens when two lists are merged in the merge sort algorithm.
10. What is the purpose of the start parameter to the select function of the selection sort algorithm?
11. What are the advantages of a linked list over a randomly accessible list implementation of a list data type?
12. What are the advantages of a randomly accessible list over a linked list implementation of a list data type?
13. How does a stack differ from a queue in how we access it?
14. What is the complexity of the radix sort algorithm?

4.14   Programming Problems

1. Write a program that times the quicksort, the merge sort, and the built-in sort algorithms in Python to discover which one is better and to see their relative speeds. To do this you should implement two sequence classes, a QSequence and a MSequence. The QSequence can inherit from the PyList class and should implement its own sort algorithm using the quicksort code presented in this chapter. The MSequence should be a similar class using the merge sort algorithm.
You can sort anything you like. If you choose to sort objects of some class you define, remember that you must implement the __lt__ method for that class. Be sure to randomize the elements in the sequence prior to sorting them using quicksort. Generate an XML file in the *plot* format to plot three sequences. Plot the time it takes to both randomize and quicksort a sequence. Then plot the time it takes to merge sort a sequence. Finally, plot the time it takes to sort the same sequence using the built-in sort method. The complexity of merge sort and quicksort is O(n log n) so by computational complexity the three algorithms are equivalent. What does the experimental data reveal about the two algorithms? Put a comment at the top of your program giving your answer.
To effectively test these three sorting algorithms you should sort items up to a list size of at least 1000 elements. You can time the sorts in increments of 100. Depending on your computer, you may need to play with the exact numbers to some degree to get a good looking graph.
2. The merge sort algorithm is not as commonly used as the quicksort algorithm because quicksort is an inplace sort while merge sort requires at least space for one extra copy of the list. In fact, merge sort can be implemented with exactly one extra copy of the list. In this exercise you are to re-implement the merge sort

algorithm to use one extra copy of the list instead of allocating a new list each time two lists are merged.

The extra list is allocated prior to calling the recursive part of the merge sort algorithm. Then, with each alternating level of recursion the merge sort algorithm copies to the other list, flipping between the two lists. To accomplish this, the *mergeSortRecursively* function should be given a new list of lists called *lists* instead of the *seq* list. At *lists* [0] is the *seq* list and at *lists* [1] is the extra copy of the list. One extra parameter is given to the *mergeSortRecursively* function. The index of the list to merge from is also provided. This index will flip back and forth between 0 and 1 as each recursive call to *mergeSortRecursively* occurs. This flipping of 0 to 1 to 0 and so on can be accomplished using modular arithmetic by writing:

```
listToMergeFromIndex = (listToMergeFromIndex + 1) % 2
```

The percent sign is the remainder after dividing by 2. Adding 1 and finding the remainder after dividing by two means that *listToMergeFromIndex* flips between 0 and 1. So, the call is made as *mergeSortRecursively(listToMergeFromIndex, lists, start, stop)*. The *mergeSortRecursively* function must return the new index of the list to merge from.

One part of this new *mergeSortRecursively* function is a little tricky. There may be one more level of recursion on the left or right side for the two recursive calls to *mergeSortRecursively*. If this is the case, then the result from either the left or right half must be copied into the same list as the other half before the two halves can be successfully merged.

When *mergeSortRecursively* returns to the *mergeSort* function the result of sorting may be in the original sequence or it may be in the copy. If it is in the copy, then the result must be copied back to the original sequence before returning.

Complete this two list version of merge sort as described in this exercise and test it thoroughly. Then time this version of merge sort and compare those timings with the version of merge sort presented in the chapter and with the quicksort implementation presented in this chapter. Construct an XML file in the format read by the PlotData.py program and plot their corresponding timing diagrams to see how this algorithm performs when compared to the other two.

3. Complete the tic tac toe program described in the section on 2-dimensional matrices. Use the code from Sect. 20.5 as your starting point. Then complete the sections that say they are left as an exercise for the student.

4. Complete the *LinkedList* datatype by implementing the delete, equality, iterate, length, and membership operations. Make sure they have the complexity given in the LinkedList complexities table. Then, implement a test program in your *main* function to thoroughly test the operations you implemented. Call the module linkedlist.py so that you can import this into other programs that may need it.

5. Implement a queue data type using a linked list implementation. Create a set of test cases to throroughly test your datatype. Place the datatype in a file called queue.py and create a main function that runs your test cases.

6. Implement a priority queue data type using a linked list implementation. In a priority queue, elements on the queue each have a priority where the lower the number the higher the priority. The priorities are usually just numbers. The priority queue has the usual enqueue, dequeue, and empty methods. When a value is enqueued it is compared to the priority of other items and placed in front of all items that have lower priority (i.e. a higher priority number).

7. Implement a stack data type using a linked list implementation. Create a set of test cases to throroughly test your datatype. Place the datatype in a file called stack.py and create a main function that runs your test cases.

8. Implement the infix evaluator program described in the chapter. You should accept input and produce output as described in that section of the text. The input tokens should will all be separated by blanks to make retrieval of the tokens easy. Don't forget to convert your number tokens from strings to floats when writing the program.

9. Implement the radix sort algorithm described in the chapter. Use the algorithm to sort a list of words you find on the internet or elsewhere. Write a main program that tests your radix sort algorithm.

10. Searching a sequence of items for a particular item takes $O(n)$ time on average where n is the number of items in the list. However, if the list is sorted first, then searching for an item within the list can be done in $O(\log n)$ time by using a divide and conquer approach. This type of search is called binary search. The binary search algorithm starts by looking for the item in the middle of the sequence. If it is not found there then because the list is sorted the binary search algorithm knows whether to look in the left or right side of the sequence. Binary search reports *True* or *False* depending on whether the item is found. It is often written recursively being given a sequence and the beginning and ending index values in which to search for the item. For instance, to search an entire sequence called *seq*, binary search might be called as *binarySearch(seq,0,len(seq)-1)*. Write a program that builds a PyList or just a Python list of values, sorts them, and then looks up random values within the list. Compute the lookup times for lists of various sizes and record your results in the *PlotData.py* format so you can visualize your results. You should see a $O(\log n)$ curve if you implemented binary search correctly.

Sets and Maps

5

In the last chapter we studied sequences which are used to keep track of lists of things where duplicate values are allowed. For instance, there can be two sixes in a sequence or list of integers. In this chapter we look at *sets* where duplicate values are not allowed. After examining sets we'll move on to talk about *maps*. *Maps* may also be called *dictionaries* or *hash tables*.

The term *hash table* actually suggests an implementation of a set or map. The primary focus of this chapter is in understanding *hashing*. Hashing is a very important concept in Computer Science because it is a very efficient method of searching for a value. To begin the chapter we'll motivate our interest in hashing, then we'll develop a hashing algorithm for finding values in a set. We'll also apply hashing to the building of sets and maps. Then we'll look at an important technique that uses hashing called *memoization* and we'll apply that technique to a couple of problems.

5.1   Chapter Goals

In this chapter you learn how to implement a couple of abstract datatypes: sets and maps. You will read about the importance of hashing for both of these datatypes. You'll also learn about the importance of understanding the difference between mutable and immutable data. By the end of the chapter you should be able to answer these questions.

- What is the complexity of finding a value in a set?
- What is the *load factor* and how does it affect the overall efficiency of lookup in a hash table?
- When would you use an immutable set?
- When might you want a mutable set?
- When is there an advantage to using memoization in a problem?
- Under what circumstances can it be useful to use a map or dictionary?

© Springer International Publishing Switzerland 2015   139
K.D. Lee and S. Hubbard, *Data Structures and Algorithms with Python*,
Undergraduate Topics in Computer Science, DOI 10.1007/978-3-319-13072-9_5

Again, there will be some interesting programming problem challenges in this chapter including optimization of the tic tac toe game first presented in the last chapter and a Sudoku puzzle solver. Read on to discover what you need to know to solve these interesting problems.

5.2   Playing Sudoku

Many people enjoy solving Sudoku puzzles. To solve a Sudoku puzzle you must find the correct numbers to fill a 9×9 matrix. All numbers must be 1–9. Each row must have one each of 1–9 in it. The same is true for each column. Finally, there are nine 3×3 squares within the 9×9 matrix that must also have each of 1–9 in them. To begin, you are given a puzzle with some of the locations known as shown in Fig. 5.1. Your job is to find the rest of the numbers given the numbers that already appear in the puzzle.

A common way to solve these puzzles is by the process of elimination. It helps to write down the possible values for a puzzle and then eliminate the possible values one by one. For instance, the puzzle above can be annotated with possible values in for the unknowns as shown in Fig. 5.2.

To begin solving the puzzle, we can immediately eliminate 8, 3 and 9 from the second column of the puzzle for those cells that do not contain 8, 3 or 9. None of those numbers could appear in any other cell in the second column because they are already known. Likewise, the numbers 8, 6 and 4 can be eliminated from some cells

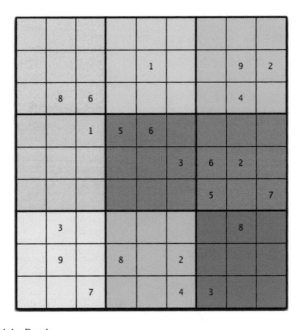

Fig. 5.1 A Sudoku Puzzle

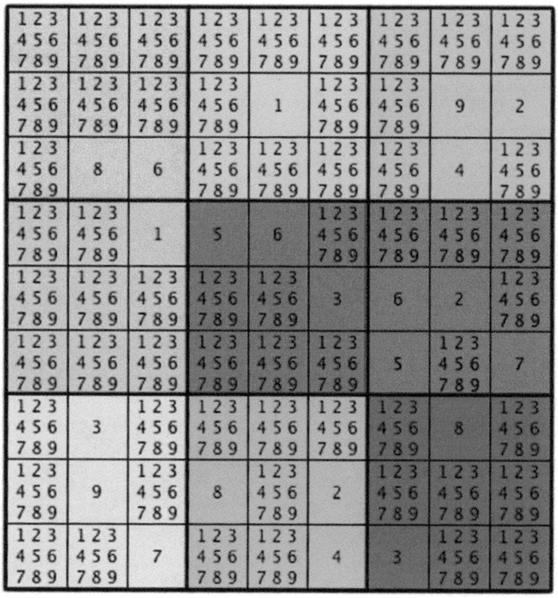

Fig. 5.2 Annotated Sudoku Puzzle

in the third row in the puzzle because those numbers already appear in other cells. Applying rules like these reduces the number of possible values for each cell in the puzzle. Figure 5.3 shows the puzzle after applying some of these rules.

If we spend some time thinking about Sudoku and how to solve it we can derive two rules that can be used to solve many Sudoku puzzles. These two rules can be applied to any group within the puzzle. A group is a collection of nine cells that appear in a row, column, or square within the puzzle. Within each cell is a set of numbers representing the possible values for the cell at some point in the process of reducing the puzzle. Here are the two rules.

- **RULE 1**. The first rule is a generalization of the process that we used above to remove some values from cells. Within a group look for cells that contain the same set of possible values. If the cardinality of the set (i.e. the number of items in the set) matches the number of duplicate sets found, then the items of the duplicate sets may safely be removed from all non-duplicate sets in the group. This rule applies even in the degenerative case where the number of duplicate sets is 1 and the size of that set is 1. The degenerative case is what we used above to remove single items from other sets. This rule can be applied to Fig. 5.3 to remove the 2 from all cells in the 7th row of the puzzle except the 7th column where 2 appears by itself.
- **RULE 2**. The second rule looks at each cell within a group and throws away all items that appear in other cells in the group. If we are left with only one value in the chosen cell, then it must appear in this cell and the cell may be updated by throwing

123 456 789	124 57	234 59	234 679	234 578 9	567 89	178	135 67	135 68
345 7	457	345	346 7	1	567 8	78	9	2
123 579	8	6	237 9	235 79	579	17	4	135
234 789	247	1	5	6	789	489	3	489
457 89	457	458 9	147 9	478 9	3	6	2	489
234 689	246	234 89	124 9	248 9	189	5	1	7
124 56	3	245	167 9	579	156 79	2	8	145 69
145 6	9	45	8	3	2	147	156 7	145 6
8	125 6	7	169	59	4	3	156	156 9

Fig. 5.3 Sudoku Puzzle After One Pass

away all other values that appear in the chosen cell. Applying this rule to the fifth row in Fig. 5.3 results in the fourth column being reduced to containing a 1 because 1 does not appear in any other cell in the 5th row. This rule also applies in the last row of the puzzle where 2 is only possible in the second column after removing 1, 5 and 6 from that cell because they appear within other cells in that row.

Note that the puzzle in Fig. 5.3 is not fully reduced. The reduction process can be applied iteratively until no more reductions are possible. The Sudoku solver algorithm keeps applying this reduction process until no more changes are made during a pass of reductions on all the groups within the puzzle. Applying these two rules in this manner will fully reduce many Sudoku puzzles.

5.3   Sets

The reduction algorithm for Sudoku puzzles manipulates sets of numbers and eliminates possible values from those sets as the reduction progresses. A set is a collection that does not allow duplicate values. Sets can be composed of any values. Integers, employee objects, characters, strings, literally any object in Python could be an element of some set. A set has a *cardinality*. The *cardinality* of a set is the number of items in it.

Operation	Complexity	Usage	Description
Set Creation	O(1)	s=set([iterable])	Calls the set constructor to create a set. Iterable is an optional initial contents in which case we have O(n) complexity.
Set Creation	O(1)	s=frozenset([iterable])	Calls the frozenset constructor for immutable set objects to create a frozenset object.
Cardinality	O(1)	len(s)	The number of elements in s is returned.
Membership	O(1)	e in s	Returns True if e is in s and False otherwise.
non-Membership	O(1)	e not in s	Returns True if e is not in s and False otherwise.
Disjoint	O(n)	s.isdisjoint(t)	Returns True if s and t share no elements, and False otherwise.
Subset	O(n)	s.issubset(t)	Returns True if s is a subset of t, and False otherwise.
Superset	O(n)	s.issuperset(t)	Returns True if s is a superset of t and False otherwise.
Union	O(n)	s.union(t)	Returns a new set which contains all elements in s and t.
Intersection	O(n)	s.intersection(t)	Returns a new set which contains only the elements in both s and t.
Set Difference	O(n)	s.difference(t)	Returns a new set which contains the elements of s that are not in t.
Symmetric Difference	O(n)	s.symmetric_difference(t)	Returns a new set which contains s.difference(t).union(t.difference(s))
Set Copy	O(n)	s.copy()	Returns a shallow copy of s.

Fig. 5.4 Set and Frozen Set Operations

Sets are objects that have several commonly defined operations on them. These operations are sometimes binary operations involving more than one set, and sometimes retrieve information about just one set. The table in Fig. 5.4 describes commonly defined operations on sets and their associated computational complexities. Python has built-in support for two types of sets, the *set* and *frozenset* classes. The *frozenset* class is immutable. Objects of the *set* class can be mutated. In Fig. 5.4 the variable s must be a set and the variable t must be an iterable sequence, which would include sets.

Infix operators are also defined as syntactic sugar for some of the operations defined in Fig. 5.4. For subset containment you can write $s <= t$. For proper subset you can write $s < t$. A proper subset is a subset that has at least one less element than its superset. For superset you can write $s >= t$ or $s > t$ for proper superset. For the union operation, writing $s \mid t$ is equivalent to writing *s.union(t)*. And for intersection, *s&t* is equivalent to writing *s.intersection(t)*. Writing $s - t$ is the same as writing *s.difference(t)* and *s^t* is equivalent to the symmetric difference operator.

The operations in Fig. 5.5 are not defined on the *frozenset* class since they mutate the set *s*. They are only defined on the *set* class.

Again, there are operators for some of the methods presented in Fig. 5.5. The mutator union method can be written *s|=t*. Intersection update can be written as *s&=t*. Finally, the symmetric difference update operator is written *s^=t*. While these operators are convenient, they are not well-known and code written by calling the methods in the table above will be more descriptive.

Operation	Complexity	Usage	Description
Union	O(n)	s.update(t)	Adds the contents of *t* to *s*.
Intersection	O(n)	s.intersection_update(t)	Updates s to contain only the intersection of the elements from *s* and *t*.
Set Difference	O(n)	s.difference_update(t)	Subtracts from *s* the elements of *t*.
Symmetric Difference	O(n)	s.symmetric_difference _update(t)	Updates *s* with the symmetric difference of *s* and *t*.
Add	O(1)	s.add(e)	Add the element *e* to the set *s*.
Remove	O(1)	s.remove(e)	Remove the element *e* from the set *s*. This raises *KeyError* if *e* does not exist in *s*.
Discard	O(1)	s.discard(e)	Remove the element *e* if it exists in *s* and ignore it otherwise.
Pop	O(1)	s.pop()	Remove an arbitrary element of *s*.
Clear	O(1)	s.clear()	Remove all the elements of *s* leaving the set empty.

Fig. 5.5 Mutable Set Operations

The computational complexities presented above are surprising! How can set membership be tested in O(1) time? From what has been presented so far, it should take O(n) time to test set membership. After all, we would have to look at all the elements in the set, or at least half on average, to know if an item was in the set. How can the union of two sets be computed in O(n) time if we are to insure there are no duplicates in the set? It would seem that the union of two sets would take $O(n^2)$ time to compute unless the set could be sorted in some way. But sorting elements of a set is not always possible since not all elements of sets have an ordering.

5.4   Hashing

If it is possible to implement a set membership test in O(1) time, then we can implement the other operations above with the complexities we have indicated. Without a O(1) membership test, taking the union of two sets would take a lot longer as indicated above. Testing set membership in O(1) time is accomplished using *hashing*. Hashing is an extremely important concept in Computer Science and is related to random access in a computer. As we saw back in Chap. 2, accessing any location within a list can be accomplished in O(1) time. This is the principle of random access. A *randomly accessible* list means any location within the list can be accessed in O(1) time. To access a location in a list we need the index of the location we wish to access. The index serves as the address of an item in the list. Once we have stored an item in the list, we must remember its index if we wish to retrieve it in O(1) time. Without the index we would have to search for the item in the list which would take O(n) time, not O(1) time.

So, if we wanted to implement a set where we could test membership in O(1) time we might think of storing the items of the set in a list. We would somehow have to remember the index where each item was stored to find it again in O(1) time. This seems improbable at first. However, what if the item could be used to figure out its address? This is the insight that led to hashing. Each object in the computer must be stored as a string of zeroes and ones since computers speak binary. These zeroes and ones can be interpreted however we like, including as the index into a list. This concept is so important that Python (and many other modern languages) has included a function called *hash* that can be called on any object to return an integer value for an object. We'll call this value the object's *hash code* or *hash value*. Consider these calls to the hash function.

```
Python 3.2 (r32:88452, Feb 20 2011, 10:19:59)
[GCC 4.0.1 (Apple Inc. build 5493)] on darwin
Type "help", "copyright", "credits" or "license" for more information.
>>> hash("abc")
-1600925533
>>> hash("123")
1911471187
>>> hash(45)
45
>>> hash(45.0)
45
>>> hash(45.3)
1503225491
>>> hash(True)
1
>>> hash(False)
0
>>> hash([1,2,3])
Traceback (most recent call last):
  File "<stdin>", line 1, in <module>
TypeError: unhashable type: 'list'
>>>
```

While most objects are hashable, not every object is. In particular, mutable objects like lists may not be hashable because when an object is mutated its hash value may also change. This has consequences when using hash values in data structures as we'll see later in this chapter. In addition to built-in types, Python let's the programmer have some control over hash codes by implementing a *__hash__* method on a class. If you write a *__hash__* method for a class you can return whatever hash value integer you like for instances of that class.

Notice that calling hash on the string "abc" returned a negative value while other calls to hash returned extremely large integers. Clearly some work has to be done to convert this hash integer into an acceptable index into a list. Read on to discover how hash values are converted into list indices.

5.5   The HashSet Class

We can use a hash value to compute an index into a list to obtain O(1) item lookup complexity. To hide the details of the list and the calling of the *hash* function to find the index of the item, a set class can be written. We'll call our set class *HashSet*, not to be confused with the built-in *set* class of Python. The built-in *set* class uses hashing, too. The *HashSet* class presented in this section shows you how the *set* class is implemented. To begin, *HashSet* objects will contain a list and the number of items in the list. Initially the list will contain a bunch of *None* values. The list must be built with some kind of value in it. *None* serves as a null value for places in the list where no value has been stored. The list isn't nearly big enough to have a location for every possible hash value. Yet, the list can't possibly be big enough for all possible hash values anyway. In fact, as we saw in the last section, some hash values are negative and clearly indices into a list are not negative. The conversion of a hash value to a list index is explained in more detail in Sect. 5.5.2. The *HashSet* constructor is given in Sect. 5.5.1.

5.5.1 The HashSet Constructor

```
1   class HashSet:
2       def __init__(self,contents=[]):
3           self.items = [None] * 10
4           self.numItems = 0
5
6           for item in contents:
7               self.add(item)
```

5.5.2 Storing an Item

To store an item in a hash set we first compute its index using the hash function. There are two problems that must be dealt with. First, the list that items are stored in must be finite in length and definitely cannot be as long as the unique hash values we would generate by calling the hash function. Since the list must be shorter than the maximum hash value, we pick a size for our list and then divide hash values by the length of this list. The remainder (i.e. the result of the % operator, called the *mod* operator) is used as the index into the list. The remainder after dividing by the length of the list will always be between 0 and the length of the list minus one even if the hash value is a negative integer. Using the *mod* operator will give us valid indices into a list of whatever size we choose.

There is another problem we must deal with. Hash values are not necessarily unique. Hash values are integers and there are only finitely many integers possible in a computer. In addition, because we divide hash values by the length of the list, the remainders, or list indices, will be even less unique than the original hash values. If the list length is 10, then a hash value of 44 and -6 will both result in trying to store a value at index 4 in the list. This isn't possible of course.

5.5.3 Collision Resolution

Consider trying to store both "Cow" and "Fox" using hashing in a list whose length is 10. The hash value of "Cow" is -1432160826 and the hash value of "Fox" is 1462539404. When we *mod* both values by 10 the remainder is 4 for both hash values indicating they should both be stored at the fifth location in a list.

When two objects need to be stored at the same index within the hash set list, because their computed indices are identical, we call this a *collision*. It is necessary to define a *collision resolution* scheme to deal with this. There are many different schemes that are possible. We'll explore a scheme called *Linear Probing*. When a collision occurs while using linear probing, we advance to the next location in the list to see if that location might be available. We can tell if a location is available if we find a *None* value in that spot in the list. It turns out that there is one other value we might find in the list that means that location is available. A special type of object called a *__Placeholder* object might also be stored in the list. The reason for this class will become evident in the next section. For now, a *None* or a *__Placeholder* object indicates an open location within the hash set list. The code in Sect. 5.5.4 takes care of adding an item into the HashSet list and is a helper function for the actual *add* method.

5.5.4 HashSet Add Helper Function

```
1   def __add(item,items):
2       idx = hash(item) % len(items)
3       loc = -1
4
5       while items[idx] != None:
6           if items[idx] == item:
7               # item already in set
8               return False
9
10
11          if loc < 0 and type(items[idx]) == HashSet.__Placeholder:
12              loc = idx
13
14          idx = (idx + 1) % len(items)
15
16      if loc < 0:
17          loc = idx
18
19      items[loc] = item
20
21      return True
```

The code in Sect. 5.5.4 does not add an item that is already in the list. The while loop is the *linear probing* part of the code. The index *idx* is incremented, mod the length of the list, until either the item is found or a *None* value is encountered. Finding a *None* value indicates the end of the linear chain and hence the end of any linear searching that must be done to determine if the item is already in the set. If the item is not in the list, then the item is added either at the location of the first *__Placeholder* object found in the search, or at the location of the *None* value at the end of the chain.

There is one more issue that must be dealt with when adding a value. Imagine that only one position was open in the hash set list. What would happen in the code above? The linear search would result in searching the entire list. If the list were full, the result would be an infinite loop. We don't want either to happen. In fact, we want to be able to add an item in amortized O(1) time. To insure that we get an amortized complexity of O(1), the list must never be full or almost full.

5.5.5 The Load Factor

The fullness of the hash set list is called its load factor. We can find the load factor of a hash set by dividing the number of items stored in the list by its length. A really small load factor means the list is much bigger than the number of items stored in it and the chance there is a collision is small. A high load factor means more efficient space utilization, but higher chance of a collision. Experimentation can help to determine optimal load factors, but a reasonable maximum load factor is 75 % full. When adding a value into the list, if the resulting load factor is greater than 75 % then all the values in the list must be transferred to a new list. To transfer the values to a new list the values must be hashed again because the new list is a different length. This process is called *rehashing*. In the hash set implementation we chose to double the size of the list when rehashing was necessary.

The code in Sect. 5.5.6 calls the *__add* function from Sect. 5.5.4. This code and the *__add* method are in the *HashSet* class. The *__add* and *__rehash* functions are hidden helper functions used by the publicly accessible *add* method.

5.5.6 HashSet Add

```
1   def __rehash(oldList, newList):
2       for x in oldList:
3           if x != None and type(x) != HashSet.__Placeholder:
4               HashSet.__add(x,newList)
5
6       return newList
7
8   def add(self, item):
9       if HashSet.__add(item,self.items):
10          self.numItems += 1
11          load = self.numItems / len(self.items)
12          if load >= 0.75:
13              self.items = HashSet.__rehash(self.items,[None]*2*len(self.items))
```

Since the load factor is managed, the amortized complexity of adding a value to the list is O(1). This means the length of any chain within the list will be a finite length independent of the number of items in the hash set.

5.5.7 Deleting an Item

Deleting a value from a hash set means first finding the item. This may involve doing a linear search in the chain of values that reside at a location in the list. If the value to be deleted is the last in a chain then it can be replaced with a None. If it is in the middle of a chain then we cannot replace it with *None* because this would cut the chain of values. Instead, the item is replaced with a *__Placeholder* object. A place holder object does not break a chain and a linear probe continues to search skipping over placeholder objects when necessary. The remove helper function is given in Sect. 5.5.8.

5.5.8 HashSet Remove Helper Function

```
1   class __Placeholder:
2       def __init__(self):
3           pass
4
5       def __eq__(self,other):
6           return False
7
8   def __remove(item,items):
9       idx = hash(item) % len(items)
10
11      while items[idx] != None:
12          if items[idx] == item:
13              nextIdx = (idx + 1) % len(items)
14              if items[nextIdx] == None:
15                  items[idx] = None
16              else:
17                  items[idx] = HashSet.__Placeholder()
18              return True
19
20          idx = (idx + 1) % len(items)
21
22      return False
```

When removing an item, the load factor may get too low to be efficiently using space in memory. When the load factor dips below 25%, the list is again rehashed to decrease the list size by one half to increase the load factor. The remove method is provided in Sect. 5.5.9.

5.5.9 HashSet Remove

```
1   def remove(self, item):
2       if HashSet.__remove(item,self.items):
3           self.numItems -= 1
4           load = max(self.numItems, 10) / len(self.items)
5           if load <= 0.25:
6               self.items = HashSet.__rehash(self.items,[None]*int(len(self.items)/2))
7       else:
8           raise KeyError("Item not in HashSet")
```

For the same reason that adding a value can be done in O(1) time, deleting a value can also be done with an amortized complexity of O(1). The *discard* method is nearly the same of the remove method presented in Sect. 5.5.9 except that no exception is raised if the item is not in the set when it is discarded.

5.5.10 Finding an Item

To find an item in a hash set involves hashing the item to find its address and then searching the possible chain of values. The chain terminates with a *None*. If the item is in the chain somewhere then the *__contains__* method will return True and False will be returned otherwise. The method in Sect. 5.5.11 is called when *item in set* is written in a program.

5.5.11 HashSet Membership

```
1  def __contains__(self, item):
2      idx = hash(item) % len(self.items)
3      while self.items[idx] != None:
4          if self.items[idx] == item:
5              return True
6
7          idx = (idx + 1) % len(self.items)
8
9      return False
```

Finding an item results in O(1) amortized complexity as well. The chains are kept short as long as most hash values are evenly distributed and the load factor is kept from approaching 1.

5.5.12 Iterating Over a Set

To iterate over the items of a set we need to define the *__iter__* method to yield the elements of the HashSet. The method traverses the list of items skipping over placeholder elements and None references. Here is the code for the iterator.

```
1  def __iter__(self):
2      for i in range(len(self.items)):
3          if self.items[i] != None and type(self.items[i]) != HashSet.__Placeholder:
4              yield self.items[i]
```

5.5.13 Other Set Operations

Many of the other set operations on the HashSet are left as an exercise for the reader. However, most of them can be implemented in terms of the methods already presented in this chapter. Consider the *difference_update* method. It can be implemented using the iterator, the membership test, and the discard method. The code in Sect. 5.5.14 provides the implementation for the *difference_update* method.

5.5.14 HashSet Difference Update

```
1  def difference_update(self, other):
2      for item in other:
3          self.discard(item)
```

The *difference_update* method presented in Sect. 5.5.14 is a mutator method because it alters the sequence referenced by *self*. Compare that with the *difference* method in Sect. 5.5.15 which does not mutate the object referenced by *self*. Instead, the *difference* method returns a new set which consists of the difference of *self* and the *other* set.

5.5.15 HashSet Difference

```
1   def difference(self, other):
2       result = HashSet(self)
3       result.difference_update(other)
4       return result
```

The *difference* method is implemented using the *difference_update* method on the *result* HashSet. Notice that a new set is returned. The hash set referenced by self is not updated. The code is simple and it has the added benefit that if *difference_update* is correctly written, so will this method. Programmers should always avoid writing duplicate code when possible and *difference* and *difference_udpate* are nearly identical except that the *difference* method performs the difference on a newly constructed set instead of the set that *self* references.

5.6 Solving Sudoku

Using a *set* or a *HashSet* datatype, we now have the tools to solve most Sudoku puzzles. A puzzle can be read from a file where known values are represented by their digit and unknown values are X's as in the puzzle below.

```
x x x x x x x x x
x x x x 1 x x 9 2
x 8 6 x x x x 4 x
x x 1 5 6 x x x x
x x x x 3 6 2 x
x x x x x 5 x 7
x 3 x x x x 8 x
x 9 x 8 x 2 x x x
x x 7 x x 4 3 x x
```

Reading the dateable can be done a line at a time. Splitting the line will provide a string with each known and unknown value as a separate item in the list. When an X is encountered a *set* containing all values 1–9 can be constructed, just as you would if solving Sudoku by hand. When a known value is found a *set* with the known number in it can be constructed.

The sets are added to a two-dimensional matrix. The matrix is a list of lists. So reading a line corresponds to reading a row of the matrix. Each line becomes a list of sets. Each list of sets is added to a list we'll call the *matrix*. So, *matrix[row][col]* is one set within the Sudoku puzzle.

There are 81 sets within a Sudoku puzzle. However, each set is a member of three groups: the row, the column, and the square in which it resides. The rules presented in the Sudoku puzzle description above each deal with reducing a set within one of these groups. After reading the input from the file and forming the matrix with the 81 sets, 27 groups are formed by creating a list of groups.

A shallow copy of each row is first appended to the list of groups. A shallow copy means that each of the sets is the same set that was created when the puzzle was read.

A deep copy would create a copy of each of the 81 sets. A shallow copy of a list does not copy the sets within the list. Calling *list* on a list will make a shallow copy.

Another group is formed for each column and those groups are appended to the list of groups. Finally, a group is formed for each square and those groups are appended to the list of groups. When all done, there is one *groups* list with 27 groups in it. When forming these groups it is critical that the same set appears in each of three groups. This is because when a row is reduced, we want the changes in that row to be reflected in the columns and squares where the elements of the row also appear.

Solving a Sudoku puzzle means reducing the number of items in each set of a group according to the two rules presented in Sect. 5.2. Writing a function called *reduceGroup* that is given a list of 9 sets to reduce can help. The function *reduceGroup* should return **True** if it was able to reduce the group and **False** if it was not. Given this *reduceGroup* function, the *reduce* function is as defined in Sect. 5.6.1.

5.6.1 The Sudoku Reduce Function

```
1    def reduce(matrix):
2        changed = True
3        groups = getGroups(matrix)
4
5        while changed:
6            changed = reduceGroups(groups)
```

This algorithm is quite simple, and yet very powerful. It is different than any other algorithms that have been presented so far in this text. The concept is quite simple: keep reducing until no more reductions are possible. We are guaranteed that it will terminate since each iteration of the algorithm reduces the number of items in some of the sets of the puzzle. We never increase the size of any of these sets. Once we return from this function we may or may not have a solution. There are some puzzles that will not be solved by this Sudoku solver because the two rules that are presented above are not powerful enough for all puzzles. There are some situations where the number of items in a set cannot be reduced by looking at just one group. You would have to look at more than one group at the same time to figure out how to reduce the number of sets. *Hold on, you don't need to figure out any more rules. The next chapter will present an algorithm for solving all Sudoku puzzles, even the very hardest of them.*

The rules presented in this chapter will solve the Sudoku puzzle given in this section and many others. Sudoku puzzles one through six on the text's website can be solved by this Sudoku solver. The *reduceGroups* function above would presumably call *reduceGroup* on each of the groups in its list and it would return *True* if any of the groups are reduced and *False* otherwise.

5.7 Maps

A *map* in computer science is not like the map you used to read when going someplace in your car. The term *map* is a more mathematical term referring to a function that maps a *domain* to a *range*. You may have already used a map in Python. Maps are called by many names including dictionaries, hash tables, and hash maps. They are all the same data structure.

A map or dictionary maps a set of unique keys to their associated values much the way a function maps a value in the domain to the range. A key is what we provide to a map when we want to look for the key/value pair. The keys of a map are unique. There can only be one copy of a specific key value in the dictionary at a time. As we saw in chapter one, Python has built-in support for dictionaries or maps. Here is some sample interaction with a dictionary in the Python shell.

```
Python 3.2 (r32:88452, Feb 20 2011, 10:19:59)
[GCC 4.0.1 (Apple Inc. build 5493)] on darwin
Type "help", "copyright", "credits" or "license" for more information.
>>> d = {}
>>> d["dog"] = "cat"
>>> d["batman"] = "joker"
>>> d["superman"] = "lex luther"
>>> for key in d:
...     print(key)
...
batman
dog
superman
>>> for key in d:
...     print(key,d[key])
...
batman joker
dog cat
superman lex luther
>>> len(d)
3
>>> d["dog"] = "skunk"
>>> d["dog"]
'skunk'
>>>
```

A map, or dictionary, is a lot like a set. A set and a dictionary both contain unique values. The set datatype contains a group of unique values. A map contains a set of unique keys that map to associated values. Like sets, we can look up a key in the map, and its associated value, in O(1) time. As you might expect, maps, like sets, are implemented using hashing. While the underlying implementation is the same, maps and sets are used differently. The table below provides the methods and operators of maps or dictionaries and their associated complexities.

The operations in the table above have the expected complexities given a hashing implementation as was presented in Sect. 5.5. The interesting difference is that key/value pairs are stored in the dictionary as opposed to just the items of a set. The key part of the key/value pair is used to determine if a key is in the dictionary as you might expect. The value is returned when appropriate.

5.7.1   The HashMap Class

A *HashMap* class, like the *dict* class in Python, uses hashing to achieve the complexities outlined in the table in Fig. 5.6. A private *__KVPair* class is defined. Instances of *__KVPair* hold the key/value pairs as they are added to the *HashMap* object. With the addition of a *__getitem__* method on the *HashSet* class, the *HashSet* class could be used for the *HashMap* class implementation. The additional *__getitem__* method for the *HashSet* is given in Sect. 5.7.3.

5.7.2   HashSet Get Item

```
1   # One extra HashSet method for use with the HashMap class.
2   def __getitem__(self, item):
3       idx = hash(item) % len(self.items)
4       while self.items[idx] != None:
5           if self.items[idx] == item:
6               return self.items[idx]
7
8           idx = (idx + 1) % len(self.items)
9
10      return None
```

Operation	Complexity	Usage	Description
Dictionary Creation	O(1)	d = {[iterable]}	Calls the constructor to create a dictionary. Iterable is an optional initial contents in which case it is O(n) complexity.
Size	O(1)	len(d)	The number of key/value pairs in the dictionary.
Membership	O(1)	k in d	Returns True if *k* is a key in *d* and False otherwise.
non-Membership	O(1)	k not in d	Returns True if *k* is not a key in *d* and False otherwise.
Add	O(1)	d[k] = v	Adds *(k,v)* as a key/value pair in *d*.
Lookup	O(1)	d[k]	Returns the value associated with the key, *k*. A *KeyError* exception is raised if *k* is not in *d*.
Lookup	O(1)	d.get(k[,default])	Returns *v* for the key/value pair *(k,v)*. If *k* is not in *d* returns *default* or *None* if not specified.
Remove Key/Value Pair	O(1)	del d[k]	Removes the *(k,v)* key value pair from *d*. Raises *KeyError* if *k* is not in *d*.
Items	O(1)	d.items()	Returns a view of the key/value pairs in *d*. The view updates as *d* changes.
Keys	O(1)	d.keys()	Returns a view of the keys in *d*. The view updates as *d* changes.
Values	O(1)	d.values()	Returns a view of the values in *d*. The view updates as *d* changes.
Pop	O(1)	d.pop(k)	Returns the value associated with key *k* and deletes the item. Raises *KeyError* if *k* is not in *d*.
Pop Item	O(1)	d.popitem()	Return an arbitrary key/value pair, *(k,v)*, from *d*.
Set Default	O(1)	d.setdefault(k[, default])	Sets *k* as a key in *d* and maps *k* to *default* or *None* if not specified.
Update	O(n)	d.update(e)	Updates the dictionary, *d*, with the contents of dictionary *e*.
Clear	O(1)	d.clear()	Removes all key/value pairs from *d*.
Dictionary Copy	O(n)	d.copy()	Returns a shallow copy of *d*.

Fig. 5.6 Dictionary Operations

Then, to implement the *HashMap* we can use a *HashSet* as shown in Sect. 5.7.3. In the __*KVPair* class definition it is necessary to define the __*eq*__ method so that keys are compared when comparing two items in the hash map. The __*hash*__ method of __*KVPair*__ hashes only the key value since keys are used to look up key/value pairs in the hash map. The implementation provided in Sect. 5.7.3 is partial. The other methods are left as an exercise for the reader.

5.7.3 The HashMap Class

```
 1  class HashMap:
 2      class __KVPair:
 3          def __init__(self,key,value):
 4              self.key = key
 5              self.value = value
 6
 7          def __eq__(self,other):
 8              if type(self) != type(other):
 9                  return False
10
11              return self.key == other.key
12
13          def getKey(self):
14              return self.key
15
16          def getValue(self):
17              return self.value
18
19          def __hash__(self):
20              return hash(self.key)
21
22      def __init__(self):
23          self.hSet = hashset.HashSet()
24
25      def __len__(self):
26          return len(self.hSet)
27
28      def __contains__(self,item):
29          return HashSet.__KVPair(item,None) in self.hSet
30
31      def not__contains__(self,item):
32          return item not in self.hSet
33
34      def __setitem__(self,key,value):
35          self.hSet.add(HashMap.__KVPair(key,value))
36
37      def __getitem__(self,key):
38          if HashMap.__KVPair(key,None) in self.hSet:
39              val = self.hSet[HashMap.__KVPair(key,None)].getValue()
40              return val
41
42          raise KeyError("Key " + str(key) + " not in HashMap")
43
44      def __iter__(self):
45          for x in self.hSet:
46              yield x.getKey()
```

The provided implementation in Sect. 5.7.3 helps to demonstrate the similarities between the implementation of the *HashSet* class and the *HashMap* class, or between the *set* and *dict* classes in Python. The two types of data structures are both implemented using hashing. Both rely heavily on a O(1) membership test. While understanding how the *HashMap* class is implemented is important, most programming languages include some sort of hash map in their library of built-in types, as does Python. It is important to understand the complexity of the methods on a hash map, but just as important is understanding when to use a hash map and how it can be used. Read on to see how you can use a hash map in code you write to make it more efficient.

5.8   Memoization

Memoization is an interesting programming technique that can be employed when you write functions that may get called more than once with the same arguments. The idea behind memoization is to do the work of computing a value in a function once. Then, we make a note to ourselves so when the function is called with the same arguments again, we return the value we just computed again. This avoids going to the work of computing the value all over again.

A powerful example of this is the recursive Fibonacci function. The Fibonacci sequence is defined as follows.

- Fib(0) = 0
- Fib(1) = 1
- Fib(n) = Fib(n−1) + Fib(n−2)

This sequence can be computed recursively by writing a Python function as follows.

```python
def fib(n):
    if n == 0:
        return 0

    if n == 1:
        return 1

    return fib(n-1) + fib(n-2)
```

However, we would never want to use this function for anything but a simple demonstration of a small Fibonacci number. The function cannot be used to computing something as big as fib(100) even. Running the function with an argument of 100 will take a very long time on even the fastest computers. Consider what happens to compute fib(5). To do that fib(4) and fib(3) must first be computed. Then the two results can be added together to find fib(5). But, to compute fib(4) the values fib(3) and fib(2) must be computed. Now we are computing fib(3) twice to compute fib(5), But to compute fib(3) we must compute fib(2) and fib(1). But, fib(2) must be computed to find fib(4) as well. Figure 5.7 shows all the calls to fib to compute fib(5).

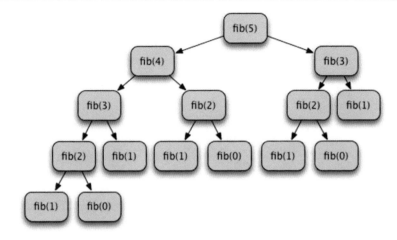

Fig. 5.7 Computing fib(5)

As you can see from Fig. 5.7, it takes a lot of calls to the *fib* function to compute fib(5). Now imagine how many calls it would take to compute fib(6). To compute fib(6) we first have to compute fib(5) and then compute fib(4). It took 15 calls to *fib* to compute fib(5) and from the figure we can see that it takes 9 calls to compute fib(4). Including the call to fib(6) it will take 25 calls to *fib* to compute fib(6). Computing fib(7) will take $15 + 25 + 1$ calls or 41 calls. Computing fib(n) this way more than doubles the number of calls to compute fib(n−2). This is called exponential growth. The complexity of the *fib* function is $O(2^n)$. A function with exponential complexity is worthless except for very small values of *n*.

All is not lost. There are better ways of computing the Fibonacci sequence. The way to improve the efficiency is to avoid all that unnecessary work. Once fib(2) has been computed, we shouldn't compute it again. We already did that work. There are at least a couple of ways of improving the efficiency. One method involves removing the recursion and computing fib(n) with a loop, which is probably the best option. However, the recursive function is closer to the original definition. We can improve the recursive version of the function with memoization. In Sect. 5.8.1, the *memo* dictionary serves as our mapping from values of *n* to their *fib(n)* result.

5.8.1   A Memoized Fibonacci Function

```
1    memo = {}
2
3    def fib(n):
4        if n in memo:
5            return memo[n]
6
7        if n == 0:
8            memo[0] = 0
```

```
9          return 0
10
11      if n == 1:
12          memo[1] = 1
13          return 1
14
15      val = fib(n-1) + fib(n-2)
16
17      memo[n] = val
18
19      return val
20
21  def main():
22      print(fib(100))
23
24  if __name__ == "__main__":
25      main()
```

The memoized *fib* function in Sect. 5.8.1 records any value returned by the function in its memo. The *memo* variable is accessed from the enclosing scope. The *memo* is not created locally because we want it to persist from one call of *fib* to the next. Each time *fib* is called with a new value of n the answer is recorded in the memo. When *fib(n)* is called a subsequent time for some n, the memoized result is looked up and returned. The result: the memoized *fib* function now has O(n) complexity and it can compute fib(100) almost instantly. Without memoization, it would take 1,146,295,688,027,634,168,201 calls to the *fib* function to compute fib(100). Assuming each function call completed in 10 microseconds, it would take roughly 363 million years to compute fib(100). With memoization it takes 100 calls to *fib* and assuming 10 microseconds per call, that's 1000 microseconds or 1/1000 of a second.

This is an extreme example of the benefit of memoization, but it can come in handy in many situations. For instance, in the tic tac toe problem of Chap. 4 the minimax function is called on many boards that are identical. The minimax function does not care if an X is placed in the upper-right corner first followed by the lower-left corner or vice-versa. Yet, the way minimax is written it will be called to compute the value of the same board multiple times. Memoizing minimax speeds up the playing of tic tac toe.

5.9   Correlating Two Sources of Information

Another use of a map or dictionary is in correlating data from different sources. Assume you are given a list of cities and the zip code or codes within those cities. You want to provide a service where people can look up the zip code for a city in the USA. So, you'll be given a city by the web page that provides you the information. You have to use that city to find a list of possible zip codes. You could search the list of cities to find the corresponding list of zip codes. Or, you could create a dictionary from city name to zip code list. Then when given a city name you check to see if it is in the dictionary and if so, you can look up the corresponding list of zip codes in O(1) time.

5.10   Chapter Summary

In this chapter we explored the implementation and some uses of sets and maps in Python. Hashing is an important concept. Hashing data structures must be able to handle collisions within the hash table by a collision resolution strategy. The resolution strategy explored in this chapter was linear probing. There are other collision resolution strategies possible. Any collision resolution strategy must have a way of handling new values being added to a chain and existing values being deleted from a chain.

The key feature of hashing is the amortized O(1) complexity for membership testing and lookup within the table. The ability to test membership or lookup a value in O(1) time makes many algorithms efficient that otherwise might not run efficiently on large data sets.

Memoization is one important use of a dictionary or map. By memoizing a function we avoid doing any redundant work. Another important use of maps or dictionaries is in correlating sources of information. When we are given information from two different sources and must match those two sources, a map or dictionary will make that correlation efficient.

5.11   Review Questions

Answer these short answer, multiple choice, and true/false questions to test your mastery of the chapter.

1. What type of value is a hash code?
2. Hash codes can be both positive and negative. How does a hash code get converted into a value that can be used in a hash table?
3. Once you find the proper location with a hash table, how do you know if the item you are looking for is in the table or not? Be careful to answer this completely.
4. Why is a collision resolution strategy needed when working with a hash table?
5. What is the difference between a map and a set?
6. In this chapter the HashSet was used to implement the HashMap class. What if we turned things around? How could a dictionary in Python be used to implement a set? Describe how this might be done by describing the add and membership methods of a set and how they would be implemented if internally the set used a dictionary.
7. How does the load factor affect the complexity of the membership test on the set datatype?
8. What is rehashing?
9. When is memoization an effective programming technique?
10. True or False: Memoization would help make the factorial function run faster? Justify your answer.

```
def fact(n):
    if n == 0:
        return 1

    return n * fact(n-1)

def main():
    x = fact(10)
    print("10! is",x)

if __name__ == "__main__":
    main()
```

5.12   Programming Problems

1. Complete the Sudoku puzzle as described in the chapter. The program should read
   a text file. Prompt the user for the name of the text file. The text file should be
   placed in the same directory or folder as the program so it can easily be found by
   your program. There are six sample Sudoku puzzles that you can solve available
   on the text's website. Write the program to read a text file like those you find on
   the text's website. Print both the unsolved and solved problem to the screen as
   shown below.

```
Please enter a Sudoku puzzle file name: sudoku2.txt
Solving this puzzle
-----------------
x x x x x x x x x
x x x x 1 x x 9 2
x 8 6 x x x x 4 x
x x 1 5 6 x x x x
x x x x x 3 6 2 x
x x x x x x 5 x 7
x 3 x x x x x 8 x
x 9 x 8 x 2 x x x
x x 7 x x 4 3 x x

Solution
-----------------
4 1 2 9 8 5 7 6 3
7 5 3 4 1 6 8 9 2
9 8 6 3 2 7 1 4 5
2 7 1 5 6 8 9 3 4
5 4 9 1 7 3 6 2 8
3 6 8 2 4 9 5 1 7
6 3 4 7 5 1 2 8 9
1 9 5 8 3 2 4 7 6
8 2 7 6 9 4 3 5 1

Valid Solution!
```

2. Complete the *HashSet* class found in the chapter by implementing the methods described in the two tables of set operations. Then, write a *main* function to test these operations. Save the class in a file called hashset.py so it can be imported into other programs. If you call your *main* function in hashset.py with the *if __name__* == "*__main__*" statement, then when you import it into another program your hashset.py *main* function will not be executed, but when you run hashset.py on its own, its *main* function will run to test your *HashSet* class.

3. Memoize the tic tac toe program from Chap. 3 to improve its performance. To do this each board must have a hash value. You should implement a *__hash__* method for the *Board* class. The hash value should be unique to a board's configuration. In other words, the X's, O's, and Dummy objects should factor into the hash value for the board so that each board has its own unique hash value. Then memoize the minimax function to remember the value found for a particular board's configuration. The minimax function should start by checking whether or not the value for this board has already been computed and the function should return it if it has.

4. Write a version of the *HashSet* class that allows you to specify the maximum and minimum allowable load factor. Then run a number of tests where you plot the average time taken to add an item to a set given different maximum load factors. Also gather information about the average time it takes to test the membership of an item in a set for different maximum load factors. From this information you should be able to see some of the space/time trade-off in hash tables. Generate XML data in the plot format from these experimental results and plot the data to see what it tells you. From the gathered information, express your opinion about the optimal load factor for the *HashSet* class. Comment on the optimal maximum load factor at the top of the program that performs your tests.

Trees

6

When we see a tree in our everyday lives the roots are generally in the ground and the leaves are up in the air. The branches of a tree spread out from the roots in a more or less organized fashion. The word *tree* is used in Computer Science when talking about a way data may be organized. Trees have some similarities to the linked list organization found in Chap. 4. In a tree there are nodes which have links to other nodes. In a linked list each node has one link, to the next node in the list. In a tree each node may have two or more links to other nodes. A tree is not a sequential data structure. It is organized like a tree, except the root is at the top of tree data structures and the leaves are at the bottom. A tree in computer science is usually drawn inverted when compared to the trees we see in nature. There are many uses for trees in computer science. Sometimes they show the structure of a bunch of function calls as we saw when examining the Fibonacci function as depicted in Fig. 6.1.

Figure 6.1 depicts a call tree of the fib function for computing fib(5). Unlike real trees it has a *root* (at the top) and *leaves* at the bottom. There are relationships between the nodes in this tree. The fib(5) call has a left *sub-tree* and a right sub-tree. The fib(4) node is a *child* of the fib(5) node. The fib(4) node is a *sibling* to the fib(3) node to the right of it. A *leaf* node is a node with no children. The leaf nodes in Fig. 6.1 represent calls to the *fib* function which matched the base cases of the function.

In this chapter we'll explore trees and when it makes sense to build and or use a tree in a program. Not every program will need a tree data structure. Nevertheless, trees are used in many types of programs. A knowledge of them is not only a necessity, proper use of them can greatly simplify some types of programs.

6.1 Chapter Goals

This chapter introduces trees and some algorithms that use trees. By the end of the chapter you should be able to answer these questions.

- How are trees constructed?
- How can we traverse a tree?

© Springer International Publishing Switzerland 2015
K.D. Lee and S. Hubbard, *Data Structures and Algorithms with Python*,
Undergraduate Topics in Computer Science, DOI 10.1007/978-3-319-13072-9_6

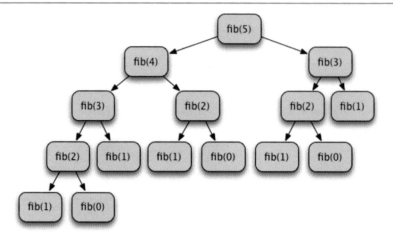

Fig. 6.1 The Call Tree for Computing fib(5)

- How are expressions and trees related?
- What is a binary search tree?
- Under what conditions is a binary search tree useful?
- What is depth first search and how does it relate to trees and search problems?
- What are the three types of tree traversals we can do on binary trees?
- What is a grammar and what can we do with a grammar?

Read on to discover trees and their uses in Computer Science.

6.2   Abstract Syntax Trees and Expressions

Trees have many applications in Computer Science. They are used in many different types of algorithms. For instance, every Python program you write is converted to a tree, at least for a little while, before it is executed by the Python interpreter. Internally, a Python program is converted to a tree-like structure called an *Abstract Syntax Tree*, often abbreviated *AST*, before it is executed. We can build our own abstract syntax trees for expressions so we can see how a tree might be evaluated and why we would want to evaluate a tree.

In Chap. 4 linked lists were presented as a way of organizing a list. Trees may be stored using a similar kind of structure. If a node in a tree has two children, then that node would have two links to its children as opposed to a linked list which has one link to the next node in the sequence.

Consider the expression $(5+4) * 6+3$. We can construct an abstract syntax tree for this expression as shown in Fig. 6.2. Since the + operation is the last operation performed when evaluating this function, the + node will be at the root of the tree. It has two subtrees, the expression to the left of the + and then 3 to the right of the +.

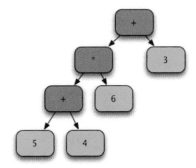

Fig. 6.2 The AST for $(5+4) * 6 + 3$

Similarly, nodes for the other operators and operands can be constructed to yield the tree shown in Fig. 6.2.

To represent this in the computer, we could define one class for each type of node. We'll define a TimesNode, a PlusNode, and a NumNode class. So we can evaluate the abstract syntax tree, each node in the tree will have one eval method defined on it. The code in Sect. 6.2.1 defines these classes, the eval methods, and a main function that builds the example tree in Fig. 6.2.

6.2.1   Constructing ASTs

```
1   class TimesNode:
2       def __init__(self, left, right):
3           self.left = left
4           self.right = right
5
6       def eval(self):
7           return self.left.eval() * self.right.eval()
8
9   class PlusNode:
10      def __init__(self, left, right):
11          self.left = left
12          self.right = right
13
14      def eval(self):
15          return self.left.eval() + self.right.eval()
16
17  class NumNode:
18      def __init__(self, num):
19          self.num = num
20
21      def eval(self):
22          return self.num
23
24  def main():
25      x = NumNode(5)
26      y = NumNode(4)
27      p = PlusNode(x,y)
28      t = TimesNode(p, NumNode(6))
29      root = PlusNode(t, NumNode(3))
30
```

```
31        print(root.eval())
32
33    if __name__ == "__main__":
34        main()
```

In Sect. 6.2.1 the tree is built from the bottom (i.e. the leaves) up to the root. The code above contains an *eval* function for each node. Calling *eval* on the root node will recursively call *eval* on every node in the tree, causing the result, 57, to be printed to the screen.

Once an AST is built, evaluating such a tree is accomplished by doing a recursive traversal of the tree. The *eval* methods together are the recursive function in this example. We say that the *eval* methods are *mutually recursive* since all the *eval* methods together form the recursive function.

6.3   Prefix and Postfix Expressions

Expressions, as we normally write them, are said to be in infix form. An *infix expression* is an expression written with the binary operators in between their operands. Expressions can be written in other forms though. Another form for expressions is postfix. In a *postfix expression* the binary operators are written after their operands. The infix expression $(5 + 4) * 6 + 3$ can be written in postfix form as $5\ 4 + 6 * 3 +$. Postfix expressions are well-suited for evaluation with a stack. When we come to an operand we push the value on the stack. When we come to an operator, we pop the operands from the stack, do the operation, and push the result. Evaluating expressions in this manner is quite easy for humans to do with a little practice. Hewlett-Packard has designed many calculators that use this postfix evaluation method. In fact, in the early years of computing, Hewlett-Packard manufactured a whole line of computers that used a stack to evaluate expressions in the same way. The HP 2000 was one such computer. In more recent times many virtual machines are implemented as stack machines including the Java Virtual Machine, or JVM, and the Python virtual machine.

As another example of a tree traversal, consider writing a method that returns a string representation of an expression. The string is built as the result of a traversal of the abstract syntax tree. To get a string representing an infix version of the expression, you perform an *inorder traversal* of the AST. To get a postfix expression you would do a *postfix* traversal of the tree. The *inorder* methods in Sect. 6.3.1 perform an inorder traversal of an AST.

6.3.1   AST Tree Traversal

```
1   class TimesNode:
2       def __init__(self, left, right):
3           self.left = left
4           self.right = right
```

```
 5
 6        def eval(self):
 7            return self.left.eval() * self.right.eval()
 8
 9        def inorder(self):
10            return "(" + self.left.inorder() + " * " + self.right.inorder() + ")"
11
12   class PlusNode:
13        def __init__(self, left, right):
14            self.left = left
15            self.right = right
16
17        def eval(self):
18            return self.left.eval() + self.right.eval()
19
20
21        def inorder(self):
22            return "(" + self.left.inorder() + " + " + self.right.inorder() + ")"
23
24   class NumNode:
25        def __init__(self, num):
26            self.num = num
27
28        def eval(self):
29            return self.num
30
31        def inorder(self):
32            return str(self.num)
```

The *inorder* methods in Sect. 6.3.1 provide for an inorder traversal because each binary operator is added to the string *in between* the two operands. To do a postorder traversal of the tree we would write a *postorder* method that would add each binary operator to the string *after* postorder traversing the two operands. Note that because of the way a postorder traversal is written, parentheses are never needed in postfix expressions.

One other traversal is possible, called a *preorder traversal*. In a preorder traversal, each binary operator is added to the string before its two operands. Given the infix expression (5 + 4) * 6 + 3 the prefix equivalent is + * + 5 4 6 3. Again, because of the way a prefix expression is written, parentheses are never needed in prefix expressions.

6.4 Parsing Prefix Expressions

Abstract syntax trees are almost never constructed by hand. They are often built automatically by an *interpreter* or a *compiler*. When a Python program is executed the Python interpreter scans it and builds an abstract syntax tree of the program. This part of the Python interpreter is called a parser. A *parser* is a program, or part of a program, that reads a file and automatically builds an abstract syntax tree of the expression (i.e. a source program), and reports a syntax error if the program or expression is not properly formed. The exact details of how this is accomplished is beyond the scope of this text. However, for some simple expressions, like prefix expressions, it is relatively easy to build a parser ourselves.

In middle school we learned when checking to see if a sentence is *properly formed* we should use the English grammar. A grammar is a set of rules that dictate how a sentence in a language can be put together. In Computer Science we have many different languages and each language has its own grammar. Prefix expressions make up a language. We call them the language of prefix expressions and they have their own grammar, called a context-free grammar. A context-free grammar for prefix expressions is given in Sect. 6.4.1.

6.4.1 The Prefix Expression Grammar

$G = (\mathcal{N}, \mathcal{T}, \mathcal{P}, E)$ where

$\qquad \mathcal{N} = \{E\}$

$\qquad \mathcal{T} = \{identifier, number, +, *\}$

$\qquad \mathcal{P}$ is defined by the set of productions

$$E \rightarrow + E\,E \mid * E\,E \mid number$$

A grammar, G, consists of three sets: a set of non-terminals symbols denoted by N, a set of terminals or tokens called T, and a set, P, of productions. One of the non-terminals is designated the start symbol of the grammar. For this grammar, the special symbol E is the start symbol and only non-terminal of the grammar. The symbol E stands for any prefix expression. In this grammar there are three *productions* that provide the rules for how prefix expressions can be constructed. The productions state that any prefix expression *is composed of* (you can read $\rightarrow$ as *is composed of*) a plus sign followed by two prefix expressions, a multiplication symbol followed by two prefix expressions, or just a number. The grammar is recursive so every time you see E in the grammar, it can be replaced by another prefix expression. This grammar is very easy to convert to a function that given a queue of tokens will build an abstract syntax tree of a prefix expression. A function, like the E function in Sect. 6.4.2, that reads tokens and returns an abstract syntax tree is called a *parser*. Since the grammar is recursive, the parsing function is recursive as well. It has a base case first, followed by the recursive cases. The code in Sect. 6.4.2 provides that function.

6.4.2 A Prefix Expression Parser

```
1   import queue
2
3   def E(q):
4       if q.isEmpty():
5           raise ValueError("Invalid Prefix Expression")
6
7       token = q.dequeue()
8
```

```
9          if token == "+":
10             return PlusNode(E(q),E(q))
11
12         if token == "*":
13             return TimesNode(E(q),E(q))
14
15         return NumNode(float(token))
16
17  def main():
18      x = input("Please enter a prefix expression: ")
19
20      lst = x.split()
21      q = queue.Queue()
22
23      for token in lst:
24          q.enqueue(token)
25
26      root = E(q)
27
28      print(root.eval())
29      print(root.inorder())
30
31  if __name__ == "__main__":
32      main()
```

In Sect. 6.4.2 the parameter q is a queue of the tokens read from the file or string. Code to call this function is provided in the *main* function of Sect. 6.4.2. The *main* function gets a string from the user and enqueues all the tokens in the string (tokens must be separated by spaces) on a queue of tokens. Then the queue is passed to the function E. This function is based on the grammar given above. The function looks at the next token and decides which rule to apply. Each call to the E function returns an abstract syntax tree. Calling E from the *main* function results in parsing the prefix expression and building its corresponding tree. This example gives you a little insight into how Python reads a program and constructs an abstract syntax tree for it. A Python program is parsed according to a grammar and an abstract syntax tree is constructed from the program. The Python interpreter then interprets the program by traversing the tree.

This parser in Sect. 6.4.2 is called a top-down parser. Not all parsers are constructed this way. The prefix grammar presented in this text is a grammar where the top-down parser construction will work. In particular, a grammar cannot have any left-recursive rules if we are to create a top-down parser for it. Left recursive rules occur in the postfix grammar given in Sect. 6.4.3.

6.4.3 The Postfix Expression Grammar

$G = (\mathcal{N}, \mathcal{T}, \mathcal{P}, E)$ where

$\mathcal{N} = \{E\}$

$\mathcal{T} = \{identifier, number, +, *\}$

$\mathcal{P}$ is defined by the set of productions

$$E \rightarrow E\,E + \mid E\,E * \mid number$$

In this grammar the first and second productions have an expression composed of an expression, followed by another expression, followed by an addition or multiplication token. If we tried to write a recursive function for this grammar, the base case would not come first. The recursive case would come first and hence the function would not be written correctly since the base case must come first in a recursive function. This type of production is called a left-recursive rule. Grammars with left-recursive rules are not suitable for top-down construction of a parser. There are other ways to construct parsers that are beyond the scope of this text. You can learn more about parser construction by studying a book on compiler construction or programming language implementation.

6.5   Binary Search Trees

A binary search tree is a tree where each node has up to two children. In addition, all values in the left subtree of a node are less than the value at the root of the tree and all values in the right subtree of a node are greater than or equal to the value at the root of the tree. Finally, the left and right subtrees must also be binary search trees. This definition makes it possible to write a class where values may be inserted into the tree while maintaining the definition. The code in Sect. 6.5.1 accomplishes this.

6.5.1   The BinarySearchTree Class

```
1   class BinarySearchTree:
2       # This is a Node class that is internal to the BinarySearchTree class.
3       class __Node:
4           def __init__(self,val,left=None,right=None):
5               self.val = val
6               self.left = left
7               self.right = right
8
9           def getVal(self):
10              return self.val
11
12          def setVal(self,newval):
13              self.val = newval
14
15          def getLeft(self):
16              return self.left
17
18          def getRight(self):
19              return self.right
20
21          def setLeft(self,newleft):
22              self.left = newleft
23
24          def setRight(self,newright):
25              self.right = newright
26
27          # This method deserves a little explanation. It does an inorder traversal
28          # of the nodes of the tree yielding all the values. In this way, we get
```

```
29              # the values in ascending order.
30          def __iter__(self):
31              if self.left != None:
32                  for elem in self.left:
33                      yield elem
34
35              yield self.val
36
37              if self.right != None:
38                  for elem in self.right:
39                      yield elem
40
41      # Below are the methods of the BinarySearchTree class.
42      def __init__(self):
43          self.root = None
44
45      def insert(self,val):
46
47              # The __insert function is recursive and is not a passed a self parameter. It is a
48              # static function (not a method of the class) but is hidden inside the insert
49              # function so users of the class will not know it exists.
50
51          def __insert(root,val):
52              if root == None:
53                  return BinarySearchTree.__Node(val)
54
55              if val < root.getVal():
56                  root.setLeft(__insert(root.getLeft(),val))
57              else:
58                  root.setRight(__insert(root.getRight(),val))
59
60              return root
61
62          self.root = __insert(self.root,val)
63
64      def __iter__(self):
65          if self.root != None:
66              return self.root.__iter__()
67          else:
68              return [].__iter__()
69
70  def main():
71      s = input("Enter a list of numbers: ")
72      lst = s.split()
73
74      tree = BinarySearchTree()
75
76      for x in lst:
77          tree.insert(float(x))
78
79      for x in tree:
80          print(x)
81
82  if __name__ == "__main__":
83      main()
```

When the program in Sect. 6.5.1 is run with a list of values (they must have an ordering) it will print the values in ascending order. For instance, if 5 8 2 1 4 9 6 7 is entered at the keyboard, the program behaves as follows.

```
Enter a list of numbers:  5 8 2 1 4 9 6 7
1.0
2.0
4.0
5.0
6.0
7.0
8.0
9.0
```

From this example it appears that a binary search tree can produce a sorted list of values when traversed. How? Let's examine how this program behaves with this input. Initially, the tree reference points to a BinarySearchTree object where the root pointer points to *None* as shown in Fig. 6.3.

Into the tree in Fig. 6.3 we insert the 5. The *insert* method is called which immediately calls the *__insert* function on the root of the tree. The *__insert* function is given a tree, which in this case is *None* (i.e. an empty tree) and the *__insert* function returns a new tree with the value inserted. The *root* instance variable is set equal to this new tree as shown in Fig. 6.4 which is the consequence of line 62 of the code in Sect. 6.5.1. In the following figures the dashed line indicates the new reference that is assigned to point to the new node. Each time the *__insert* function is called a new tree is returned and the *root* instance variable is re-assigned on line 62. Most of the time it is re-assigned to point to the same node.

Now, the next value to be inserted is the 8. Inserting the 8 calls *__insert* on the root node containing 5. When this is done, it recursively calls *__insert* on the right subtree, which is *None* (and not pictured). The result is a new right subtree is created and the right subtree link of the node containing 5 is made to point to it as shown in Fig. 6.5 which is the consequence of line 58 in Sect. 6.5.1. Again the dashed arrows indicate the new references that are assigned during the insert. It doesn't hurt anything to reassign the references and the code works very nicely. In the recursive *__insert* we always reassign the reference on lines 56 and 58 after inserting a new value into the tree. Likewise, after inserting a new value, the *root* reference is reassigned to the new tree after inserting the new value on line 62 of the code in Sect. 6.5.1.

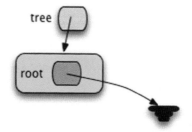

Fig. 6.3 An empty BinarySearchTree object

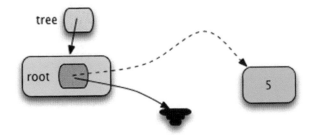

Fig. 6.4 The Tree After Inserting 5

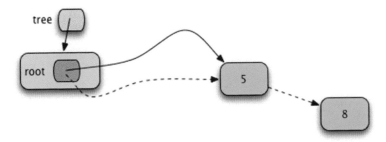

Fig. 6.5 The Tree After Inserting 8

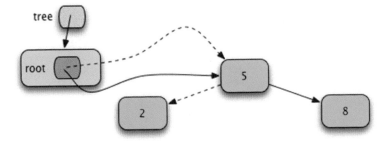

Fig. 6.6 The Tree After Inserting 2

Next, the 2 is inserted into the tree as shown in Fig. 6.6. The 8 ended up to the right of the 5 to preserve the binary search tree property. The 2 is inserted into the left subtree of the 5 because 2 is less than 5.

The 1 is inserted next and because it is less than the 5, it is inserted into the left subtree of the node containing 5. Because that subtree contains 2 the 1 is inserted into the left subtree of the node containing 2. This is depicted in Fig. 6.7.

Inserting the 4 next means the value is inserted to the left of the 5 and to the right of the 2. This preserves the binary search tree property as shown in Fig. 6.8.

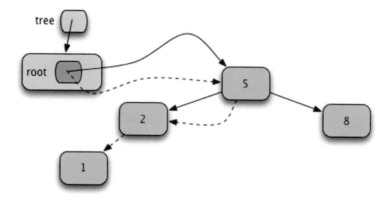

Fig. 6.7 The Tree After Inserting 1

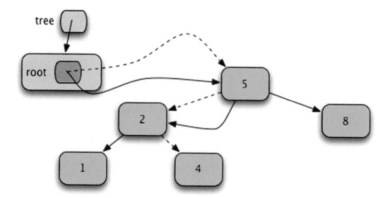

Fig. 6.8 The Tree After Inserting 4

To insert the 9 it must go to the right of all nodes inserted so far since it is greater than all nodes in the tree. This is depicted in Fig. 6.9.

The 6 goes to the right of the 5 and to the left of the 8 in Fig. 6.10.

The only place the 7 can go is to the right of the 5, left of the 8, and right of the 6 in Fig. 6.11.

The final tree is pictured in Fig. 6.12. This is a binary search tree since all nodes with subtrees have values less than the node in the left subtree and values greater than or equal to the node in the right subtree while both subtrees also conform to the binary search tree property.

The final part of the program in Sect. 6.5.1 iterates over the *tree* in the main function. This calls the __*iter*__ method of the BinarySearchTree class. This __*iter*__ method returns an iterator over the root's __*Node* object. The __*Node*'s __*iter*__ method is interesting because it is a recursive traversal of the tree. When *for elem in self.left* is written, this calls the __*iter*__ method on the left subtree. After all the elements in the left subtree are yielded, the value at the root of the tree is yielded,

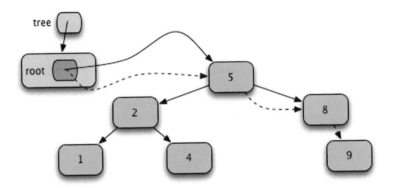

Fig. 6.9 The Tree After Inserting 9

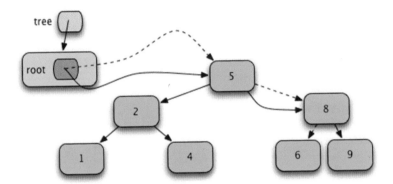

Fig. 6.10 The Tree After Inserting 6

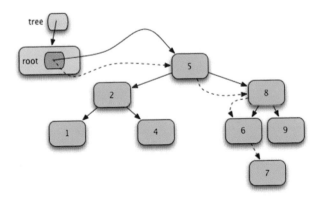

Fig. 6.11 The Tree After Inserting 7

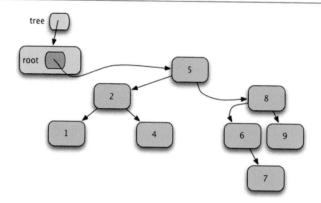

Fig. 6.12 The Final BinarySearchTree Object Contents

then the values in the right subtree are yielded by writing *for elem in self.right*. The result of this recursive function is an *inorder* traversal of the tree.

Binary search trees are of some academic interest. However, they are not used much in practice. In the average case, inserting into a binary search tree takes O(log n) time. To insert *n* items into a binary search tree would take O(n log n) time. So, in the average case we have an algorithm for sorting a sequence of ordered items. However, it takes more space than a list and the quicksort algorithm can sort a list with the same big-Oh complexity. In the worst case, binary search trees suffer from the same problem that quicksort suffers from. When the items are already sorted, both quicksort and binary search trees perform poorly. The complexity of inserting *n* items into a binary search tree becomes O(n^2) in the worst case. The tree becomes a stick if the values are already sorted and essentially becomes a linked list.

There are a couple of nice properties of binary search trees that a random access list does not have. Inserting into a tree can be done in O(log n) time in the average case while inserting into a list would take O(n) time. Deleting from a binary search tree can also be done in O(log n) time in the average case. Looking up a value in a binary search tree can also be done in O(log n) time in the average case. If we have lots of insert, delete, and lookup operations for some algorithm, a tree-like structure may be useful. But, binary search trees cannot guarantee the O(log n) complexity. It turns out that there are implementations of search tree structures that can guarantee O(log n) complexity or better for inserting, deleting, and searching for values. A few examples are Splay Trees, AVL-Trees, and B-Trees which are all studied later in this text.

6.6   Search Spaces

Sometimes we have a problem that may consist of many different states. We may want to find a particular state of the problem which we'll call the *goal*. Consider Sudoku puzzles. A Sudoku puzzle has a state, reflecting how much of it we have solved. We are seeking a goal which is the solution of the puzzle. We could randomly try a value in a cell of the puzzle and try to solve the puzzle after having made that guess. The guess would lead to a new state of the puzzle. But, if the guess were wrong we may have to go back and undo our guess. A wrong guess could lead to a dead end.

This process of guessing, trying to finish the puzzle, and undoing bad guesses is called *depth first search*. Looking for a goal by making guesses is called a depth first search of a problem space. When a dead end is found we may have to *backtrack*. Backtracking involves undoing bad guesses and then trying the next guess to see if the problem can be solved by making the new guess. The description here leads to the depth first search algorithm in Sect. 12.2.1.

6.6.1   Depth-First Search Algorithm

```
def dfs(current, goal):
  if current == goal:
    return [current]

  for next in adjacent(current):
    result = dfs(next)
    if result != None:
      return [current] + result

  return None
```

The depth first search algorithm may be written recursively. In this code the depth first search algorithm returns the path from the current node to the goal node. The backtracking occurs if the for loop completes without finding an appropriate adjacent node. In that case, *None* is returned and the previous recursive call of *dfs* goes on to the next adjacent node to look for the goal on that path.

In the last chapter an algorithm was presented for solving Sudoku puzzles that works for many puzzles, but not all. In these cases, depth first search can be applied to the puzzle *after* reducing the problem as far as possible. It is important to first apply the rules of the last chapter to reduce the puzzle because otherwise the search space is too big to search in a reasonable amount of time. The solve function in Sect. 6.6.2 includes a depth first search that will solve any Sudoku puzzle assuming that the reduce function applies the rules of the last chapter to all the groups within a puzzle. The *copy* module must be imported for this code to run correctly.

6.6.2   Sudoku Depth-First Search

```
def solutionViable(matrix):
  # Check that no set is empty
  for i in range(9):
    for j in range(9):
      if len(matrix[i][j]) == 0:
        return False

  return True

def solve(matrix):
```

```
11
12      reduce(matrix)
13
14      if not solutionViable(matrix):
15        return None
16
17      if solutionOK(matrix):
18        return matrix
19
20      print("Searching...")
21
22      for i in range(9):
23        for j in range(9):
24          if len(matrix[i][j]) > 1:
25            for k in matrix[i][j]:
26              mcopy = copy.deepcopy(matrix)
27              mcopy[i][j] = set([k])
28
29              result = solve(mcopy)
30
31              if result != None:
32                return result
33
34      return None
```

In the *solve* function of Sect. 6.6.2, *reduce* is called to try to solve the puzzle with the rules of the last chapter. After calling *reduce* we check to see if the puzzle is still solvable (i.e. no empty sets). If not, the *solve* function returns *None*. The search proceeds by examining each location within the matrix and each possible value that the location could hold. The *for k* loop tries all possible values for a cell with more than one possibility. If the call to *reduce* solves the puzzle, the *solutionOK* function will return *True* and the *solve* function will return the matrix. Otherwise, the *depth first search* proceeds by looking for a cell in the matrix with more than one choice. The function makes a copy of the matrix called *mcopy* and makes a guess as to the value in that location in *mcopy*. It then recursively calls *solve* on *mcopy*.

The *solve* function returns *None* if no solution is found and the solved puzzle if a solution is found. So, when *solve* is called recursively, if *None* is returned, the function continues to search by trying another possible value. Initially calling *solve* can be accomplished as shown in Sect. 6.6.3 assuming that *matrix* is a 9×9 matrix of sets representing a Sudoku puzzle.

6.6.3 Calling Sudoku's Solve Function

```
1      print("Begin Solving")
2
3      matrix = solve(matrix)
4
5      if matrix == None:
6        print("No Solution Found!!!")
7        return
```

If a non-None matrix is returned, then the puzzle is solved and the solution may be printed. This is one example where no tree is ever constructed, yet the search space is shaped like a tree and depth first search can be used to search the problem space.

6.7 Chapter Summary

Tree-like structures appear in many problems in Computer Science. A tree datatype can hold information and allow quick insert, delete, and search times. While binary search trees are not used in practice, the principles governing them are used in many advanced data structures like B-trees, AVL-trees, and Splay Trees. Understanding how references point to objects and how this can be used to build a datatype like a tree is an important concept for computer programmers to understand.

Search spaces are often tree-like when making a decision between several choices leads to another decision. A search space is not a datatype, so in this case no tree is built. However, the space that is searched has a tree-like structure. The key to doing a depth first search of a space is to remember where you were so you can backtrack when a choice leads to a dead end. Backtracking is often accomplished using recursion.

Many algorithms that deal with trees are naturally recursive. Depth first search, tree traversals, parsing, and abstract syntax evaluation may all be recursively implemented. Recursion is a powerful mechanism to have in your toolbox for solving problems.

6.8 Review Questions

Answer these short answer, multiple choice, and true/false questions to test your mastery of the chapter.

1. Is the root of a tree in Computer Science at the top or bottom of a tree?
2. How many roots can a tree have?
3. A full binary tree is a tree that is full at each level of the tree, meaning there is no room for another node at any level of the tree, except at the leaves. How many nodes are in a full binary tree with three levels? How about 4 levels? How about 5 levels?
4. In a full binary tree, what is the a relationship between the number of leaves in the tree and the total number of nodes in the tree?
5. When constructing a tree, for which is it easiest to write code, a bottom-up or top-down construction of the tree?
6. What term is used when a wrong choice is made and another choice must be attempted when searching for a value in a tree?
7. How does a search space differ from a tree datatype?

8. Describe a non-recursive algorithm for doing an inorder traversal of a tree. HINT: Your algorithm will need a stack to get this to work.
9. Write some code to build a tree for the infix expression 5 * 4 + 3 * 2. Be sure to follow the precedence of operators and in your tree. You may assume the PlusNode and TimesNode classes from the chapter are already defined.
10. Provide the prefix and postfix forms of 5 * 4 + 3 * 2.

6.9   Programming Problems

1. Write a program that asks the user to enter a prefix expression. Then, the program should print out the infix and postfix forms of that expression. Finally, it should print the result of evaluating the expression. Interacting with the program should look like this.

```
Please enter a prefix expression: + + * 4 5 6 7
The infix form is: (((4 * 5) + 6) + 7)
The postfix form is: 4 5 * 6 + 7 +
The result is: 33
```

If the prefix expression is malformed, the program should print that the expression is malformed and it should quit. It should not try to print the infix or postfix forms of the expression in this case.

2. Write a program that reads a list of numbers from the user and lets the user insert, delete, and search for values in the tree. The program should be menu driven allowing for inserting, searching, and deleting from a binary search tree. Inserting into the tree should allow for multiple inserts as follows.

```
Binary Search Tree Program
--------------------------
Make a choice...
1. Insert into tree.
2. Delete from tree.
3. Lookup Value.
Choice? 1
insert? 5
insert? 2
insert? 8
insert? 6
insert? 7
insert? 9
insert? 4
insert? 1
insert?

Make a choice...
1. Insert into tree.
2. Delete from tree.
3. Lookup Value.
Choice? 3
Value? 8
Yes, 8 is in the tree.
```

```
Make a choice...
1. Insert into tree.
2. Delete from tree.
3. Lookup Value.
Choice? 2
Value? 5
5 has been deleted from the tree.

Make a choice...
1. Insert into tree.
2. Delete from tree.
3. Lookup Value.
Choice? 2
Value? 3
3 was not in the tree.
```

The hardest part of this program is deleting from the tree. You can write a recursive function to delete a value. In some ways, the delete from tree function is like the insert function given in the chapter. You will want to write two functions, one that is a method to call on a binary search tree to delete a value, the other would be a hidden recursive delete from tree function. The recursive function should be given a tree and a value to delete. It should return the tree after deleting the value from the tree. The recursive delete function must be handled in three cases as follows.

- **Case 1**. The value to delete is in a node that has no children. In this case, the recursive function can return an empty tree (i.e. None) because that is the tree after deleting the value from it. This would be the case if the 9 were deleted from the binary search tree in Fig. 6.12. In Fig. 6.13 the right subtree of the node containing 8 is now *None* and therefore the node containing 9 is gone from the tree.
- **Case 2**. The value to delete is in a node that has one child. In this case, the recursive function can return the child as the tree after deleting the value. This would be the case if deleting 6 from the tree in Fig. 6.13. In this case, to delete

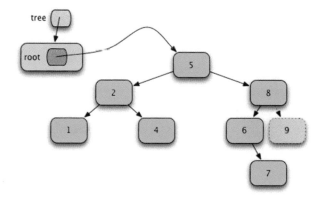

Fig. 6.13 The Tree After Deleting 9

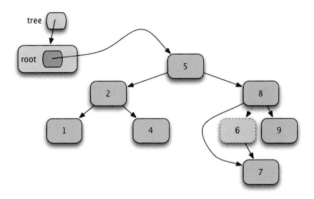

Fig. 6.14 The Tree After Deleting 6

the node containing 6 from the tree you simply return the tree for the node containing 7 so it ends up being linked to the node containing 8. In Fig. 6.14 the node containing 6 is eliminated by making the left subtree of the node containing 8 point at the right subtree of the node containing 6.

- **Case 3**. This is is hardest case to implement. When the value to delete is in a node that has two children, then to delete the node we want to use another function, call it *getRightMost*, to get the right-most value of a tree. Then you use this function to get the right-most value of the left subtree of the node to delete. Instead of deleting the node, you replace the value of the node with the right-most value of the left subtree. Then you delete the right-most value of the left subtree from the left subtree. In Fig. 6.15 the 5 is eliminated by setting the node containing 5 to 4, the right-most value of the left subtree. Then 4 is deleted from the left subtree.

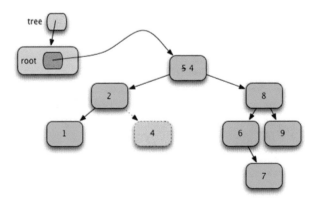

Fig. 6.15 The Tree After Deleting 5

3. Complete the Sudoku program as described in Chap. 5 and augment it with the depth first search described in Sect. 6.6.2 to complete a Sudoku program that is capable of solving any Sudoku puzzle. It should solve these puzzles almost instantly. If it is taking a long time to solve a puzzle it is likely because your reduce function is not reducing the puzzle as described in Chap. 5.

   To complete this exercise you will need two functions, the *solutionOK* function and the *solutionViable* function. The *solutionViable* function is given in the chapter and returns *True* if none of the sets in the matrix are empty. The *solutionOK* function returns *True* if the solution is a valid solution. This can be checked very easily. If any of the sets in the matrix do not contain contain exactly 1 element then the solution is not okay and *False* should be returned. If the union of any group within a Sudoku puzzle does not contain 9 elements then the solution is not okay and *False* should be returned. Otherwise, the solution is okay and *True* should be returned.

   After completing this program you should be able to solve Sudoku problems like sudoku7.txt or sudoku8.txt which are available for download on the text's website.

4. Design an OrderedTreeSet class which can be used to insert items, delete items, and lookup items in an average case of O(log n) time. Implement the *in* operator on this class for set containment. Also implement an iterator that returns the items of the set in ascending order. The design of this set should allow items of any type to be added to the set as long as they implement the __lt__ operator. This OrderedTreeSet class should be written in a file called orderedtreeset.py. The main function of this module should consist of a test program for your OrderedTreeSet class that thoroughly tests your code. The *main* function should be called using the standard *if* statement that distinguishes between the module being imported or run itself.

5. Design an OrderedTreeMap class which uses an OrderedTreeSet class in its implementation. To organize this correctly you should create two modules: an orderedtreeset.py module and an orderedtreemap.py module. Have the Ordered TreeMap class use the OrderedTreeSet class in its implementation the way *Hash-Set* and *HashMap* were implemented in Chap. 5. Design test cases to thoroughly test your OrderedTreeMap class.

Graphs

7

Many problems in Computer Science and Mathematics can be reduced to a set of states and a set of transitions between these states. A graph is a mathematical representation of problems like these. In the last chapter we saw that trees serve a variety of purposes in Computer Science. Trees are graphs. However, graphs are more general than trees. Abstracting away the details of a problem and studying it in its simplest form often leads to new insight. As a result, many algorithms have come out of the research in graph theory. Graph theory was first studied by mathematicians. Many of the algorithms in graph theory are named for the mathematician that developed or discovered them. Dijkstra and Kruskal are two such mathematicians and this chapter covers algorithms developed by them.

Representing a graph can be done one of several different ways. The correct way to represent a graph depends on the algorithm being implemented. Graph theory problems include graph coloring, finding a path between two states or nodes in a graph, or finding a shortest path through a graph among many others. There are many algorithms that have come from the study of graphs. To understand the formulation of these problems it is good to learn a little graph notation which is presented in this chapter as well.

7.1   Chapter Goals

This chapter covers the representation of graphs. It also covers a few graph algorithms. Depth first search of a graph is presented, along with breadth first search. Dijkstra's algorithm is famous in Computer Science and has many applications from networking to construction planning. Kruskal's algorithm is another famous algorithm used to find a minimum weighted spanning tree. By the end of the chapter you should have a basic understanding of graph theory and how many problems in Computer Science can be posed in the form of graphs.

To begin we'll study some notation and depth first search of a graph. Then we'll examine a couple of *Greedy Algorithms* that answer some interesting questions about graphs. Greedy algorithms are algorithms that never make a wrong choice in finding

© Springer International Publishing Switzerland 2015   185
K.D. Lee and S. Hubbard, *Data Structures and Algorithms with Python*,
Undergraduate Topics in Computer Science, DOI 10.1007/978-3-319-13072-9_7

a solution. We'll examine two of these algorithms called Kruskal's Algorithm and Dijkstra's Algorithm, both named for the people that formulated the algorithm to solve their respective problems.

7.2   Graph Notation

A little notation will help in the graph definitions in this chapter. A set is an unordered collection of items. For instance, $V = \{0, 1, 2, 3, 4, 5, 6, 7, 8, 9, 10, 11, 12\}$ is the set of the first 13 natural numbers. A *subset* of a set is some collection, possibly empty, of items from its *superset*. The set $U = \{5, 8, 2\}$ is a subset of V. The *cardinality* of a set is its size or number of elements. The cardinality of the set V is written as $|V|$. The cardinality of V is 13 and U is 3, so $|V| = 13$ and $|U| = 3$.

A graph $G = (V,E)$ is defined by a set of vertices, named V, and a set of edges, named E. The set of edges are subsets of V where each member of E has *cardinality* 2. In other words, edges are denoted by pairs of vertices. Consider the simple, undirected graph given in Fig. 7.1. The sets $V = \{0, 1, 2, 3, 4, 5, 6, 7, 8, 9, 10, 11, 12\}$ and $E = \{\{0, 1\},\{0, 3\},\{0, 10\},\{1, 10\},\{1, 4\},\{2, 3\},\{2, 8\},\{2, 6\},\{3, 9\},\{5, 4\},\{5, 12\},\{5, 7\},\{11, 12\},\{11, 10\},\{9, 10\}\}$ define this graph. Since each edge is itself a set of cardinality 2, the order of the vertices in each edge set does not matter. For instance, $\{1, 4\}$ is the same edge as $\{4, 1\}$.

Many problems can be formulated in terms of a graph. For instance, we might ask how many colors it would take to color a map so that no two countries that shared a border were colored the same. In this problem the vertices in Fig. 7.1 would represent countries and two countries that share a border would have an edge between them. The problem can then be restated as finding the minimum number of colors required to color each vertex in the graph so that no two vertices that share an edge have the same color.

A directed graph $G = (V,E)$ is defined in the same way as an undirected graph except that the set of edges, E, is a set of tuples instead of subsets. By defining $E = \{(v_i, v_j) \; where \; v_i, v_j \in V\}$ means that edges can be traversed in one direction

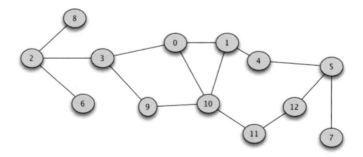

Fig. 7.1 An Undirected Graph

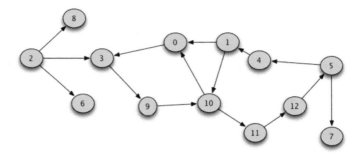

Fig. 7.2 A Directed Graph

only. In Fig. 7.2 we can move from vertex 10 to vertex 0 along the edge (10,0), but we cannot move from vertex 0 to 10, at least not without going through some other vertices, because the edge (0,10) is not in the set E.

A *path* in a graph is a series of edges, none repeated, that can be traversed in order to travel from one vertex to another in a graph. A *cycle* in a graph is a path which begins and ends with the same vertex. The last chapter covered trees in computer science. Now armed with some notation from graph theory we can give a formal definition of a tree. A *tree* is a *directed, connected acyclic graph*. An acyclic graph is a graph without any cycles.

Sometimes in graph theory a tree is defined as an *acyclic connected graph* dropping the requirement that it be a directed graph. In this case, a tree may be defined as a graph which is fully connected, but has only one path between any two vertices.

Both directed and undirected graphs can be used to model many different kinds of problems. The graph in Fig. 7.1 might represent register allocation in a CPU. The vertices could represent symbolically named registers and two registers that were both in use at the same time would have an edge between them. The question that might be asked is, "How many physical registers of the machine are required for the symbolic registers of this computation?".

It turns out that register allocation and map coloring represent the same problem. When we abstract away the details, the problem boils down to a graph coloring problem. An answer to "How many colors are required to color the map?" would answer "How many physical registers are required for this computation?" and vice-versa.

A weighted graph is a graph where every edge has a weight assigned to it. More formally, a weighted graph $G = (V,E,w)$ is a graph with the given set of vertices, V, and edges, E. In addition, a weighted graph has a weight function, w, that maps edges to real numbers. So the signature of w is given by $w: E \rightarrow Real$. Weighted graphs can be used to represent the state of many different problems. For instance, a weighted graph might provide information about roads and intersections. Cost/benefit analysis can sometimes be expressed in terms of a weighted graph. The weights can represent the available capacity of network connections between nodes in a network.

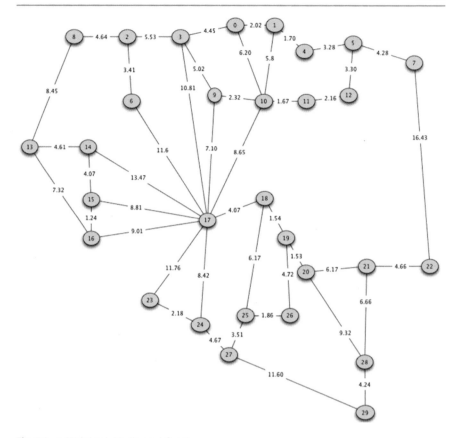

Fig. 7.3 A Weighted, Undirected Graph

A weighted graph can be used to represent the state of many different kinds of problems. Figure 7.3 depicts a weighted graph which represents roads and intersections.

7.3   Searching a Graph

Many problems have been formulated in terms of graph theory. One of the more common problems is discovering a path from one vertex to another in a graph. The question might be, does a path exist from vertex v_i to v_j and if so, what edges must you traverse to get there? Performing depth first search on a graph is similar to the algorithm first presented in Chap. 6, but we must be wary of getting stuck in a cycle within a graph.

Consider searching for a path from vertex 0 to vertex 1 in the directed graph of Fig. 7.2. The blue lines in Fig. 7.4 highlight the path between these vertices. In the

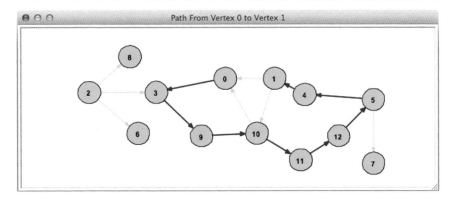

Fig. 7.4 A Path from Vertex 0 to Vertex 1

graph, there seems to be only one choice in most cases. However, when the search reaches vertex 10 we must choose between two edges. One edge takes us back to vertex 0 which we have already visited. The other edge takes us closer to the final path. Another choice is made at vertex 5. If the edge to 7 is wrongly examined, we must have a way of backing up and trying the other edge to vertex 4.

Searching a graph in this manner is also called *depth first search*, as first discussed in Chap. 6, and requires the ability to backtrack. Consider when vertex 5 is encountered. If a choice is made to go to vertex 7, we must be able to back up to fix that choice and go to vertex 4 instead. A stack data structure or recursion handles the backtracking.

Depth first search must also avoid possible cycles within the graph. The avoidance of cycles is accomplished by maintaining a set of *visited* vertices. When a vertex is visited, it is added to the *visited* set. If a vertex is in the visited set, then it is not examined again later in the search should a cycle take the search back to the same vertex.

An iterative (i.e. non-recursive) graph depth first search algorithm begins by initializing the *visited* set to the empty set and by creating a stack for backtracking. The start vertex is pushed onto the stack to begin the algorithm. Steps similar to those taken in Sect. 7.3.1 are executed to find the goal. This code is pseudo-code, but presents the necessary details.

7.3.1   Iterative Depth First Search of a Graph

```
1   def graphDFS(G, start, goal):
2       # G = (V,E) is the graph with vertices, V, and edges, E.
3       V,E = G
4       stack = Stack()
5       visited = Set()
6       stack.push(start)
7
8       while not stack.isEmpty():
9           # A vertex is popped from the stack. This is called the current vertex.
10          current = stack.pop()
```

```
11    # The current vertex is added to the visited set.
12    visited.add(current)
13
14    # If the current vertex is the goal vertex, then we discontinue the
15    # search reporting that we found the goal.
16    if current == goal:
17      return True # or return path to goal perhaps
18
19    # Otherwise, for every adjacent vertex, v, to the current vertex
20    # in the graph, v is pushed on the stack of vertices yet to search
21    # unless v is already in the visited set in which case the edge
22    # leading to v is ignored.
23    for v in adjacent(current,E):
24      if not v in visited:
25        stack.push(v)
26
27    # If we get this far, then we did not find the goal.
28    return False # or return an empty path
```

If the while loop in Sect. 7.3.1 terminates the stack was empty and therefore no path to the goal exists. This algorithm implements depth first search of a graph. It can also be implemented recursively if pushing on the stack is replaced with a recursive call to *depth first search*. When implemented recursively, the *depth first search* function is passed the current vertex and a mutable *visited* set and it returns either the path to the goal or alternatively a boolean value indicating that the goal or target was found. Given the graph in Fig. 7.4 the search returned *True*.

The iterative version of *depth first search* can be modified to do a *breadth first search* of a graph if the stack is replaced with a queue. Breadth first search is an exhaustive search, meaning that it looks at all paths at the same time, but will also find the shortest path, with the least number of edges, between any two vertices in a graph. Performing breadth first search on large graphs may take too long to be of practical use.

7.4   Kruskal's Algorithm

Consider for a moment a county which is responsible for plowing roads in the winter but is running out of money due to an unexpected amount of snow. The county supervisor has been told to reduce costs by plowing only the necessary roads for the rest of the winter. The supervisor wants to find the shortest number of total miles that must be plowed so any person can travel from one point to any other point in the county, but not necessarily by the shortest route. The county supervisor wants to minimize the miles of plowed roads, while guaranteeing you can still get anywhere you need to in the county.

Joseph Kruskal was an American computer scientist and mathematician who lived from 1928 to 2010. He imagined this problem, formalized it in terms of a weighted graph, and devised an algorithm to solve this problem. His algorithm was first published in the *Proceedings of the American Mathematical Society* [5] and is commonly called *Kruskal's Algorithm*.

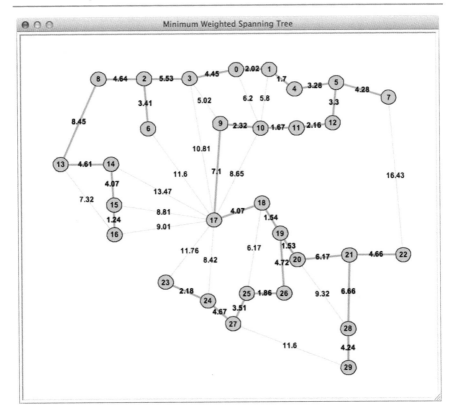

Fig. 7.5 A Minimum Weighted Spanning Tree

The last chapter introduced trees by using them in various algorithms like binary search. The definition doesn't change from the last chapter. But trees, in the context of graph theory, are a subset of the set of all possible graphs. A tree is just a graph without any cycles. In addition, it is relatively easy to prove that a tree must contain one less edge than its number of vertices. Otherwise, it would not be a tree.

Clearly the graph in Fig. 7.3 is not a tree. There are many cycles within the graph. Kruskal's paper presented an algorithm to find a minimum weighted spanning tree for such a graph. Figure 7.5 contains a minimum weighted spanning tree for the graph in Fig. 7.3 with the tree edges highlighted in orange. We don't say *the* minimum weighted spanning tree because in general there could be more than one minimum weighted spanning tree. In this case, there is likely only one possible.

Kruskal's algorithm is a *greedy algorithm*. The designation *greedy* means that the algorithm always chooses the first alternative when presented with a list of alternatives and never makes a mistake, or wrong choice, when choosing. In other words, no backtracking is required in Kruskal's algorithm.

The algorithm begins by sorting all the edges in ascending order of their weights. Assuming that the graph is fully connected, the spanning tree will contain $|V|-1$ edges. The algorithm forms sets of all the vertices in the graph, one set for each vertex, initially containing just that vertex that corresponds to the set. In the example in Fig. 7.3 there are initially 30 sets each containing one vertex.

The algorithm proceeds as follows until |V|−1 edges have been added to the set of spanning tree edges.

1. The next shortest edge is examined. If the two vertex end points of the edge are in different sets, then the edge may be safely added to the set of spanning tree edges. A new set is formed from the union of the two vertex sets and the two previous sets are dropped from the list of vertex sets.
2. If the two vertex endpoints of the edge are already in the same set, the edge is ignored.

That's the entire algorithm. The algorithm is *greedy* because it always chooses the next smallest edge unless doing so would form a cycle. If a cycle would be formed by adding an edge, it is known right away without having to undo any mistake or backtrack.

Consider Fig. 7.6. In this snapshot the algorithm has already formed a forest of trees, but not a spanning tree yet. The edges in orange are part the spanning tree.

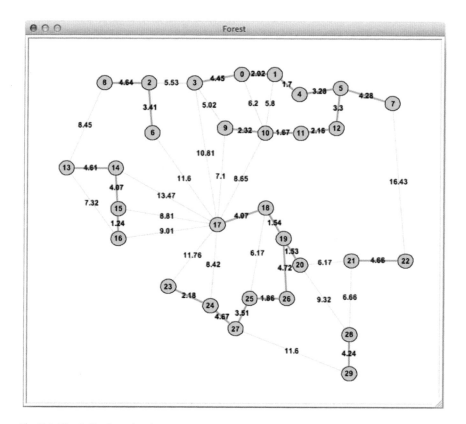

Fig. 7.6 Kruskal's: Snapshot 1

The next shortest edge, the edge from vertex 3 to vertex 9 is currently being considered. The set containing 3 and 9 is the set {3, 0, 1, 4, 5, 12, 11, 10, 9}. Adding the edge with end points 3 and 9 cannot be done because vertices 3 and 9 are already in the same set. So, this edge is skipped. It cannot be a part of the minimum weighted spanning tree.

The next shortest edge is the edge between vertices 2 and 3. Since 2 is a member of {8, 2, 6} and 3 is a member of its set in the previous paragraph, the edge {2, 3} is added to the minimum weighted spanning tree edges and the new set {8, 2, 6, 3, 0, 1, 4, 5, 12, 11, 10, 9} is formed replacing its previous two subsets as depicted in Fig. 7.7.

The next shortest edge is the edge between vertices 1 and 10. This edge again cannot be added since 1 and 10 are in the same set and therefore adding the edge would form a cycle. The next shortest edge is the edge between vertices 18 and 25, but again adding it would form a cycle so it is skipped. The algorithm proceeds in this manner until the resulting spanning tree is formed with |V|−1 edges (assuming the graph is fully connected).

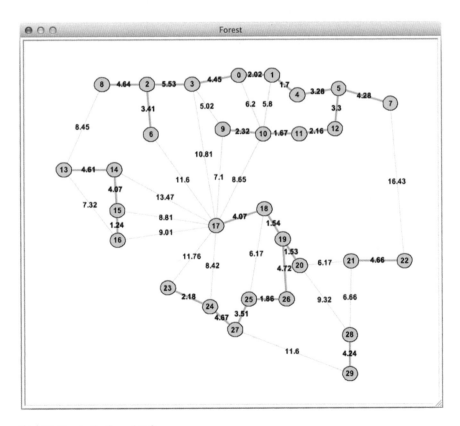

Fig. 7.7 Kruskal's: Snapshot 2

7.4.1   Proof of Correctness

Proving Kruskal's algorithm correctly finds a minimum weighted spanning tree can be done with a proof by contradiction. The proof starts by recognizing that there must be $|V|-1$ edges in the spanning tree. Then we assume that some other edge would be better to add to the spanning tree than the edges picked by the algorithm. The new edge must be a part of one and only one cycle. If adding the new edge formed two or more cycles then there would have had to be a cycle in the tree before adding the new edge. One of the edges in this newly formed cycle must be deleted from the minimum weighted spanning tree to once again make it a tree. And, the deleted edge must have weight greater than the newly added edge. This is only possible if the new edge and the deleted old edge have exactly the same weight since all the old edges in the cycle were chosen before the new edge and the new edge was skipped because choosing it would have formed a cycle. So dropping the same weighted edge of the older edges will result in a minimum weighted spanning tree with the same weight. Therefore, the new spanning tree has the same weight as the original spanning tree and that contradicts our assumption that a better edge could be found.

7.4.2   Kruskal's Complexity Analysis

The complexity of Kruskal's algorithm depends on sorting the list of edges and then forming the union of sets as the algorithm proceeds. Sorting a list, as was shown in Chap. 4 when we looked at the complexity of quicksort, is $O(|E|\log|E|)$.

Sorting the list is one half of Kruskal's algorithm. The other half is choosing the correct edges. Recall that each edge starts in a set by itself and that an edge belongs to the minimum weighted spanning tree if the two endpoint vertices are in separate sets. If so, then the union is formed for the two sets containing the endpoints and this union of two sets replaces the previous two sets going forward.

Three operations are required to implement this part of the algorithm.

1. First we must discover the set for each endpoint of the edge being considered for addition to the spanning tree.
2. Then the two sets must be compared for equality.
3. Finally, the union of the two sets must be formed and any necessary updates must be performed so the two endpoint vertices now refer to the union of the two sets instead of their original sets.

One way to implement these operations would be to create a list of sets where each position in the list corresponded to one vertex in the graph. The vertices are conveniently numbered 0–29 in the example in the text but vertices can be reassigned integer identifiers starting at 0 otherwise. The set corresponding to a vertex can be determined in $O(1)$ time since indexed lookup in a list is a constant time operation.

If we make sure there is only one copy of each set, we can determine if two sets are the same or not in $O(1)$ time as well. We can just compare their references to see whether they are the same set or not. The keyword *is* in Python will accomplish this. So if we want to know that x and y refer to the same set we can write x *is* y and this operation is $O(1)$.

The third operation requires forming a new set from the previous two. This operation will be performed $|V|-1$ times. In the worst case the first time this operation occurs 1 vertex will be added to an existing set. The second time, two vertices will be added to an existing set, and so on. So in the end, the overall worst case complexity of this operation is $O(|V|^2)$ assuming once again that the graph is connected. Clearly, this is the expensive operation of this algorithm. The next section presents a data structure that improves on this considerably.

7.4.3   The Partition Data Structure

To improve on the third required operation, the merging of two sets into one set, a specialized data structure called a *Partition* may be used. The partition data structure contains a list of integers with one entry for each vertex. Initially, the list simply contains a list of integers which match their indices:

```
  0  1  2  3  4  5  6  7  8  9 10 11 12 13 14 15 16 17 18 19 20 21 22 23 24 25 26 27 28 29
[ 0,  1,  2,  3,  4,  5,  6,  7,  8,  9,10,11,12,13,14,15,16,17,18,19,20,21,22,23,24,25,26,27,28,29]
```

Think of this list as a list of trees, representing the sets of connected edges in the spanning forest constructed so far. A tree's root is indicated when the value at a location within the list matches its index. Initially, each vertex within the partition is in its own set because each vertex is the root of its own tree.

Discovering the set for a vertex means tracing a tree back to its root. Consider what happens when the edge from vertex 3 to vertex 9 is considered for adding to the minimum weighted spanning tree as pictured in Fig. 7.6. The partition at that time looks like this.

```
  0  1  2  3  4  5  6  7  8  9 10 11 12 13 14 15 16 17 18 19 20 21 22 23 24 25 26 27 28 29
[ 4,  4,  2,  7,  5,11,  2,  7,  2,11,11,  7,11,16,16,16,16,19,19,19,19,22,22,24,26,26,19,26,29,29]
```

Vertex 3 is not the root of its own tree at this time. Since 7 is found at index 3 we next look at index 7 of the partition list. That position in the partition list matches its value. The 3 is in the set (i.e. tree) rooted at location 7. Looking at vertex 9 next, index 9 in the list contains 11. Index 11 in the list contains 7. Vertex 9 is also in the set (i.e. tree) rooted at index 7. Therefore vertex 3 and 9 are already in the same set and the edge from 3 to 9 cannot be added to the minimum spanning tree since a cycle would be formed.

The next edge to be considered is the edge between vertices 2 and 3. The root of the tree containing 2 is at index 2 of the partition. The root of the vertex containing 3 is at index 7 as we just saw. These two vertices are not in the same set so the edge from 2 to 3 is added to the minimum spanning tree edges.

The third operation that must be performed is the merging of the sets containing 2 and 3. This is where the partition comes in handy. Having found the root of the two trees, we simply make the root of one of the trees point to the root of the other tree. We end up with this partition after merging these two sets.

```
 0  1  2  3  4  5  6  7  8  9 10 11 12 13 14 15 16 17 18 19 20 21 22 23 24 25 26 27 28 29
[ 4, 4, 2, 7, 5,11, 2, 2, 2,11,11, 7,11,16,16,16,16,19,19,19,19,22,22,24,26,26,19,26,29,29]
```

At this point in the algorithm, the tree rooted at 7 has been altered to be rooted at 2 instead. That's all that was needed to merge the two sets containing vertex 2 and 3! The root of one tree can be made to point to the root of the other tree when two sets are merged into one.

The partition data structure combines the three required operations from Sect. 7.4.2 into one method called *sameSetAndUnion*. This method is given two vertex numbers. The method returns true if the two vertices are in the same set (i.e. have the same root). If they do not have the same root, then the root of one tree is made to point to the other and the method returns false.

The *sameSetAndUnion* method first finds the roots of the two vertices given to it. In the worst case this could take $O(|V|)$ time leading to an overall complexity of $O(|V|^2)$. However, in practice these *set trees* are very flat. For instance, in the example presented in this chapter, the average depth of the *set trees* is 1.7428, meaning that on average it takes 1.7428 comparisons to find the root of a *set tree* in a graph with 30 vertices and 45 edges to consider adding to the minimum weighted spanning tree. Another example containing 133 vertices and 8778 edges had an average *set tree* depth of 7.5656. The average complexity of this *sameSetAndUnion* method is much better than the solution considered in Sect. 7.4.2. The average case complexity of *sameSetAndUnion* is much closer to $O(\log|V|)$. This means that the second part of Kruskal's algorithm, using this partition data structure, exhibits $O(|E|\log|V|)$ complexity in the average case.

In a connected graph the number of edges must be no less than one less than the total number of vertices. Sorting the edges takes $O(|E|\log|E|)$ time and the second part of Kruskal's algorithm takes $O(|E|\log|V|)$ time. Since the number of edges is at least on the same order as the number of vertices in a connected graph the complexity $O(|E|\log|V|) \leq O(|E|\log|E|)$. So we can say that the overall average complexity of Kruskal's algorithm is $O(|E|\log|E|)$. In practice, Kruskal's algorithm is very efficient and finds a minimum weighted spanning tree quickly even for large graphs with many edges.

7.5   Dijkstra's Algorithm

Edsger Dijkstra was a Dutch computer scientist who lived from 1930 to 2002. In 1959 he published a short paper [4] that commented on Kruskal's solution to the minimum spanning tree problem and provided an alternative that might in some cases be more efficient. More importantly, he provided an algorithm for finding the

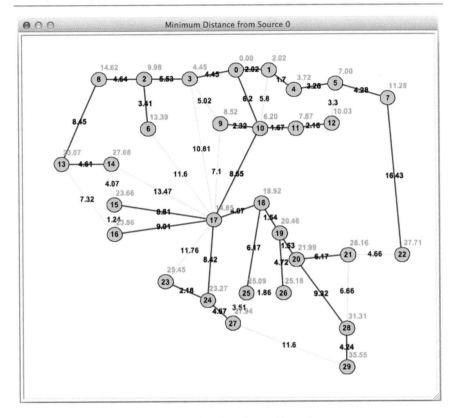

Fig. 7.8 Minimum Cost Paths and Total Cost from Source Vertex 0

minimum cost path between any two vertices in a weighted graph. This algorithm can be, and sometimes is, generalized to find the minimum cost path between a *source* vertex and all other vertices in a graph. This algorithm is known as Dijkstra's algorithm. Figure 7.8 shows the result of running Dijkstra's algorithm on the graph first presented in Fig. 7.3. The purple edges show the minimum cost paths from source vertex 0 to all other vertices in the graph. The orange values are the minimum cost of reaching each vertex from source vertex 0.

Efficiently finding a minimum cost path from one vertex to another is used in all kinds of problems including network routing, trip planning, and other planning problems where vertices represent intermediate goals and edges represent the cost of transitioning between intermediate goals. These kind of planning problems are very common.

Dijkstra's algorithm proceeds in a greedy fashion from the single *source* vertex. Each vertex, *v*, in the graph is assigned a cost which is the sum of the weighted edges on the path from the *source* to *v*. Initially the *source* vertex is assigned cost 0. All other vertices are initially assigned infinite cost. Anything greater than the sum of all weights in the graph can serve as an infinite value.

Dijkstra's algorithm shares some commonality with depth first search. The algorithm proceeds as depth first search proceeds, but starts with a single source eventually visiting every node within the graph. There are two sets that Dijkstra's algorithm maintains. The first is an *unvisited* set. This is a set of vertices that yet need to be considered while looking for minimum cost paths. The *unvisited* set serves the same purpose as the stack when performing *depth first search* on a graph. The *visited* set is the other set used by the algorithm. The *visited* set contains all vertices which already have their minimum cost and path computed. The *visited* set serves the same purpose as the *visited* set in depth first search of a graph.

To keep track of the minimum cost path from the source to a vertex, v, it is only necessary to keep track of the previous vertex on the path to v. For each vertex, v, we keep track of the previous vertex on its path from the source.

Initially the *source* vertex, with its cost of 0, is added to the *unvisited* set. Then the algorithm proceeds as follows as long as there is at least one vertex in the *unvisited* set.

1. Remove the vertex we'll call *current* from the *unvisited* set with the least cost. All other paths to this vertex must have greater cost because otherwise they would have been in the *unvisited* set with smaller cost.
2. Add *current* to the *visited* set.
3. For every vertex, *adjacent*, that is adjacent to *current*, check to see if *adjacent* is in the *visited* set or not. If *adjacent* is in the *visited* set, then we know the minimum cost of reaching this vertex from the source so don't do anything.
4. If *adjacent* is not in the *visited* set, compute a new cost for arriving at *adjacent* by traversing the edge, e, from *current* to *adjacent*. A new cost can be found by adding the cost of getting to *current* and e's weight. If this new cost is better than the current cost of getting to *adjacent*, then update *adjacent*'s cost and remember that *current* is the previous vertex of *adjacent*. Also, add *adjacent* to the *unvisited* set.

When this algorithm terminates the cost of reaching all vertices in the graph has been computed assuming that all vertices are reachable from the source vertex. In addition, the minimum cost path to each vertex can be determined from the *previous vertex* information that was maintained as the algorithm executed.

7.5.1   Dijkstra's Complexity Analysis

In the first step of Dijkstra's algorithm, the next *current* vertex is always the unvisited vertex with smallest cost. By always picking the vertex with smallest cost so far, we can be guaranteed that no other cheaper path exists to this vertex since we always proceed by considering the next cheapest vertex on our search to find cheapest paths in the graph.

The number of edges of any vertex in a simple, undirected graph will always be less than the number of total vertices in the graph. Each vertex becomes the *current* vertex exactly once in the algorithm in step 1. Assume finding the next *current* takes

$O(|V|)$ time. Since this happens $|V|$ times, the complexity of the first step is $O(|V|^2)$ over the course of running the algorithm. The rest of the steps consider those edges adjacent to *current*. Since the number of edges of any vertex in a simple, undirected graph will always be less than $|V|$, the rest of the algorithm runs in less than $O(|V|^2)$ time. So, the complexity of Dijkstra's Algorithm is $O(|V|^2)$ assuming that the first step takes $O(|V|)$ to find the next *current* vertex.

It turns out that selecting the next *current* can be done in $O(\log|V|)$ time if we use a priority queue for our *unvisited* set. Priority queues and their implementation are discussed in Chap. 9. Using a priority queue, Dijkstra's Algorithm will run in $O(|V|\log|V|)$ time.

7.6   Graph Representations

How a graph, $G = (V,E)$, is represented within a program depends on what the program needs to do. Consider the directed graph in Fig. 7.2. The graph itself can be stored in an XML file containing vertices and edges as shown in Sect. 7.6.1. A weighted graph would include a weight attribute for each edge in the graph. In this XML file format the vertexId is used by the edges to indicate which vertices they are attached to. The labels, which appear in Fig. 7.2 are only labels and are not used within the XML file to associate edges with vertices.

7.6.1   A Graph XML File

```
1   <?xml version="1.0" encoding="UTF-8"?>
2   <Graph width="595.80" height="229.20" directed="True" weighted="False">
3     <Vertices>
4       <Vertex vertexId="12" x="343.15" y="156.10" label="10"/>
5       <Vertex vertexId="11" x="246.15" y="161.10" label="9"/>
6       <Vertex vertexId="10" x="288.15" y="58.10" label="0"/>
7       <Vertex vertexId="9" x="374.15" y="58.10" label="1"/>
8       <Vertex vertexId="8" x="135.15" y="156.10" label="6"/>
9       <Vertex vertexId="7" x="49.65" y="83.10" label="2"/>
10      <Vertex vertexId="6" x="167.15" y="83.05" label="3"/>
11      <Vertex vertexId="5" x="121.15" y="19.10" label="8"/>
12      <Vertex vertexId="4" x="419.15" y="204.10" label="11"/>
13      <Vertex vertexId="3" x="426.15" y="87.10" label="4"/>
14      <Vertex vertexId="2" x="546.15" y="96.10" label="5"/>
15      <Vertex vertexId="1" x="546.15" y="210.10" label="7"/>
16      <Vertex vertexId="0" x="485.15" y="161.10" label="12"/>
17    </Vertices>
18    <Edges>
19      <Edge tail="12" head="10"/>
20      <Edge tail="10" head="6"/>
21      <Edge tail="6" head="11"/>
22      <Edge tail="7" head="6"/>
23      <Edge tail="7" head="8"/>
24      <Edge tail="7" head="5"/>
```

```
25      <Edge tail="11" head="12"/>
26      <Edge tail="12" head="4"/>
27      <Edge tail="4" head="0"/>
28      <Edge tail="0" head="2"/>
29      <Edge tail="2" head="1"/>
30      <Edge tail="2" head="3"/>
31      <Edge tail="3" head="9"/>
32      <Edge tail="9" head="10"/>
33      <Edge tail="9" head="12"/>
34    </Edges>
35  </Graph>
```

The *x* and *y* vertex attributes are not required in any graph representation, but to draw a graph it is nice to have location information for the vertices. All this information is stored in the XML file, but what about the three algorithms presented in this chapter? What information is actually needed by each algorithm.

When searching a graph by depth first search vertices are pushed onto a stack as the search proceeds. In that case the vertex information must be stored for use by the search. In this case, since edges have the *vertexId* of their edge endpoints, it would be nice to have a method to quickly lookup vertices within the graph. A map or dictionary from *vertexId* to vertices would be convenient. It makes sense to create a class to hold the vertex information like the class definition of Sect. 7.6.2.

7.6.2   A Vertex Class

```
1  class Vertex:
2      def __init__(self,vertexId,x,y,label):
3          self.vertexId = vertexId
4          self.x = x
5          self.y = y
6          self.label = label
7          self.adjacent = []
8          self.previous = None
```

In this *Vertex* class definition for directed graphs it makes sense to store the edges with the vertex since edges connect vertices. The *adjacent* list can hold the list of adjacent vertices. When running *depth first search* a map of *vertexId* to *Vertex* for each of the vertices in the graph provides the needed information for the algorithm.

When implementing Kruskal's algorithm, a list of edges is the important feature of the graph. The class definition of Sect. 7.6.3 provides a *less-than* method which allows edge objects to be sorted, which is crucial for Kruskal's algorithm. The vertices themselves are not needed by the algorithm. A list of edges and the *partition* data structure suffice for running Kruskal's algorithm.

7.6.3 An Edge Class

```
1   class Edge:
2       def __init__(self,v1,v2,weight=0):
3           self.v1 = v1
4           self.v2 = v2
5           self.weight = weight
6
7       def __lt__(self,other):
8           return self.weight < other.weight
```

Running Dijkstra's algorithm benefits from having both the edge and vertex objects. The weight of each edge is needed by the algorithm so storing the weight in the edge and associating vertices and edges is useful.

There are other potential representations for graphs. For instance, a two-dimensional *matrix* could be used to represent edges between vertices. The rows and columns of the matrix represent the vertices. The weight of an edge from vertex v_i to vertex v_j would be recorded at *matrix[i][j]*. Such a representation is called an *adjacency matrix*. Adjacency matrices tend to be sparsely populated and are not used much in practice due to their wasted space.

The chosen graph representation depends on the work being done. Vertices with adjacency information may be enough. An edge list is enough for the Kruskal's algorithm. Vertex and edge information is required for Dijkstra's algorithm. An adjacency matrix may be required for some situations. As programmers we need to be mindful about wasted space, algorithm needs, and efficiency of our algorithms and the implications that the choice of data representation has on our programs.

7.7 Chapter Summary

Graph notation was covered in this chapter. Several terms and definitions were given for various types of graphs including weighted and directed graphs. The chapter presented three graph theory algorithms: depth first search, Kruskal's algorithm, and Dijkstra's algorithm. Through looking at those algorithms we also explored graph representations and their use in these various algorithms.

After reading this chapter you should know the following.

- A graph is composed of vertices and edges.
- A graph may be directed or undirected.
- A tree is a graph where one path exists between any two vertices.
- A spanning tree is a subset of a graph which includes all the vertices in a connected graph.
- A minimum weighted spanning tree is found by running Kruskal's algorithm.
- Dijkstra's algorithm finds the minimum cost of reaching all vertices in a graph from a given source vertex.
- Choosing a graph representation depends on the work to be done.

- Some typical graph representations are a vertex list with adjacency information, an edge list, or an adjacency matrix.

7.8   Review Questions

Answer these short answer, multiple choice, and true/false questions to test your mastery of the chapter.

1. In the definition of a graph, $G = (V, E)$, what does the V and the E stand for?
2. What is the difference in the definition of E in directed and undirected graphs?
3. In depth first search, what is the purpose of the *visited* set?
4. How is backtracking accomplished in depth first search of a graph? Explain how the backtracking happens.
5. What is a path in a graph and how does that differ from a cycle?
6. What is a tree? For the graph in Fig. 7.2 provide three trees that include the vertices 0, 1, and 10.
7. Why does Kruskal's algorithm never make a mistake when selecting edges for the minimum weighted spanning tree?
8. Why does Dijkstra's algorithm never make a mistake when computing the cost of paths to vertices?
9. What graph representation is best for Kruskal's algorithm? Why?
10. Why is the previous vertex stored by Dijkstra's algorithm? What purpose does the previous vertex have and why is it stored?

7.9   Programming Problems

1. Write a program to find a path between vertex 9 and 29 in the graph shown in Fig. 7.9. Be sure to print the path (i.e. the sequence of vertices) that must be traversed in the path between the two vertices. An XML file describing this graph can be found on the text website.
2. Modify the first problem to find the shortest path between vertices 9 and 29 in terms of the number of edges traversed. In other words, ignore the weights in this problem. Use breadth first search to find this solution.
3. Write the code and perform Dijkstra's algorithm on the graph in Fig. 7.9 to find the minimum cost of visiting all other vertices from vertex 9 of the graph.
4. Write the code and perform Kruskal's algorithm on either the directed graph in Fig. 7.9 or the undirected example found in the chapter. XML files for both graphs can be found on the text website.
5. Not every graph must be represented explicitly. Sometimes it is just as easy to write a function that given a vertex, will compute the vertices that are adjacent to it (that have edges between them). For instance, consider the water bucket

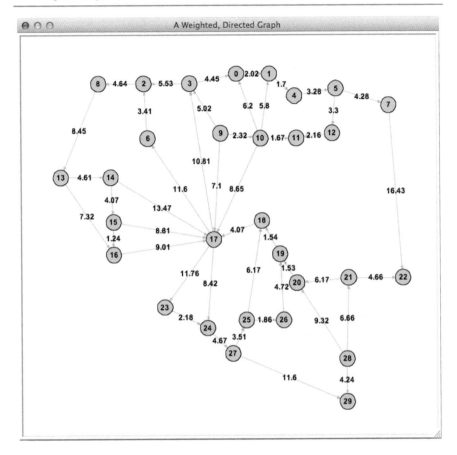

Fig. 7.9 A Sample Weighted, Directed Graph

problem. There are two buckets in this problem: a 3 gallon bucket and a 5 gallon bucket. Your job is to put exactly 4 gallons in the 5 gallon bucket. The rules of the game say that you can completely fill a bucket of water, you can pour one bucket into another, and you can completely dump a bucket out on the ground. You cannot partially fill up a bucket, but you can pour one bucket into another. You are to write a program that tells you how to start with two empty buckets and end with 4 gallons in the 5 gallon bucket.

To complete this problem you must implement depth first search of a graph. The vertices in this problem consist of the state of the problem which is given by the amount of water in each bucket. Along with the search algorithm you must also implement an adjacent function that given a vertex containing this state information will return a list of states that may be adjacent to it. It may be easier to generate some extra adjacent states and then filter out the unreasonable ones before returning the list from adjacent. For instance, it may be easier to generate a state with 6 gallons in the 5 gallon bucket and then throw that state out later by removing states from the list which have more gallons than allowed in that bucket.

The program should print out the list of actions to take to get from no water in either bucket to four gallons in the five gallon pail. The solution may not be the absolute best solution, but it should be a valid solution that is printed when the program is completed.

6. A bipartite graph is a graph where the vertices may be divided into two sets such that no two vertices in the same set have an edge between them. All edges in the graph go between vertices that appear in different sets. A program can test to see if a graph is bipartite by doing a traversal of the graph, like a depth first search, and looking for odd cycles. A graph is bipartite if and only if it does not contain an odd cycle. Write a program that given a graph decides if it is bipartite or not. The program need only print *Yes, it is bipartite*, or *No, it is not bipartite*.

7. Extend the program from the previous exercise to print the set of vertices in each of the two bipartite sets if the graph is found to be bipartite.

Membership Structures

8

In Chap. 5 we covered data structures that support insertion, deletion, membership testing, and iteration. For some applications testing membership may be enough. Iteration and deletion may not be necessary. The classic example is that of a spell checker. Consider the job of a spell checker. A simple one may detect errors in spelling while a more advanced spell checker may suggest alternatives of *correctly* spelled words.

Clearly a spell checker is provided with a large dictionary of words. Using the list of words the spell checker determines whether a word you have is in the dictionary and therefore a correct word. If the word does not appear in the dictionary the word processor or editor may underline the word indicating it may be incorrectly spelled. In some cases the word processor may suggest an alternative, correctly spelled word. In some cases, the word processor may simply correct the misspelling. How do these spell checkers/correctors work? What kind of data structures do they use?

8.1 Chapter Goals

At first glance, a hash set (i.e. a Python dictionary) might seem an appropriate data structure for spell checking. Lookup time within the set could be done in $O(1)$ time. However, the tradeoff is in the size of this hash map. A typical English dictionary might contain over 100,000 words. The amount of space required to store that many words would be quite large.

In this chapter we'll cover two data structures that are designed to test membership within a set. The first, a bloom filter, has significantly smaller space requirements and provides a very fast membership test. The other is a trie (pronounced try) data structure which has features that would not be readily available to a hash set implementation and may take up less space than a hash set.

© Springer International Publishing Switzerland 2015
K.D. Lee and S. Hubbard, *Data Structures and Algorithms with Python*,
Undergraduate Topics in Computer Science, DOI 10.1007/978-3-319-13072-9_8

8.2   Bloom Filters

Bloom filters are named for their creator, Burton Howard Bloom, who originally proposed this idea in 1970. Since then many authors have covered the implementations of bloom filters including Alan Tharp [7]. Wikipedia, while not always the authoritative source, has a very good discussion of bloom filters as well [8].

A bloom filter shares some ideas with hash sets while using considerably less space. A bloom filter is a data structure employing statistical probability to determine if an item is a member of a set of values. Bloom filters are not 100 % accurate. A bloom filter will never report a false negative for set membership, meaning that they will never report that an item doesn't belong to a set when it actually does. However, a bloom filter will sometimes report a false positive. It may report an item is in a set when it is actually not.

Consider the problem of spell checking. A spell checker needs to know if a typed word is correctly typed by looking it up in the dictionary. With a bloom filter, the typed word can be given to the bloom filter which will report that it is or is not a correctly typed word. In some cases it may report a word is correct when it is not.

A bloom filter is an array of bits along with a set of hashing functions. The number of bits in the filter and the number of hashing functions influences the accuracy of the bloom filter. The exact number of bits and hash functions will be discussed later. Consider a bloom filter with 20 bits and 3 independent hash functions. Initially all the bits in the filter are set to 0 as shown in Fig. 8.1.

Consider adding the word *cow* to the bloom filter. Assume that three independent hash functions hash the word cow, modulo 20, to 18, 9, and 3 respectively. The bits at indices 18, 9, and 3 are set to 1 to *remember* that *cow* has been added to the filter as shown in Fig. 8.2.

Now consider adding the word *cat* to the same filter. Assume the hash values from the three hash functions, modulo 20, are 0, 3, and 9. Inserting *cat* into the filter results in setting the bit at index 0 to a 1. The other two were already set by inserting *cow*. Finally, inserting *dog* into the filter results in the bloom filter shown in Fig. 8.3. The hash values for *dog* are 10, 9, and 8.

Fig. 8.1 An Empty Bloom Filter

0	1	2	3	4	5	6	7	8	9	10	11	12	13	14	15	16	17	18	19
0	0	0	1	0	0	0	0	0	1	0	0	0	0	0	0	0	0	1	0

Fig. 8.2 After Inserting *cow* into the Bloom Filter

Fig. 8.3   After Inserting *cow*, *cat*, and *dog* into the Bloom Filter

Looking up an item in a bloom filter requires hashing the value again with the same hash functions generating the indices into the bit array. If the value at all indices in the bit array are one, then the lookup function reports success and otherwise failure.

Consider looking up a value that is not in the bloom filter of Fig. 8.3. If we look up *fox* the three hash function calls return 3, 12, and 18. The digit at indices 3 and 18 is a *1*. However, the digit at index 12 is a 0 and the lookup function reports that *fox* is not in the bloom filter.

Consider looking up the value *rabbit* in the same bloom filter. Hashing *rabbit* with the three hash functions results in values 8, 9, and 18. All three of the digits at these locations within the bloom filter contain a *1* and the bloom filter incorrectly reports that *rabbit* has been added to the filter. This is a false positive and while not desirable, must be acceptable if a bloom filter is to be used.

If a bloom filter is to be useful, it must never report a false negative. From these examples it should be clear that false negatives are impossible. False positives must be kept to a minimum. In fact, it is possible to determine on average how often a bloom filter will report a false positive. The probability calculation depends on three factors: the hashing functions, the number of items added to the bloom filter, and the number of bits used in the bloom filter. The analysis of these factors are covered in the next sections.

8.2.1   The Hashing Functions

Each item added to a bloom filter must be hashed by some number of hash functions which are completely independent of each other. Each hashing function must also be evenly distributed over the range of bit indices in the bit array. This second requirement is true of hashing functions for hash sets and hash tables as well. Uniform distribution is guaranteed by the built-in hash functions of Python and most other languages.

In the examples above, three hashing functions were required. Sometimes the required number of hashing functions can be much higher, depending on the number of items being inserted and the number of bits in the bit array. Creating the required number of independent, uniformly distributed hashing functions might seem like a daunting problem, but it can be solved in at least a couple of ways. Some hashing functions allow a seed value to be provided. In this case, different seed values could be used to create different hashing functions.

Another equally effective way of generating independent hashing functions is to append some known value to the end of each item before it is hashed. For instance, a *0* might be appended to the item before hashing it to get the first hash function. A *1* could be appended to the item before hashing to get the second hash function. Likewise, a *2* might be appended to get the third hash function value. So looking up *rabbit* in the bloom filter is accomplished by first hashing *rabbit0*, *rabbit1*, and *rabbit2* with the same hashing function. Since the hashing function is uniformly distributed, the values returned by the three hashed values will be independent of each other. And, all items with *0* appended will themselves be uniformly distributed. Likewise for items with *1* appended and with *2* appended.

8.2.2   The Bloom Filter Size

It is possible to find the required bloom filter size given a number of items to insert and a desired false positive probability. The probability of any one location within a bloom filter not being set by a hash function while inserting an item is given by the following formula where the filter consists of *m* bits.

$$1 - \frac{1}{m}$$

If the bloom filter uses *k* hash functions, then the probability that a bit in the bit array is not set by any of the hash functions required for inserting an item is given by this formula.

$$\left(1 - \frac{1}{m}\right)^k$$

If *n* items are inserted into the bloom filter then raising this formula to *n* will provide the probability that a bit within the bloom filter's bit array is still a zero after inserting all *n* items. So we have

$$\left(1 - \frac{1}{m}\right)^{nk}$$

So, the probability that a bit in the bloom filter is a *1* after inserting *n* items while using *k* hashing functions is given by this formula.

$$1 - \left(1 - \frac{1}{m}\right)^{nk}$$

Now consider looking up an item that was not added to the bloom filter. The probability that it will report a false positive can be found by computing the likelihood that each location within the bloom filter is a 1 for all *k* hashing functions. This is expressed as follows.

$$p = \left(1 - \left(1 - \frac{1}{m}\right)^{nk}\right)^k$$

This formula contains a sequence that can be approximated using the natural log [8] as

$$p = \left(1 - e^{kn/m}\right)^k$$

Using this formula it is possible to solve for m given an n and desired probability, p, of false positives. The formula is as follows.

$$m = -\frac{n \ln p}{(\ln 2)^2}$$

Finally, solving for k above results in the following formula.

$$k = \frac{m}{n}\ln 2$$

These two formulas tell us how many bits are required in our filter to guarantee a maximum specified rate of false positives. We can also compute the required number of hash functions. For instance, for an English dictionary containing 109,583 words and a desired false postive percentage of no more than 1 % (expressed as 0.01 in the formula) requires a bit array of 1,050,360 bits and seven hashing functions.

The number of bits in this example may seem excessive. However, recall that they are bits. An efficient implementation requires roughly 128 KB of storage. The number of characters in the English dictionary used in these examples totals 935,171. Assuming 1 byte per character, storing all these words would require a minimum of 914 KB. The bloom filter represents quite a savings in space. In addition, during experiments the lookup time using the bloom filter never took longer than 160 μs. The lookup time is bounded by the number and efficiency of the hash functions used to compute the desired values. Assuming that the hash functions are dependent on the length of the string being hashed, then the lookup time is O(lk) where l is given by the length of the item being looked up and k is the number of hash functions.

8.2.3   Drawbacks of a Bloom Filter

Besides the obvious false positive potential, the bloom filter can only report *yes* or *no*. It can't suggest alternatives for items that might be close to being spelled correctly. A bloom filter has no memory of which bits were set by which items so a *yes* or *no* answer is the best we can get with even a *yes* answer not being correct in some circumstances. The next section presents a *Trie* data structure that will not report false positives and can be used to find alternatives for incorrectly spelled words.

8.3   The Trie Datatype

A trie is a data structure that is designed for re*TRIE*val. The data structure is pronounced like the word *try*. A trie is not meant to be used when deleting values from a data structure is required. It is meant only for retrieval of items based on a key value.

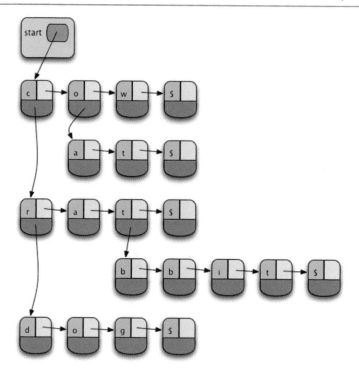

Fig. 8.4 After Inserting *cow*, *cat*, *rat*, *rabbit*, and *dog* into a Trie

Tries are appropriate when key values are made up of more than one unit and when the individual units of a key may overlap with other item keys. In fact, the more overlap the key units have, the more compact the trie data structure.

In the problem of spell checking, words are made up of characters. These characters are the individual units of the keys. Many words overlap in a dictionary like *a*, *an*, and *ant*. A trie may be implemented in several different ways. In this text we'll concentrate on the linked trie which is a series of link lists making up a matrix. Matrix implementations lead to sparsely populated arrays which take up much more room with empty locations. A linked trie has overhead for pointers, but is not sparsely populated.

The trie data structure begins with an empty linked list. Each node in the linked trie list contains three values: a unit of the key (in the spellchecker instance this is a character of the word), a next pointer that points to the next node in the list which would contain some other unit (i.e. character) appearing at the same position within a key (i.e. word), and a follows pointer which points at a node that contains the next unit within the same key. In Fig. 8.4 the follows pointer is in yellow while the next pointer field is in red.

When items are inserted into the trie a sentinel unit is added. In the case of the spell checker, a '$' character is appended to the end of every word. The sentinel is needed because words like *rat* are prefixes to words like *ratchet*. Without the sentinel character it would be unclear whether a word ended or was only a prefix of some other word.

In a trie keys with a common prefix share that prefix and are not repeated. The *next* pointer is used when more than one possible next character is possible. This saves space in the data structure. The trade-off is that the *next* and *follows* pointers take extra space in each node.

8.3.1 The Trie Class

```
 1  class Trie:
 2      def __insert(node,item):
 3          # This is the recursive insert function.
 4
 5      def __contains(node,item):
 6          # This is the recursive membership test.
 7
 8
 9      class TrieNode:
10          def __init__(self,item,next = None, follows = None):
11              self.item = item
12              self.next = next
13              self.follows = follows
14
15      def __init__(self):
16          self.start = None
17
18      def insert(self,item):
19          self.start = Trie.__insert(self.start,item)
20
21      def __contains__(self,item):
22          return Trie.__contains(self.start,item)
```

8.3.2 Inserting into a Trie

Inserting values into a trie can be done either iteratively, with a loop, or recursively. To recursively insert into a trie the *insert* method can call an *__insert* function. It is easier to write the recursive code as a function and not a method of the *Trie* class because the *node* value passed to the function may be *None*. To insert into the trie, the *__insert* function operates as follows.

1. If the key is empty (i.e. no units are left in the key), return *None* as the empty node.
2. If the node is *None* then a new node is created with the next unit of the key and the rest of the key is inserted and added to the *follows* link.

3. If the first unit of the key matches the unit of the current node, then the rest of the key is inserted into the *follows* link of the node.
4. Otherwise, the key is inserted into the *next* link of the node.

Building the trie recursively is simple. However, an iterative version would work just as well. The iterative version would require a loop and a pointer to the current node along with remaining key to insert. The iterative insert algorithm would behave in a similar fashion to the step outlined above but would need to keep track of the previous node as well as the current node so that links could be set correctly.

8.3.3   Membership in a Trie

Checking membership in a trie can also be accomplished recursively. The steps include a base case which might not be completely intuitive at first. The empty key is reported as a member of any trie because it works when checking membership. With the sentinel unit added to the trie, returning *True* for an empty key is completely safe because any real key will at least consist of the sentinel character. In the algorithm outlined here the sentinel is assumed to have already been added to the key. The steps for membership testing are as follows.

1. If the length of the key is 0, then report success by returning *True*.
2. If the node we are looking at is *None* then report failure by returning *False*.
3. If the first unit of the key matches the unit in the current node, then check membership of the rest of the key starting with the *follows* node.
4. Otherwise, check membership of the key starting with the *next* node in the trie.

Again, this code might be implemented iteratively with a while loop keeping track of the current node and the remainder of the key. Either a recursive or iterative implementation will work equally well.

8.3.4   Comparing Tries and Bloom Filters

Bloom filters are clearly faster for testing membership than a trie. However, the trie works acceptably well. While the longest bloom filter lookup time in a simple experiment was $160\,\mu s$, the longest trie lookup was $217\,\mu s$. Of course the trie takes more space, but common prefixes share nodes in a trie saving some space over storing each word distinctly in a data structure, as in a hash set.

For purposes of spell checking a trie has distinct advantages, since spelling alternatives can be easily found. Common typographical errors fall into one of four categories.

- Transposition of characters like *teh* instead of *the*
- Dropped characters like *thei* instead of *their*
- Extra characters like *thre* instead of *the*
- Incorrect characters like *thare* instead of *there*

If in searching in a trie a word is not found, these alternatives can also be searched for to find a selection of alternative spellings. What's more, these alternative spellings can be searched in parallel in a trie to quickly put together a list of alternatives. A bloom filter cannot be used to find alternative spellings since that information is lost once entered into the filter. Of course, a trie will never report a false positive either as is possible with a bloom filter.

8.4 Chapter Summary

Tries and bloom filters are two data structures for testing membership. Bloom filters are relatively small and will produce false positives some percentage of the time. Tries are larger, don't produce false positives, and can be used to find alternative key values that *are close* to the key being sought. While either data structure will work for spell checking, spelling correction would be aided by a trie while a bloom filter would not help.

As far as efficiency goes, bloom filters more efficiently test set membership, subject to the false positives that are sometimes produced. However, a trie also operates efficiently while also taking more space than a bloom filter. Both the bloom filter and the trie tested membership of words in the dictionary in microseconds. The bloom filter's worst time was $160\,\mu s$ while the trie's worst time was $217\,\mu s$ for the informal test performed on both.

Size requirements are also a concern of course. The example dictionary used in the development of both the bloom filter and the trie in this chapter contained 109,583 words. The bloom filter for this dictionary of words was approximately 128 KB in size. Assuming that the *next* and *follows* pointers take 4 bytes each and the key units (i.e. word characters) take 1 byte each, the size of the trie is roughly 3.1 MB in size. While the bloom filter is much smaller than the trie, both are well within the limits of what computers are capable of storing.

8.5 Review Questions

Answer these short answer, multiple choice, and true/false questions to test your mastery of the chapter.

1. Which datatype, the trie or the bloom filter, is susceptible to false positives?
2. What is a false positive in this context?

3. A bloom filter requires more or less storage than a trie?
4. When spell checking, which data type can be used for spelling correction?
5. How can you generate more than one hashing function for use in a bloom filter?
6. Add the words "a", "an", "ant", "bat", and "batter" to a trie. Draw the trie data structure showing its structure after inserting the words in the order given here.
7. Why is a sentinel needed in a trie?
8. Why is a sentinel not needed in a bloom filter?
9. What must be true of keys to be able to store them in a trie?
10. Which datatype, *trie* or *bloom filter*, is more efficient in terms of space? Which is more efficient in terms of speed?

8.6   Programming Problems

1. Go to the text website and download the dictionary of words. Build a bloom filter for this list of words and use it to spellcheck the declaration of independence, printing all the misspelled words to the screen.
2. Go to the text website and download the dictionary of words. Build a trie datatype for this list of words and use it to spellcheck the declaration of independence, printing all misspelled words to the screen.
3. Create a trie as in the previous exercise, but also print suggested replacements for all misspelled words. This is a tough assignment. Suggested replacements should not differ from the original in more than one of the ways suggested in the chapter.

Heaps

9

The word *heap* is used in a couple of different contexts in Computer Science. A heap sometimes refers to an area of memory used for dynamic (i.e. run-time) memory allocation. Another meaning, and the topic of this chapter, is a data structure that is conceptually a complete binary tree. Heaps are used in implementing priority queues, the heapsort algorithm, and some graph algorithms. Heaps are somewhat like binary search trees in that they maintain an ordering of the items within the tree. However, a heap does not maintain a complete ordering of its items. This has some implications for how a heap may be used.

9.1 Chapter Goals

By the end of this chapter you should be able to answer the following questions:

- What is a heap and how is it used?
- What is the computational complexity of adding and deleting items from a heap?
- Would you use a heap to look up items or not?
- When would you use a heap?
- In the heapsort algorithm, why is it advantageous to construct a largest-on-top heap?

9.2 Key Ideas

To understand heaps we'll start with a definition. A *largest-on-top heap* is a complete ordered tree such that every node is ≥ all of its children (if it has any). An example will help illustrate this definition. Conceptually, a heap is a tree that is full on all levels except possibly the lowest level which is filled in from left to right. It takes the general shape shown in Fig. 9.1.

© Springer International Publishing Switzerland 2015
K.D. Lee and S. Hubbard, *Data Structures and Algorithms with Python*,
Undergraduate Topics in Computer Science, DOI 10.1007/978-3-319-13072-9_9

Fig. 9.1 Heap Shape

Conceptually a heap is a tree, but heaps are generally not stored as trees. A *complete* tree is a tree that is full on all levels except the lowest level which is filled in from left to right. Because heaps are complete trees, they may be stored in an array. An example will help in understanding heaps and the complete property better. Consider a largest on top heap with the root node stored at index 0 in an array. Conceptually, Fig. 9.2 is a heap containing integers.

The data in this conceptual version is stored in an array by traversing the tree level by level starting from the root node to the heap. The conceptual heap in Fig. 9.2 would be stored in an array as organized in Fig. 9.3.

There are two properties that a heap exhibits. They are:

- *Heap Structure Property*: The elements of the heap form a complete ordered tree.
- *Heap Order Property*: Every parent ≥ all children (including all descendants).

The heap in Fig. 9.2 maintains these two properties. The array implementation of this heap in Fig. 9.3 also maintains these properties. To see how the properties are maintained in the array implementation we need to be able to compute the location

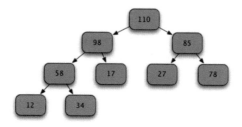

Fig. 9.2 Sample Heap

Fig. 9.3 Heap Organization

of children and parents. The children of any element of the array can be calculated from the index of the parent.

$$leftChildIndex = 2 * parentIndex + 1$$

$$rightChildIndex = 2 * parentIndex + 2$$

Using these formulae on Fig. 9.3 we can see that the children of the root node (i.e. index 0) are 98 (at index 1) and 85 (at index 2). Likewise, the children of 85 are located at index 5 and 6 which are the values 27 and 78, which we can verify are the same children as in the conceptual model.

Of course, not every node has a child or even two children. If the computed *leftChildIndex* or *rightChildIndex* are greater than or equal to the number of values in the heap, then the node in question is a leaf node.

It is also possible to go in the other direction. Given a child's index, we can discover where the parent is located.

$$parentIndex = (childIndex - 1)//2$$

The // in the previous formula represents integer division. It means that the result is always an integer. If there were a fractional part we round down to the next lower integer. So, the index of the parent of the 34 in Fig. 9.3 is computed as

$$parentIndex = (8 - 1)//2 = 3$$

Consulting the conceptual model in Fig. 9.2, we see that the value at index 3 in the array, the 58, is indeed the parent of the 34. It should be noted that not every node in a heap has a parent. In particular, the root node, at index 0, does not have a parent. All other nodes in a heap have parents.

9.3   Building a Heap

Now that we've seen what a heap looks like, we'll investigate building a heap. Heaps can be built either largest on top or smallest on top. We'll build a largest on top heap. A *Heap* class will encapsulate the data and methods needed to build a heap. Heap objects contain a list and count of the number of items currently stored in the heap. We'll call this count the *size* of the heap. To encapsulate the data we'll want a method that will take a sequence of values and build a heap from it. We'll call this method *buildFrom*. A private method will also be useful. The *buildFrom* method will call the _*siftUpFrom* to get each successive element of the sequence into its correct position within the heap.

9.3.1   The buildFrom Method

```
1    def buildFrom(self, aSequence):
2            '''aSequence is an instance of a sequence collection which
3            understands the comparison operators. The elements of
4            aSequence are copied into the heap and ordered to build
5            a heap. '''
```

```
6  def __siftUpFrom(self, childIndex):
7      '''childIndex is the index of a node in the heap. This method sifts
8      that node up as far as necessary to ensure that the path to the root
9      satisfies the heap condition. '''
```

The sequence of values passed to the *buildFrom* method will be copied into the heap. Then, each subsequent value in the list will be sifted up into its final location in the heap. Consider the list of values [71, 15, 36, 57, 101]. We'll trace this through showing the resulting heap at each stage. To begin the list is copied into the heap object in the order given here. Then *siftUpFrom* is called on each subsequent element. To begin, *siftUpFrom* is called on the second element, the 57 in this case. Calling *siftUpFrom* on the root of the heap would have no effect. Normally, the parent index of the node is computed. The parent will already be greater than the other child (if there is one). If the value at the current child index is greater than the value at the parent index, then the two are swapped and the process repeats. This process repeats as many times as are necessary: either until the root node is reached (i.e. index 0 of the list) or until the new node is in the proper location to maintain the heap property.

The first time some movement occurs is when 57 is added to the heap. The 57 is swapped with the 15 to arrive at its final location resulting in the heap in Fig. 9.4.

The first four elements of the list now make up a heap. But, the 101 is not in its final position. We need to sift it up in the heap to get it to its final position. Looking at the conceptual view of the heap (i.e. the tree), you can see that 101 is a child of the node containing 57. Clearly, that violates the heap property. So, 101 and 57 are swapped to sift the 101 up as shown in Fig. 9.5.

Without looking at the conceptual model you can still compute the parent of the node containing 101 in part one of Fig. 9.5. When 101 was at index 4 in the list, the parent index was computered as follows.

$$parentIndex = (4 - 1)//2 = 1$$

So, the 101 is compared to the 57 at index 1 in part one above. Then, the swap is made because 101 is greater than 57 in part two. However, the 101 is still not in the

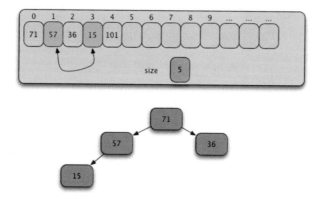

Fig. 9.4 Building a Heap Part One

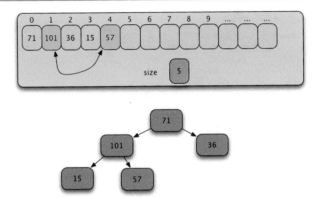

Fig. 9.5 Building a Heap Part Two

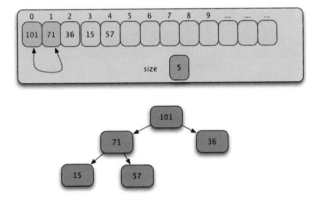

Fig. 9.6 Building a Heap Part Three

right place.

$$parentIndex = (1-1)//2 = 0$$

We compare 101 with the 71 and swap the two elements. This is the last iteration of sifting up because 101 has now reached the root (i.e. index 0) of the heap. After swapping the two values we get the heap in Fig. 9.6.

9.4 The Heapsort Algorithm Version 1

Heaps have two basic operations. You can add a value to a heap. You can also delete, and retrieve, the maximum value from a heap if the heap is a largest on top heap. Using these two operations, or variations of them, we can devise a sorting algorithm by building a heap with a list of values and then removing the values one by one in descending order. We'll call these two parts of the algorithm phase I and phase II. To implement phase I we'll need one new method in our Heap class.

9.4.1 The addToHeap Method

```
1   def addToHeap(self,newObject):
2       '''If the heap is full, double its current capacity.
3        Add the newObject to the heap, maintaining it as a
4        heap of the same type.  Answer newObject.'''
```

This new method can use the __siftUpFrom private method to get the new element to its final destination within the heap. Version 1 of Phase I calls *addToHeap n* times. This results in O(n log n) complexity. The specific steps of phase I include:

1. double the capacity of the heap if necessary.
2. data[size] = newObject
3. __siftUpFrom(size)
4. size += 1.

As you can see, __siftUpFrom will be called *n* times, once for each element of the heap. Each time __siftUpFrom is called, the heap will have grown by 1 element. Consider the heap in Fig. 9.7 just before pass #9.

We are about to sift the 98 up to its rightful location within the heap. Conceptually we have the picture of the heap shown in Fig. 9.8.

To move the 98 to the correct location we must compute the parent index from the child indices as shown in Table 9.1.

Fig. 9.7 Adding 98 to the Heap

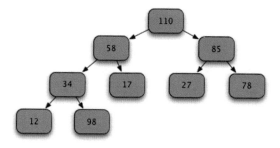

Fig. 9.8 Conceptual View While Adding 98 to the Heap

Table 9.1 Child and Parent Indices

childIndex	parentIndex = (childIndex − 1)//2
8	3 (swap)
3	1 (swap)
1	0 (stop)

Fig. 9.9 Heap After Moving 98 to Correct Location

Sifting up the 98 in the heap's list results in two swaps before it reaches its final location. Figure 9.9 shows the 98 is swapped with the 34 at index 3. Then it is swapped again with the 58 at index 1. At this point no more swaps are done because 101 is greater than 98. The 98 has reached its proper position within the heap.

9.5 Analysis of Version 1 Phase I

The approach taken in version 1 of phase I is slow as we shall see. Consider a perfect complete binary tree. One which is completely full on all levels with h levels as shown in Fig. 9.10.

Consider the relationship between the number of levels and the number of items in the heap as shown in Table 9.2.

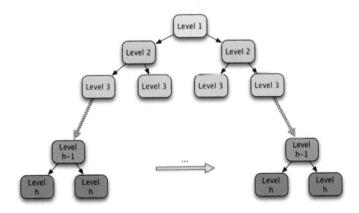

Fig. 9.10 A Perfect Binary Tree

Table 9.2 Heap levels versus Heap size

Level	# of nodes at level
1	$(2^{1-1} = 1)$
2	$(2^{2-1} = 2)$
3	$(2^{3-1} = 4)$
...	...
h	(2^{h-1})

For a heap with n items in it, the value of n can be computed by adding up all the nodes at each level in the heap's tree. To simplify our argument we'll assume that the heap is a full binary tree.

$$n = 1 + 2^1 + 2^2 + \cdots + 2^{h-1} \text{ for some } h$$

This is the sum of a geometric sequence. The sum of a geometric sequence can be computed as follows.

$$1 + r + r^2 + r^3 + \cdots + r^m = \frac{r^{m+1} - 1}{r - 1} \text{ if } r \neq 1$$

Applying this formula to our equation above the number of nodes in a complete binary tree (i.e. a full binary heap) with h levels is given by this formula below.

$$n = 1 + 2^1 + 2^2 + \cdots + 2^{h-1} = \frac{2^h - 1}{2 - 1} = 2^h - 1$$

This implies that $n + 1 = 2^h$. We can solve this equation for h. Doing so we get

$$h = \lceil log_2(n + 1) \rceil$$

The brackets above are the ceiling operator and it simply means that we should round up to the next highest integer. Rounding up takes into account that not every heap tree is completely full so there may be some values of n that won't give us an integer for h if we didn't round up. The following inequality will be useful in determining the computational complexity of phase I of the heapsort algorithm.

$$log_2 I \leq \lceil log_2(I + 1) \rceil \leq log_2 I + 1 \ \forall I \geq 2$$

So far we have been able to determine that the height of a complete binary tree (i.e. the number of levels) is equivalent to the ceiling of the log, base 2, of the number of elements in the tree +1. Phase I of our algorithm appends each value to the end of the list where it is sifted up to its final location within the heap. Since sifting up will go through at most h levels and since the heap grows by one each time, the following summation describes an upper limit of a value that is proportional to the amount of work that must be done in Phase I.

$$\sum_{I=2}^{N} \lceil log_2(I + 1) \rceil$$

But applying the inequality presented above we have the following. The $N - 1$ term comes from the last summation from 2 to N. From the inequality above there are $N - 1$ ones that are a part of the summation. These can be factored out as $N - 1$.

$$\sum_{I=2}^{N} log_2 I \leq \sum_{I=2}^{N} \lceil log_2(I+1) \rceil \leq \sum_{I=2}^{N} (log_2 I + 1) = \left(\sum_{I=2}^{N} log_2 I\right) + (N - 1)$$

We now have a lower and upper bound for our sum. The same summation appears in both the lower and upper bound. But what does $\sum_{I=2}^{N} log_2 I$ equal? The following equivalences will help in determining this summation.

$$y = log_2 x \Leftrightarrow 2^y = x \Leftrightarrow y \, ln \, 2 = ln \, x \Leftrightarrow log_2 x = y = \frac{1}{ln \, 2} ln \, x$$

To determine what the summation above is equal to we can establish a couple of inequalities that bound the sum from above and below. In Fig. 9.11, the summation can be visualized as the green area. The first term in the summation would provide the first green rectangle, the second green rectangle corresponds to the second term in the summation and so on. The black line in the figure is the plot of the log base 2 of x. Clearly the area covered by the green rectangles is bigger than the area under

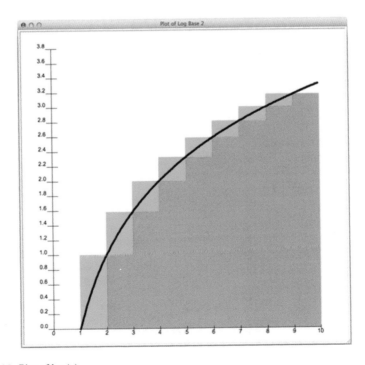

Fig. 9.11 Plot of log(n)

the curve of the log. The area under the curve can be found by taking the definite integral from 1 to N, which in the picture is 9 but in general would be N. From this we get the following inequality.

$$\int_1^N log_2\, x\, dx \le \sum_{I=2}^N log_2\, I$$

Now, consider shifting the entire green area to the right by one. In the figure above, that's the orange area. The orange and green areas are exactly the same size. The orange is just shifted right by one. Now look at the plot of the log base 2 of x. The area below the curve is now clearly bigger than the orange area. If we imagine this graph going out to N, then we'll have to include $N+1$ in our definite integral (since we shifted the orange area to the right). So we get the following inequality.

$$\sum_{I=2}^N log_2\, I \le \int_2^{N+1} log_2\, x\, dx$$

Putting the two inequalities together we have a lower and upper bound for our summation.

$$\int_1^N log_2\, x\, dx \le \sum_{I=2}^N log_2\, I \le \int_2^{N+1} log_2\, x\, dx$$

It is easier to integrate using natural log so we'll rewrite the integral as follows.

$$\int_1^N log_2\, x\, dx = \int_1^N \frac{1}{ln\, 2} ln\, x\, dx$$

The constant term in the integral can be factored out. So we'll look at the following integral.

$$\int_1^N ln\, x\, dx$$

We can find the result of the definite integral that appears above by doing integration by parts. The integration by parts rule is as follows.

$$\int_a^b u\, dv = uv\Big|_a^b - \int_a^b v\, du$$

Applying this to our integral we have the following

$$u = \ln x \text{ and } dv = dx$$

$$du = \frac{1}{x}dx \text{ and } v = x$$

$$\Rightarrow \int_1^N \ln x \, dx = x \ln x \Big|_1^N - \int_1^N x \frac{1}{x}dx$$

$$= x \ln x \Big|_1^N - \int_1^N 1 dx = x \ln x \Big|_1^N - x \Big|_1^N$$

$$= N \ln N - (N - 1)$$

We have proved that the lower bound is proportional to $N \log N$. Similarly, we could prove that the upper bound is also proportional to $N \log N$. Therefore the work done by inserting N elements into a heap using the __siftUpFrom method is $\theta(N \log N)$. We can do better! If the values in the heap were in the correct order we could achieve $O(N)$ complexity. Using a different approach we will be able to achieve $O(N)$ complexity in all cases.

9.6   Phase II

Later, we will investigate how to improve the performance of phase I. Recall that phase I of the heapsort algorithm builds a heap from a list of values. Phase II takes the elements out of the heap, one at a time, and places them in a list. To save space, the same list that was used for the heap may be used for the list of values to be returned. Each pass of phase II takes one item from the list and places it where it belongs and the size of the heap is decremented by one. The key operation is the __siftDownFromTo method (Fig. 9.12).

9.6.1   The siftDownFromTo Method

```
1   def __siftDownFromTo(self, fromIndex, lastIndex):
2           '''fromIndex is the index of an element in the heap.
3           Pre: data[fromIndex..lastIndex] satisfies the heap condition,
4           except perhaps for the element data[fromIndex].
5           Post:  That element is sifted down as far as neccessary to
6           maintain the heap structure for data[fromIndex..lastIndex].'''
```

To illustrate this method, let's take our small heap example and start extracting the values from it. Consider the heap in Fig. 9.13 where both the conceptual view and the organization of that heap are shown. 101 is at the top of the heap and is also the largest value.

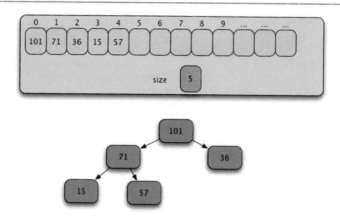

Fig. 9.12 Just Before Phase II

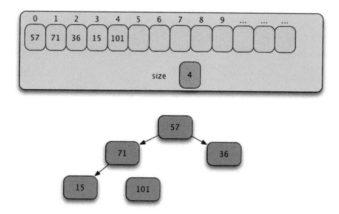

Fig. 9.13 After Swapping First and Last Values

If sorted, the 101 would go at the end of the list. Since there are 5 elements in the heap, we'll swap the 57 and the 101. By doing this, 101 is at its final position within a sorted list. The 57 is not in the correct location within the heap. So, we call the __siftDownFromTo method to sift the 57 down from the 0 position within the heap to at most the *size-1* location.

The __siftDownFromTo method does its work and swaps the 57 with the bigger of the two children, the 71. The 57 does not need to sift down any further since it is bigger than the 15. So we have the view of the heap in Fig. 9.14 after the first pass of Phase II.

The second pass of Phase II swaps the 15 and the 71, moving the 71 to its final location in the sorted list. It then sifts the 15 down to its rightful location within the heap, producing the picture you see in Fig. 9.15.

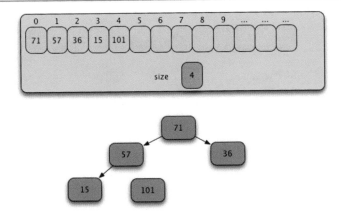

Fig. 9.14 After the First Pass of Phase II

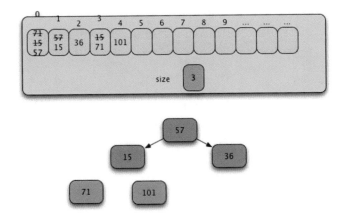

Fig. 9.15 After the Second Pass of Phase II

During the third pass of Phase II the 57 is put in its final location and swapped with the 36 to make room for it. Although __*siftDownFromTo* is called, no movement of values within the heap occurs because the 36 is at the top and is the largest value in the heap (Fig. 9.16).

During the fourth and final pass, the 36 is swapped with the 15. No call to **_sift-DownFromTo** is necessary this time since the heap is only of size 1 after the swap. Since a heap of size 1 is already sorted and in the right place, we can decrement the size to 0. The list is now sorted in place without using an additional array as shown in Fig. 9.17.

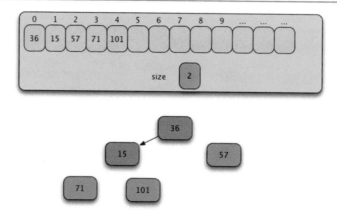

Fig. 9.16 After the Third Pass of Phase II

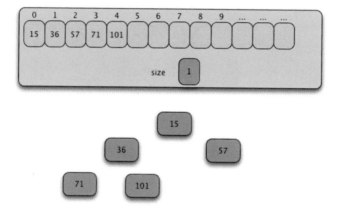

Fig. 9.17 After the Fourth and Final Pass of Phase II

9.7   Analysis of Phase II

The work of Phase II is in the calls to the *__siftDownFromTo* method which is called
$N - 1$ times. Each call must sift down an element in a tree that shrinks by one element
each time. Earlier in this chapter we did the analysis to determine that the amount of
work in the average and worst case is proportional to

$$\sum_{I=2}^{N} \lceil log_2(I + 1) \rceil \equiv \theta(NlogN)$$

The best case of Phase II would require that all values in the heap are identical. In
that case the computational complexity would be O(N) since the values would never

sift down. This best case scenario brings up a good point. If we could limit how far down the value is sifted, we might be able to speed up Phase I. That's the topic or our next section.

9.8 The Heapsort Algorithm Version 2

In version one, the heapsort algorithm attained O(N log N) complexity during Phase I and Phase II. In version two, we will be able to speed up Phase I of the heapsort algorithm up to O(N) complexity. We do this by limiting how far each newly inserted value must be sifted down. The idea is pretty simple, but yet a powerful technique. Rather than inserting each element at the top of the heap, we'll build the heap, or heaps, from the bottom up. This means that we'll approach the building of our heap by starting at the end of the list rather than the beginning. An example will help make this more clear. Consider the list of values in Fig. 9.18 that we wish to sort using heapsort.

Rather than starting from the first element of the list, we'll start from the other end of the list. There is no need to start with the last element as we will see. We need to pick a node that is a parent of some node in the tree. Since the final heap is a binary heap, the property we have is that half the nodes of the tree are leaf nodes and cannot be parents of any node within the heap. We can compute the first parent index as follows.

$$parentIndex = (size - 2)//2$$

The size above is the size of the list to be sorted. Note that because the list has indices 0 to size-1 we must subtract two to compute the proper parentIndex in all cases. In this case, that *parentIndex* is 2. We need to start with index 2 in the list to start building our heaps from the bottom up. Index 2 will be the first *parent* and we'll sift it down as far as necessary.

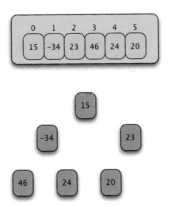

Fig. 9.18 A List to be Heapsorted

$$childIndex1 = 2 * parentIndex + 1 = 2 * 2 + 1 = 5$$
$$childIndex2 = 2 * parentIndex + 2 = 2 * 2 + 2 = 6$$

Since the second of these indices is beyond the last index of the list, the __siftDown-FromTo method will not consider childIndex2. After considering the 20 and the 23 we see that those two nodes do in fact form a heap as shown in Fig. 9.19. We will show this in the following figures by joining them with an arrow. We now have 5 heaps, one less than we started with. More importantly, we only had to sift the parent down one position at the most.

Next, we move back one more in the list to index 1. We call __siftDownFromTo specifying to start from this node. Doing so causes the sift down method to pick the larger of the two children to swap with, forming a heap out of the three values −34, 46, and 24 as a result. This is depicted in Fig. 9.20.

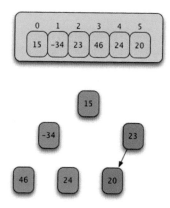

Fig. 9.19 After Forming a Sub-Heap

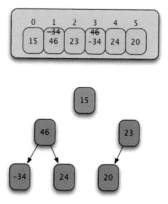

Fig. 9.20 After Forming a Second Sub-Heap

Finally, we move backward in the list one more element to index 0. This time we only need to look at the values of the two children because they will already be the largest values in their respective heaps. Calling __*siftDownFromTo* on the first element of the list will pick the maximum value from 15, 46, and 23 and will swap the 15 with that value resulting in the situation in Fig. 9.21.

This doesn't form a complete heap yet. We still need to move the 15 down again and __*siftDownFromTo* takes care of moving the 15 to the bottom of the heap as shown in Fig. 9.22.

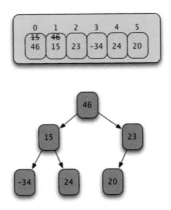

Fig. 9.21 Sifting the 15 Down

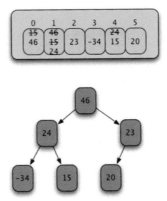

Fig. 9.22 The Final Heap using Version 2 of Phase I

9.9   Analysis of Heapsort Version 2

Recall that Phase II is when the values are in a heap and extracted one at a time to form the sorted list. Version 2 Phase II of the heapsort algorithm is identical to version 1 and has the same complexity, O(N log N).

Version 2 Phase I on the other hand has changed from a top down approach to building the heap in version 1 to building the heap from the bottom up in version 2. We claimed that the complexity of this new phase I is O(N) where N is the number of nodes in the list. Stated more formally we have this claim. *For a perfect binary tree of height h, containing (2^h-1) nodes, the sums of the lengths of its maximum comparison paths is $(2^h - 1-h)$.*

Consider binary heaps of heights 1, 2, etc. up to height h. From the example for version 2 of the algorithm it should be clear the maximum path length for any call to __siftDownFromTo will be determined as shown in Table 9.3).

Notice that (2^{h-1}) represents half the nodes in the final heap (the leaf nodes) and that the max path length for half the nodes in the heap will be 0. It is this observation that leads to a more efficient algorithm for building a heap from the bottom up. If we could add up all these maximum path lengths, then we would have an upper bound for the amount of work to be done during phase I of version 2 of this algorithm.

$$S = 1 * (h - 1) + 2 * (h - 2) + 2^2 * (h - 3) + \cdots + 2^{h-3} * 2 + 2^{h-2} * 1$$

The value S would be an upper bound of the work to be done, the sum of the maximum path lengths. We can eliminate most of the terms in this sum with a little manipulation of the formula. The value of S could be computed as $2S - S = S$. Using this formula we can write it as

$$S = 2 * S - S = 2 * (h - 1) + 2^2 * (h - 2) + \cdots + 2^{h-2} * 2 + 2^{h-1} * 1$$
$$- [(h - 1) + 2 * (h - 2) + 2^2 * (h - 3) + \cdots + 2^{h-2} * 1]$$

If we line up the terms in the equation above (as they are lined up right now), we can subtract like terms. In the first like term we see $h - 1 - (h - 2)$. This simplifies to

Table 9.3 Maximum path length for __siftDownFromTo

Level	Max path length	# of nodes at level
1	$h - 1$	1
2	$h - 2$	2
3	$h - 3$	4
...	...	...
$h - 2$	2	2^{h-3}
$h - 1$	1	2^{h-2}
h	0	2^{h-1}

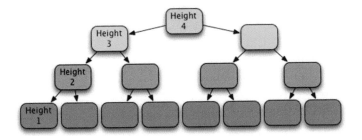

Fig. 9.23 A Binary Heap of Height 4

$h - h - 1 + 2 = 1$. Similarly, the other like terms simplify so we end up with the following formula for S.

$$S = 2 * S - S = 2 + 2^2 + \cdots + 2^{h-2} + 2^{h-1} - (h - 1)$$
$$= 1 + 2 + 2^2 + \cdots + 2^{h-2} + 2^{h-1} - h$$
$$= 2^h - 1 - h \equiv O(N) \ where \ N = 2^h - 1 \ nodes.$$

In the last step of the simplification above we have the sum of the first $h-1$ powers of 2, also known as the sum of a geometric sequence. This sum is equal to 2 raised to the h power, minus one. This can be proven with a simple proof by induction. So, we have just proved that version 2 of phase I is $O(N)$. Phase II is still $O(N \log N)$ so the overall complexity of heap sort is $O(N \log N)$.

Consider a binary heap of height 4 (Fig. 9.23).

In such a heap, using the sift down method the first sifting occurs at height 2 in the tree where we have four nodes that may travel down one level in the tree. At height 3 we have two nodes that may travel down two levels. Finally, the root node may travel down three levels. We have the following sum of maximum path lengths.

$$1 + 1 + 1 + 1 + 2 + 2 + 3 =$$
$$11 =$$
$$2^4 - 1 - 4 =$$
$$2^h - 1 - h$$

9.10   Comparison to Other Sorting Algorithms

The heapsort algorithm operates in $O(N \log N)$ time, the same complexity as the quicksort algorithm. A key difference is in the movement of individual values. In quicksort, values are always moved toward their final location. Heapsort moves values first to form a heap, then moves them again to arrive at their final location

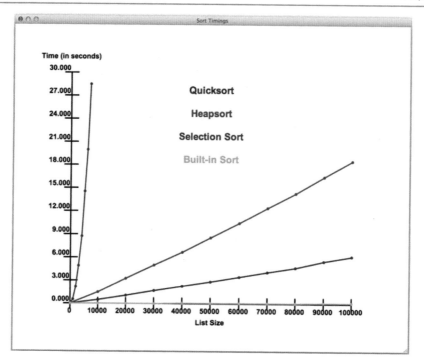

Fig. 9.24 Comparison of Several Sorting Algorithms

within a sorted list. Quicksort is more efficient than heapsort even though they have the same computational complexity.

Examining Fig. 9.24 we see selection sort operating with $\theta(N^2)$ complexity, which is not acceptable except for very short lists. The quicksort algorithm behaves more favorably than the heapsort algorithm as is expected. The built-in sort, which is quicksort implemented in C, runs the fastest, due to being implemented in C.

9.11   Chapter Summary

This chapter introduced heaps and the heapsort algorithm. Building a heap can be done efficiently in O(N) time complexity. A heap guarantees the top element will be either the biggest or smallest element of an ordered collection of values. Using this principle we can implement many algorithms and datatypes using heaps. The heapsort algorithm was presented in this chapter as one example of a use for heaps.

Heaps are not good for looking up values. Looking up a value in a heap would take O(N) time and would be no better than linear search of a list for a value. This is because there is no ordering of the elements within a heap except that the largest (or smallest) value is on top. You cannot determine where in a heap a value is located without searching the entire heap, unless it happens to be equal or greater to the largest value and you have a largest on top heap. Likewise, if you have a smallest on top heap and are looking for a value, you would have to look at all values unless the value you are searching for is equal or smaller than the smallest value.

Commonly, heaps are used to implement priority queues where the elements of a queue are ordered according to some kind of priority value. An element can be added to an existing heap in O(log N) time. An element can be removed from a heap in O(log N) time as well. This makes a heap the logical choice for a priority queue implementation. Priority queues are useful in message passing frameworks and especially in some graph algorithms and heuristic search algorithms.

9.12   Review Questions

Answer these short answer, multiple choice, and true/false questions to test your mastery of the chapter.

1. State the heap property for a largest on top heap.
2. When removing a value from a heap, which value are you likely to remove? Why?
3. After removing a value from a heap, what steps do you have to take to ensure you still have a heap?
4. If you had a heap of height 6, what would be the total maximum travel distance for all nodes in the heap as you built it using version 2, phase I of the heapsort algorithm.
5. Use __siftUpFrom() from version 1 of the heapsort algorithm, adding a new element to a growing heap on each pass to construct a largest-on-top heap from the following integers:

    70, 30, 25, 90, 15, 85, 35, 87, 100

   Sketch a new picture of the binary heap each time the structure changes.
6. Use __siftDownFromTo() from version 2 of the heapsort algorithm on the same data as in the previous problem, sketching a new picture of the binary tree each time the structure changes.
7. Using the final heap from problem 6, execute phase II version 2 of the heapsort algorithm, using __siftDownFromTo to sort the data in increasing order. Sketch a new picture of the binary tree each time the structure changes.
8. Redo problems 6 and 7, this time showing the data in arrays (i.e. lists) with starting index 0, rather than drawing the tree structures. Show the new values of the structure after each pass. Use the following data:

    37, 45, 91, 5, 57, 74, 83, 45, 99

9. Why does heapsort operate less efficiently than quicksort?
10. When is a heap commonly used?

9.13 Programming Problems

1. Implement version 2 of the heapsort algorithm. Run your own tests using heapsort and quicksort to compare the execution time of the two sorting algorithms. Output your data in the plot format and plot your data using the PlotData.py program provided on the text website.

2. Implement version 1 and version 2 of the program and compare the execution times of the two heapsort variations. Gather experimental data in the XML format accepted by the PlotData.py program and plot that data to see the difference between using version 1 and version 2 of the heap sort algorithm.

3. Implement a smallest on top heap and use it in implementing a priority queue. A priority queue has enqueue and dequeue methods. When enqueueing an item on a priority queue, a priority is provided. Elements enqueued on the queue include both the data item and the priority. Write a test program to test your priority queue data structure.

4. Use the priority queue from the last exercise to implement Dijkstra's algorithm from Chap. 7. The priority queue implementation of Dijkstra's algorithm is more efficient. The priority of each element is the cost so far of each vertex added to the priority queue. By dequeueing from the priority queue we automatically get the next lowest cost vertex from the queue without searching, resulting in a $O(|V|\log|V|)$ complexity instead of $O(|V|^2)$.

5. Use the heapsort algorithm, either version 1 or version 2, to implement Kruskal's algorithm from Chap. 7. Use one of the sample graph XML files found on the text website as your input data to test your program.

Balanced Binary Search Trees

10

In Chap. 6 binary search trees were defined along with a recursive insert algorithm. The discussion of binary search trees pointed out they have problems in some cases. Binary search trees can become unbalanced, actually quite often. When a tree is unbalanced the complexity of insert, delete, and lookup operations can get as bad as $\Theta(n)$. This problem with unbalanced binary search trees was the motivation for the development of height-balanced AVL trees by G.M. Adelson-Velskii and E.M. Landis, two Soviet computer scientists, in 1962. AVL trees were named for these two inventors. Their paper on AVL trees [1] described the first algorithm for maintaining balanced binary search trees.

Balanced binary search trees provide $\Theta(log\ n)$ insert, delete, and lookup operations. In addition, a balanced binary search tree maintains its items in sorted order. An infix traversal of a binary search tree will yield its items in ascending order and this traversal can be accomplished in $\Theta(n)$ time assuming the tree is already built.

The HashSet and HashMap classes provide very efficient insert, delete, and lookup operations as well, more efficient than the corresponding binary search tree operations. Heaps also provide $\Theta(log\ n)$ insert and delete operations. But neither hash tables nor heaps maintain their elements as an ordered sequence. If you want to perform many insert and delete operations and need to iterate over a sequence in ascending or descending order, perhaps many times, then a balanced binary search tree data structure may be more appropriate.

10.1 Chapter Goals

This chapter describes why binary search trees can become unbalanced. Then it goes on to describe several implementations of two types of height-balanced trees, AVL trees and splay trees. By the end of this chapter you should be able to implement your own AVL or splay tree datatype, with either iteratively or recursively implemented operations.

© Springer International Publishing Switzerland 2015

K.D. Lee and S. Hubbard, *Data Structures and Algorithms with Python*,

Undergraduate Topics in Computer Science, DOI 10.1007/978-3-319-13072-9_10

10.2   Binary Search Trees

A binary search tree comes in handy when a large number of insert, delete, and lookup operations are required by an application while at times it is necessary to traverse the items in ascending or descending order. Consider a website like Wikipedia that provides access to a large set of online materials. Imagine the designers of the website want to keep a log of all the users that have accessed the website within the last hour. The website might operate as follows.

- Each visitor accesses the website with a unique cookie.
- When a visitor accesses the site their cookie along with a date and time is recorded in a log on the site's server.
- If they have accessed the site within the last two hours their cookie and access time may already be recorded. In that case, their last access date and time is updated.
- Every hour a snapshot is generated as to who is currently accessing the site.
- The snapshot is to be generated in ascending order of the unique cookie numbers.
- After a patron has been inactive for at least an hour, according to the snapshot, their information is deleted from the record of website activity log.

Since the site is quite large with thousands, if not tens of thousands or more, people accessing it every hour, the data structure to hold this information must be fast. It must be fast to insert, lookup, and delete entries. It must also be quick to take snapshot since the website will hold up all requests while the snapshot is taken.

If the number of users that come and go during an hour on a site like Wikipedia is typically higher than the number that stay around for long periods of time, if may be most efficient to rebuild the tree from the activity log rather than delete each entry after it has been inactive for at least an hour. This would be true if the number of people still active on the site is much smaller than the number of inactive entries in the snapshot of the log. In this case, rebuilding the log after deleting inactive patrons must be fast as well.

A binary search tree is a logical choice for the organization of this log if we could guarantee $\Theta(log\, n)$ lookup, insert, and delete along with $\Theta(n)$ time to take a snapshot. However, a binary search tree has one big problem. Recall that as the snapshot is taken the log may be rebuilt with only the recently active users and furthermore the cookies will be accessed in ascending order while rebuilding the log.

Consider the insert operation on binary search trees shown in Sect. 10.2.1. When the binary search tree is rebuilt the items to insert into the new tree will be added in ascending order. The result is an unbalanced tree.

10.2.1   Binary Search Tree Insert

```
1   def __insert(root,val):
2       if root == None:
3           return BinarySearchTree.__Node(val)
```

```
4        if val < root.getVal():
5            root.setLeft(BinarySearchTree.__insert(root.getLeft(),val))
6        else:
7            root.setRight(BinarySearchTree.__insert(root.getRight(),val))
8        return root
```

If items are inserted into a binary search tree in ascending order the effect is that execution always progresses from line 2 to 4, 6, 7 and 8. The result on line 7 puts the new value in the right most location of the binary search tree, since it is the largest value inserted so far. The resulting tree is a stick extending down and to the right. Without any balance to the tree, inserting the next bigger value will result in traversing each and every value that has already been inserted to find the location of the new value. This means that the first value takes zero comparisons to insert, while the second requires one comparison to find its final location, the third value requires two comparisons, and so on. The total number of comparisons to build the tree is $\Theta(n^2)$ as proved in Chap. 2. This complexity will be much too slow for any site getting a reasonable amount of activity in an hour. In addition, when the height of the binary search tree is n, where n is the number of values in the tree, the look up, insert, and delete times are $\Theta(n)$ for both the worst and average cases. When the tree is a stick or even close to being a stick the efficiency characteristics of a binary search tree are no better than that of a linked list.

10.3   AVL Trees

A binary search tree that stays balanced would provide everything that is required by the website log described in the last section. AVL trees are binary search trees with additional information to maintain their balance. The height of an AVL tree is guaranteed to be $\Theta(log\ n)$ thus guaranteeing that lookup, insert, and delete operations will all complete in $\Theta(log\ n)$ time. With these guarantees, an AVL tree can be built in $\Theta(n\ log\ n)$ time from a sequence of n items. Moreover, AVL trees, like binary search trees, can be traversed using an inorder traversal, yielding their items in ascending order in $\Theta(n)$ time.

10.3.1 Definitions

To understand how AVL trees work, a few definitions are in order.

Height(*Tree*): The height of a tree is one plus the maximum height of its subtrees. The height of a leaf node is one.
Balance(*Tree*): The balance of a node in a binary tree is height(right subtree)—height(left subtree).
AVL Tree: An AVL tree is a binary tree in which the balance of every node in the tree is −1, 0 or 1.

10.3.2 Implementation Alternatives

Looking back at Chap. 6 and the implementation of binary search trees, inserting a value into a tree can be written recursively. Inserting into an AVL tree can also be implemented recursively. It is also possible to implement inserting a value into an AVL tree iteratively, using a loop and a stack. This chapter explores both alternatives.

Additionally, the balance of an AVL tree can be maintained using either the height of each node in the tree or the balance of each node in the tree. Implementations of AVL tree nodes store either their balance or their height. As values are inserted into the tree, the balance or height values of affected nodes are updated to reflect the addition of the new item in the tree.

10.3.3 AVLNode with Stored Balance

```
1   class AVLTree:
2       class AVLNode:
3           def __init__(self,item,balance=0,left=None,right=None):
4               self.item = item
5               self.left = left
6               self.right = right
7               self.balance = balance
8
9           def __repr__(self):
10              return "AVLTree.AVLNode("+repr(self.item)+",balance="+
11                  repr(self.balance)+",left="+repr(self.left)+
12                  ",right="+repr(self.right)+")"
```

Whether implementing insert recursively or iteratively, the *Node* class of Chap. 6 must be extended slightly to accommodate either the balance or the height of the node. Consider the code fragment in Sect. 10.3.3. The first implementation of AVLTree that we'll explore is a balance storing iterative version of the algorithm. Notice that the AVLNode implementation is buried inside the AVLTree class to *hide* it from users of the AVLTree class. While Python does not actually prevent access to the AVLNode class from outside the AVLTree class, by convention users of the AVLTree data structure should know to leave the internals of the tree alone. AVL trees are created by users of this data structure, but not AVL nodes. The creation of nodes is handled by the ALVTree class.

The AVLNode constructor has default values for balance, left, and right which makes it easy to construct AVLTrees when debugging code. The *repr* function prints the AVLNode in a form that can be used to construct such a node. Calling *print(repr(node))* will print a node so it can be provided to Python to construct a sample tree. The *repr(self.left)* and *repr(self.right)* are recursive calls to the *repr* function, so the entire tree is printed rooted at *self*. From Chap. 6 the same *iter* function will work to traverse an AVLTree. The iterator function will yield all the values of the tree in ascending order.

Examples in this chapter will refer to balance of nodes in an AVL Tree. It turns out that storing the balance of a node is sufficient to correctly implement height balanced

AVL Trees, but perhaps a bit more difficult to maintain than maintaining the height of each node in the tree. Later in the chapter modifications to these algorithms are discussed that maintain the height of each node. Whether storing height or balance in AVL Trees, the complexity of the tree operations is not affected.

10.3.4 AVL Tree Iterative Insert

As described in the last section, there are two variants to the insert algorithm for height balanced AVL trees. Insert can be performed iteratively or recursively. The balance can also be stored explicitly or it can be computed from the height of each subtree. This section describes how to maintain the balance explicitly without maintaining the height of each node.

Iteratively inserting a new value in a height balanced AVL tree requires keeping track of the path to the newly inserted value. To maintain that path, a stack is used. We'll call this stack the *path stack* in the algorithm. To insert a new node, we follow the unique search path from the root to the new node's location, pushing each node on the path stack as we proceed, just as if we were adding it to a binary search tree.

As we proceed along the path to the new node's destination, we push all the nodes we encounter onto the *path stack*. We insert the new item where it should be according to the binary search tree property. Then, the algorithm proceeds popping values from the path stack and adjusting their balances until a node is found that has a balance not equal to zero before being adjusted. This node, which is the closest ancestor with non-zero balance, is called the *pivot*. Based on the pivot and the location of the new value there are three mutually exclusive cases to consider which are described below. After making the adjustments in case 3 below there may be a new root node for the subtree rooted at the pivot. If this is the case, the parent of the pivot is the next node on the path stack and can be linked to the new subtree. If the path stack is empty after popping the pivot, then the root of the tree was the pivot. In this case, the root node of the AVL tree can be made to point to the new root node in the tree. As mentioned above, one of three cases will arise when inserting a new value into the tree.

Case 1: No Pivot There is no pivot node. In other words the balance of each node along the path was 0. In this case just adjust the balance of each node on the search path based on the relative value of the new key with respect to the key of each node. You can use the *path stack* to examine the path to the new node.

This case is depicted in Fig. 10.1 where 39 is to be added to the AVL tree. In each node the value is on the left and the balance is given on the right. Each of the nodes containing 10, 18, and 40 are pushed onto the *path stack*. The balance of the new node containing 39 is set to 0. The new balance of the node containing 40 is −1. The node containing 18 has a new balance of 1. The balance of the root node after the insert is 1 because 39 is inserted to the right of it and therefore its balance increases by one. The new value is inserted to the left of the node containing 40, so its balance decreases by one. Figure 10.2 depicts the tree after inserting the new value.

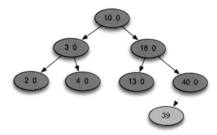

Fig. 10.1 AVL Tree Case 1—No Pivot Node

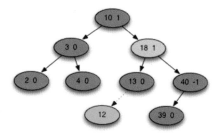

Fig. 10.2 AVL Tree Case 2—No Rotate

Case 2: Adjust Balances The pivot node exists. Further, the subtree of the pivot node in which the new node was added has the smaller height. In this case, just change the balance of the nodes along the search path from the new node up to the pivot node. The balances of the nodes above the pivot node are unaffected. This is true because the height of the subtree rooted at the pivot node is not changed by the insertion of the new node.

Figure 10.2 depicts this case. The item with *key* 12 is about to be added to the AVL tree. The node containing the 18 is the pivot node. Since the value to be inserted is less than 18 and the balance of the node containing 18 is 1, the new node could possibly help to better balance the tree. The AVL tree remains an AVL tree. The balance of nodes up to the pivot must be adjusted. Balances above the pivot need not be adjusted because they are unaffected. Figure 10.3 depicts what the tree looks like after inserting 12 into the tree.

Case 3: The pivot node exists. This time, however, the new node is added to the subtree of the pivot of larger height (the subtree in the direction of the imbalance). This will cause the pivot node to have a balance of −2 or 2 after inserting the new node, so the tree will no longer be an AVL tree. There are two subcases here, requiring either a *single rotation* or a *double rotation* to restore the tree to AVL status. Call the child of the pivot node in the direction of the imbalance the *bad child*.

Subcase A: Single Rotation This subcase occurs when the new node is added to the subtree of the bad child which is also in the direction of the imbalance. The *solution*

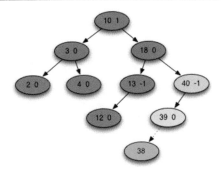

Fig. 10.3 AVL Tree Case 3A—Single Rotation

is a rotation at the pivot node in the opposite direction of the imbalance. After the rotation the tree is still a binary search tree. In addition, the subtree rooted at the pivot will be balanced once again, decreasing its overall height by one.

Figure 10.3 illustrates this subcase. The value 38 is to be inserted into the tree to the left of the node containing 39. However, doing so would result in the balance of the node containing 40 to decrease to -2, which is the closest ancestor with improper balance and the pivot node. The yellow node is the *bad child*. In addition, the 38 is being inserted in the same direction as the imbalance. The imbalance is on the left and new new value is being inserted on the left. The solution is to rotate the subtree rooted at 40 to the right, resulting in the tree pictured in Fig. 10.4.

Subcase B: Double Rotation This subcase occurs when the new node is added to the subtree of the bad child which is in the opposite direction of the imbalance. For this subcase, call the child node of the bad child which lies on the search path the *bad grandchild*. In some cases, there may not be a bad grandchild. In Fig. 10.4 the bad grandchild is the purple node. The solution is as follows:

1. Perform a single rotation at the bad child in the direction of the imbalance.
2. Perform a single rotation at the pivot away from the imbalance.

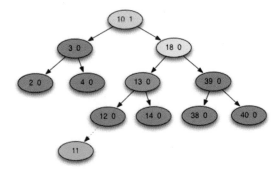

Fig. 10.4 AVL Tree Case 3B—Double Rotation

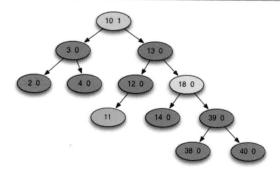

Fig. 10.5 AVL Tree Case 3B Step 1 Rotate Toward

Again, the tree is still a binary search tree and the height of the subtree in the position of the original pivot node is not changed by the double rotation. Figure 10.4 illustrates this situation. The pivot in this case is the root of the tree. The node containing 18 is the bad child. The bad grandchild is the node containing 13 (Fig. 10.5).

The imbalance in the tree is to the right of the pivot. Yet the 11 is being inserted to the left of the bad child. The first step is a rotation to the right at the bad child. This *brings the* 11 *up*, somewhat helping to balance the right side of the tree. The second step, depicted in Fig. 10.6 rotates to the left at the pivot bringing the whole tree into balance again.

The trickiest part of this algorithm is updating the balances correctly. First, the pivot, bad child, and bad grandchild contain the balances that may change. If there is no bad grandchild then the pivot's and bad child's balances will be zero. If there is a bad grandchild, as is the case here, then there is a little more work to determining the balances of the pivot and the bad child. When the bad grandchild exists, its balance is 0 after the double rotation. The balances of the bad child and pivot depend on the direction of the rotation and the value of the new item and the bad grandchild's item. This can be analyzed on a case by case basis to determine the balances of both the pivot and bad grandchild in these cases. In the next section we examine how the balances are calculated.

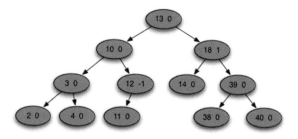

Fig. 10.6 AVL Tree Case 3B Step 2 Rotate Away

10.3.5 Rotations

Both cases 1 and 2 are trivial to implement as they simply adjust balances. Case 3 is by far the hardest of the cases to implement. Rotating a subtree is the operation that keeps the tree balanced as new nodes are inserted into it. For case 3 A the tree is in a state where a new node is going to be added to the tree causing an imbalance that must be dealt with. There are two possibilities. Figure 10.7 depicts the first of these possible situations. The new node may be inserted to the left of the bad child, A, when the subtree anchored at the pivot node is already weighted to the left. The pivot node, B, is the nearest ancestor with a non-zero balance. For node B to have balance -1 before inserting the new node its right subtree must have height h while its left subtree has height $h + 1$. Adding the new node into the subtree of the bad child would result in the pivot having balance -2 which is not allowed. The right rotation resolves the problem and maintains the binary search tree property. The subtree $T2$ moves in the rotation but before the rotation all values in $T2$ must have been less then B and greater than A. After the rotation this would also be true which means it remains a binary search tree.

Inserting a value to the right of the bad child when the imbalance is to the right results in an analogous situation requiring a left rotation. Notice that in either rotation the balance of nodes A and B are zero. This only applies to case 3 A and does not hold in the case of a double rotation (Fig. 10.8).

Again, the balance of both nodes, the pivot and the bad child, become zero after the rotation in either direction. Case 3 A is not possible under any other circumstances.

For case 3B we must deal not only with a pivot and bad child, but also a bad grandchild. As described in the previous section, this case occurs when inserting a

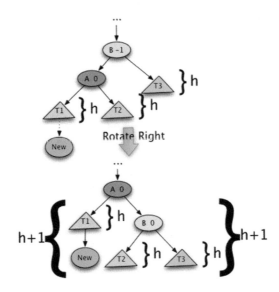

Fig. 10.7 AVL Tree Case 3A Right Rotation

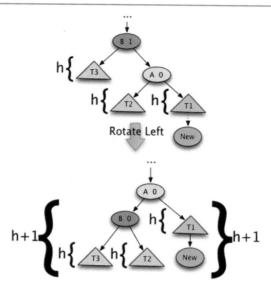

Fig. 10.8 AVL Tree Case 3A Left Rotation

new value under a bad child in the opposite direction of the imbalance. For instance, the subtree in Fig. 10.9 is weighted to the left and the new node is inserted to the right of the bad child. An analogous situation occurs when the subtree is weighted to the right and the new node is inserted into the left subtree of the bad child. When either situation occurs a double rotation is needed to bring it back into balance.

Figure 10.9 show that there are two possible subcases. There are actually three possible subcases. It is possible there is no bad grandchild. In that case, the newly inserted node will end up in the location that would have been occupied by the bad grandchild. Otherwise the new node might be inserted to the left or right of the bad grandchild, which is node C in Fig. 10.9. Either way, the first step in Fig. 10.9 is to rotate left at the bad child, node A. Then a right rotation at the pivot, node B, completes the rebalancing of the tree.

Again, the trickiest part of this implementation is the calculation of the balance of each node. The bad grandchild and new pivot node, node C in Fig. 10.9, always has a balance of 0. If there is no bad grandchild, then the new pivot node is the newly inserted value. If there was a bad grandchild, and if the new item was less than the bad grandchild's item, the balance of the bad child is 0 and the balance of the old pivot is 1. If the new item was inserted to the right of the bad grandchild then the balance of the bad child is -1 and the balance of the old pivot is 0. All other balances remain the same including balances above the pivot because the overall height of the tree before inserting the new value and after inserting the new value has not changed.

Again, an analogous situation occurs in the mirror image of Fig. 10.9. When a new value is inserted into a left subtree of a bad child which is in the right subtree of the pivot and which is already weighted more heavily to the right, then a double rotation is also required, rotating first right at the bad child and then left at the pivot.

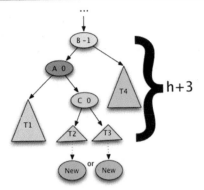

Step 1: Rotate Left at A

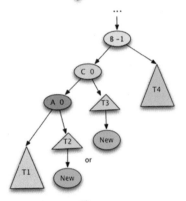

Step2: Rotate Right at B

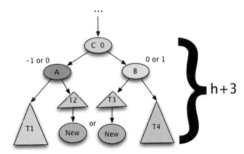

Fig. 10.9 AVL Tree Case 3B Steps 1 and 2

10.3.6 AVL Tree Recursive Insert

When implementing a recursive function it is much easier to write as a stand-alone function as opposed to a method of a class. This is because a stand-alone method may be called on nothing (i.e. *None* in the case of Python) while a method must always have a non-null *self* reference. Writing recursive functions as methods leads to special cases for *self*. For instance, the *insert* method, if written recursively, is easier to implement if it calls __insert_ as its recursive function. The __insert_ function of Sect. 10.2.1 won't suffice for height balanced AVL trees. The insert algorithm must take into account the current balance of the tree and operate to maintain the balance as we discussed in the three cases presented in the previous section.

10.3.7 The Recursive Insert AVL Tree Class Declaration

```
1    class AVLTree:
2        class AVLNode:
3            def __init__(self,item,balance=0,left=None,right=None):
4                self.item = item
5                self.left = left
6                self.right = right
7                self.balance = balance
8
9                # Other methods to be written here like __iter__ and
10               # __repr__. See Chap. 6
11
12       def __init__(self,root=None):
13           self.root = root
14
15       def insert(self, item):
16
17           def __insert(root,item):
18               ... # Code to be written here
19
20               return root
21
22           self.pivotFound = False
23           self.root = __insert(self.root,item)
24
25       def __repr__(self):
26           return "AVLTree(" + repr(self.root) + ")"
27
28       def __iter__(self):
29           return iter(self.root)
```

    The shell of the recursive implementation is given in Sect. 10.3.7. The algorithm proceeds much like a combination of the three cases presented above along with the implementation of insert presented in Sect. 10.2.1. There is no *path stack* in the recursive implementation. Instead, the run-time stack serves that purpose. Between lines 5 and 6 or lines 7 and 8 of Sect. 10.2.1 there is an opportunity to rebalance the tree as the code returns and works its way back up from the recursive calls. As each call returns, the balances of each node can be adjusted accordingly. Adjusting balances before returning implements cases one and two as described earlier in the chapter. Case three is detected when a balance of −2 or 2 results from rebalancing. In that case the pivot is found and rebalancing according to case 3 can occur.

Should a pivot be found, no balancing need occur above the pivot. This is the use of the *self.pivotFound* variable initialized on line 22 of the code in Sect. 10.3.7. This flag can be set to *True* to avoid any balancing above the pivot node, should it be found. Balances are adjusted just as described in the case by case analysis earlier in the chapter. In the worst case the balances of the pivot and bad child will need to be adjusted.

Implementing both the iterative and the recursive versions of insert into AVL trees helps illustrate the special cases that must be handled in the iterative version, while the recursive version will not need special cases. The recursive version does not need special case handling because of the way the *__insert* works. The function always is given the root node of a tree in which to insert the new item and returns the root node of the tree after inserting that item. Since it works in such a regular way, special case handling is not necessary.

10.3.8 Maintaining Balance Versus Height

The two implementations presented in this chapter, the recursive and iterative insert algorithms for AVL trees, maintained the balance of each node. As an alternative, the height of each node could be maintained. In this case, the height of a leaf node is 1. The height of any other node is 1 plus the maximum height of its two subtrees. The height of an empty tree or *None* is 0.

10.3.9 AVLNode with Stored Height

```
1   class AVLNode:
2       def __init__(self,item,height=1,left=None,right=None):
3           self.item = item
4           self.left = left
5           self.right = right
6           self.height = height
7
8       def balance(self):
9           return AVLTree.height(self.right) - AVLTree.height(self.left)
```

If the height of nodes is maintained instead of balances, all heights on the path to the new item's inserted location must be adjusted on the way back up the tree. Unlike balances, it is not possible to stop adjusting heights at the pivot node. After rotation the height of the pivot and bad child must also be recomputed as the rotation may change their height. Since heights are computed bottom-up, all heights on the path, including the heights of the pivot and bad child should be recomputed in a bottom-up fashion. The code in Sect. 10.3.9 provides a partial declaration of an AVLNode storing the height of the tree tree rooted at the node. In this implementation the balance of any node can be computed from the heights of the two subtrees.

10.3.10   Deleting an Item from an AVL Tree

Deleting a value from an AVL tree can be accomplished in the same way as described in programming problem 2 from Chap. 6. However, it is necessary to adjust balances on the way back from deleting the final leaf node. This can be done either by maintaining a *path stack* if delete is implemented iteratively or by adjusting balances or heights while returning from the recursive calls in a recursive implementation of delete.

In either case, when adjusted balance of a node on the path reaches 2, a left rotation is required to rebalance the tree. If the adjusted balance of a node on the path results in −2, then a right rotation is required. These rotations may cascade back up the path to the root of the tree.

10.4   Splay Trees

AVL trees are always balanced since the balance of each node is computed and maintained to be either −1, 1 or 0. Because they are balanced they guarantee $\Theta(log\ n)$ lookup, insert, and delete time. An AVL tree is a binary search tree so it also maintains its items in sorted order allowing iteration from the smallest to largest item in $\Theta(n)$ time. While there doesn't seem to be many downsides to this data structure there is a possible improvement in the form of splay trees.

One of the criticisms of AVL trees is that each node must maintain its balance. The extra work and extra space that are required for this balance maintenance might be unnecessary. What if a binary search tree could maintain its balance *good enough* without storing the balance in each node. Storing the balance of each node or the height of each node increases the size of the data in memory. This was a bigger concern when memory sizes were smaller. But, maintaining the extra information takes extra time as well. What if we could not only reduce the overall data size but eliminate some of the work in maintaining the balance of a binary search tree.

The improvement to AVL trees incorporates the concept of *spatial locality*. This idea reflects the nature of interaction with large data sets. Access to a large data set is often localized, meaning that the same piece or several pieces of data might be accessed several times over a short period of time and then may not be accessed for some time while some other relatively small subset of the data is accessed by either inserting new values or looking up old values. *Spatial Locality* means that a relatively small subset of data is accessed over a short period of time.

In terms of our example at the beginning of this chapter, a tree containing cookies may have cookies that are assigned when a user first visits a website. A user coming into the website will interact for a while and then leave, probably not coming back soon again. The set of users who are interacting with the web server will change over time but it is always a relatively small subset compared to the overall number of entries in the tree. If we could store the cookies of the recent users closer to the top of the tree, we might be able to improve the overall time for looking up and inserting a new value in the tree. The complexity won't improve. Inserting an item will still take $\Theta(log\ n)$ time. But the overall time to insert or lookup an item might improve a little bit. This is the motivation for a splay tree.

In a splay tree, each insert or lookup moves the inserted or looked up value to the root of the tree through a process called *splaying*. When deleting a value, the parent may be splayed to the root of the tree. A splay tree is still a binary search tree. Splay trees usually remain well-balanced but unlike an AVL tree, a splay tree does not contain any balance or height information. Splaying a node to the root involves a series of rotates, much like the rotates of AVL trees, but with a slight difference.

It is interesting to note that while splay trees are designed to exploit *spatial locality* in the data, they are not dependent on spatial locality to perform well. Splay trees function as well or better than AVL trees in practice on completely random data sets.

There are several things that are interesting about splay trees.

- First, the splaying process does not require the balance or any other information about the height of subtrees. The binary search tree structure is good enough.
- Splay trees don't stay perfectly balanced all the time. However, because they stay relatively balanced, they are balanced enough to get an average case complexity of $\Theta(log\ n)$ for insert, lookup, and delete operations. This idea that they are good enough is the basis for what is called *amortized complexity* which is discussed later in Chap. 2 and later in this chapter.
- Splaying is relatively simple to implement.

In this text we cover two bottom-up splay tree implementations. Splay trees can be implemented either iteratively or recursively and we examine both implementations. In Chap. 6 binary search tree insert was implemented recursively. If splaying is to be done recursively, the splay can be part of the insert function. If written iteratively, a stack can be used in the splaying process. The following sections cover both the iterative and recursive implementations. But first we examine the rotations that are used in splaying.

10.4.1 Splay Rotations

Each time a value is inserted or looked up the node containing that value is splayed to the top through a series of rotate operations. Unlike AVL trees, a splay tree employs a double rotation to move a node up to the level of its grandparent if a grandparent exists. Through a series of double rotations the node will either make it to the root or to the child of the root. If the splayed node makes it to the child of the root, a single rotation is used to bring it to the root.

The single rotate functions are often labelled a *zig* or a *zag* while the double rotations are called *zig-zig* or *zig-zag* operations depending on the direction of the movement of the splayed node. Sometimes the node moves with a zig-zag motion while other times it moves with a zig-zig motion.

Splaying happens when a value is inserted into, looked up, or deleted from a splay tree. When a value is looked up either the searched value is splayed to the top or the would-be parent of the value if the value is not found in the tree. Deletion from the tree can be implemented like delete from any other binary search tree as described in problem 2 of Chap. 6. When a value is deleted from a binary search tree the parent of the deleted node is splayed to the root of the tree.

The example in Fig. 10.14 depicts the splay operations that result from inserting the green nodes into a splay tree. When 30 is inserted, it is splayed to the root of the tree as appears in the second version of the tree (the red nodes). When 5 is inserted, it is splayed to the root as well. Moving 5 to the root is accomplished through a zig-zig rotation called a double-right rotation. Splaying the 8 to the root is the result of a zig-zag rotation called a right-left rotation. When the 42 is splayed to the root it is a double-left rotation followed by a single left rotation.

Splaying the 15 to the root is accomplished by doing a double-right rotation followed by a left-right rotation. The double-right is often called a zig-zig rotation as is the double-left rotation. The left-right and right-left rotations are often called zig-zag rotations. The end result in each case has the newly inserted node, or looked up node, splayed to the root of the tree.

Figures 10.10, 10.11, 10.12 and 10.13 depict these splay operations. Figures 10.12 and 10.13 give some intuitive understanding of why splay trees work as well as they

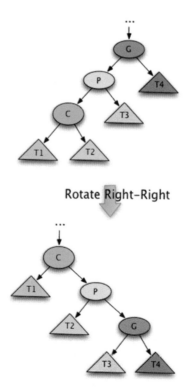

Fig. 10.10 Splay Tree Double-Right Rotate

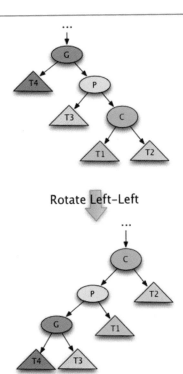

Fig. 10.11 Splay Tree Double-Left Rotate

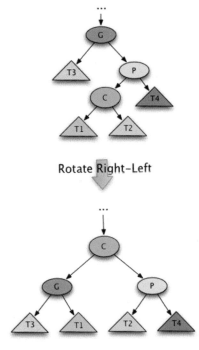

Fig. 10.12 Splay Tree Right-Left Rotate

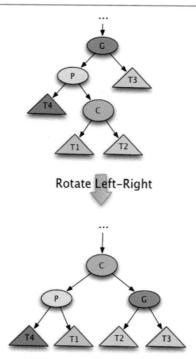

Fig. 10.13 Splay Tree Left-Right Rotate

do. After the rotate operations depicted in Figs. 10.12 and 10.13 the subtree rooted at the child appears to be more balanced than before those rotations.

Notice that doing a left-right rotation is not the same as doing a left rotation followed by a right rotation. The splay left-right rotate yields a different result. Likewise, the splay right-left rotate yields a different result than a right followed by a left rotation. Splay zig-zag rotates are designed this way to help balance they tree. Figures 10.12 and 10.13 depict trees that might be slightly out of balance before the rotation, brought into much better balance by the right-left rotation or the left-right rotation.

10.5 Iterative Splaying

Each time a value is inserted or looked up it is splayed to the root of the splay tree through a series of rotations as described in the previous section. The double rotation operations will either move the value to the root or the child of the root of the tree. If the double rotates result in the newly inserted value at the child of the root of the tree, a single rotate is used to move the newly inserted value to the root as depicted in Fig. 10.14 when 30 and 15 are inserted into the splay tree.

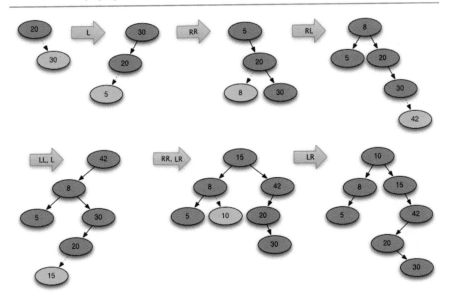

Fig. 10.14 Splay Tree Example

Inserting a new value into a binary search tree without recursion is possible using a while loop. The while loop moves from the root of the tree to the leaf node which will become the new node's parent at which point the loop terminates, the new node is created, and the parent is hooked up to its new child.

After inserting the new node, it must be splayed to the top. To splay it is necessary to know the path that was taken through the tree to the newly inserted node. This path can be recorded using a stack. As the insert loop passes through another node in the tree, it is pushed onto the stack. The end result is that all nodes, from the root to the new child, on the path to the new child are pushed onto this path stack.

Finally, splaying can occur by emptying this path stack. First the child is popped from the stack. Then, the rest of the stack is emptied as follows.

- If two more nodes are available on the stack they are the parent and grandparent of the newly inserted node. In that case a double rotate can be performed resulting in the root of the newly rotated subtree being the newly inserted node. Which double rotation is required can be determined from the values of the grandparent, parent, and child.
- If only one node remains on the stack it is the parent of the newly inserted node. A single rotation will bring the newly inserted node to the root of the splay tree.

Implementing splay in the manner described here works well when looking up a value in the tree, whether it is found or not. When a value is found it will be added to the path stack. When a value is not found, the parent should be splayed to the top, which naturally occurs when the looked up value is not found because the parent will be left on the top of the path stack when splaying is performed.

One method of deleting a node from a splay tree is accomplished by deleting just as you would in a binary search tree. If the node to delete has zero or one child it is trivial to delete the node. If the node to delete has two children, then the leftmost value in its right subtree can replace the value in the node to delete and the leftmost value can be deleted from the right subtree. The parent of the deleted node is splayed to the top of the tree.

Another method of deletion requires splaying the deleted node to the root of the tree first. Then the rightmost value of the left subtree is splayed to the root. After splaying the left subtree, its root node's right subtree is empty and the original right subtree can be added to it. The original left subtree becomes the root of the newly constructed splay tree.

10.6 Recursive Splaying

Implementing splaying recursively follows the recursive insert operation on binary search trees. The splaying is combined with this recursive insert function. As the recursive insert follows the path down the tree it builds a rotate string of "R" and "L". If the new item is inserted to the right of the current root node, then a left rotate will be required to splay the newly inserted node up the tree and an "L" is added to the rotate string. Otherwise, a right rotate will be required and an "R" is added to the rotate string.

As the recursive insert function returns, the path to the newly inserted node is retraced by the returning function. The last two characters in the rotate string dictate what double rotation is required. A dictionary or hash table takes care of mapping "RR", "RL", "LR", and "LL" to the appropriate rotate functions. The hash table lookup is used to call the appropriate rotation and the rotate string is truncated (or re-initialized to the empty string depending on when "R" and "L" are added to the rotate string). When the recursive insert is finished, any required single rotation will be recorded in the rotate string and can be performed.

It should be noted that implementing splaying using a rotate string and hash table like this requires about one half the conditional statements to determine the required rotations as compared to the iterative algorithm described above. When inserting a new node the path must be determined by comparing the value to insert to each node on the path to its location in the tree. In the iterative description above, the values on the path are again compared during splaying. In this recursive description the new item is only compared to each item on the path once. This has an impact on performance as shown later in the chapter.

Looking up a value using this recursive implementation works similarly to insert either splaying the found value or its parent if it is not found to the root of the tree. Deleting a value again can be done recursively by first looking up the value to delete resulting in it being splayed to the root of the tree and then performing the method of root removal described in the previous section.

10.7   Performance Analysis

In the worst case a splay tree may become a stick resulting in $\Theta(n)$ complexity for each lookup, insert, and delete operation while AVL trees guarantee $\Theta(log\ n)$ time for lookup, insert, and delete operations. It would appear that AVL trees might have better performance. However, this does not seem to be the case in practice. Close to 100,000 insert and 900,000 random lookups were performed in an experiment using a pre-generated dataset. The insert and lookup operations were identified in the dataset with all looked up values being found in the tree. The average combined insert and lookup time were recorded in Fig. 10.15 for an AVL tree, a splay tree implemented iteratively, and the recursive implementation of splay tree insert and lookup. The results show that the recursive splay tree implementation performs better on a random set of values than the AVL tree implementation. The experiment suggests that splay trees also exhibit $\Theta(log\ n)$ complexity in practice for insert and lookup operations.

In Figs. 10.13 and 10.12 we got an intuitive understanding of how splay trees maintain balance through their specialized double rotations. However, it is not a very convincing argument to say that the double rotations appear to make the tree more balanced. This idea is formalized using *amortized complexity*. Amortization, first encountered in Chap. 2, is an accounting term used when an expense is spread over a number of years as opposed to expensing it all in one year. This same principle can be applied to the expense in finding or inserting a value in a Splay Tree. The complete

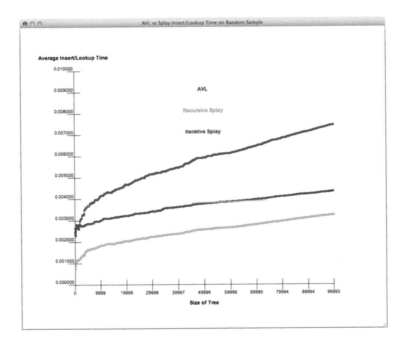

Fig. 10.15 Average Insert/Lookup Time

analysis of this is done on a case by case basis and is not present in this text but may be found in texts on-line. These proofs show that splay trees do indeed operate as efficiently as AVL trees on randomly accessed data. In addition, the splaying operation used when inserting or looking up a value exploits *spatial locality* in the data. Data values that are frequently looked up will make their way toward the top of the tree so as to be more efficiently looked up in the future. While taking advantage of spatial locality is certainly desirable if present in the data, it does not improve the overall computational complexity of splay tree insert and lookup operations.

However, this does not happen in the average case on randomly inserted and looked up values. In fact, the recursive implementation of splay trees presented in the previous section exhibits $\Theta(\log n)$ average insert and lookup time on a randomly distributed set of values and performs better in a random sample than the AVL tree implementation.

Insert, lookup, and delete operations on an AVL tree can be completed in $\Theta(\log n)$ time. In the average case this holds for splay trees as well. Traversal of an AVL or splay tree runs in $\Theta(n)$ time and yields its items in ascending or descending order (depending on how the iterator is written). While the quicksort algorithm can sort the items of a list just as efficiently, AVL and splay trees are data structures that allow many insert and delete operations while still maintaining the ordering of their elements. An AVL or splay tree may be a practical choice if a data structure is needed that efficiently implements lookup, delete, and insert operations while also allowing the sequence of values to be iterated over in ascending or descending order. The advantage of AVL trees lies in their ability to maintain the ordering of elements while guaranteeing efficient lookup, insert, and delete complexity. Splay trees work just as well in almost all cases and in the case of the recursive splay tree implementation described in this chapter it performs even better than the AVL Tree implementation on random data sets. The difference in performance between the AVL tree and the recursive splay tree performance numbers is the difference between maintaining the balance explicitly in the AVL tree and getting *good enough* balance in the splay tree.

10.8   Chapter Summary

This chapter presented several implementations of height-balanced AVL trees and splay trees. Recursive and iterative insert algorithms were presented. Both balance maintaining and height maintaining AVL nodes were discussed. The recursive insert algorithms for both AVL and splay trees result in very clean code without many special cases, while the iterative versions needs a few more if statements to handle some conditions. In some instance the iterative version may be slightly more efficient than the recursive version since there is a cost associated with function calls in any language, but the experimental results obtained from the experiments performed in this chapter seem to suggest that the recursive implementations operate very efficiently when written in Python.

10.9   Review Questions

Answer these short answer, multiple choice, and true/false questions to test your
mastery of the chapter.

1. What is the balance of a node in an AVL tree?
2. How does the balance of a node relate to its height?
3. How does an AVL tree make use of the balance of a node?
4. What is a pivot node?
5. What is a bad child in relationship to AVL trees?
6. What is the path stack and when is it necessary?
7. After doing a right rotation, where is the pivot node and the bad child in the
   subtree that was originally rooted at the pivot?
8. Why is the balance of the root of a subtree always 0 after code for case 3 is
   executed?
9. In the two subcases for case 3, what node becomes the root node of the subtree
   rooted at the pivot after executing the algorithm on each of the subcases?
10. Why does the AVL tree insert algorithm always completes in $\Theta(log\ n)$ time?
    Do a case by case analysis to justify your answer for each of the three cases
    involved in inserting a value.
11. What is the purpose of the rotate string in the recursive insert splay tree imple-
    mentation?
12. Why does it seem that the recursive splay tree insert and lookup implementation
    operates faster than the AVL tree implementation?

10.10   Programming Problems

1. Write an AVL tree implementation that maintains balances in each node and
   implements insert iteratively. Write a test program to thoroughly test your program
   on some randomly generated data.
2. Write an AVL tree implementation that maintains balances in each node and
   implements insert recursively. Write a test program to thoroughly test your program on some randomly generated data.
3. Write an AVL tree implementation that maintains heights in each node and implements insert recursively. Write a test program to thoroughly test your program on
   some randomly generated data.
4. Write an AVL tree implementation that maintains heights in each node and implements insert iteratively. Write a test program to thoroughly test your program on
   some randomly generated data.
5. Complete programming problem 3. Then implement the delete operation for AVL
   Trees. Finally, write a test program to thoroughly test your data structure. As
   values are inserted and deleted from your tree you should test your code to make
   sure it maintains all heights correctly and the ordering of all values in the tree.

6. Implement two of the programming problems 1–4 in this chapter and then write a test program that generates a random list of integers. Time inserting the values into the first implementation and then time inserting each value into the second implementation. Record all times in the XML format needed by the PlotData.py program from chapter two. Plot the timing of the two algorithms to compare their relative efficiency.

7. Write a splay tree implementation with recursive insert and lookup functions. Implement an AVL tree either iteratively or recursively where the height of each node is maintained. Run a test where trees are built from the same list of values. When you generate the list of values, duplicate values should be considered a lookup. Write the data file with an *L* or an *I* followed by a value which indicates either a *lookup* or *insert* operation should be performed. Generate an XML file in the format used by the PlotData.py program to compare your performance results.

8. Write a splay tree implementation with recursive insert and lookup functions. Compare it to one of the other balanced binary tree implementations detailed in this chapter. Run a test where trees are built from the same list of values. When you generate the list of values, duplicate values should be considered a lookup. Write the data file with an *L* or an *I* followed by a value which indicates either a *lookup* or *insert* operation should be performed. Generate an XML file in the format used by the PlotData.py program to compare your performance results.

B-Trees

11

This chapter covers one of the more important data structures of the last thirty years. B-Trees are primarily used by relational databases to efficiently implement an operation called *join*. B-Trees have other properties that are also useful for databases including ordering of rows within a table, fast delete capability, and sequential access.

11.1 Chapter Goals

This chapter introduces some terminology from relational databases to motivate the need for B-Trees. The chapter goes on to introduce the B-Tree data structure and its implementation. By the end of this chapter you should have an understanding of B-Trees, their advantages over other data structures, and you should be able to demonstrate your understanding by implementing a B-Tree that can be used to efficiently process *joins* in relational databases.

11.2 Relational Databases

While this is not a database text we will cover a bit of database terminology to demonstrate the need for a B-Tree and its use in a relational database. A relational database consists of entities and relationships between these entities. A database schema is a collection of entities and their relationships. A schema is specified by a *Entity Relationship* diagram, often abbreviated *ER*-diagram, or a Logical Data Structure [2]. Figure 11.1 provides an ER-diagram for a database called the *Dairy Database*. It is used to formulate rations for dairy cattle to maximize milk production.

Each box in Fig. 11.1 represents an entity in the database. Of particular interest in this text are the Feed, FeedAttribute, and FeedAttribType entities. A feed, like corn silage or alfalfa, is composed of many different nutrients. Nutrients are things like calcium, iron, phosphorus, protein, sugar, and so on. In the *Dairy Database*

© Springer International Publishing Switzerland 2015
K.D. Lee and S. Hubbard, *Data Structures and Algorithms with Python*,
Undergraduate Topics in Computer Science, DOI 10.1007/978-3-319-13072-9_11

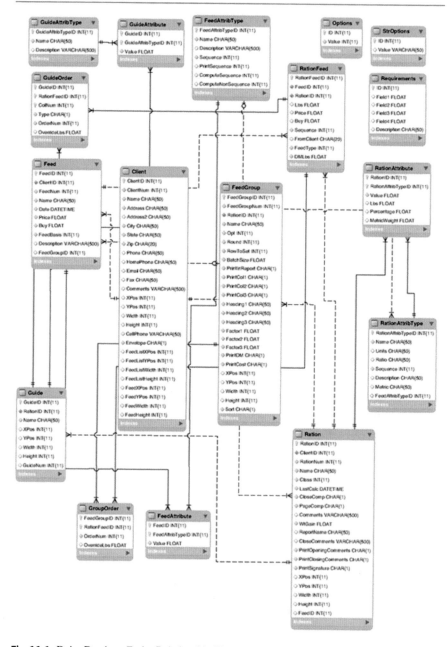

Fig. 11.1 Dairy Database Entity Relationship Diagram

these nutrients are called FeedAttribTypes. There is a many-to-many relationship between Feeds and FeedAttribTypes. A feed has many feed attributes, or nutrients. Each nutrient or feed attribute type appears in more than one feed. This relationship

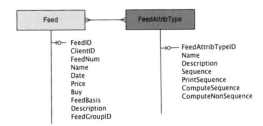

Fig. 11.2 A Many to Many Relationship

is depicted in Fig. 11.2. The forks on the two ends of the line represent the many-to-many relationship between feeds and feed attribute types.

Many-to-Many relationships cannot be represented in a relational database without going through a process called reification. *Reification* introduces new entities that remove many-to-many relationships. When a many-to-many relationship appears within a logical data structure it indicates there may be missing attributes. In this case, the quantity of each nutrient within a feed was missing. The new *FeedAttribute* entity eliminates the many-to-many relationship by introducing two one-to-many relationships. One-to-many relationships can be represented in relational databases.

Every entity in a relational database must have a unique identifier. In Fig. 11.3 the Feed entities are uniquely identified by their *FeedID* attribute. The other attributes are important, but do not have to be unique. Each *FeedID* must be unique and it cannot be null or empty for any feed. Likewise, a *FeedAttribTypeID* field uniquely identifies each feed nutrient. There is a unique FeedAttribTypeID for calcium, iron, and so on. The FeedAttribute entity has a unique id made up of two fields. Together, the *FeedID* and the *FeedAttribTypeID* identify a unique instance of a nutrient for a particular feed. The *Value* was the missing attribute in Fig. 11.2 that was introduced by reifying the many-to-many relationship as depicted in Fig. 11.3. The Logical Data Structure in Fig. 11.3 describes the schema for feeds and nutrients in the *Dairy Database*.

A relational database is composed of tables and the shema provides the definition of these tables. The *Feed* table consists of rows and columns. Each row in the *Feed* table describes one feed. The columns of the Feed table are each of the attributes of a feed provided in Fig. 11.3. The example in Sect. 11.2.1 provides a subset of this table

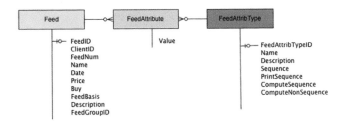

Fig. 11.3 Logical Data Structure

with a subset of the columns of this table. The ellipses (i.e. the ...) indicate omitted rows within the database. The full table is available as *Feed.tbl* on the text website.

11.2.1 The Feed Table

1	...			
2	1316	512	10'Corn Silag'	2/28/2002 12:00:00 AM
3	1317	512	11'Almond Hul'	7/15/1989 12:00:00 AM
4	1318	512	12'MolassWet'	5/19/1989 12:00:00 AM
5	1319	512	13'LIQ CIT PL'	3/2/2002 12:00:00 AM
6	1320	512	14'Whey'	9/4/1997 12:00:00 AM
7	1321	512	16'SF CORN'	9/29/1998 12:00:00 AM
8	1322	512	18'Dry Min'	10/17/2002 12:00:00 AM
9	1323	512	19'Min Plts'	11/17/2002 12:00:00 AM
10	1324	512	20'Mineral'	2/28/2002 12:00:00 AM
11	1372	525	1'Hay lact'	9/15/2003 12:00:00 AM
12	1373	525	2'DRY HAY'	11/30/1999 12:00:00 AM
13	1374	525	3'Oat hay'	11/10/1998 12:00:00 AM
14	1375	525	4'Hlg'	4/12/2004 12:00:00 AM
15	1376	525	5'CUPHay'	9/17/2003 12:00:00 AM
16	1377	525	6'Hay #1'	3/27/2001 12:00:00 AM
17	1378	525	8'BMR CSilage'	4/1/2004 12:00:00 AM
18	1379	525	9'Wheat Sil'	9/15/2003 12:00:00 AM
19	1380	525	10'Corn Silag'	10/30/2003 12:00:00 AM
20	1381	525	11'Almond Hul'	7/10/2000 12:00:00 AM
21	1382	525	14'ClosePlt'	1/13/2003 12:00:00 AM
22	1383	525	16'Corn1%fat'	9/3/2002 12:00:00 AM
23	1384	525	18'Dry Min'	7/12/2000 12:00:00 AM
24	1385	525	19'Comm Mix'	12/13/2003 12:00:00 AM
25	1386	525	20'On Farm'	10/30/2003 12:00:00 AM
26	1438	529	1'Big Sq155'	6/21/1999 12:00:00 AM
27	1439	529	2'Hay#1-200'	2/1/2000 12:00:00 AM
28	1440	529	3'Hay#2-145'	2/1/2000 12:00:00 AM
29	...			

Normally a relational database would store a table like the *Feed* table in a binary format that would be unreadable except by a computer. The *Feed.tbl* file is written in ASCII format to be human readable with a simple text editor, but the principles are the same. Each row within the table represents one record of the table which is one instance of a feed in this case. The records are each the same size to make reading the table easy. Within any record we can find the name of the feed by going to the correct column for feed name, which is the fourth field within each record and starts 30 bytes or characters into each record. Ten bytes or characters are allocated to each integer field (the first column was edited to better fit on the page). There are 107 records or feeds within the sample *Feed.tbl* table provided on the text website.

11.2.2 The FeedAttribType Table

1	...		
2	10'P'	'Phosphorus as % of DM'	15
3	11'Ca'	'Calcium as % of DM'	16
4	12'RFV'	'Relative Feed Value (calculated)'	17
5	13'S'	'Sulfur as % of DM'	18
6	14'K'	'Potassium as % of DM'	19

7	15'Mg'	'Magnesium as % of DM'	20
8	16'Fat'	'Fat as % of DM'	14
9	...		

The table in Sect. 11.2.2 contains a subset of the records in the *FeedAttrib-Type* table, available as *FeedAttribType.tbl* on the text website. The full table has 57 different rows each containing 7 fields. As with the *Feed* table, the *FeedAttrib-Type* table is organized into rows and columns.

A subset of the *FeedAttribute* table is provided in Sect. 11.2.3. Each feed attribute is comprised of the corresponding *FeedID*, the *FeedAttribTypeID*, and the amount of that nutrient for the given feed which is called the *Value* column within the table.

11.2.3 The FeedAttribute Table

1	...		
2	1316	10	0.250000
3	1316	11	0.210000
4	1316	12	128.000000
5	1316	13	0.150000
6	1316	14	1.200000
7	1316	15	0.200000
8	1316	16	3.000000
9	...		
10	1317	10	0.110000
11	1317	11	0.220000
12	1317	12	129.000000
13	1317	13	0.110000
14	1317	14	0.530000
15	1317	15	0.130000
16	1317	16	2.000000
17	...		

Storing the feed data this way is flexible. New nutrients can easily be added. Feeds can be added as well. Feed attributes can be stored if available or omitted. Occasionally, programs that use relational databases need access to data from more than one table but need to correlate the data between the tables. For instance, it may be convenient to temporarily construct a table that contains the feed number, feed name, nutrient name, and value of that nutrient for the corresponding feed into a table like that in Sect. 11.2.4. We may want to compute the average phosphorous content within all feeds. In fact, we may wish to calculate the average content for each nutrient type within the database. In that case a table like the one in Sect. 11.2.4 would be very useful.

11.2.4 A Temporary Table

1	...
2	10 Corn Silag P 0.25
3	10 Corn Silag Ca 0.21
4	10 Corn Silag RFV 128.0
5	10 Corn Silag S 0.15

```
6    10 Corn Silag K 1.2
7    10 Corn Silag Mg 0.2
8    10 Corn Silag Fat 3.0
9    ...
10   11 Almond Hul P 0.11
11   11 Almond Hul Ca 0.22
12   11 Almond Hul RFV 129.0
13   11 Almond Hul S 0.11
14   11 Almond Hul K 0.53
15   11 Almond Hul Mg 0.13
16   11 Almond Hul Fat 2.0
17   ...
```

Relational databases are often called *SQL* databases. *SQL* stands for *System Query Language*. SQL is a language for querying relational databases. SQL can be used to build temporary tables like the one in Sect. 11.2.4. The *SQL* statement to build this table would be written as

```
SELECT Feed.FeedNum, Feed.Name, FeedAttribType.Name, FeedAttribute.Value WHERE
       Feed.FeedID = FeedAttribute.FeedID AND
       FeedAttribute.FeedAttribTypeID = FeedAttribType.FeedAttribTypeID
```

This SQL statement is known as a *join* of three tables because three tables will be joined together to form the result. It is up to the relational database to translate this query into commands that read the three tables and efficiently construct a new temporary table as the result of the join.

If we were to implement our own relational database, the join operation for these three tables might be programmed similarly to the code appearing in Sect. 11.2.5. Don't be misled. Relational databases don't program specific joins like this one, but the joining of the three tables might be functionally equivalent to this code. The entire program is available as *joinquery.py* on the text's website. The *readField* function here in the text is abbreviated for space, but reads any type of field from a table file. The join algorithm picks one of the tables and read it from beginning to end. In this case, the FeedAttribute table is read from beginning to end. For each feed attribute, the matching feed id from the feed table must be located. In the code in Sect. 11.2.5 this involves reading, on average, half the feed table to supply the feed number and feed name for each line of the query. Likewise, to supply the feed attribute name, on average half the FeedAttribType table is read to supply the feed attribute name for each line of the query output.

The complexity of this operation is $O(n*m)$ where n is the number of records in *FeedAttribute.tbl* and m is the maximum of the number of records in *FeedAttribType.tbl* and *Feed.tbl*. This is $O(n^2)$ performance if n is roughly equivalent to m. Whether the two are roughly equivalent or not, the performance of this query, even on our small sample table, is not great. It takes about 4.993 s to run the query as written on a 2.66 GHz Intel Core i7 processor with 8 GB of RAM and a solid state hard drive.

11.2.5 Programming the Joining of Tables

```
1    import datetime
2    def readField(record,colTypes,fieldNum):
```

```
3      # fieldNum is zero based
4      # record is a string containing the record
5      # colTypes is the types for each of the columns in the record
6      offset = 0
7      for i in range(fieldNum):
8          colType = colTypes[i]
9
10         if colType == "int":
11             offset+=10
12         elif colType[:4] == "char":
13             size = int(colType[4:])
14             offset += size
15         elif colType == "float":
16             offset+=20
17         ...
18     return val
19 def main():
20     # SELECT Feed.FeedNum, Feed.Name, FeedAttribType.Name, FeedAttribute.Value WHERE
21     # Feed.FeedID = FeedAttribute.FeedID AND
22     # FeedAttribute.FeedAttribTypeID = FeedAttribType.FeedAttribTypeID
23     attribTypeCols = ["int","char20","char60","int","int","int","int"]
24     feedCols = ["int","int","int","char50","datetime","float","float","int","char50","int"]
25     feedAttributeCols = ["int","int","float"]
26     before = datetime.datetime.now()
27     feedAttributeTable = open("FeedAttribute.tbl","r")
28     for record in feedAttributeTable:
29         feedID = readField(record,feedAttributeCols,0)
30         feedAttribTypeID = readField(record,feedAttributeCols,1)
31         value = readField(record,feedAttributeCols,2)
32         feedTable = open("Feed.tbl","r")
33         feedFeedID = -1
34         while feedFeedID != feedID:
35             feedRecord = feedTable.readline()
36             feedFeedID = readField(feedRecord,feedCols,0)
37         feedNum = readField(feedRecord,feedCols,2)
38         feedName = readField(feedRecord,feedCols,3)
39         feedAttribTypeTable = open("FeedAttribType.tbl", "r")
40         feedAttribTypeIDID = -1
41         while feedAttribTypeIDID != feedAttribTypeID:
42             feedAttribTypeRecord = feedAttribTypeTable.readline()
43             feedAttribTypeIDID = readField(feedAttribTypeRecord,attribTypeCols,0)
44         feedAttribTypeName = readField(feedAttribTypeRecord,attribTypeCols,1)
45         print(feedNum,feedName,feedAttribTypeName,value)
46     after = datetime.datetime.now()
47     deltaT = after - before
48     milliseconds = deltaT.total_seconds() * 1000
49     print("Time for the query without indexing was",milliseconds,"milliseconds.")
50
51 if __name__ == "__main__":
52     main()
```

The code in Sect. 11.2.5 suffers because the two tables, *Feed.tbl* and *FeedAttrib-Type.tbl* are read sequentially each time through the outer loop to find the matching feed and feed attribute type, respectively. We can improve the efficiency of this query if we recognize that disk drives are *random access* devices. That means that we can position the read head of a disk drive anywhere within a file. We don't have to start at the beginning of a table to begin looking for a matching feed or feed attribute type. We can jump around within the table to find the matching record.

11.2.6 The readRecord Function

```
 1   def readRecord(file,recNum,recSize):
 2       file.seek(recNum*recSize)
 3       record = file.read(recSize)
 4       return record
```

Python includes a *seek* method on files to position the read head of a disk to a byte offset within a file. The *read* method on files reads a given number of bytes and returns them as a string. To test this *readRecord* function, and the functionality of the *seek* method, a program was written to randomly access the records in the *FeedAttribute.tbl* file. The results of that experiment are shown in Fig. 11.4. The data shows that accessing any record within the file took about the same amount of time regardless of its position within the file. As with any experiment, there were a few anomalies. But, the vast majority of records were accessed in the same amount of time or nearly the same amount of time.

Let's say we were to organize the *Feed.tbl* and the *FeedAttribType.tbl* files so that the records were sorted in increasing order by their keys. The *Feed.tbl* file would be sorted by *FeedID* and the *FeedAttribType.tbl* would be sorted by *FeedAttribTypeID*. Then we could use binary search on these two files to find the matching records for each feed attribute in the code of Sect. 11.2.5. Since the tables are randomly accessible, the query time could be reduced from O(n*m) to O(n log m). However,

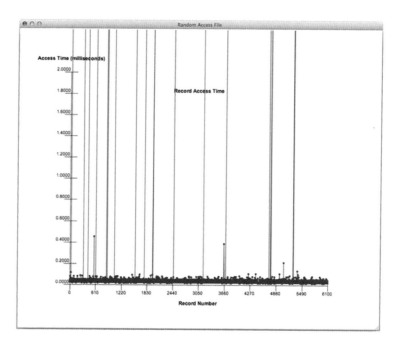

Fig. 11.4 Access Time for Randomly Read Records in a File

we can't assume that a database table will always, or ever, be sorted according to one field. Databases can have new records added and old records deleted at any time.

This is where the need for a B-Tree comes from. A B-Tree is a tree structure that is built over the top, so to speak, of a database table to provide O(log n) lookup time to any record within the database table. While the records themselves may be in any order, the B-Tree provides the O(log n) search complexity into the table.

A B-Tree is built by inserting records or items into the tree. Once built, the index provides the efficient lookup of any record based on the key value stored in the B-Tree. Consider the code in Sect. 11.2.7. Lines 18–23 build the *Feed.tbl* index and lines 39–44 build the *FeedAttribType.tbl* index. Once built, the indices are used when programming the query. The loop beginning on line 55 no longer contains two while loops to lookup the corresponding records in the two tables. Instead, the B-Trees are consulted to find the corresponding records in the two tables. When programmed this way, the query in Sect. 11.2.7 runs in approximately 1.628 s, three times faster than the original, non-indexed query. The sample query here uses relatively small tables. Imagine the speed up possible when either of the *Feed.tbl* or *FeedAttribType.tbl* tables contained millions of records. In that case, the original query would not have completed in an acceptable amount of time while the indexed query given here would have completed in roughly the same amount of time or perhaps a second longer at worst.

11.2.7 Efficient Join

```
1  def main():
2      # Select Feed.FeedNum, Feed.Name, FeedAttribType.Name, FeedAttribute.Value where
3      # Feed.FeedID = FeedAttribute.FeedID and FeedAttribute.FeedAtribTypeID = FeedAttribType.ID
4      attribTypeCols = ["int","char20","char60","int","int","int","int"]
5      feedCols = ["int","int","int","char50","datetime","float","float","int","char50","int"]
6      feedAttributeCols = ["int","int","float"]
7
8      feedAttributeTable = open("FeedAttribute.tbl","r")
9
10     if os.path.isfile("Feed.idx"):
11         indexFile = open("Feed.idx","r")
12         feedTableRecLength = int(indexFile.readline())
13         feedIndex = eval(indexFile.readline())
14     else:
15         feedIndex = BTree(3)
16         feedTable = open("Feed.tbl","r")
17         offset = 0
18         for record in feedTable:
19             feedID = readField(record,feedCols,0)
20             anItem = Item(feedID,offset)
21             feedIndex.insert(anItem)
22             offset+=1
23             feedTableRecLength = len(record)
24
25         print("Feed Table Index Created")
26         indexFile = open("Feed.idx","w")
27         indexFile.write(str(feedTableRecLength)+"\n")
28         indexFile.write(repr(feedIndex)+"\n")
29         indexFile.close()
30
31     if os.path.isfile("FeedAttribType.idx"):
32         indexFile = open("FeedAttribType.idx","r")
```

```
33              attribTypeTableRecLength = int(indexFile.readline())
34              attribTypeIndex = eval(indexFile.readline())
35          else:
36              attribTypeIndex = BTree(3)
37              attribTable = open("FeedAttribType.tbl","r")
38              offset = 0
39              for record in attribTable:
40                  feedAttribTypeID = readField(record,attribTypeCols,0)
41                  anItem = Item(feedAttribTypeID,offset)
42                  attribTypeIndex.insert(anItem)
43                  offset+=1
44                  attribTypeTableRecLength = len(record)
45
46              print("Attrib Type Table Index Created")
47              indexFile = open("FeedAttribType.idx","w")
48              indexFile.write(str(attribTypeTableRecLength)+"\n")
49              indexFile.write(repr(attribTypeIndex)+"\n")
50              indexFile.close()
51
52          feedTable = open("Feed.tbl","rb")
53          feedAttribTypeTable = open("FeedAttribType.tbl", "rb")
54          before = datetime.datetime.now()
55          for record in feedAttributeTable:
56
57              feedID = readField(record,feedAttributeCols,0)
58              feedAttribTypeID = readField(record,feedAttributeCols,1)
59              value = readField(record,feedAttributeCols,2)
60
61              lookupItem = Item(feedID,None)
62              item = feedIndex.retrieve(lookupItem)
63              offset = item.getValue()
64              feedRecord = readRecord(feedTable,offset,feedTableRecLength)
65              feedNum = readField(feedRecord,feedCols,2)
66              feedName = readField(feedRecord,feedCols,3)
67
68              lookupItem = Item(feedAttribTypeID,None)
69              item = attribTypeIndex.retrieve(lookupItem)
70              offset = item.getValue()
71              feedAttribTypeRecord = readRecord(feedAttribTypeTable,offset,attribTypeTableRecLength)
72              feedAttribTypeName = readField(feedAttribTypeRecord,attribTypeCols,1)
73
74              print(feedNum,feedName,feedAttribTypeName,value)
75          after = datetime.datetime.now()
76          deltaT = after - before
77          milliseconds = deltaT.total_seconds() * 1000
78          print("Time for the query with indexing was",milliseconds,"milliseconds.")
```

Clearly we need the functionality of a B-Tree to make queries possible and efficient in relational database joins. The next section goes on to explain the organization of a B-Tree, the advantages of B-Trees, and how they are implemented.

11.3   B-Tree Organization

A B-Tree is a balanced tree. Each node in a B-Tree consists of alternating pointers and items as shown in Fig. 11.5. B-Trees consist of nodes. Each node in a B-Tree contains pointers to other nodes and items in an alternating sequence. The items in a node are arranged sequentially in order of their keys. In Fig. 11.5 the key is the first value in each tuple. A pointer to the left of an item points to another B-Tree node

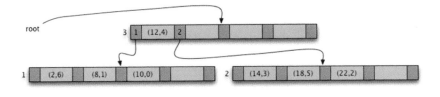

Record	FeedID	Rest of Feed Record
0	10	...
1	8	...
2	22	...
3	14	...
4	12	...
5	18	...
6	2	...

Fig. 11.5 A Sample B-Tree

that contains items that are all less than the item to the right of the pointer. A pointer to the right of an item points to a node where all the items are greater than the item. In Fig. 11.5 the items in node 1 are all less than 12 while the items in node 2 are all greater than 12.

B-Trees are always balanced, meaning that all the leaf nodes appear on the same level of the tree. A B-Tree may contain as many items and pointers as desired in each node. There will always be one more pointer than items in a node. B-Trees don't have to fill each node. The *degree* of a B-Tree is the minimum number of items that a B-Tree node may contain, except for the root node. The *capacity* of a node is always twice its *degree*. In Fig. 11.5 the degree is 2 and the capacity is 4.

The requirements of a B-Tree are as follows:

1. Every node except the root node must contain between *degree* and *2*degree* items.
2. Every node contains one more pointer than the number of items in the node.
3. All leaf nodes are at the same level within a B-Tree.
4. The items within a B-Tree node are ordered in ascending (or descending) order. All nodes have their items in the same order, either ascending or descending.
5. The items in the subtree to the left of an item are all less than that item.
6. The items in the subtree to the right of an item are all greater than that item.

To maintain these properties, inserting and deleting items from the tree must be done with some care. Inserting an item can cause splitting of a node. Deleting from a tree sometimes requires rebalancing of the tree. Looking up an item in a B-Tree is performed much the same way lookup is performed in a binary search tree. The node is examined to find the item. If it is not found, then the pointer is followed that lies between the items that are less than and greater than the item to be found. If this leads to a leaf node and the item is not found in the leaf node, the item is reported as not in the tree.

11.4   The Advantages of B-Trees

A B-Tree may contain entire records instead of just key/value pairs as appear in
Fig. 11.5 where the key/value pairs are the FeedID and record number of each record
in the Feed table. For instance, the entire record for FeedID 10 might be stored
directly in the B-Tree where (10,0) currently appears. In the examples in this text the
B-Tree and the database table are stored separately. This has the advantage that more
than one B-Tree index could be built over the Feed table. The B-Tree in Fig. 11.5 is
built over the FeedID field. Some other unique field might be used to build another
B-Tree over the table if desired. By storing the B-Tree and the table separately,
multiple indices are possible.

As mentioned earlier in the chapter, B-Trees provide $O(\log_d n)$ lookup time where
d is the degree of the B-Tree and n is the number of items in the tree. Hash tables
provide faster lookup time than a B-Tree. So why not use a hash table instead?

Unlike a hash table, a B-Tree provides ordered sequential access to the index.
You can iterate over the items in a B-Tree much like binary trees provide iteration.
Iteration over a B-Tree provides the items or keys in ascending (or descending) order.
A hash table does not provide an ordering of its keys.

B-Trees provide $O(\log n)$ insert, delete, and lookup time as well. While not as
efficient as hash tables in this regard, B-Trees nodes are often quite large providing
a very flat tree. In this case, the time for these three operations often comes close to
that of a hash table.

B-Trees are often constructed with literally millions of items. When a B-Tree
reaches this size, holding all the nodes in memory at one time may consume a lot of
RAM. This is a great advantage of B-Trees over hash tables. A B-Tree may be stored
in a file itself. Since files are randomly accessible on a disk, a B-Tree's node may be
thought of as a record in a file. Consider the B-Tree in Fig. 11.5. The nodes 1, 2, and 3
could be thought of as three records within a file. The record number are the pointer
values, so to search the B-Tree it is only necessary to start with the root node in
memory. Then, to search when a pointer is followed during search, the record corresponding to the new node is read into memory during the search. A search can proceed
in this way, reading one record at a time from disk. Typically a pool of records would
be held in memory for a B-Tree and records would be replaced in memory using some
sort of node replacement scheme. In this way a fixed amount of RAM can be allocated
to hold a B-Tree that would typically be much smaller than the total size of the tree.

In addition, since a B-Tree can be stored in a file, it is not necessary to reconstruct
the B-Tree each time it is needed. The code in Sect. 11.2.7 stores the B-Trees in two
files named *Feed.idx* and *FeedAttribType.idx* and reads the index from the file the
next time the program is run.

Deleting a record from a table with a million records or more in it could be an
expensive operation if the table has to be completely rewritten. If sequential access
to the underlying table is handled through the B-Tree or if the entire file is stored in
the nodes of the B-Tree, deletion of a row or record in the table gets much simpler.
For instance, in Fig. 11.6 the feed with FeedID of 10 remains in the Feed.tbl file, but

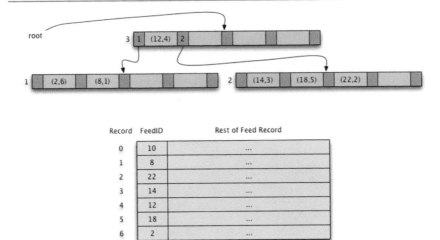

Fig. 11.6 A Sample B-Tree with Key 10 Deleted

has been deleted from the B-Tree. If sequential access is always handled through the B-Tree, it would appear that the feed with FeedID 10 has been deleted from the table. Deleting an item from the table in this way is a O(log n) operation while deleting by rewriting the entire file would take O(n) time. When *n* is millions of records, the difference between O(log n) and O(n) is significant.

The same goes for inserting a new row or record within the Feed table. Adding one new record to the end of a file can be done quickly, without rewriting the entire file. When a B-Tree is used the newly inserted item automatically maintains its sorted position within the file.

To summarize, B-Trees have several characteristics that make them attractive to use in relational databases and for providing access to large quantities or ordered data. These properties include:

- Ordered sequential access over the key value on O(n) time.
- O(log n) insert time, while maintaining the ordering of the items.
- O(log n) delete time of items within the B-Tree.
- If sequential access is handled through the B-Tree then O(log n) delete time is provided for the underlying table as well.
- B-Trees can be stored in a file and B-Tree nodes can be read on an as needed basis allowing B-Trees to be larger than available memory.
- A B-Tree index stored in a file does not have to be rebuilt each time it is needed in a program.

It is this final point that make B-Trees and their derivatives so valuable to relational database implementations. Relational databases need B-Trees and their derivative implementations to efficiently process *join* operations while also providing many of the advantages listed above.

11.5   B-Tree Implementation

Looking up a value in a B-Tree is relatively simple and is left as an exercise for the reader. Inserting and deleting values are where all the action is. Alan Tharp [7] provides a great discussion of both inserting and deleting values in a B-Tree. In this text we provide new examples and suggest both iterative and recursive implementations of both operations.

11.6   B-Tree Insert

Inserting an item in a B-Tree involves finding the leaf node which should contain the item. It may also involve splitting if no room is left in the leaf node. When a leaf node reaches its capacity, which is two times its degree and a new item is being inserted, the 2*degree+1 items are sorted and the median value (i.e. the middle value) is promoted up the tree to the parent node. In this way, splitting may cascade up the tree.

To see the splitting process in action, consider building the tree given in Fig. 11.5 with the keys given in this order [10, 8, 22, 14, 12, 18, 2, 50, 15]. The first item to be inserted is the 10. When this occurs, the B-Tree is empty, consisting of one empty node. The (10,4) item is added into that node as shown in Fig. 11.7.

The items with keys 8, 14, and 22 are inserted in a similar fashion as shown in Fig. 11.8. The node is now full. The next item to be inserted will cause a split.

The next item inserted is a 12 causing the node to split into two nodes. The left subtree node is the original node. The right subtree contains the new node. The middle value, 12 in this case, is promoted up to the parent. In this case, there is no parent since we split the root node. In this special case a new root node is created to hold the promoted value. After taking these steps, the tree appears as shown in Fig. 11.9.

The three values 18, 2, and 50 are inserted resulting in the tree as shown in Fig. 11.10.

When 15 is inserted B-Tree node number 2 is going to split and promote the middle value, 18 in this case, up to the parent. This time there is room in the parent so the new item is added resulting in the tree shown in Fig. 11.11.

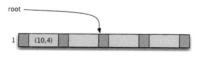

Fig. 11.7 Inserting 10 into an empty B-Tree

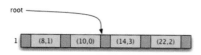

Fig. 11.8 After Inserting 8, 14, and 22

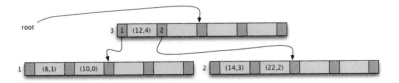

Fig. 11.9 After Splitting as a Result of Inserting 12

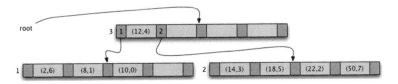

Fig. 11.10 After Inserting 18, 2, and 50

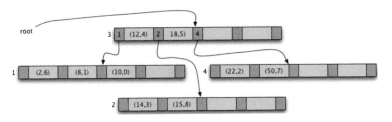

Fig. 11.11 Inserting 15 into the B-Tree Causes Splitting

Inserting an item causes one of two possible outcomes. Either the leaf node has room in it to add the new item or the leaf node splits resulting in a middle value and a new node being promoted to the parent. This suggests a recursive implementation is appropriate for inserting a new item. The recursive algorithm is given an item to insert and returns two values, the promoted key and the new right node if there is one and proceeds as follows.

1. If this is a leaf node and there is room for it, make room and store the item in the node.
2. Otherwise. if this is a leaf node, make a new node. Sort the new item and old items. Choose the middle item to promote to the parent. Take the items after the middle and put them into the new node. Return a tuple of the middle item and new right node.
3. If this is a non-leaf node, call insert recursively on the appropriate subtree. Consult the return value of the recursive call to see if there is a newly promoted key and right subtree. If so, take the appropriate action to store the new item and subtree pointer in the node. If there is no room to store the promoted value, split again as described in step 2.

Step 3 above automatically handles any cascading splits that must occur. After the recursive call the algorithm looks for any promoted value and handles it by either adding it into the node or by splitting again. An iterative version of insert would proceed in a similar manner as the recursive version except that the path to the newly inserted item would have to be maintained on a stack. Then, after inserting or splitting the leaf node, the stack of nodes on the path to the leaf would be popped one at a time, handling any promoted values, until the stack was emptied.

When writing insert as a recursive function it makes sense to implement it as a method of a B-Tree node class. Then the insert method on a B-Tree class can call the recursive insert on the B-Tree node class. In this way, if the root node is split, the B-Tree insert method can deal with this by creating a new root node from the promoted value and the left and right subtrees. Recall that the old root is the new left subtree in the newly created node.

11.7   B-Tree Delete

Deleting from a B-Tree can be written recursively or iteratively like the insert algorithm. When an item is deleted from a B-Tree there may be rebalancing required. Recall that every node, except the root node, of a B-Tree must contain at least *degree* items. There are just a few rules that can be followed to delete items from the tree while maintaining the balance requirements.

1. If the node containing the item is a leaf node and the node has more than degree items in it then the item may simply be deleted.
2. If the node containing the item is a leaf node and has *degree* or fewer items in it before deleting the value, then rebalancing is required.
3. If the node is a non-leaf node then the least value of the right subtree can replace the item in the node.

Rebalancing can be accomplished in one of two ways.

1. If a sibling of the unbalanced node contains more than *degree* items, then some of those items can be rotated into the current node.
2. If no rotation from a sibling is possible, then a sibling and the unbalanced node, along with the item that separates them in the parent, can be coalesced into one node. This reduces by one the number of items in the parent which in turn may cause cascading rotations or coalescing to occur.

Another example will help to illustrate the delete and rebalancing algorithm. Consider deleting the item containing 14 from the B-Tree in Fig. 11.11. This causes

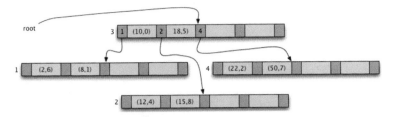

Fig. 11.12 After Deleting the Item Containing 14

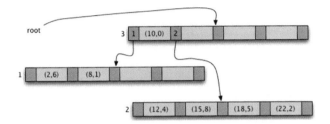

Fig. 11.13 After Deleting the Item Containing 50

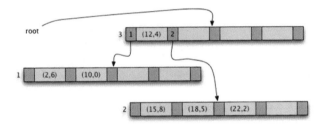

Fig. 11.14 After Deleting the Item Containing 8

the node containing 14 to become unbalanced. Rebalancing is accomplished by borrowing items from its left sibling. This is depicted in Fig. 11.12.

In Fig. 11.12 notice that the 10 rotates to the parent and the item containing 12 rotates into node 2 of the tree. This is necessary to maintain the ordering within the nodes. The rotation travels through the parent to redistribute the items between the two nodes. Next, consider deleting the item containing 50. In this case there is no sibling on the right and the sibling on the left doesn't have enough items to redistribute them. So, nodes 2 and 4 are coalesced into one node along with the item containing 18 from the root node, producing the B-Tree shown in Fig. 11.13.

Next, 8 is deleted from the B-Tree. This causes a left rotation with the right sibling resulting in the B-Tree depicted in Fig. 11.14.

Continuing the example assume that the item containing a key of 12 is deleted from the tree. The item is in a non-leaf node so in this case the least value from the right subtree replaces the item containing 12. This must be followed up with deleting

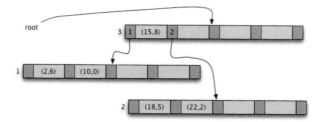

Fig. 11.15 After Deleting the Item Containing 12

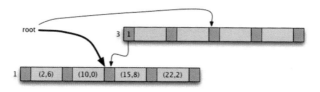

Fig. 11.16 After Deleting the Item Containing 18

that value, the item containing 15 in this case, from the right subtree. The result is depicted in Fig. 11.15.

Deleting 18 next causes the two sibling nodes to coalesce along with the separating item in the parent (the root in this case). The result is an empty root node as shown in Fig. 11.16. In this case, the delete method in the B-Tree class must recognize this situation and update the root node pointer to point to the correct node. B-Tree node 3 is no longer the root node of the B-Tree. Deleting any more of the nodes simply reduces the number of items in the root node.

Again, the delete method on B-Tree nodes may be implemented recursively. The B-Tree node delete method is given the item to delete and does not need to return anything. The recursive algorithm proceeds as follows.

1. If the item to delete is in the current node then we do one of two things depending on whether it is a leaf node or not.

   a. If the node is a leaf node, the item is deleted from the node without regard to rebalancing.
   b. If the node is a non-leaf node, then the smallest valued item from the right subtree replaces the item and the smallest valued item is deleted from the right subtree.

2. If the item is not in the current node then delete is called recursively on the correct subtree.
3. After delete returns, rebalancing of the child on the path to the deleted item may be needed. If the child node is out of balance first try rotating a value from a left

or right sibling. If that can't be done, then coalesce the child node with a left or right sibling.

If the algorithm is implemented iteratively instead of recursively a stack is needed to keep track of the path from the root node to the node containing the item to delete. After deleting the item the stack is emptied and as each node is popped from the stack rebalancing of the child node on the path may be required as described in the steps above.

11.8 Chapter Summary

B-Trees are very important data structures, especially for relational databases. In order for *join* operations to be implemented efficiently, indices are needed over at least some tables in a relational database. B-Trees are also important because they can be stored in record format on disk meaning that the entire index does not need to be present in RAM at any one time. This means that B-Trees can be created even for tables that consist of millions of records.

B-Trees have many important properties including O(log n) lookup, insert, and delete time. B-Trees always remain balanced, regardless of the order of insertions and deletions. B-Trees can also provide sequential access of records within a table in a sorted order, either ascending or descending.

Due to the balance requirement in B-Trees splitting of nodes may be required during item insertion. Rebalancing of nodes may be required during item deletion. Rebalancing takes the form of rotation of items or coalescing of nodes. Rotation to redistribute items is the preferred method of rebalancing.

Both the insert and delete operations may be implemented either recursively or iteratively. In either case the splitting or rebalancing may result in cascading splitting or rebalancing as the effects ripple up through the tree on the path taken to insert or delete the item. If implemented iteratively, both the insert and delete algorithms require a stack to record the path from the root node to the inserted or deleted item so that this ripple affect can be handled. In the recursive case no stack is required since the run-time stack remembers the path from the root node to the inserted or deleted item.

There are derivative implementations of B-Trees that have been created. B+-Trees and B#-Trees are two other variations that are not covered in this text. Alan Tharp [7], among others, covers both these derivative implementations.

11.9 Review Questions

Answer these short answer, multiple choice, and true/false questions to test your mastery of the chapter.

1. How does the use of an index improve the efficiency of the sample join operation presented in Sect. 11.2.7?
2. What advantages does a B-Tree have over a hash table implementation of an index?
3. What advantages does a hash table have over a B-Tree implementation of an index?
4. How can a B-Tree index be created over a table with millions of records and still be usable? What challenges could this pose and how does a B-Tree provide a means to deal with those challenges?
5. Starting with Fig. 11.13 insert an item with key 13 and draw a picture of the resulting B-Tree.
6. Starting with Fig. 11.10 delete the item containing 12 and draw a picture of the resulting B-Tree.
7. When does a node get coalesced? What does that mean? Provide a short example different from any example in the text.
8. When does a rotation correct imbalance in a node? Provide a short example different from any example in the text.
9. Insert the values 1 through 10 into an empty B-Tree of degree 4 to demonstrate your understanding of the insert algorithm. Draw pictures, but you can combine pictures that don't require splitting. At each split be sure to draw a completely new picture.
10. Delete the values 7, 8 and 9 from the tree you constructed in the previous review question showing the rebalanced tree after each deletion.

11.10 Programming Problems

1. Write a B-Tree class and a B-Tree node class. Implement the insert and delete algorithms described in this chapter. Implement a lookup method as well. Use this implementation to efficiently run the join operation presented in Sect. 11.2.7. Compare the time this algorithm takes to run to the time the non-indexed join, from Sect. 11.2.5, takes to run. Write the two methods recursively.
2. Write the B-Tree class with iterative, non-recursive, implementations of insert and delete. In this case the insert and delete methods of the B-Tree class don't necessarily have to call insert and delete on B-Tree nodes.
3. Since the example tables in this chapter are rather small, after completing exercise 1 or 2, run the query code again using a dictionary for the index. Compare the amount of time taken to implement the query in this way with the B-tree implementation. Comment on the experiment results.

Heuristic Search

12

This text has focused on the interaction of algorithms with data structures. Many of the algorithms presented in this text deal with search and how to organize data so searching can be done efficiently. Many problems involve searching for an answer among many possible solutions, not all of which are correct. Sometimes, there are so many possibilities, no algorithm can be written that will efficiently find a correct solution amongst all the possible solutions. In these cases, we may be able to use a *rule of thumb*, most often called a *heuristic* in computer science, to eliminate some of these possibilities from our search space. If the *heuristic* does not eliminate possible solutions, it may at least help us order the possible solutions so we look at *better* possible solutions first, whatever *better* might mean.

In Chap. 7 depth first search of a graph was presented. Sometimes search spaces for graphs or other problems grow to such an enormous size, it is impossible to blindly search for a goal node. This is where a heuristic can come in handy. This chapter uses searching a maze, which is really just a type of graph, as an example to illustrate several search algorithms that are related to depth first or breadth first search. Several applications of these search algorithms are also presented or discussed.

Heuristic search is often covered in texts on Artificial Intelligence [3]. As problems in AI are better understood, algorithms arise that become more commonplace over time. The heuristic algorithms presented in this chapter are covered in more detail in an AI text, but as data sizes grow, heuristic search will become more and more necessary in all sorts of applications. AI techniques may be useful in many search problems and so are covered in this chapter to provide an introduction to search algorithms designed to deal with large or infinite search spaces.

12.1 Chapter Goals

By the end of this chapter you will have been presented with examples of depth first and breadth first search. Hill climbing, best first search, and the A* (pronounced A star) algorithm will also be presented. In addition, heuristics will be applied to the search in two person game playing as well.

© Springer International Publishing Switzerland 2015
K.D. Lee and S. Hubbard, *Data Structures and Algorithms with Python*,
Undergraduate Topics in Computer Science, DOI 10.1007/978-3-319-13072-9_12

While heuristic search is not the solution to every problem, as data sizes grow, the use of heuristics will become more important. This chapter provides the necessary information to choose between at least some of these techniques to improve performance and solve some interesting large problems that would otherwise be unsolvable in a reasonable amount of time.

12.2   Depth First Search

We first encountered depth first search in Chap. 6 where we discuss search spaces and using depth first search to find a solution to some sudoku puzzles. Then, in Chap. 7 the depth first search algorithm was generalized a bit to handle search spaces that include cycles. To prevent getting *stuck* in a cycle, a visited set was used to avoid looking at vertices that had already been considered. A slightly modified version of the depth first search for graphs is presented in Sect. 12.2.1. In this version the path from the start to the goal is returned if the goal is found. Otherwise, the empty list is returned to indicate the goal was not found.

12.2.1 Iterative Depth First Search of a Graph

```
1    def graphDFS(G, start, goal):
2      # G = (V,E) is the graph with vertices, V, and edges, E.
3      V,E = G
4      stack = Stack()
5      visited = Set()
6      stack.push([start]) # The stack is a stack of paths
7
8      while not stack.isEmpty():
9        # A path is popped from the stack.
10       path = stack.pop()
11       current = path[0] # the last vertex in the path.
12       if not current in visited:
13         # The current vertex is added to the visited set.
14         visited.add(current)
15
16         # If the current vertex is the goal vertex, then we discontinue the
17         # search reporting that we found the goal.
18         if current == goal:
19           return path # return path to goal
20
21         # Otherwise, for every adjacent vertex, v, to the current vertex
22         # in the graph, v is pushed on the stack of paths yet to search
23         # unless v is already in the path in which case the edge
24         # leading to v is ignored.
25         for v in adjacent(current,E):
26           if not v in path:
27             stack.push([v]+path)
28
29     # If we get this far, then we did not find the goal.
30     return [] # return an empty path
```

The algorithm in Sect. 12.2.1 consists of a while loop that finds a path from a *start* node to a *goal* node. When there is a choice of direction on this path, all choices are pushed onto the stack. By pushing all choices, if a path leads to a dead end, the algorithm just doesn't push anything new onto the stack. The next time through the loop, the next path is popped from the stack, resulting in the algorithm *backtracking* to a point where it last made a decision on the direction it was going.

12.2.2 Maze Representation

How should the maze be represented? Data representation is such an important part of any algorithm. The maze consists of rows and columns. We can think of each location in the maze as a tuple of (row, column). These tuples can be added to a hash set for lookup in O(1) time. By using a hash set we can determine the adjacent (row,column) locations in O(1) time as well for any location within the maze. When a maze is read from a file, the (row, column) pairs can be added to a hash set. The adjacent function then must be given a location and the maze hash set to determine the adjacent locations.

12.2.3 DFS Example

Consider searching the maze in Fig. 12.1. Let's assume that our depth first search algorithm prefers to go up if possible when searching a maze. If it can't go up, then it prefers to go down. Next preference is given to going left in the maze, followed lastly by going right. Assume we start at the top of the maze and want to exit at the bottom. Note that going on the diagonal is not considered in the examples presented in this chapter since otherwise moves where two corners in the maze meet would be

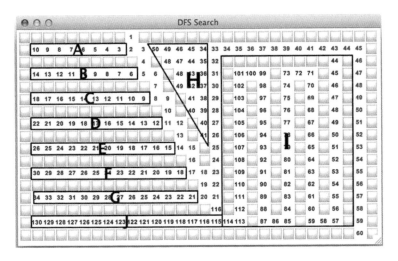

Fig. 12.1 Depth First Search of a Maze

possible. Diagonal moves would have the affect of moving through what looks like walls in the maze in some circumstances.

According to our direction preference, the algorithm proceeds by making steps 1 and 2 in red. Then it proceeds to travel to the left into region A. When it gets to 10 in region A, there are no possible moves adjacent to step 10 that have not already been visited. The code in lines 23–25 cannot find anything to push onto the stack.

However, when step 2 was originally considered, all the other choices were pushed onto the stack including the red three that appears to the right of step 2. When nothing is pushed onto the stack while looking at step 10 in region A, the next top value on the stack is the red step 3. The unvisited nodes adjacent to the red step 3 are then pushed onto the stack. The last location pushed is the red step 4, which leads to the red step 5 being pushed and considered next. Then the depth first search proceeds to the left again, examining all the locations in region B.

When region B is exhausted, backtracking occurs again, resulting in taking the red step 6. This leads to the search entering region D next, exhausting the possibilities on this path and backtracking occurring to take the search to step 12 in red. Likewise, regions E, F, and G are explored. When the search gets to red step 21 the depth first search prefers to go up and proceeds to the top of the maze and enters region H.

We can tell by looking at the maze that entering region H will lead nowhere. But depth first search does not know or care about this. It just blindly considers the next possible path to the goal until that path leads to the goal or we have exhausted all possible next steps and backtrack. Backtracking out of region H leads to step 34 in red. When we reach step 44 the algorithm prefers to go down first and proceeds on a wild goose chase leading from region I to region J where it runs out of possible next steps and backtracks to the red step 44. Finally, that path leads to the goal.

There are some things to notice about this search. First, as mentioned before, it was a blind search that uses backtracking to eventually find the goal. In this example the depth first search examined every location in the maze, but that is not always the case. Depth first search did find a solution, but it wasn't the optimal solution. If the depth first search were programmed to go right first it would have found a solution much faster and found the optimal solution for this maze. Unfortunately of course, that won't work for all mazes.

While the maze search space is finite, what if the *maze* was infinite in size and we went to the left while we should have started going right? The algorithm would blindly proceed going left forever, never finding a solution. The drawbacks of depth first search are as follows.

- Depth first search cannot handle infinite search spaces unless it gets lucky and proceeds down a path that leads to the goal.
- It does not necessarily find an optimal solution.
- Unless we are lucky, the search order in a finite space may lead to exhaustively trying every possible path.

We may be able to do better using either breadth first search or a heuristic search. Read on to see how these algorithms work.

12.3   Breadth First Search

Breadth First Search was first mentioned in Chap. 7. The code for breadth first search differs in a small way from depth first search. Instead of a stack, a queue is used to store the alternative choices. The change to the code is small, but the impact on the performance of the algorithm is quite big.

Depth first search goes down one path until the path leads to the goal or no more steps can be taken. When a path is exhausted and does not end at the goal, backtracking occurs. In contrast, breadth first search explores all paths from the starting location at the same time. This is because each alternative is enqueued onto the queue and then each alternative is dequeued too. This has an effect on how the search proceeds.

12.3.1 BFS Example

Breadth first search takes a step on each path each time through the while loop in Sect. 12.2.1. So, after step 2 in Fig. 12.1 the two step 3's occur next. Then the three step 4's occur. The three step 5's are next. The five step 6's are all done on the next five iterations of the while loop.

You can see that the number of alternatives is growing in this maze. There were 2 step 2's on up to five step 6's. The number of choices at each step is called the *branching factor* of a problem. A *branching* factor of one would mean that there is no choice from one step to the next. A branching factor of two means the problem doubles in size at each step.

Since breadth first search takes a step in each direction at each step, a branching factor of two would be bad. A branching factor of two means the size of the search space grows exponentially (assuming no repeated states). Breadth first search is not a good search in this case unless the goal node is very near the start node.

The breadth first search shown in Fig. 12.2 covers nearly as much of the maze as the blind depth first search did. Only a few locations are left unvisited. The breadth first search found the optimal solution to this maze. In fact, breadth first search will always find the optimal solution if it is given enough time.

Breadth first search also deals well with infinite search spaces. Because breadth first search branches out from the source exploring all possible paths simultaneously, it will never get stuck going down some infinite path forever. It may help to visualize pouring water into the maze. The water will fill the maze from the source and find the shortest way to the goal.

The advantages and disadvantages of breadth first search are as follows.

- Breadth first search can deal with infinite search spaces.
- Breadth first search will always find the optimal goal.
- It may not perform well at all when the problem has too high a branching factor. In fact, it may take millions of years or more to use breadth first search on some problems.

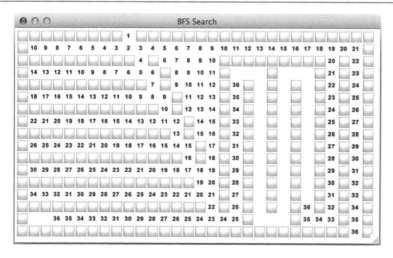

Fig. 12.2 Breadth First Search of a Maze

While it would be nice to be able to find optimal solutions to problems, breadth first search is not really all that practical to use. Most interesting problems have high enough branching factors that breadth first search is impractical.

12.4 Hill Climbing

Depth first search was impractical because it blindly searched for a solution. If the search is truly blind then sometimes we'll get lucky and find a solution quickly while other times we might not find a solution at all depending on the size of the search space, especially when there are infinite branches.

If we had some more information about where the goal is, then we might be able to improve the depth first search algorithm. Think of trying to summit a mountain. We can see the peak of the mountain so we know the general direction we want to take to get there. We want to climb the hill. That's where the name of this algorithm comes from.

Anyone who has climbed mountains knows that sometimes what appears to be a route up the mountain leads to a dead end. Sometimes what appears to be a route to the top only leads to a smaller peak close by. These false peaks are called localized maxima and hill climbing can suffer from finding a localized maximum and thinking that it is the overall goal that was sought.

12.4.1 Hill Climbing Example

Figure 12.3 features the same maze with hill climbing applied to the search. To climb the hill we apply a heuristic to help. In searching a maze, if we know the exit point of

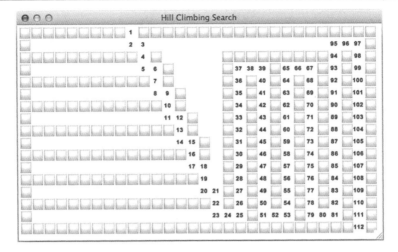

Fig. 12.3 Hill Climbing Search of a Maze

the maze we can employ the *Manhattan distance* as a heuristic to guide us towards the goal. We don't know the length of the path that will lead to the solution since we don't know all the details of the maze, but we can estimate the distance from where we are to the goal if we know the location of the goal and our current location.

The *Manhattan distance* is a measure of the number of rows and columns that separate any two locations on a maze or map. In Fig. 12.3 the Manhattan distance from the start to the goal is 36. We have to go down one row, then right 20 columns, and down 15 rows. This distance is called the Manhattan distance because it would be like walking between buildings in Manhattan or city blocks in any city.

The Manhattan distance would be either exact or an under-estimate of the total distance to the goal. In Fig. 12.3 it is an exact estimate, but in general a direct route to the goal may not be possible in which case the Manhattan distance would be an under-estimate. This is important because over-estimating the distance will mean that hill climbing will end up working like depth first search again. The heuristic would not affect the performance of the algorithm. For instance, if we took the easy approach and said that our distance was always 100 from the goal, hill climbing would not really occur.

The example in Fig. 12.3 shows that the algorithm chooses to go down first if possible. Then it goes right. The goal location is known and the minimum Manhattan distance orders the choices to be explored. Going left or up is not an option unless nothing else is available. So the algorithm proceeds down and to the right until it reaches step 25 where it has no choice on this path but to go up.

Hill climbing performs like depth first search in that it won't give up on a path until it reaches a dead end. While hill climbing does not find the optimal solution in Fig. 12.3, it does find a solution and examines far fewer locations in this case than breadth first or depth first search. The advantages and disadvantages of hill climbing are as follows.

- The location of the goal must be known prior to starting the search.
- You must have a heuristic that can be applied that will either under-estimate or provide an exact length of the path to the goal. The better the heuristic, the better the hill climbing search algorithm.
- Hill climbing can perform well even in large search spaces.
- Hill climbing can handle infinite search branches if the heuristic can avoid them.
- Hill climbing may suffer from local maxima or peaks.
- Hill climbing may not find an optimal solution like breadth first search.

To implement hill climbing the alternative choices at each step are sorted according to the heuristic before they are placed on the stack. Otherwise, the code is exactly the same as that of depth first search.

12.4.2 Closed Knight's Tour

Hill climbing can be used in solving the closed Knight's Tour problem. Solving this problem involves moving a knight from the game of chess around a chess board (or any size board). The knight must be moved two squares followed by one square in the perpendicular direction, forming an L on the chessboard. The closed knight tour problem is to find a path that visits every location on the board through a sequence of legal knight moves that starts and ends in the same location with no square being visited twice except the starting and ending location.

Since we want to find a path through the board, the solution can be represented as a path from start to finish. Each node in the path is a move on the board. A move is valid if it is on the board and is not already in the path. In this way, the board itself never has to be explicitly built.

Generating possible moves for a knight could be rather complex if you try to write code to deal with the edges of the board. In general, when adjacent nodes have to be generated and special cases occur on boundaries, it is far easier to generate a set of possibly invalid moves along with the valid moves. In the case of moving a knight around, there are eight possible moves in the general case. After generating all possible moves, the invalid moves are obvious and can be filtered out. Using this technique, boundary conditions are handled in a uniform manner once instead of with each separate possible move. The code is much cleaner and the logic is much easier to understand.

Figure 12.4 provides a solution to the closed knight's tour problem for a 12×12 board. The tour starts in the lower left corner where two edges were not drawn so you can see where the tour began and ended while it was being computed. The tour took a few minutes to find using a heuristic to sort the choices of next location. A least constrained heuristic was applied to sort the new choices before adding them to the stack. The least constrained next choice was the choice that would have the most choices next. Sorting the next moves in this fashion avoids looking at paths that lead to dead ends by generally staying closer to the edges of the board where the next move has the most choices. In other words, it avoids moving to the middle

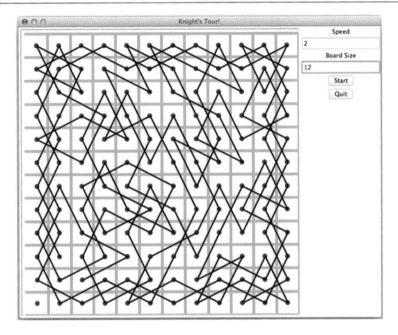

Fig. 12.4 A Closed 12×12 Knight's Tour

and getting stuck in the middle of the board. This heuristic is not perfect and some backtracking is still required to find the solution. Nevertheless, without this heuristic there would be no hope in solving the problem in a reasonable amount of time for a 12×12 board. In fact, the 8×8 solution can't be found in a reasonable amount of time with simple depth first search, unless you get lucky and search in the correct direction at each step. With the heuristic and hill climbing applied, the 8×8 solution can be found in just a few seconds.

12.4.3 The N-Queens Problem

To solve the N-Queens problem, N queens must be placed on an $N \times N$ chess board so that no two queens are in the same column, row, or diagonal. Solving this using depth first search would not work. The search space is too large and you would simply have to get very lucky to find a solution using brute force.

The N-Queens problem does have the unique feature that when a queen is placed on the board, all other locations in the row, column, or the diagonals it was placed in are no longer possible candidates for future moves. Removing these possible moves from the list of available locations is called *forward checking*. This forward checking decreases the size of the search space at each step.

The choice of the next row to place a queen is another unique feature of the N-Queens problem. The solution won't be easier to find if a random row is picked or if we simply pick the next row in the sequence of rows. So the search for the solution is only what column to place the next queen in.

To aide in forward checking, the board can be represented as a tuple: (queen locations, available locations). The first item in the tuple is the list of placed queens. The second item of the tuple is the list of available locations on the board. The forward checking can pick one of the available locations for the next row. At this point all locations in the second part of the tuple that conflict with the choice of the next queen placement can be eliminated. Thus forward checking removes all the possible locations that are no longer viable given a choice of placement for a queen.

The hill climbing part of solving the N-Queens problem comes into play when the choice of which column to place a queen is made. The column chosen is the one that least constrains future choices. Like the Knight's Tour, the N-Queens problem benefits when the next choice made leaves the maximum number of choices later. Using this heuristic, forward checking, and the simple selection of the next row in which to place a queen, it is possible to solve the 25-Queens problem in a reasonable amount of time. One solution is shown in Fig. 12.5.

To review, implementing hill climbing requires the alternative choices at each step be sorted according to the heuristic before they are placed on the stack. Otherwise, the code is exactly the same as that of depth first search. In some cases, like the Knight's Tour and the N-Queens problem, any solution is an optimal solution. But, as noted above when searching a maze, hill climbing does not necessarily find an optimal solution. Wouldn't it be nice if we could combine breadth first search and hill climbing.

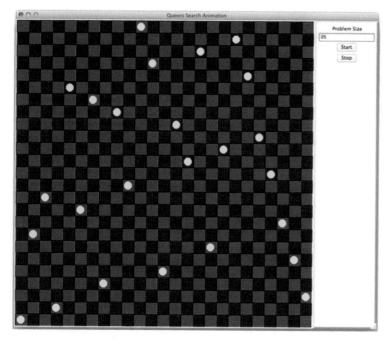

Fig. 12.5 A 25-Queens Solution

12.5 Best First Search

So, breadth first search can find an optimal solution and deal with infinite search spaces, but it is not very efficient and can only be used in some smaller problems. Hill climbing is more efficient, but may not find an optimal solution. Combining the two we get best first search. In best first search we order the entire queue according to the distance of each current node to the goal using the same heuristic as hill climbing.

12.5.1 Best First Example

Consider the example in Fig. 12.6. Step 3 moves closer by moving down one row to step 4. Now, to the right of step 3 is an equally good move (actually better knowing the optimal solution), but the next step is *better* at step 5 than to the right of 3 because it is closer to the eventual goal. So best first proceeds down and to the right like hill climbing until it gets to step 26 in red. At this step it is forced to move up and away from the goal. In this case red step 28 looks just as good as blue step 24 along the bottom. The Manhattan distance of both is 14. When we reach red step 29 then blue step 22 in the middle of the maze looks just as good. The effect of heading away from the goal is to start search all paths simultaneously. That's how best first works. It explores one path while it is moving towards the goal and multiple paths when moving away from the goal.

The code for best first search is a lot like breadth first except that a priority queue is used to sort the possible next steps on the queue according to their estimated distance from the goal. Best first has the advantage of considering multiple paths, like breadth first search, when heading away from the goal while performing like hill climbing when heading toward the goal.

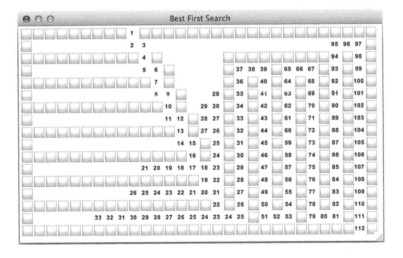

Fig. 12.6 Best First Search of a Maze

In the example shown here we did not do better than hill climbing. Of course, that is only this example. In general hill climbing may do worse than best first. It all depends on the order that locations are searched in the search space. However, neither hill climbing or best first found the optimal solution like breadth first search. They both got stuck heading into the long path in the middle of the maze.

12.6 A* Search

Wouldn't it be nice to be able to give up on some paths if they seem too long? That's the idea behind the A* algorithm. In this search, the next choices are sorted by their estimate of the distance to the goal (the Manhattan distance in our maze examples) and the distance of the path so far. The effect of this is that paths are abandoned (for a while anyway) if they appear to be taking too long to reach the goal.

12.6.1 A* Example

In Fig. 12.7 the same path is first attempted by going down and to the right until step 25 at the bottom of the maze is reached. Then that path is abandoned because the length of the path plus the Manhattan distance at step 4 in red is *better* than taking another step (step 26) at the bottom of the maze. Again the search goes down and to the right eventually filling the same region H from Fig. 12.1. At this point the search continues across the top to step 19 where it again goes down to step 33 at which point step 20 in red looks better than taking step 34 to the left. The search gives up on the blue path at step 33 and then proceeds to the goal from red step 20.

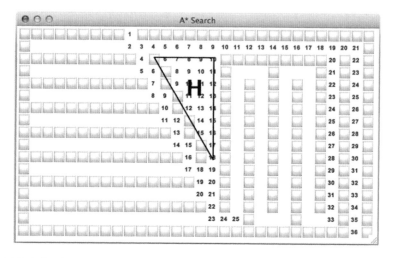

Fig. 12.7 A-Star Search of a Maze

The A* algorithm finds an optimal solution in this example because it gives up on two paths that are getting *too long* according to the heuristic plus total cost so far. Of course the optimality of the solution depends on the heuristic and the total cost. For instance, the heuristic should be good enough to return 0 as the cost of getting from the goal to the goal. The heuristic cannot over-estimate the cost of getting to the goal from the current node.

The A* algorithm was used to solve a problem in the Infinite Mario AI competition. In this competition programmers from around the world were given the task of writing code that would guide Mario through a programmable version of the Nintendo game *Mario Brothers*. The idea was that machine learning techniques would be employed to *teach* Mario to make good decisions while navigating the game's *world*. Instead of using machine learning, Robin Baumgarten solved the problem of getting Mario through the game by implementing the A* algorithm. In Robin's solution Mario makes choices based on the path length so far plus a heuristically computed cost to get to the goal. The A* implementation solved the problem and was a hit on the internet. You can read more about Robin's solution and how he developed it at http://aigamedev.com/open/interviews/mario-ai/.

12.7 Minimax Revisited

In Chap. 4 tictactoe was presented as a demonstration of two dimensional arrays. The outline of the minimax algorithm was presented. The minimax algorithm is used by computer games to provide a computer opponent. Minimax only applies in two person games of what is called *perfect information*. These are games where everyone can see everything. Poker is not a game of perfect information. Tic tac toe is a game of perfect information.

The game of tic tac toe is small enough that adults can generally look far enough ahead so they never lose, unless they make a careless mistake. Children on the other hand sometimes can't get enough! If you don't have children or younger brothers and sisters, someday you will understand. Tic tac toe is also small enough to be solvable by a computer. The minimax algorithm can play the game to its conclusion to insure that it never loses, just like an adult.

The game of connect four is a bit different. In this game, black and red checkers are dropped down slots in a vertically positioned board. The board is seven checkers wide by six checkers tall. Checkers always drop as far down as possible so there are at most seven choices at each turn in the game. The goal is to get four of your checkers in a row, a column, or on a diagonal. In Fig. 12.8 the computer has won with the four black checkers on the diagonal.

Playing connect four is not as easy as playing tic tac toe. With a branching factor of approximately seven at each turn, the number of possible boards quickly grows past what can be considered exhaustively in a reasonable amount of time. In these situations a heuristic must be added to the minimax algorithm to cut off the search. The algorithm is not repeated here. See Sect. 4.9 for a complete description of the

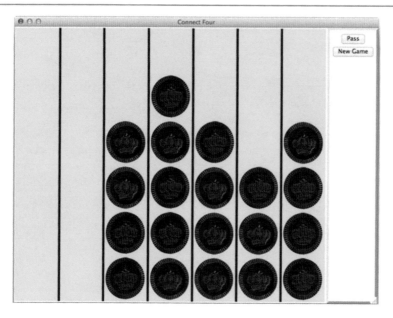

Fig. 12.8 The Connect Four Game

algorithm. The base cases for minimax are then modified as follows to incorporate the search cutoff heuristic.

1. The current board is a win for the computer. In that case minimax returns a 1 for a computer win.
2. The current board is a win for the human. In that case minimax returns a −1 for a human win.
3. The current board is full. In that case, since neither human or computer won, minimax returns a 0.
4. The maximum depth has been reached. Evaluate the board with no more search and report a number between −1.0 and 1.0. A negative value indicates the human is more likely to win given this board. A positive value indicates the computer is more likely to win.

To implement this last base case for the algorithm, a new depth parameter is passed to the minimax algorithm and possibly some other parameters as well. Early in a game the maximum depth may not be very deep. However, later in a game, when less choices are available, the maximum depth may be deeper. Increasing the depth of search is the best way to improve the computer's ability to win at games like this. A good heuristic can also help in earlier stages of the game when deeper search is not possible. Coming up with a good heuristic is a challenge. The trick is to keep it relatively simple to compute while encouraging moves in some fashion on the board.

We have developed a connect four implementation based on these ideas that runs on standard hardware without any special multiprocessing. Our version beats all commercially available apps and applications presently available when playing against them. Your challenge, should you care to take it on, is to build a better one. A front-end for this game is available in Sect. 20.6 or on the text's website so you can build your own connect four game.

12.8   Chapter Summary

This chapter covered heuristics and how they play a part in problems when the search space grows too large for an exhaustive search. Many problems that would otherwise be unsolvable are solvable when heuristics are applied. However, the nature of a heuristic is that sometimes they work well and other times they may not. If a heuristic worked every time, it would be called a technique and not a heuristic.

We must think carefully about whether heuristic search is really required or not when solving problems. Choosing the right problem representation, data structure, or algorithm is much more important than a brute force approach and applying a heuristic. It may be that a problem that seems too big to solve can be reduced to something that can be solved by the right algorithm. When there is no such reduction possible, heuristic search may be the answer.

The search algorithms hill climbing, best first, and A* are best remembered by comparing their algorithms to depth first search and breadth first search. Hill climbing is like depth first search except that a heuristic is applied to order the newly added nodes to the stack. Best first is like breadth first search except that all the nodes on the queue are ordered according to the heuristic. It is often implemented with a priority queue. The A* algorithm is like best first except that the queue is ordered by the sum of the heuristically estimated distance to the goal plus the distance travelled so far.

The minimax algorithm too uses a heuristic when the search space is too large. An effective game engine will always search as deep as possible, but when the search must be cut off, a good heuristic will help in estimating the worth of a move in the game.

12.9   Review Questions

Answer these short answer, multiple choice, and true/false questions to test your mastery of the chapter.

1. Which is faster, depth first search or breadth first search?
2. Which search, depth first or breadth first, may not complete in some situations? When could that happen?
3. When hill climbing, what could prevent the algorithm from finding a goal node?

4. Will the best first search algorithm find an optimal solution? Why or why not?
5. Will the A* algorithm find an optimal solution? Why or why not?
6. When would hill climbing be better to use than the A* algorithm?
7. What is forward checking and how does that help solve a problem?
8. Describe what happens in the depth first search algorithm when backtracking occurs. Be specific about how the algorithm behaves at the point when backtracking occurs in Sect. 12.2.1.
9. Name a game that cannot use the minimax algorithm other than poker.
10. What is the best way to insure that minimax behaves as desired: a really good heuristic or deeper search?

12.10 Programming Problems

1. Write a program that uses the five search algorithms in this chapter to search a maze as shown in the examples. Construct sample mazes by writing a text file where each space represents an open location in the maze and each non-space character represents a wall in the maze. Start the maze with the number of rows and columns of the maze on the first two lines of the file. Assume that you search the maze from top to bottom to find a way through it. There should be only one entry and one exit from your maze. Compare and contrast the different algorithms and their performance on your sample mazes. Be sure to download the maze searching front-end from the text's website so you can visualize your results. The architecture for communication between the front-end and your back-end code is provided in the front-end program file.
2. Write a program to solve the Knight's Tour problem. Be sure to use a heuristic in your search to narrow the search space. Make sure you can solve the tour quickly for an 8 × 8 board. Draw your solution using turtle graphics.
3. Write a program to solve the N-Queens problem. Use forward checking and a heuristic to solve the N-Queens problem for an 8 × 8 board. For an extra challenge try to solve it for a 25 × 25 board. The program will likely need to run for a while (a half hour?) to solve this one. Be sure to use the N-Queens front-end code provided on the text's website to visualize your result. The back-end code you write should follow the architecture presented at the top of the front-end program file.
4. Write the connect four program to challenge another student's connect four. You both must write programs that have a *pass* button. A flip of a coin can determine who goes first. The one who goes first should begin by pressing their pass button. Then you and the other student can flip back and forth while your computer programs compete. To keep things moving, your game must make a move within 30 s or it forfeits. You can use the front-end code presented in Sect. 20.6 as your front-end. You must write the back-end code. Follow the architecture to communicate with the front-end code presented at the top of the front-end program file.
5. For an extra challenge, write the connect four program and beat the program provided by the authors on text website. To run the author's code you must have

Python version 3 and Common Lisp installed. Both the front-end code and the author's back-end code must be in the same directory or folder to run the author's version of the program. You can get the author's front-end and back-end code from the text's website.

Appendix A: Integer Operators

13

This documentation was generated from the Python documentation available by typing *help(int)* in the Python shell. In this documentation the variables *x*, *y*, and *z* refer to integers. The official Python 3 documentation is at http://docs.python.org/3/.

Operator	Returns	Comments
x+y	int	Returns the sum of x and y
x−y	int	Returns the difference of x and y
x*y	int	Returns the product of x and y
x/y	float	Returns the quotient of x divided by y
x//y	int	Returns the integer quotient of x divided by y
x%y	int	Returns x modulo y. This is the remainder of dividing x by y
−x	int	Returns the negation of x
x&y	int	Returns the bit-wise *and* of x and y
x|y	int	Returns the bit-wise *or* of x and y
xy	int	Returns the bit-wise *exclusive or* of x and y
x<<y	int	Returns a bit-wise shift left of x by y bits. Shifting left by 1 bit multiplies x by 2
x>>y	int	Returns a bit-wise right shift of x by y bits
~x	int	Returns an integer where each bit in the x has been inverted. $x + x = -1$ for all x
abs(x)	int	Returns the absolute value of x
divmod(x, y)	(q,r)	Returns the quotient q and the remainder r as a tuple
float(x)	float	Returns the float representation of x
hex(x)	str	Returns a hexadecimal representation of x as a string
int(x)	int	Returns x
oct(x)	str	Return an octal representation of x as a string
pow(x, y[, z])	int	Returns x to the y power modulo z. If z is not specified then it returns x to the y power
repr(x)	str	Returns a string representation of x
str(x)	str	Returns a string representation of x

© Springer International Publishing Switzerland 2015
K.D. Lee and S. Hubbard, *Data Structures and Algorithms with Python*,
Undergraduate Topics in Computer Science, DOI 10.1007/978-3-319-13072-9_13

Appendix B: Float Operators

14

This documentation was generated from the Python documentation available by typing *help(float)* in the Python shell. In this documentation at least one of the variables *x* and *y* refer to floats. The official Python 3 documentation is at http://docs.python.org/3/.

Operator	Returns	Comments
x + y	float	Returns the sum of x and y
x − y	float	Returns the difference of x and y
x*y	float	Returns the product of x and y
x/y	float	Returns the quotient of x divided by y
x//y	float	Returns the quotient of integer division of x divided by y. However, the result is still a float
x%y	float	Returns x modulo y. This is the remainder of dividing x by y
abs(x)	int	Returns the absolute value of x
divmod(x, y)	(q,r)	Returns the quotient q and the remainder r as a tuple. Both q and r are floats, but integer division is performed. The value r is the whole and fractional part of any remainder. The value q is a whole number
float(x)	float	Returns the float representation of x
int(x)	int	Returns the floor of x as an integer
pow(x, y)	float	Returns x to the y power
repr(x)	str	Returns a string representation of x
str(x)	str	Returns a string representation of x

© Springer International Publishing Switzerland 2015
K.D. Lee and S. Hubbard, *Data Structures and Algorithms with Python*,
Undergraduate Topics in Computer Science, DOI 10.1007/978-3-319-13072-9_14

Appendix C: String Operators and Methods

15

This documentation was generated from the Python documentation available by typing *help(str)* in the Python shell. In the documentation found here the variables *s* and *t* are references to strings. The official Python 3 documentation is at http://docs.python.org/3/.

Method	Returns	Comments
s+t	str	Return a new string which is the concatenation of s and t
s in t	bool	Returns True if s is a substring of t and False otherwise
s==t	bool	Returns True if s and t refer to strings with the same sequence of characters
s>=t	bool	Returns True if s is lexicographically greater than or equal to t
s<=t	bool	Returns True if s is lexicographically less than or equal to t
s>t	bool	Returns True if s is lexicographically greater than t
s<t	bool	Returns True if s is lexicographically less than t
s!=t	bool	Returns True if s is lexicographically not equal to t
s[i]	str	Returns the character at index i in the string. If i is negative then it returns the character at index len(s)−i
s[[i]:[j]]	str	Returns the slice of characters starting at index i and extending to index j−1 in the string. If i is omitted then the slice begins at index 0. If j is omitted then the slice extends to the end of the list. If i is negative then it returns the slice starting at index len(s)+i (and likewise for the slice ending at j)
s * i	str	Returns a new string with s repeated i times
i * s	str	Returns a new string with s repeated i times
chr(i)	str	Return the ASCII character equivalent of the integer i
float(s)	float	Returns the float contained in the string s
int(s)	int	Returns the integer contained in the string s
len(s)	int	Returns the number of characters in s
ord(s)	int	Returns the ASCII decimal equivalent of the single character string s
repr(s)		Returns a string representation of s. This adds an extra pair of quotes to s
str(s)	str	Returns a string representation of s. In this case you get just the string s
s.capitalize()	str	Returns a copy of the string s with the first character upper case

(continued)

© Springer International Publishing Switzerland 2015
K.D. Lee and S. Hubbard, *Data Structures and Algorithms with Python*,
Undergraduate Topics in Computer Science, DOI 10.1007/978-3-319-13072-9_15

(continued)

Method	Returns	Comments
s.center(width[, fillchar])	str	Returns s centered in a string of length width. Padding is done using the specified fill character (default is a space)
s.count(sub[, start[, end]])	int	Returns the number of non-overlapping occurrences of substring sub in string s[start:end]. Optional arguments start and end are interpreted as in slice notation
s.encode([encoding[, errors]])	bytes	Encodes s using the codec registered for encoding. Encoding defaults to the default encoding. Errors may be given to set a different error handling scheme. Default is 'strict' meaning that encoding errors raise a UnicodeEncodeError. Other possible values are 'ignore', 'replace' and 'xmlcharrefreplace' as well as any other name registered with codecs.register_error that can handle UnicodeEncodeErrors
s.endswith(suffix[, start[, end]])	bool	Returns True if s ends with the specified suffix, False otherwise. With optional start, test s beginning at that position. With optional end, stop comparing s at that position. Suffix can also be a tuple of strings to try
s.expandtabs([tabsize])	str	Returns a copy of s where all tab characters are expanded using spaces. If tabsize is not given, a tab size of 8 characters is assumed
s.find(sub[, start[, end]])	int	Returns the lowest index in s where substring sub is found, such that sub is contained within s[start:end]. Optional arguments start and end are interpreted as in slice notation. Return −1 on failure
s.format(*args, **kwargs)	str	
s.index(sub[, start[, end]])	int	Like s.find() but raise ValueError when the substring is not found
s.isalnum()	bool	Returns True if all characters in s are alphanumeric and there is at least one character in s, False otherwise
s.isalpha()	bool	Returns True if all characters in s are alphabetic and there is at least one character in s, False otherwise
s.isdecimal()	bool	Returns True if there are only decimal characters in s, False otherwise
s.isdigit()	bool	Returns True if all characters in s are digits and there is at least one character in s, False otherwise
s.isidentifier()	bool	Returns True if s is a valid identifier according to the language definition
s.islower()	bool	Returns True if all cased characters in s are lowercase and there is at least one cased character in s, False otherwise

(continued)

(continued)

Method	Returns	Comments
s.isnumeric()	bool	Returns True if there are only numeric characters in s, False otherwise
s.isprintable()	bool	Returns True if all characters in s are considered printable in repr() or s is empty, False otherwise
s.isspace()	bool	Returns True if all characters in s are whitespace and there is at least one character in s, False otherwise
s.istitle()	bool	Returns True if s is a titlecased string and there is at least one character in s, i.e. upper- and titlecase characters may only follow uncased characters and lowercase characters only cased ones. Return False otherwise
s.isupper()	bool	Returns True if all cased characters in s are uppercase and there is at least one cased character in s, False otherwise
s.join(sequence)	str	Returns a string which is the concatenation of the strings in the sequence. The separator between elements is s
s.ljust(width[, fillchar])	str	Returns s left-justified in a Unicode string of length width. Padding is done using the specified fill character (default is a space)
s.lower()	str	Returns a copy of the string s converted to lowercase
s.lstrip([chars])	str	Returns a copy of the string s with leading whitespace removed. If chars is given and not None, remove characters in chars instead
s.partition(sep)	(h,sep,t)	Searches for the separator sep in s, and returns the part before it, the separator itself, and the part after it. If the separator is not found, returns s and two empty strings
s.replace (old, new[, count])	str	Returns a copy of s with all occurrences of substring old replaced by new. If the optional argument count is given, only the first count occurrences are replaced
s.rfind(sub[, start[, end]])	int	Returns the highest index in s where substring sub is found, such that sub is contained within s[start:end]. Optional arguments start and end are interpreted as in slice notation. Returns −1 on failure
s.rindex(sub[, start[, end]])	int	Like s.rfind() but raise ValueError when the substring is not found
s.rjust(width[, fillchar])	str	Returns s right-justified in a string of length width. Padding is done using the specified fill character (default is a space)
s.rpartition(sep)	(t,sep,h)	Searches for the separator sep in s, starting at the end of s, and returns the part before it, the separator itself, and the part after it. If the separator is not found, returns two empty strings and s

(continued)

(continued)

Method	Returns	Comments
s.rsplit([sep[, maxsplit]])	string list	Returns a list of the words in s, using sep as the delimiter string, starting at the end of the string and working to the front. If maxsplit is given, at most maxsplit splits are done. If sep is not specified, any whitespace string is a separator
s.rstrip([chars])	str	Returns a copy of the string s with trailing whitespace removed. If chars is given and not None, removes characters in chars instead
s.split([sep[, maxsplit]])	string list	Returns a list of the words in s, using sep as the delimiter string. If maxsplit is given, at most maxsplit splits are done. If sep is not specified or is None, any whitespace string is a separator and empty strings are removed from the result
s.splitlines([keepends])	string list	Returns a list of the lines in s, breaking at line boundaries. Line breaks are not included in the resulting list unless keepends is given and true
s.startswith(prefix[, start[, end]])	bool	Returns True if s starts with the specified prefix, False otherwise. With optional start, test s beginning at that position. With optional end, stop comparing s at that position. prefix can also be a tuple of strings to try
s.strip([chars])	str	Returns a copy of the string s with leading and trailing whitespace removed. If chars is given and not None, removes characters in chars instead
s.swapcase()	str	Returns a copy of s with uppercase characters converted to lowercase and vice versa
s.title()	str	Returns a titlecased version of s, i.e. words start with title case characters, all remaining cased characters have lower case
s.translate(table)	str	Returns a copy of the string s, where all characters have been mapped through the given translation table, which must be a mapping of Unicode ordinals to Unicode ordinals, strings, or None. Unmapped characters are left untouched. Characters mapped to None are deleted
s.upper()	str	Returns a copy of s converted to uppercase
s.zfill(width)	str	Pad a numeric string s with zeros on the left, to fill a field of the specified width. The string s is never truncated

Appendix D: List Operators and Methods

16

This documentation was generated from the Python documentation available by typing *help(list)* in the Python shell. In the documentation found here the variables *x* and *y* are references to lists. The official Python 3 documentation is at http://docs.python.org/3/.

Method	Returns	Comments
list()	list	Returns a new empty list. You can also use [ ] to initialize a new empty list
list(sequence)	list	Returns new list initialized from sequence's items
[item [,item]+]	list	Writing a number of comma-separated items in square brackets constructs a new list of those items
x+y	list	Returns a new list containing the concatenation of the items in x and y
e in x	bool	Returns True if the item e is in x and False otherwise
del x[i]		Deletes the item at index i in x. This is not an expression and does not return a value
x==y	bool	Returns True if x and y contain the same number of items and each of those corresponding items are pairwise equal
x>=y	bool	Returns True if x is greater than or equal to y according to a lexicographical ordering of the elements in x and y. If x and y have different lengths their items are == up to the shortest length, then this returns True if x is longer than y
x<=y	bool	Returns True if x is lexicographically before y or equal to y and False otherwise
x>y	bool	Returns True if x is lexicographically after y and False otherwise
x<y	bool	Returns True if x is lexicographically before y and False otherwise
x!=y	bool	Returns True if x and y are of different length or if some item of x is not == to some item of y. Otherwise it returns False
x[i]	item	Returns the item at index i of x

(continued)

© Springer International Publishing Switzerland 2015
K.D. Lee and S. Hubbard, *Data Structures and Algorithms with Python*,
Undergraduate Topics in Computer Science, DOI 10.1007/978-3-319-13072-9_16

(continued)

Method	Returns	Comments
x[[i]:[j]]	list	Returns the slice of items starting at index i and extending to index j−1 in the string. If i is omitted then the slice begins at index 0. If j is omitted then the slice extends to the end of the list. If i is negative then it returns the slice starting at index len(x)+i (and likewise for the slice ending at j)
x[i]=e		Assigns the position at index i the value of e in x. The list x must already have an item at index i before this assignment occurs. In other words, assigning an item to a list in this way will not extend the length of the list to accommodate it
x+=y		This mutates the list x to append the items in y
x*=i		This mutates the list x to be i copies of the original x
iter(x)	iterator	Returns an iterator over x
len(x)	int	Returns the number of items in x
x*i	list	Returns a new list with the items of x repeated i times
i*x	list	Returns a new list with the items of x repeated i times
repr(x)	str	Returns a string representation of x
x.append(e)	None	This mutates the value of x to add e as its last element. The function returns None, but the return value is irrelevant since it mutates x
x.count(e)	int	Returns the number of occurrences of e in x by using == equality
x.extend(iter)	None	Mutates x by appending elements from the iterable, iter
x.index(e,[i,[j]])	int	Returns the first index of an element that == e between the the start index, i, and the stop index, j−1. It raises ValueError if the value is not present in the specified sequence. If j is omitted then it searches to the end of the list. If i is omitted then it searches from the beginning of the list
x.insert(i, e)	None	Insert e before index i in x, mutating x
x.pop([index])	item	Remove and return the item at index. If index is omitted then the item at len(x)−1 is removed. The pop method returns the item and mutates x. It raises IndexError if list is empty or index is out of range
x.remove(e)	None	remove first occurrence of e in x, mutating x. It raises ValueError if the value is not present
x.reverse()	None	Reverses all the items in x, mutating x
x.sort()	None	Sorts all the items of x according to their natural ordering as determined by the item's __cmp__ method, mutating x. Two keyword parameters are possible: key and reverse. If reverse=True is specified, then the result of sorting will have the list in reverse of the natural ordering. If key=f is specified then f must be a function that takes an item of x and returns the value of that item that should be used as the key when sorting

Appendix E: Dictionary Operators and Methods

17

This documentation was generated from the Python documentation available by typing *help(dict)* in the Python shell. In the documentation found here the variable *D* is a reference to a dictionary. A few methods were omitted here for brevity. The official Python 3 documentation is at http://docs.python.org/3/.

Method	Returns	Comments
dict()	dict	new empty dictionary
dict(mapping)	dict	new dictionary initialized from a mapping object's (key, value) pairs
dict(seq)	dict	new dictionary initialized as if via: D = {} for k, v in seq: D[k] = v
dict(**kwargs)	dict	new dictionary initialized with the name=value pairs in the keyword arg list. For example: dict(one=1, two=2)
k in D	bool	True if D has key k, else False
del D[k]		Deletes key k from dictionary D
D1==D2	bool	Returns True if dictionaries D1 and D2 have same keys mapped to same values
D[k]	value type	Returns value k maps to in D. If k is not mapped, it raises a KeyError exception
iter(D)	iterator	Returns an iterator over D
len(D)	int	Returns the number of keys in D
D1!=D2	bool	Returns True if D1 and D2 have any different keys or keys map to different values
repr(D)	str	Returns a string representation of D
D[k]=e		Stores the key, value pair k,e in D
D.clear()	None	Remove all items from D
D.copy()	dict	a shallow copy of D
D.get(k[,e])	value type	D[k] if k in D, else e. e defaults to None
D.items()	items	a set-like object providing a view on D's items

(continued)

© Springer International Publishing Switzerland 2015
K.D. Lee and S. Hubbard, *Data Structures and Algorithms with Python*,
Undergraduate Topics in Computer Science, DOI 10.1007/978-3-319-13072-9_17

(continued)

Method	Returns	Comments
D.keys()	keys	a set-like object providing a view on D's keys
D.pop(k[,e])	v	remove specified key and return the corresponding value. If key is not found, e is returned if given, otherwise KeyError is raised
D.popitem()	(k, v)	remove and return some (key, value) pair as a 2-tuple; but raise KeyError if D is empty
D.setdefault(k[,e])	D.get(k,e)	Returns D.get(k,e) and also sets d[k]=e if k not in D
D.update(E, **F)	None	Update D from dict/iterable E and F If E has a .keys() method, does: for k in E: D[k] = E[k] If E lacks .keys() method, does: for (k, v) in E: D[k] = v In either case, this is followed by: for k in F: D[k] = F[k]
D.values()	values	an object providing a view on D's values

Appendix F: Turtle Methods

18

This documentation was generated from the Python documentation available by typing

from turtle import *
help (Turtle)

in the Python shell. In the documentation found here the variable *turtle* is a reference to a Turtle object. This is a subset of that documentation. The official Python 3 documentation is at http://docs.python.org/3/.

Method Description

turtle.back(distance)
    Aliases: backward bk
 	
    Argument:
    distance – a number
 	
    Move the turtle backward by distance, opposite to the direction the
    turtle is headed. Do not change the turtle's heading.
 	
    Example (for a Turtle instance named turtle):
    >>> turtle.position()
    (0.00, 0.00)
    >>> turtle.backward(30)
    >>> turtle.position()
    (−30.00, 0.00)

turtle.begin_fill()
    Called just before drawing a shape to be filled.
 	
    Example (for a Turtle instance named turtle):
    >>> turtle.color("black","red")
    >>> turtle.begin_fill()
    >>> turtle.circle(60)
    >>>turtle.end_fill()

© Springer International Publishing Switzerland 2015
K.D. Lee and S. Hubbard, *Data Structures and Algorithms with Python*,
Undergraduate Topics in Computer Science, DOI 10.1007/978-3-319-13072-9_18

Method Description

turtle.begin_poly()

    Start recording the vertices of a polygon. Current turtle position
    is first point of polygon.

    Example (for a Turtle instance named turtle):
    >>> turtle.begin_poly()

turtle.circle(radius, extent=None, steps=None)

    Arguments:
    radius – a number
    extent (optional) – a number
    steps (optional) – an integer

    Draw a circle with given radius. The center is radius units left
    of the turtle; extent - an angle - determines which part of the
    circle is drawn. If extent is not given, draw the entire circle.
    If extent is not a full circle, one endpoint of the arc is the
    current pen position. Draw the arc in counterclockwise direction
    if radius is positive, otherwise in clockwise direction. Finally
    the direction of the turtle is changed by the amount of extent.

    As the circle is approximated by an inscribed regular polygon,
    steps determines the number of steps to use. If not given,
    it will be calculated automatically. Maybe used to draw regular
    polygons.

    call: circle(radius) # full circle
    –or: circle(radius, extent) # arc
    –or: circle(radius, extent, steps)
    –or: circle(radius, steps=6) # 6-sided polygon

    Example (for a Turtle instance named turtle):
    >>> turtle.circle(50)
    >>> turtle.circle(120, 180) # semicircle

turtle.clear()

    Delete the turtle's drawings from the screen. Do not move turtle.
    State and position of the turtle as well as drawings of other
    turtles are not affected.

    Examples (for a Turtle instance named turtle):
    >>> turtle.clear()

turtle.color(*args)

    Arguments:
    Several input formats are allowed.
    They use 0, 1, 2, or 3 arguments as follows:

    color()
    Return the current pencolor and the current fillcolor
    as a pair of color specification strings as are returned
    by pencolor and fillcolor.

Method Description

color(colorstring), color((r,g,b)), color(r,g,b)
 inputs as in pencolor, set both, fillcolor and pencolor,
 to the given value.
 color(colorstring1, colorstring2),
 color((r1,g1,b1), (r2,g2,b2))
 equivalent to pencolor(colorstring1) and fillcolor(colorstring2)
 and analogously, if the other input format is used.
 If turtleshape is a polygon, outline and interior of that polygon
 is drawn with the newly set colors.
 For mor info see: pencolor, fillcolor
 	
 Example (for a Turtle instance named turtle):
 >>> turtle.color('red', 'green')
 >>> turtle.color()
 ('red', 'green')
 >>> colormode(255)
 >>> color((40, 80, 120), (160, 200, 240))
 >>> color()
 ('#285078', '#a0c8f0')

turtle.degrees()

Set the angle measurement units to degrees.
 	
 Example (for a Turtle instance named turtle):
 >>> turtle.heading()
 1.5707963267948966
 >>> turtle.degrees()
 >>> turtle.heading()
 90.0

turtle.dot(size=None, *color)

Optional arguments:
 size – an integer +>+= 1 (if given)
 color – a colorstring or a numeric color tuple
 	
 Draw a circular dot with diameter size, using color.
 If size is not given, the maximum of pensize+4 and 2*pensize is used.
 	
 Example (for a Turtle instance named turtle):
 >>> turtle.dot()
 >>> turtle.fd(50); turtle.dot(20, "blue"); turtle.fd(50)

turtle.end_fill()

Fill the shape drawn after the call begin_fill().
 	
 Example (for a Turtle instance named turtle):
 >>> turtle.color("black","red")
 >>> turtle.begin_fill()
 >>> turtle.circle(60)
 >>> turtle.end_fill()

Method Description

turtle.end_poly()

    Stop recording the vertices of a polygon. Current turtle position is
    last point of polygon. This will be connected with the first point.

    Example (for a Turtle instance named turtle):
    >>> turtle.end_poly()

---

turtle.filling()

    Return fillstate (True if filling, False else).

    Example (for a Turtle instance named turtle):
    >>> turtle.begin_fill()
    >>> if turtle.filling():
        turtle.pensize(5)
      else:
        turtle.pensize(3)

---

turtle.fillcolor(*args)

    Return or set the fillcolor.

    Arguments:
    Four input formats are allowed:
    - fillcolor()
    Return the current fillcolor as color specification string,
    possibly in hex-number format (see example).
    May be used as input to another color/pencolor/fillcolor call.
    - fillcolor(colorstring)
    s is a Tk color specification string, such as "red" or "yellow"
    - fillcolor((r, g, b))
    a tuple of r, g, and b, which represent, an RGB color,
    and each of r, g, and b are in the range 0..colormode,
    where colormode is either 1.0 or 255
    - fillcolor(r, g, b)
    r, g, and b represent an RGB color, and each of r, g, and b
    are in the range 0..colormode

    If turtleshape is a polygon, the interior of that polygon is drawn
    with the newly set fillcolor.

    Example (for a Turtle instance named turtle):
    >>> turtle.fillcolor('violet')
    >>> col = turtle.pencolor()
    >>> turtle.fillcolor(col)
    >>> turtle.fillcolor(0, .5, 0)

---

turtle.forward(distance)

    Aliases: fd

    Argument:
    distance – a number (integer or float)

Method Description

Move the turtle forward by the specified distance, in the direction the turtle is headed.
 	
Example (for a Turtle instance named turtle):
>>> turtle.position()
(0.00, 0.00)
>>> turtle.forward(25)
>>> turtle.position()
(25.00,0.00)
>>> turtle.forward(−75)
>>> turtle.position()
(−50.00,0.00)

turtle.get_poly()

Return the lastly recorded polygon.

Example (for a Turtle instance named turtle):
>>> p = turtle.get_poly()
>>> turtle.register_shape("myFavouriteShape", p)

turtle.get_shapepoly()

Return the current shape polygon as tuple of coordinate pairs.

Examples (for a Turtle instance named turtle):
>>> turtle.shape("square")
>>> turtle.shapetransform(4, −1, 0, 2)
>>> turtle.get_shapepoly()
((50, −20), (30, 20), (−50, 20), (−30, −20))

turtle.getscreen()

Return the TurtleScreen object, the turtle is drawing on.
So TurtleScreen-methods can be called for that object.

Example (for a Turtle instance named turtle):
>>> ts = turtle.getscreen()
>>> ts
<turtle.TurtleScreen object at 0x0106B770>
>>> ts.bgcolor("pink")

turtle.goto(x, y=None)

Aliases: setpos setposition

Arguments:
x – a number or a pair/vector of numbers
y – a number None

call: goto(x, y) # two coordinates
–or: goto((x, y)) # a pair (tuple) of coordinates
–or: goto(vec) # e.g. as returned by pos()

Move turtle to an absolute position. If the pen is down,
a line will be drawn. The turtle's orientation does not change.

Method Description

Example (for a Turtle instance named turtle):
>>> tp = turtle.pos()
>>> tp
(0.00, 0.00)
>>> turtle.setpos(60,30)
>>> turtle.pos()
(60.00,30.00)
>>> turtle.setpos((20,80))
>>> turtle.pos()
(20.00,80.00)
>>> turtle.setpos(tp)
>>> turtle.pos()
(0.00,0.00)

turtle.heading()
Return the turtle's current heading.
 	
Example (for a Turtle instance named turtle):
>>> turtle.left(67)
>>> turtle.heading()
67.0

turtle.hideturtle() Makes the turtle invisible. Aliases: ht It's a good idea to do this while you're in the middle of a complicated drawing, because hiding the turtle speeds up the drawing observably. Example (for a Turtle instance named turtle): >>> turtle.hideturtle()

turtle.isdown()
Return True if pen is down, False if it's up.
 	
Example (for a Turtle instance named turtle):
>>> turtle.penup()
>>> turtle.isdown()
False
>>> turtle.pendown()
>>> turtle.isdown()
True

turtle.isvisible()
Return True if the Turtle is shown, False if it's hidden.
 	
Example (for a Turtle instance named turtle):
>>> turtle.hideturtle()
>>> print(turtle.isvisible())
False

Method Description
turtle.left(angle)
Aliases: lt
Argument:
angle – a number (integer or float)
Turn turtle left by angle units. (Units are by default degrees,
but can be set via the degrees() and radians() functions.)
Angle orientation depends on mode. (See this.)
Example (for a Turtle instance named turtle):
>>> turtle.heading()
22.0
>>> turtle.left(45)
>>> turtle.heading()
67.0
turtle.onclick(fun, btn=1, add=None)
Bind fun to mouse-click event on this turtle on canvas.
Arguments:
fun – a function with two arguments, to which will be assigned
the coordinates of the clicked point on the canvas.
num – number of the mouse-button defaults to 1 (left mouse button).
add – True or False. If True, new binding will be added, otherwise
it will replace a former binding.
Example for the anonymous turtle, i. e. the procedural way:
>>> def turn(x, y):
turtle.left(360)
>>> onclick(turn) # Now clicking into the turtle will turn it.
>>> onclick(None) # event-binding will be removed
turtle.ondrag(fun, btn=1, add=None)
Bind fun to mouse-move event on this turtle on canvas.
Arguments:
fun – a function with two arguments, to which will be assigned
the coordinates of the clicked point on the canvas.
num – number of the mouse-button defaults to 1 (left mouse button).
Every sequence of mouse-move-events on a turtle is preceded by a
mouse-click event on that turtle.
Example (for a Turtle instance named turtle):
>>> turtle.ondrag(turtle.goto)
Subsequently clicking and dragging a Turtle will
move it across the screen thereby producing handdrawings
(if pen is down).

Method Description

turtle.onrelease(fun, btn=1, add=None)

Bind fun to mouse-button-release event on this turtle on canvas.

Arguments:
fun – a function with two arguments, to which will be assigned
the coordinates of the clicked point on the canvas.
num – number of the mouse-button defaults to 1 (left mouse button).

turtle.pencolor(*args)

Return or set the pencolor.

Arguments:
Four input formats are allowed:
- pencolor()
Return the current pencolor as color specification string,
possibly in hex-number format (see example).
May be used as input to another color/pencolor/fillcolor call.
- pencolor(colorstring)
s is a Tk color specification string, such as "red" or "yellow"
- pencolor((r, g, b))
a tuple of r, g, and b, which represent, an RGB color,
and each of r, g, and b are in the range 0..colormode,
where colormode is either 1.0 or 255
- pencolor(r, g, b)
r, g, and b represent an RGB color, and each of r, g, and b
are in the range 0..colormode

If turtleshape is a polygon, the outline of that polygon is drawn
with the newly set pencolor.

Example (for a Turtle instance named turtle):
>>> turtle.pencolor('brown')
>>> tup = (0.2, 0.8, 0.55)
>>> turtle.pencolor(tup)
>>> turtle.pencolor()
'#33cc8c'

turtle.pendown()

Pull the pen down – drawing when moving.

Aliases: pd down

Example (for a Turtle instance named turtle):
>>> turtle.pendown()

turtle.pensize(width=None)

Set or return the line thickness.

Aliases: width

Argument:
width – positive number

Method Description
Set the line thickness to width or return it. If resizemode is set to "auto" and turtleshape is a polygon, that polygon is drawn with the same line thickness. If no argument is given, current pensize is returned. Example (for a Turtle instance named turtle): >>> turtle.pensize() 1 turtle.pensize(10) # from here on lines of width 10 are drawn

turtle.penup()
Pull the pen up – no drawing when moving. Aliases: pu up Example (for a Turtle instance named turtle): >>> turtle.penup()

turtle.radians()

Set the angle measurement units to radians.
 	
Example (for a Turtle instance named turtle):
>>> turtle.heading()
90
>>> turtle.radians()
>>> turtle.heading()
1.5707963267948966

turtle.reset()

Delete the turtle's drawings from the screen, re-center the turtle and set variables to the default values.
 	
Example (for a Turtle instance named turtle):
>>> turtle.position()
(0.00,−22.00)
>>> turtle.heading()
100.0
>>> turtle.reset()
>>> turtle.position()
(0.00,0.00)
>>> turtle.heading()
0.0

turtle.setheading(to_angle)
Set the orientation of the turtle to to_angle. Aliases: seth Argument: to_angle – a number (integer or float) Set the orientation of the turtle to to_angle. Here are some common directions in degrees:

Method Description

standard - mode: logo-mode:

0 - east 0 - north
90 - north 90 - east
180 - west 180 - south
270 - south 270 - west

Example (for a Turtle instance named turtle):
>>> turtle.setheading(90)
>>> turtle.heading()
90

turtle.shape(name=None)

Set turtle shape to shape with given name / return current shapename.

Optional argument:
name – a string, which is a valid shapename

Set turtle shape to shape with given name or, if name is not given,
return name of current shape.
Shape with name must exist in the TurtleScreen's shape dictionary.
Initially there are the following polygon shapes:
'arrow', 'turtle', 'circle', 'square', 'triangle', 'classic'.
To learn about how to deal with shapes see Screen-method register_shape.

Example (for a Turtle instance named turtle):
>>> turtle.shape()
'arrow'
>>> turtle.shape("turtle")
>>> turtle.shape()
'turtle'

turtle.showturtle()

Makes the turtle visible.

Aliases: st

Example (for a Turtle instance named turtle):
>>> turtle.hideturtle()
>>> turtle.showturtle()

turtle.speed(speed=None)

Return or set the turtle's speed.

Optional argument:
speed – an integer in the range 0..10 or a speedstring (see below)

Set the turtle's speed to an integer value in the range 0 .. 10.
If no argument is given: return current speed.

If input is a number greater than 10 or smaller than 0.5,
speed is set to 0.

Method Description
turtle.undo()
Undo (repeatedly) the last turtle action.
Number of available undo actions is determined by the size of
the undobuffer.
Example (for a Turtle instance named turtle):
>>> for i in range(4):
turtle.fd(50); turtle.lt(80)
>>> for i in range(8):
turtle.undo()
turtle.write(arg, move=False, align='left', font=('Arial', 8, 'normal'))
Write text at the current turtle position.
Arguments:
arg – info, which is to be written to the TurtleScreen
move (optional) – True/False
align (optional) – one of the strings "left","center"or right"
font (optional) – a triple (fontname, fontsize, fonttype)
Write text - the string representation of arg - at the current
turtle position according to align ("left","center"or right")
and with the given font.
If move is True, the pen is moved to the bottom-right corner
of the text. By default, move is False.
Example (for a Turtle instance named turtle):
>>> turtle.write('Home = ', True, align="center")
>>> turtle.write((0,0), True)
turtle.xcor()
Return the turtle's x coordinate.
Example (for a Turtle instance named turtle):
>>> reset()
>>> turtle.left(60)
>>> turtle.forward(100)
>>> print(turtle.xcor())
50.0
turtle.ycor()
Return the turtle's y coordinate
Example (for a Turtle instance named turtle):
>>> reset()
>>> turtle.left(60)
>>> turtle.forward(100)
>>> print(turtle.ycor())
86.6025403784

Appendix G: TurtleScreen Methods

19

This documentation was generated from the Python documentation available by typing

from turtle import *
help (TurtleScreen)

in the Python shell. In the documentation found here the variable *turtle* is a reference to a Turtle object and *screen* is a reference to the *TurtleScreen* object. This is a subset of that documentation. The official Python 3 documentation is at http://docs.python. org/3/.

Method Description
screen.addshape(name)
Same thing as screen.register_shape(name)
screen.bgcolor(*args)

Set or return backgroundcolor of the TurtleScreen.
 	
    Arguments (if given): a color string or three numbers
    in the range 0..colormode or a 3-tuple of such numbers.
 	
    Example (for a TurtleScreen instance named screen):
    >>> screen.bgcolor("orange")
    >>> screen.bgcolor()
    'orange'
    >>> screen.bgcolor(0.5,0,0.5)
    >>> screen.bgcolor()
    '#800080'

© Springer International Publishing Switzerland 2015
K.D. Lee and S. Hubbard, *Data Structures and Algorithms with Python*,
Undergraduate Topics in Computer Science, DOI 10.1007/978-3-319-13072-9_19

Method Description

screen.bgpic(picname=None)

Set background image or return name of current backgroundimage.

Optional argument:
picname – a string, name of a gif-file or "nopic".

If picname is a filename, set the corresponding image as background.
If picname is "nopic", delete backgroundimage, if present.
If picname is None, return the filename of the current backgroundimage.

Example (for a TurtleScreen instance named screen):
>>> screen.bgpic()
'nopic'
>>> screen.bgpic("landscape.gif")
>>> screen.bgpic()
'landscape.gif'

screen.clear()

Delete all drawings and all turtles from the TurtleScreen.

Reset empty TurtleScreen to its initial state: white background,
no backgroundimage, no eventbindings and tracing on.

Example (for a TurtleScreen instance named screen):
screen.clear()

Note: this method is not available as function.

screen.colormode(cmode=None)

Return the colormode or set it to 1.0 or 255.

Optional argument:
cmode – one of the values 1.0 or 255

r, g, b values of colortriples have to be in range 0..cmode.

Example (for a TurtleScreen instance named screen):
>>> screen.colormode()
1.0
>>> screen.colormode(255)
>>> turtle.pencolor(240,160,80)

screen.delay(delay=None)

Return or set the drawing delay in milliseconds.

Optional argument:
delay – positive integer

Example (for a TurtleScreen instance named screen):
>>> screen.delay(15)
>>> screen.delay()
15

Method Description

screen.getcanvas()

Return the Canvas of this TurtleScreen.

Example (for a Screen instance named screen):
>>> cv = screen.getcanvas()
>>> cv
<turtle.ScrolledCanvas instance at 0x010742D8>

screen.getshapes()

Return a list of names of all currently available turtle shapes.

Example (for a TurtleScreen instance named screen):
>>> screen.getshapes()
['arrow', 'blank', 'circle', ... , 'turtle']

screen.listen(xdummy=None, ydummy=None)

Set focus on TurtleScreen (in order to collect key-events)

Dummy arguments are provided in order
to be able to pass listen to the onclick method.

Example (for a TurtleScreen instance named screen):
>>> screen.listen()

screen.mode(mode=None)

Set turtle-mode ('standard', 'logo' or 'world') and perform reset.

Optional argument:
mode – on of the strings 'standard', 'logo' or 'world'

Mode 'standard' is compatible with turtle.py.
Mode 'logo' is compatible with most Logo-Turtle-Graphics.
Mode 'world' uses userdefined 'worldcoordinates'. *Attention*: in
this mode angles appear distorted if x/y unit-ratio doesn't equal 1.
If mode is not given, return the current mode.

Mode Initial turtle heading positive angles

'standard' to the right (east) counterclockwise
'logo' upward (north) clockwise

Examples:
>>> mode('logo') # resets turtle heading to north
>>> mode()
'logo'

Method Description

screen.onclick(fun, btn=1, add=None)

Bind fun to mouse-click event on canvas.

Arguments:
fun – a function with two arguments, the coordinates of the
clicked point on the canvas.
num – the number of the mouse-button, defaults to 1

Example (for a TurtleScreen instance named screen
and a Turtle instance named turtle):

```
>>> screen.onclick(turtle.goto)
```

```
### Subsequently clicking into the TurtleScreen will
### make the turtle move to the clicked point.
>>> screen.onclick(None)
```

```
### event-binding will be removed
```

screen.onkey(fun, key)

Bind fun to key-release event of key.

Arguments:
fun – a function with no arguments
key – a string: key (e.g. "a") or key-symbol (e.g. "space")

In order to be able to register key-events, TurtleScreen
Must have focus. (See method listen.)

Example (for a TurtleScreen instance named screen
and a Turtle instance named turtle):

```
>>> def f():
        turtle.fd(50)
        turtle.lt(60)
```

```
>>> screen.onkey(f, "Up")
>>> screen.listen()
```

```
### Subsequently the turtle can be moved by
### repeatedly pressing the up-arrow key,
### consequently drawing a hexagon
```

Method Description

screen.onkeypress(fun, key=None)

Bind fun to key-press event of key if key is given,
or to any key-press-event if no key is given.

Arguments:
fun – a function with no arguments
key – a string: key (e.g. "a") or key-symbol (e.g. "space")

In order to be able to register key-events, TurtleScreen
must have focus. (See method listen.)

Example (for a TurtleScreen instance named screen
and a Turtle instance named turtle):

```
>>> def f():
        turtle.fd(50)


>>> screen.onkey(f, "Up")
>>> screen.listen()

### Subsequently the turtle can be moved by
### repeatedly pressing the up-arrow key,
### or by keeping pressed the up-arrow key.
### consequently drawing a hexagon.
```

screen.ontimer(fun, t=0)

Install a timer, which calls fun after t milliseconds.

Arguments:
fun – a function with no arguments.
t – a number >= 0

Example (for a TurtleScreen instance named screen):

```
>>> running = True
>>> def f():
    if running:
            turtle.fd(50)
            turtle.lt(60)
            screen.ontimer(f, 250)

>>> f() ### makes the turtle marching around
>>> running = False
```

Method Description

screen.register_shape(name, shape=None)

Adds a turtle shape to TurtleScreen's shapelist.

Arguments:
(1) name is the name of a gif-file and shape is None.
Installs the corresponding image shape.
!! Image-shapes DO NOT rotate when turning the turtle,
!! so they do not display the heading of the turtle!
(2) name is an arbitrary string and shape is a tuple
of pairs of coordinates. Installs the corresponding
polygon shape
(3) name is an arbitrary string and shape is a
(compound) Shape object. Installs the corresponding
compound shape.
To use a shape, you have to issue the command shape(shapename).

call: register_shape("turtle.gif")
–or: register_shape("tri", ((0,0), (10,10), (-10,10)))

Example (for a TurtleScreen instance named screen):
>>> screen.register_shape("triangle", ((5,-3),(0,5),(-5,-3)))

screen.reset()

Reset all Turtles on the Screen to their initial state.

Example (for a TurtleScreen instance named screen):
>>> screen.reset()

screen.screensize(canvwidth=None, canvheight=None, bg=None)

Resize the canvas the turtles are drawing on.

Optional arguments:
canvwidth – positive integer, new width of canvas in pixels
canvheight – positive integer, new height of canvas in pixels
bg – colorstring or color-tupel, new backgroundcolor
If no arguments are given, return current (canvaswidth, canvasheight)

Do not alter the drawing window. To observe hidden parts of
the canvas use the scrollbars. (Can make visible those parts
of a drawing, which were outside the canvas before!)

Example (for a Turtle instance named turtle):
>>> turtle.screensize(2000,1500)
e. g. to search for an erroneously escaped turtle ;-)

Method Description

screen.setworldcoordinates(llx, lly, urx, ury)

Set up a user defined coordinate-system.

Arguments:
llx – a number, x-coordinate of lower left corner of canvas
lly – a number, y-coordinate of lower left corner of canvas
urx – a number, x-coordinate of upper right corner of canvas
ury – a number, y-coordinate of upper right corner of canvas

Set up user coodinat-system and switch to mode 'world' if necessary.
This performs a screen.reset. If mode 'world' is already active,
All drawings are redrawn according to the new coordinates.

But ATTENTION: in user-defined coordinatesystems angles may appear
distorted. (see Screen.mode())

Example (for a TurtleScreen instance named screen):
>>> screen.setworldcoordinates(-10,-0.5,50,1.5)
>>> for _ in range(36):
        turtle.left(10)
        turtle.forward(0.5)

screen.title(titlestr)

Set the title of the Turtle Graphics screen. The title appears in the title bar
of the window.

screen.tracer(n=None, delay=None)

Turns turtle animation on/off and set delay for update drawings.

Optional arguments:
n – nonnegative integer
delay – nonnegative integer

If n is given, only each n-th regular screen update is really performed.
(Can be used to accelerate the drawing of complex graphics.)
Second arguments sets delay value (see RawTurtle.delay())

Example (for a TurtleScreen instance named screen):
>>> screen.tracer(8, 25)
>>> dist = 2
>>> for i in range(200):
        turtle.fd(dist)
        turtle.rt(90)
        dist += 2

screen.turtles()

Return the list of turtles on the screen.

Example (for a TurtleScreen instance named screen):
>>> screen.turtles()
[<turtle.Turtle object at 0x00E11FB0>]

Method Description
screen.update()
Perform a TurtleScreen update.
screen.window_height()
Return the height of the turtle window. Example (for a TurtleScreen instance named screen): >>> screen.window_height() 480
screen.window_width()
Return the width of the turtle window. Example (for a TurtleScreen instance named screen): >>> screen.window_width() 640
screen.mainloop()
Starts event loop - calling Tkinter's mainloop function. Must be last statement in a turtle graphics program. Must NOT be used if a script is run from within IDLE in -n mode (No subprocess) - for interactive use of turtle graphics. Example (for a TurtleScreen instance named screen): >>> screen.mainloop()
screen.numinput(title, prompt, default=None, minval=None, maxval=None)
Pop up a dialog window for input of a number. Arguments: title is the title of the dialog window, prompt is a text mostly describing what numerical information to input. default: default value minval: minimum value for imput maxval: maximum value for input The number input must be in the range minval .. maxval if these are given. If not, a hint is issued and the dialog remains open for correction. Return the number input. If the dialog is canceled, return None. Example (for a TurtleScreen instance named screen): >>> screen.numinput("Poker", "Your stakes:", 1000, minval=10, maxval=10000)
screen.textinput(title, prompt)
Pop up a dialog window for input of a string. Arguments: title is the title of the dialog window, prompt is a text mostly describing what information to input. Return the string input If the dialog is canceled, return None. Example (for a TurtleScreen instance named screen): >>> screen.textinput("NIM", "Name of first player:")

Appendix H: Complete Programs

20

20.1 The Draw Program

This is the sample drawing application from the first chapter. It illustrates the use of the tkinter library including many widgets and mouse handling. This program can be downloaded from the text's website.

```python
# The imports include turtle graphics and tkinter modules.
# The colorchooser and filedialog modules let the user
# pick a color and a filename.
import turtle
import tkinter
import tkinter.colorchooser
import tkinter.filedialog
import xml.dom.minidom

# The following classes define the different commands that
# are supported by the drawing application.
class GoToCommand:
    def __init__(self,x,y,width=1,color="black"):
        self.x = x
        self.y = y
        self.width = width
        self.color = color

    # The draw method for each command draws the command
    # using the given turtle
    def draw(self,turtle):
        turtle.width(self.width)
        turtle.pencolor(self.color)
        turtle.goto(self.x,self.y)

    # The __str__ method is a special method that is called
    # when a command is converted to a string. The string
    # version of the command is how it appears in the graphics
    # file format.
    def __str__(self):
        return '<Command x="' + str(self.x) +'" y="' + str(self.y) + \
               '" width="' + str(self.width) \
               + '" color="' + self.color +'">GoTo</Command>'

class CircleCommand:
    def __init__(self,radius, width=1,color="black"):
        self.radius = radius
        self.width = width
```

© Springer International Publishing Switzerland 2015

K.D. Lee and S. Hubbard, *Data Structures and Algorithms with Python*,
Undergraduate Topics in Computer Science, DOI 10.1007/978-3-319-13072-9_20

```
39              self.color = color
40
41      def draw(self,turtle):
42          turtle.width(self.width)
43          turtle.pencolor(self.color)
44          turtle.circle(self.radius)
45
46      def __str__(self):
47          return '<Command_radius="' + str(self.radius) +'"_width="' + \
48                  str(self.width) +'"_color="' + self.color +'">Circle </Command>'
49
50  class BeginFillCommand:
51      def __init__(self,color):
52          self.color = color
53
54      def draw(self,turtle):
55          turtle.fillcolor(self.color)
56          turtle.begin_fill()
57
58      def __str__(self):
59          return '<Command_color="' + self.color +'">BeginFill </Command>'
60
61  class EndFillCommand:
62      def __init__(self):
63          pass
64
65      def draw(self,turtle):
66          turtle.end_fill()
67
68      def __str__(self):
69          return "<Command>EndFill </Command>"
70
71  class PenUpCommand:
72      def __init__(self):
73          pass
74
75      def draw(self,turtle):
76          turtle.penup()
77
78      def __str__(self):
79          return "<Command>PenUp </Command>"
80
81  class PenDownCommand:
82      def __init__(self):
83          pass
84
85      def draw(self,turtle):
86          turtle.pendown()
87
88      def __str__(self):
89          return "<Command>PenDown </Command>"
90
91  # This is the PyList container object. It is meant to hold a
92  class PyList:
93      def __init__(self):
94          self.gcList = []
95
96      # The append method is used to add commands to the sequence.
97      def append(self,item):
98          self.gcList = self.gcList + [item]
99
100     # This method is used by the undo function. It slices the sequence
101     # to remove the last item
102     def removeLast(self):
103         self.gcList = self.gcList[:-1]
104
105     # This special method is called when iterating over the sequence.
106     # Each time yield is called another element of the sequence is returned
107     # to the iterator (i.e. the for loop that called this.)
```

```
108          def __iter__(self):
109              for c in self.gcList:
110                  yield c
111
112          # This is called when the len function is called on the sequence.
113          def __len__(self):
114              return len(self.gcList)
115
116   # This class defines the drawing application. The following line says that
117   # the DrawingApplication class inherits from the Frame class. This means
118   # that a DrawingApplication is like a Frame object except for the code
119   # written here which redefines/extends the behavior of a Frame.
120   class DrawingApplication(tkinter.Frame):
121          def __init__(self, master=None):
122              super().__init__(master)
123              self.pack()
124              self.buildWindow()
125              self.graphicsCommands = PyList()
126
127          # This method is called to create all the widgets, place them in the GUI,
128          # and define the event handlers for the application.
129          def buildWindow(self):
130
131              # The master is the root window. The title is set as below.
132              self.master.title("Draw")
133
134              # Here is how to create a menu bar. The tearoff=0 means that menus
135              # can't be separated from the window which is a feature of tkinter.
136              bar = tkinter.Menu(self.master)
137              fileMenu = tkinter.Menu(bar,tearoff=0)
138
139              # This code is called by the "New" menu item below when it is selected.
140              # The same applies for loadFile, addToFile, and saveFile below. The
141              # "Exit" menu item below calls quit on the "master" or root window.
142              def newWindow():
143                  # This sets up the turtle to be ready for a new picture to be
144                  # drawn. It also sets the sequence back to empty. It is necessary
145                  # for the graphicsCommands sequence to be in the object (i.e.
146                  # self.graphicsCommands) because otherwise the statement:
147                  # graphicsCommands = PyList()
148                  # would make this variable a local variable in the newWindow
149                  # method. If it were local, it would not be set anymore once the
150                  # newWindow method returned.
151                  theTurtle.clear()
152                  theTurtle.penup()
153                  theTurtle.goto(0,0)
154                  theTurtle.pendown()
155                  screen.update()
156                  screen.listen()
157                  self.graphicsCommands = PyList()
158
159              fileMenu.add_command(label="New",command=newWindow)
160
161              # The parse function adds the contents of an XML file to the sequence.
162              def parse(filename):
163                  xmldoc = xml.dom.minidom.parse(filename)
164
165                  graphicsCommandsElement = xmldoc.getElementsByTagName("GraphicsCommands")[0]
166
167                  graphicsCommands = graphicsCommandsElement.getElementsByTagName("Command")
168
169                  for commandElement in graphicsCommands:
170                      print(type(commandElement))
171                      command = commandElement.firstChild.data.strip()
172                      attr = commandElement.attributes
173                      if command == "GoTo":
174                          x = float(attr["x"].value)
175                          y = float(attr["y"].value)
176                          width = float(attr["width"].value)
```

```
177                    color = attr["color"].value.strip()
178                    cmd = GoToCommand(x,y,width,color)
179
180                elif command == "Circle":
181                    radius = float(attr["radius"].value)
182                    width = float(attr["width"].value)
183                    color = attr["color"].value.strip()
184                    cmd = CircleCommand(radius,width,color)
185
186                elif command == "BeginFill":
187                    color = attr["color"].value.strip()
188                    cmd = BeginFillCommand(color)
189
190                elif command == "EndFill":
191                    cmd = EndFillCommand()
192
193                elif command == "PenUp":
194                    cmd = PenUpCommand()
195
196                elif command == "PenDown":
197                    cmd = PenDownCommand()
198                else:
199                    raise RuntimeError("Unknown_Command:_" + command)
200
201                self.graphicsCommands.append(cmd)
202
203        def loadFile():
204
205            filename = tkinter.filedialog.askopenfilename(title="Select_a_Graphics_File")
206
207            newWindow()
208
209            # This re-initializes the sequence for the new picture.
210            self.graphicsCommands = PyList()
211
212            # calling parse will read the graphics commands from the file.
213            parse(filename)
214
215            for cmd in self.graphicsCommands:
216                cmd.draw(theTurtle)
217
218            # This line is necessary to update the window after the picture is drawn.
219            screen.update()
220
221
222        fileMenu.add_command(label="Load ...",command=loadFile)
223
224        def addToFile():
225            filename = tkinter.filedialog.askopenfilename(title="Select_a_Graphics_File")
226
227            theTurtle.penup()
228            theTurtle.goto(0,0)
229            theTurtle.pendown()
230            theTurtle.pencolor("#000000")
231            theTurtle.fillcolor("#000000")
232            cmd = PenUpCommand()
233            self.graphicsCommands.append(cmd)
234            cmd = GoToCommand(0,0,1,"#000000")
235            self.graphicsCommands.append(cmd)
236            cmd = PenDownCommand()
237            self.graphicsCommands.append(cmd)
238            screen.update()
239            parse(filename)
240
241            for cmd in self.graphicsCommands:
242                cmd.draw(theTurtle)
243
244
245
```

```
246                  screen.update()
247
248          fileMenu.add_command(label="Load_Into...",command=addToFile)
249
250          # The write function writes an XML file to the given filename
251          def write(filename):
252              file = open(filename, "w")
253              file.write('<?xml_version="1.0"_encoding="UTF-8"_standalone="no"_?>\n')
254              file.write('<GraphicsCommands>\n')
255              for cmd in self.graphicsCommands:
256                  file.write('____'+str(cmd)+"\n")
257
258              file.write('</GraphicsCommands>\n')
259
260              file.close()
261
262          def saveFile():
263              filename = tkinter.filedialog.asksaveasfilename(title="Save_Picture_As...")
264              write(filename)
265
266          fileMenu.add_command(label="Save_As...",command=saveFile)
267
268
269          fileMenu.add_command(label="Exit",command=self.master.quit)
270
271          bar.add_cascade(label="File",menu=fileMenu)
272
273          # This tells the root window to display the newly created menu bar.
274          self.master.config(menu=bar)
275
276          # Here several widgets are created. The canvas is the drawing area on
277          # the left side of the window.
278          canvas = tkinter.Canvas(self,width=600,height=600)
279          canvas.pack(side=tkinter.LEFT)
280
281          # By creating a RawTurtle, we can have the turtle draw on this canvas.
282          # Otherwise, a RawTurtle and a Turtle are exactly the same.
283          theTurtle = turtle.RawTurtle(canvas)
284
285          # This makes the shape of the turtle a circle.
286          theTurtle.shape("circle")
287          screen = theTurtle.getscreen()
288
289          # This causes the application to not update the screen unless
290          # screen.update() is called. This is necessary for the ondrag event
291          # handler below. Without it, the program bombs after dragging the
292          # turtle around for a while.
293          screen.tracer(0)
294
295          # This is the area on the right side of the window where all the
296          # buttons, labels, and entry boxes are located. The pad creates some empty
297          # space around the side. The side puts the sideBar on the right side of the
298          # this frame. The fill tells it to fill in all space available on the right
299          # side.
300          sideBar = tkinter.Frame(self,padx=5,pady=5)
301          sideBar.pack(side=tkinter.RIGHT, fill=tkinter.BOTH)
302
303          # This is a label widget. Packing it puts it at the top of the sidebar.
304          pointLabel = tkinter.Label(sideBar,text="Width")
305          pointLabel.pack()
306
307          # This entry widget allows the user to pick a width for their lines.
308          # With the widthSize variable below you can write widthSize.get() to get
309          # the contents of the entry widget and widthSize.set(val) to set the value
310          # of the entry widget to val. Initially the widthSize is set to 1. str(1) is
311          # needed because the entry widget must be given a string.
312          widthSize = tkinter.StringVar()
313          widthEntry = tkinter.Entry(sideBar,textvariable=widthSize)
314          widthEntry.pack()
```

```
315          widthSize.set(str(1))
316
317          radiusLabel = tkinter.Label(sideBar,text="Radius")
318          radiusLabel.pack()
319          radiusSize = tkinter.StringVar()
320          radiusEntry = tkinter.Entry(sideBar,textvariable=radiusSize)
321          radiusSize.set(str(10))
322          radiusEntry.pack()
323
324          # A button widget calls an event handler when it is pressed. The circleHandler
325          # function below is the event handler when the Draw Circle button is pressed.
326          def circleHandler():
327              # When drawing, a command is created and then the command is drawn by calling
328              # the draw method. Adding the command to the graphicsCommands sequence means the
329              # application will remember the picture.
330              cmd = CircleCommand(float(radiusSize.get()), float(widthSize.get()), penColor.get())
331              cmd.draw(theTurtle)
332              self.graphicsCommands.append(cmd)
333
334              # These two lines are needed to update the screen and to put the focus back
335              # in the drawing canvas. This is necessary because when pressing "u" to undo,
336              # the screen must have focus to receive the key press.
337              screen.update()
338              screen.listen()
339
340          # This creates the button widget in the sideBar. The fill=tkinter.BOTH causes the button
341          # to expand to fill the entire width of the sideBar.
342          circleButton = tkinter.Button(sideBar, text = "Draw_Circle", command=circleHandler)
343          circleButton.pack(fill=tkinter.BOTH)
344
345          # The color mode 255 below allows colors to be specified in RGB form (i.e. Red/
346          # Green/Blue). The mode allows the Red value to be set by a two digit hexadecimal
347          # number ranging from 00-FF. The same applies for Blue and Green values. The
348          # color choosers below return a string representing the selected color and a slice
349          # is taken to extract the #RRGGBB hexadecimal string that the color choosers return.
350          screen.colormode(255)
351          penLabel = tkinter.Label(sideBar,text="Pen_Color")
352          penLabel.pack()
353          penColor = tkinter.StringVar()
354          penEntry = tkinter.Entry(sideBar,textvariable=penColor)
355          penEntry.pack()
356          # This is the color black.
357          penColor.set("#000000")
358
359          def getPenColor():
360              color = tkinter.colorchooser.askcolor()
361              if color != None:
362                  penColor.set(str(color)[-9:-2])
363
364          penColorButton = tkinter.Button(sideBar, text = "Pick_Pen_Color", command=getPenColor)
365          penColorButton.pack(fill=tkinter.BOTH)
366
367          fillLabel = tkinter.Label(sideBar,text="Fill_Color")
368          fillLabel.pack()
369          fillColor = tkinter.StringVar()
370          fillEntry = tkinter.Entry(sideBar,textvariable=fillColor)
371          fillEntry.pack()
372          fillColor.set("#000000")
373
374          def getFillColor():
375              color = tkinter.colorchooser.askcolor()
376              if color != None:
377                  fillColor.set(str(color)[-9:-2])
378
379          fillColorButton = \
380              tkinter.Button(sideBar, text = "Pick_Fill_Color", command=getFillColor)
381          fillColorButton.pack(fill=tkinter.BOTH)
382
383
```

```
384        def beginFillHandler ():
385            cmd = BeginFillCommand ( fillColor . get ())
386            cmd . draw ( theTurtle )
387            self . graphicsCommands . append (cmd)
388
389        beginFillButton = tkinter . Button ( sideBar , text = "Begin_Fill" , command=beginFillHandler )
390        beginFillButton . pack ( fill=tkinter .BOTH)
391
392        def endFillHandler ():
393            cmd = EndFillCommand ()
394            cmd . draw ( theTurtle )
395            self . graphicsCommands . append (cmd)
396
397        endFillButton = tkinter . Button ( sideBar , text = "End_Fill" , command=endFillHandler )
398        endFillButton . pack ( fill=tkinter .BOTH)
399
400        penLabel = tkinter . Label ( sideBar , text="Pen_Is_Down" )
401        penLabel . pack ()
402
403        def penUpHandler ():
404            cmd = PenUpCommand ()
405            cmd . draw ( theTurtle )
406            penLabel . configure ( text="Pen_Is_Up" )
407            self . graphicsCommands . append (cmd)
408
409        penUpButton = tkinter . Button ( sideBar , text = "Pen_Up" , command=penUpHandler )
410        penUpButton . pack ( fill=tkinter .BOTH)
411
412        def penDownHandler ():
413            cmd = PenDownCommand ()
414            cmd . draw ( theTurtle )
415            penLabel . configure ( text="Pen_Is_Down" )
416            self . graphicsCommands . append (cmd)
417
418        penDownButton = tkinter . Button ( sideBar , text = "Pen_Down" , command=penDownHandler )
419        penDownButton . pack ( fill=tkinter .BOTH)
420
421        # Here is another event handler. This one handles mouse clicks on the screen.
422        def clickHandler (x ,y ):
423            # When a mouse click occurs , get the widthSize entry value and set the width of the
424            # pen to the widthSize value. The float (widthSize .get ()) is needed because
425            # the width is a float , but the entry widget stores it as a string.
426            cmd = GoToCommand (x ,y , float ( widthSize . get ()) , penColor . get ())
427            cmd . draw ( theTurtle )
428            self . graphicsCommands . append (cmd)
429            screen . update ()
430            screen . listen ()
431
432        # Here is how we tie the clickHandler to mouse clicks.
433        screen . onclick ( clickHandler )
434
435        def dragHandler (x ,y ):
436            cmd = GoToCommand (x ,y . float ( widthSize . get ()) , penColor . get ())
437            cmd . draw ( theTurtle )
438            self . graphicsCommands . append (cmd)
439            screen . update ()
440            screen . listen ()
441
442        theTurtle . ondrag ( dragHandler )
443
444        # the undoHandler undoes the last command by removing it from the
445        # sequence and then redrawing the entire picture.
446        def undoHandler ():
447            if len ( self . graphicsCommands ) > 0:
448                self . graphicsCommands . removeLast ()
449                theTurtle . clear ()
450                theTurtle . penup ()
451                theTurtle . goto (0 ,0)
452                theTurtle . pendown ()
```

```
453                  for cmd in self.graphicsCommands:
454                      cmd.draw(theTurtle)
455                  screen.update()
456                  screen.listen()
457
458              screen.onkeypress(undoHandler, "u")
459              screen.listen()
460
461      # The main function in our GUI program is very simple. It creates the
462      # root window. Then it creates the DrawingApplication frame which creates
463      # all the widgets and has the logic for the event handlers. Calling mainloop
464      # on the frames makes it start listening for events. The mainloop function will
465      # return when the application is exited.
466      def main():
467          root = tkinter.Tk()
468          drawingApp = DrawingApplication(root)
469
470          drawingApp.mainloop()
471          print("Program_Execution_Completed.")
472
473      if __name__ == "__main__":
474          main()
```

20.2   The Scope Program

This is the sample program from the first chapter that illustrates the use of scope within a program. This program can be downloaded from the text's website.

```
1    import math
2
3
4    PI = math.pi
5
6    def area(radius):
7        global z
8        z = 6
9        theArea = PI * radius ** 2
10
11       return theArea
12
13
14   def main():
15       global z
16
17       historyOfPrompts = []
18       historyOfOutput = []
19
20       def getInput(prompt):
21           x = input(prompt)
22           historyOfPrompts.append(prompt)
23
24           return x
25
26       def showOutput(val):
27           historyOfOutput.append(val)
28           print(val)
29
30       rString = getInput("Please_enter_the_radius_of_a_circle:")
```

```
31
32          r = float(rString)
33
34          val = area(r)
35          print(z)
36          showOutput("The area of the circle is" + str(val))
37
38    if __name__ == "__main__":
39          main()
```

20.3   The Sort Animation

```
1     import tkinter
2     import turtle
3     import random
4     import time
5     import math
6
7     class Point(turtle.RawTurtle):
8         def __init__(self, canvas, x, y):
9             super().__init__(canvas)
10            canvas.register_shape("dot",((3,0),(2,2),(0,3),(−2,2),(−3,0),(−2,−2),(0,−3),(2,−2)))
11            self.shape("dot")
12            self.speed(0)
13            self.penup()
14            self.goto(x,y)
15
16        def __str__(self):
17            return "("+str(self.xcor())+","+str(self.ycor())+")"
18
19        def __lt__(self, other):
20            return self.ycor() < other.ycor()
21
22    # This class defines the animation application. The following line says that
23    # the SortAnimation class inherits from the Frame class.
24    class SortAnimation(tkinter.Frame):
25        def __init__(self, master=None):
26            super().__init__(master)
27            self.pack()
28            self.buildWindow()
29            self.paused = False
30            self.stop = False
31            self.running = False
32
33
34        def buildWindow(self):
35
36            def partition(seq, start, stop):
37                pivotIndex = start
38                pivot = seq[pivotIndex]
39
40                theTurtle.color("red")
41                theTurtle.penup()
42                theTurtle.goto(start,pivot.ycor())
43                theTurtle.pendown()
44                theTurtle.goto(stop,pivot.ycor())
45                screen.update()
46
47                # Why twice? Because once doesn't seem to display
48                # the line the first time through for some reason
```

```
49          theTurtle.color("red")
50          theTurtle.penup()
51          theTurtle.goto(start,pivot.ycor())
52          theTurtle.pendown()
53          theTurtle.goto(stop,pivot.ycor())
54          screen.update()
55
56          i = start+1
57          j = stop-1
58
59          while i <= j:
60              while i <= j and not pivot < seq[i]:
61                  i+=1
62              while i <= j and pivot < seq[j]:
63                  j-=1
64
65              if i < j:
66                  tmp = seq[i]
67                  seq[i] = seq[j]
68                  seq[i].goto(i,seq[i].ycor())
69                  seq[j] = tmp
70                  seq[j].goto(j,seq[j].ycor())
71                  screen.update()
72                  i+=1
73                  j-=1
74
75          seq[pivotIndex] = seq[j]
76          seq[pivotIndex].goto(pivotIndex,seq[pivotIndex].ycor())
77          seq[j] = pivot
78          seq[j].goto(j,seq[j].ycor())
79          seq[j].color("green")
80          screen.update()
81
82          theTurtle.color("white")
83          theTurtle.penup()
84          theTurtle.goto(0,pivot.ycor())
85          theTurtle.pendown()
86          theTurtle.goto(len(seq),pivot.ycor())
87          screen.update()
88
89          return j
90
91
92      def quicksortRecursively(seq, start, stop):
93          if start >= stop:
94              return
95
96          if stopping():
97              return
98
99          pivotIndex = partition(seq, start, stop)
100
101         if stopping():
102             return
103
104         quicksortRecursively(seq, start, pivotIndex)
105
106         if stopping():
107             return
108
109         quicksortRecursively(seq, pivotIndex+1, stop)
110
111     def quicksort(seq):
112         quicksortRecursively(seq, 0, len(seq))
113
114     def merge(seq, start, mid, stop):
115         length = stop - start
```

```
116                    log = math.log(length,2)
117
118                    theTurtle.color("blue")
119                    theTurtle.penup()
120                    theTurtle.goto(start,-3*log)
121                    theTurtle.pendown()
122                    theTurtle.forward(length)
123                    screen.update()
124
125                    lst = []
126                    i = start
127                    j = mid
128
129                    # Merge the two lists while each has more elements
130                    while i < mid and j < stop:
131                        if seq[i] < seq[j]:
132                            lst.append(seq[i])
133                            seq[i].goto(i,seq[i].ycor())
134                            i+=1
135                        else:
136                            lst.append(seq[j])
137                            seq[j].goto(j,seq[j].ycor())
138                            j+=1
139                        #screen.update()
140
141                    # Copy in the rest of the start to mid sequence
142                    while i < mid:
143                        lst.append(seq[i])
144                        seq[i].goto(i,seq[i].ycor())
145                        i+=1
146                        #screen.update()
147
148                    # Copy in the rest of the mid to stop sequence
149                    while j < mid:
150                        lst.append(seq[j])
151                        seq[j].goto(j,seq[j].ycor())
152                        j+=1
153                        #screen.update()
154
155                    # Copy the elements back to the original sequence
156                    for i in range(len(lst)):
157                        seq[start+i]=lst[i]
158                        lst[i].goto(start+i,lst[i].ycor())
159                        lst[i].color("green")
160                        screen.update()
161
162                def mergeSortRecursively(seq, start, stop):
163                    # We must use >= here only when the sequence we are sorting
164                    # is empty. Otherwise start == stop-1 in the base case.
165                    if start >= stop-1:
166                        return
167
168                    mid = (start + stop) // 2
169
170                    if stopping():
171                        return
172
173                    length = stop-start
174                    log = math.log(length,2)
175
176                    theTurtle.color("red")
177                    theTurtle.penup()
178                    theTurtle.goto(start,-3*log)
179                    theTurtle.pendown()
180                    theTurtle.forward(length)
181                    screen.update()
182
```

```
183              # Why twice? Because once doesn't seem to display
184              # the line the first time through for some reason
185              theTurtle.color("red")
186              theTurtle.penup()
187              theTurtle.goto(start,-3*log)
188              theTurtle.pendown()
189              theTurtle.forward(length)
190              screen.update()
191
192              mergeSortRecursively(seq, start, mid)
193
194              if stopping():
195                  return
196
197              mergeSortRecursively(seq, mid, stop)
198
199              if stopping():
200                  return
201
202              theTurtle.color("blue")
203              theTurtle.penup()
204              theTurtle.goto(start,-3*log)
205              theTurtle.pendown()
206              theTurtle.forward(length)
207              screen.update()
208
209              merge(seq, start, mid, stop)
210
211              screen.update()
212              theTurtle.color("white")
213              theTurtle.goto(start -1,-3*log)
214              theTurtle.pendown()
215              theTurtle.forward(length+2)
216              screen.update()
217
218      def mergeSort(seq):
219              mergeSortRecursively(seq, 0, len(seq))
220
221      def select(seq, start):
222              minIndex = start
223              seq[minIndex].color("green")
224
225              for i in range(start, len(seq)):
226                  if seq[minIndex] > seq[i]:
227                      seq[minIndex].color("black")
228                      minIndex = i
229                      seq[minIndex].color("green")
230
231              return minIndex
232
233      def selectionSort(seq):
234              for i in range(len(seq)):
235                  minIndex = select(seq, i)
236                  if stopping():
237                      return
238                  tmp = seq[i]
239                  seq[i] = seq[minIndex]
240                  seq[minIndex] = tmp
241                  seq[i].goto(i,seq[i].ycor())
242                  seq[minIndex].goto(minIndex,seq[minIndex].ycor())
243                  seq[i].color("green")
244
245      def pause():
246              while self.paused:
247                  time.sleep(1)
248                  screen.update()
249                  screen.listen()
```

```
250
251        def stopping ():
252            if self.paused:
253                pause()
254
255            if self.stop:
256                self.pause = False
257                self.running = False
258                screen.update()
259                screen.listen()
260                return True
261
262            return False
263
264        self.master.title("Sort_Animations")
265
266        bar = tkinter.Menu(self.master)
267        fileMenu = tkinter.Menu(bar,tearoff=0)
268
269        def clear ():
270            screen.clear()
271            screen.update()
272            screen.listen()
273
274        def newWindow ():
275            clear()
276            if self.running:
277                self.stop = True
278
279        fileMenu.add_command(label="Clear",command=newWindow)
280        fileMenu.add_command(label="Exit",command=self.master.quit)
281        bar.add_cascade(label="File",menu=fileMenu)
282        self.master.config(menu=bar)
283
284        canvas = tkinter.Canvas(self,width=600,height=600)
285        canvas.pack(side=tkinter.LEFT)
286
287        theTurtle = turtle.RawTurtle(canvas)
288        theTurtle.ht()
289        theTurtle.speed(0)
290        screen = theTurtle.getscreen()
291        screen.tracer(0)
292
293        sideBar = tkinter.Frame(self,padx=5,pady=5)
294        sideBar.pack(side=tkinter.RIGHT, fill=tkinter.BOTH)
295
296        speedLabel = tkinter.Label(sideBar,text="Animation_Speed")
297        speedLabel.pack()
298        speed = tkinter.StringVar()
299        speedEntry = tkinter.Entry(sideBar,textvariable=speed)
300        speedEntry.pack()
301        speed.set("10")
302
303        def selSortHandler ():
304            self.running = True
305            clear()
306            screen.setworldcoordinates(0,0,200,200)
307            screen.tracer(0)
308            self.master.title("Selection_Sort_Animation")
309            seq = []
310            for i in range(200):
311                if stopping():
312                    return
313
314                p = Point(screen,i,i)
315                p.color("green")
316                seq.append(p)
```

```
317
318            screen.update()
319            screen.tracer(1)
320
321            for i in range(200):
322                if stopping():
323                    return
324
325                j = random.randint(0,199)
326
327                p = seq[i]
328                seq[i] = seq[j]
329                seq[j] = p
330                seq[i].goto(i,seq[i].ycor())
331                seq[j].goto(j,seq[j].ycor())
332                seq[i].color("black")
333                seq[j].color("black")
334
335            selectionSort(seq)
336            self.running = False
337            self.stop = False
338
339         button = tkinter.Button(sideBar, text = "Selection_Sort", command=selSortHandler)
340         button.pack(fill=tkinter.BOTH)
341
342         def mergeSortHandler():
343            self.running = True
344            clear()
345            screen.setworldcoordinates(0,-25,200,200)
346            theTurtle.width(5)
347            screen.tracer(0)
348            self.master.title("Merge_Sort_Animation")
349            seq = []
350            for i in range(200):
351                if stopping():
352                    return
353
354                p = Point(screen,i,i)
355                p.color("green")
356                seq.append(p)
357
358            screen.update()
359            screen.tracer(1)
360            for i in range(200):
361                if stopping():
362                    return
363
364                j = random.randint(0,199)
365
366                p = seq[i]
367                seq[i] = seq[j]
368                seq[j] = p
369                seq[i].goto(i,seq[i].ycor())
370                seq[j].goto(j,seq[j].ycor())
371                seq[i].color("black")
372                seq[j].color("black")
373
374            screen.tracer(0)
375            mergeSort(seq)
376            self.running = False
377            self.stop = False
378
379         button = tkinter.Button(sideBar, text = "Merge_Sort", command=mergeSortHandler)
380         button.pack(fill=tkinter.BOTH)
381
382         def quickSortHandler():
383            self.running = True
```

```
384                    clear ()
385                    screen . setworldcoordinates (0 ,0 ,200 ,200)
386                    theTurtle . width (5)
387                    screen . tracer (0)
388                    self . master . title (" Quicksort_Animation ")
389                    seq = []
390                    for  i  in range (200):
391                        if  stopping ():
392                            return
393
394                        p = Point (screen ,i ,i )
395                        p . color (" green ")
396                        seq . append (p)
397
398                    screen . update ()
399                    screen . tracer (1)
400                    for  i  in range (200):
401                        if  stopping ():
402                            return
403
404                        j  = random . randint (0 ,199)
405
406                        p = seq [i]
407                        seq [i] = seq [j]
408                        seq [j] = p
409                        seq [i] . goto (i ,seq [i] . ycor ())
410                        seq [j] . goto (j ,seq [j] . ycor ())
411                        seq [i] . color (" black ")
412                        seq [j] . color (" black ")
413
414                    screen . tracer (1)
415                    quicksort (seq)
416                    self . running = False
417                    self . stop = False
418
419
420                button = tkinter . Button (sideBar , text = " Quicksort ", command=quickSortHandler )
421                button . pack ( fill =tkinter .BOTH)
422
423                def  pauseHandler ():
424                    self . paused = not  self . paused
425
426                button = tkinter . Button (sideBar , text = " Pause ", command=pauseHandler )
427                button . pack ( fill =tkinter .BOTH)
428
429                def  stopHandler ():
430                    if not  self . paused and  self . running :
431                        self . stop = True
432
433                button = tkinter . Button (sideBar , text = " Stop ", command=stopHandler )
434                button . pack ( fill =tkinter .BOTH)
435
436                screen . listen ()
437
438    # The  main  function  in  our  GUI  program  is  very  simple . It  creates  the
439    # root  window . Then  it  creates  the  SortAnimation  frame  which  creates
440    # all  the  widgets  and  has  the  logic  for  the  event  handlers . Calling  mainloop
441    # on  the  frames  makes  it  start  listening  for  events . The  mainloop  function  will
442    # return  when  the  application  is  exited .
443    def main ():
444        root = tkinter . Tk ()
445        anim = SortAnimation (root)
446
447        anim . mainloop ()
448
449    if  __name__ == " __main__ ":
450        main ()
```

20.4   The PlotData Program

This is the plot program that is used throughout the text to plot experimentally
gathered data so it can be visualized. This program can be downloaded from the
text's website.

```python
1    import turtle
2    import tkinter
3    import tkinter.colorchooser
4    import tkinter.filedialog
5    import xml.dom.minidom
6    import math
7    import sys
8
9    class PlotApplication(tkinter.Frame):
10       def __init__(self, master=None, datafile=None):
11           super().__init__(master)
12           self.datafile = datafile
13           self.pack()
14           self.buildWindow()
15
16
17       def buildWindow(self):
18
19           self.master.title("Plot")
20
21           bar = tkinter.Menu(self.master)
22           fileMenu = tkinter.Menu(bar, tearoff=0)
23
24           def loadFile(filename=None):
25
26               if filename == None:
27                   filename = tkinter.filedialog.askopenfilename(title="Select_a_Plot_File")
28
29               theTurtle.clear()
30               theTurtle.penup()
31               theTurtle.goto(0,0)
32               theTurtle.pendown()
33               screen.update()
34               theTurtle.color("black")
35
36               xmldoc = xml.dom.minidom.parse(filename)
37
38               plotElement = xmldoc.getElementsByTagName("Plot")[0]
39
40               attr = plotElement.attributes
41               self.master.title(attr["title"].value)
42
43               axesElement = plotElement.getElementsByTagName("Axes")[0]
44
45               xAxisElement = axesElement.getElementsByTagName("XAxis")[0]
46               xAxisLabel = xAxisElement.firstChild.data.strip()
47
48               yAxisElement = axesElement.getElementsByTagName("YAxis")[0]
49               yAxisLabel = yAxisElement.firstChild.data.strip()
50
51               xAttr = xAxisElement.attributes
52               yAttr = yAxisElement.attributes
53
54               minX = float(xAttr["min"].value)
55               maxX = float(xAttr["max"].value)
56               minY = float(yAttr["min"].value)
57               maxY = float(yAttr["max"].value)
58
59               xSize = maxX - minX
60               ySize = maxY - minY
61               xCenter = xSize / 2.0 + minX
62               yCenter = ySize / 2.0 + minY
63
```

```
64              xPlaces = max(4−round(math.log(xSize,10)),0)
65              yPlaces = max(4−round(math.log(ySize,10)),0)
66
67              labelYVal = maxY − 0.10 * ySize
68
69              screen.setworldcoordinates(minX−0.20 * xSize,minY − 0.20 * ySize, \
70                  maxX + 0.20 * xSize,maxY + 0.20 * ySize)
71
72              theTurtle.ht()
73
74              theTurtle.penup()
75              theTurtle.goto(minX,minY)
76              theTurtle.pendown()
77              theTurtle.goto(maxX,minY)
78              theTurtle.penup()
79              theTurtle.goto(minX,minY)
80              theTurtle.pendown()
81              theTurtle.goto(minX,maxY)
82              theTurtle.penup()
83
84              theTurtle.goto(xCenter, minY − ySize * 0.10)
85              theTurtle.write(xAxisLabel,align="center",font=("Arial",14,"bold"))
86
87              theTurtle.goto(minX, maxY + 0.05 * ySize)
88              theTurtle.write(yAxisLabel,align="center",font=("Arial",14,"bold"))
89
90              for i in range(0,101,10):
91                  x = minX + xSize * i / 100.0
92                  y = minY + ySize * i / 100.0
93
94                  theTurtle.penup()
95                  theTurtle.goto(x,minY+ySize * 0.025)
96                  theTurtle.pendown()
97                  theTurtle.goto(x,minY−ySize * 0.025)
98                  theTurtle.penup()
99                  theTurtle.goto(x,minY−ySize * 0.05)
100
101                 theTurtle.write(("%1."+str(xPlaces)+"f")%x,align="center",font=("Arial",12,"normal"))
102
103                 theTurtle.penup()
104                 theTurtle.goto(minX+xSize * 0.025, y)
105                 theTurtle.pendown()
106                 theTurtle.goto(minX−xSize * 0.025, y)
107                 theTurtle.goto(minX−xSize * 0.001, y)
108                 theTurtle.write(("%1."+str(yPlaces)+"f")%y,align="right",font=("Arial",12,"normal"))
109
110
111             sequences = plotElement.getElementsByTagName("Sequence")
112
113             for sequence in sequences:
114                 attr = sequence.attributes
115
116                 label = attr["title"].value.strip()
117                 color = attr["color"].value
118                 theTurtle.color(color)
119                 theTurtle.penup()
120                 theTurtle.goto(xCenter, labelYVal)
121                 labelYVal = labelYVal − 0.10 * ySize
122                 theTurtle.write(label,align="center",font=("Arial",14,"bold"))
123
124                 dataPoints = sequence.getElementsByTagName("DataPoint")
125
126                 first = dataPoints[0]
127                 attr = first.attributes
128                 x = float(attr["x"].value)
129                 y = float(attr["y"].value)
130                 theTurtle.goto(x,y)
131                 theTurtle.dot()
132                 theTurtle.pendown()
133
134
```

```
135                        for dataPoint in dataPoints:
136                            attr = dataPoint.attributes
137                            x = float(attr["x"].value)
138                            y = float(attr["y"].value)
139                            theTurtle.goto(x,y)
140                            theTurtle.dot()
141
142                        screen.update()
143
144
145
146            fileMenu.add_command(label="Load_Plot_Data ... ",command=loadFile)
147
148            fileMenu.add_command(label="Exit",command=self.master.quit)
149
150            bar.add_cascade(label="File",menu=fileMenu)
151
152            self.master.config(menu=bar)
153
154            canvas = tkinter.Canvas(self,width=1000,height=800)
155            canvas.pack(side=tkinter.LEFT)
156
157            theTurtle = turtle.RawTurtle(canvas)
158
159            screen = theTurtle.getscreen()
160
161            screen.tracer(0)
162
163            if self.datafile != None:
164                loadFile(self.datafile.strip())
165
166    def main():
167        root = tkinter.Tk()
168        datafile = None
169        if len(sys.argv) > 1:
170            datafile = sys.argv[1]
171        plotApp = PlotApplication(root, datafile)
172
173        plotApp.mainloop()
174        print("Program_Execution_Completed.")
175
176    if __name__ == "__main__":
177        main()
```

20.5   The Tic Tac Toe Application

This is the starter code for an exercise in constructing a tic tac toe game. This program can be downloaded from the text's website.

```
1    from turtle import *
2    import tkinter.messagebox
3    import tkinter
4    import random
5    import math
6    import datetime
7    import time
8    import sys
9
10   screenMin = 0
11   screenMax = 300
12   Human = -1
13   Computer = 1
14
15   class Board:
16       # When a board is constructed, you may want to make a copy of the board.
```

```
17          # This can be a shallow copy of the board because Turtle objects are
18          # Immutable from the perspective of a board object.
19          def __init__(self, board=None, screen=None):
20              self.screen = screen
21              if screen == None:
22                  if board!=None:
23                      self.screen = board.screen
24
25              self.items = []
26              for i in range(3):
27                  rowlst = []
28                  for j in range(3):
29                      if board==None:
30                          rowlst.append(Dummy())
31                      else:
32                          rowlst.append(board[i][j])
33
34                  self.items.append(rowlst)
35
36          # Accessor method for the screen
37          def getscreen(self):
38              return self.screen
39
40          # The getitem method is used to index into the board. It should
41          # return a row of the board. That row itself is indexable (it is just
42          # a list) so accessing a row and column in the board can be written
43          # board[row][column] because of this method.
44          def __getitem__(self, index):
45              return self.items[index]
46
47          # This method should return true if the two boards, self and other,
48          # represent exactly the same state.
49          # READER EXERCISE: YOU MUST COMPLETE THIS FUNCTION
50          def __eq__(self, other):
51              pass
52
53          # This method will mutate this board to contain all dummy
54          # turtles. This way the board can be reset when a new game
55          # is selected. It should NOT be used except when starting
56          # a new game.
57          def reset(self):
58
59              self.screen.tracer(1)
60              for i in range(3):
61                  for j in range(3):
62                      self.items[i][j].goto(-100,-100)
63                      self.items[i][j] = Dummy()
64
65              self.screen.tracer(0)
66
67          # This method should return an integer representing the
68          # state of the board. If the computer has won, return 1.
69          # If the human has won, return -1. Otherwise, return 0.
70          # READER EXERCISE: YOU MUST COMPLETE THIS FUNCTION
71          def eval(self):
72              pass
73
74          # This method should return True if the board
75          # is completely filled up (no dummy turtles).
76          # Otherwise, it should return False.
77          # READER EXERCISE: YOU MUST COMPLETE THIS FUNCTION
78          def full(self):
79              pass
80
81          # This method should draw the X's and O's
82          # Of this board on the screen.
83          def drawXOs(self):
84
```

```
85              for row in range (3):
86                  for col in range (3):
87                      if self [row][col].eval() != 0:
88                          self [row][col].st()
89                          self [row][col].goto (col*100+50,row*100+50)
90
91              self.screen.update ()
92
93      # This class is just for placeholder objects when no move has been made
94      # yet at a position in the board. Having eval () return 0 is convenient when no
95      # move has been made.
96      class Dummy:
97          def __init__ (self ):
98              pass
99
100         def eval (self ):
101             return 0
102
103         def goto (self ,x ,y ):
104             pass
105
106     # In the X and O classes below the constructor begins by initializing the
107     # RawTurtle part of the object with the call to super ().__init__ (canvas). The
108     # super () call returns the class of the superclass (the class above the X or O
109     # in the class hierarchy). In this case, the superclass is RawTurtle. Then,
110     # calling __init__ on the superclass initializes the part of the object that is
111     # a RawTurtle. class X(RawTurtle ):
112         def __init__ (self , canvas ):
113             super ().__init__ (canvas)
114             self.ht ()
115             self.getscreen ().register_shape ("X",((-40,-36),(-40,-44),(0,-4),(40,-44),(40,-36), \
116                                 (4 ,0),(40,36),(40,44),(0,4),(-40,44),(-40,36),(-4,0),(-40,-36)))
117             self.shape ("X")
118             self.penup ()
119             self.speed (5)
120             self.goto (-100,-100)
121
122         def eval (self ):
123             return Computer
124
125     class O(RawTurtle ):
126         def __init__ (self , canvas ):
127             super ().__init__ (canvas)
128             self.ht ()
129             self.shape ("circle")
130             self.penup ()
131             self.speed (5)
132             self.goto (-100,-100)
133
134         def eval (self ):
135             return Human
136
137     # The minimax function is given a player (1 = Computer, -1 = Human) and a
138     # board object. When the player = Computer, minimax returns the maximum
139     # value of all possible moves that the Computer could make. When the player =
140     # Human then minimax returns the minimum value of all possible moves the Human
141     # could make. Minimax works by assuming that at each move the Computer will pick
142     # its best move and the Human will pick its best move. It does this by making a
143     # move for the player whose turn it is, and then recursively calling minimax.
144     # The base case results when, given the state of the board, someone has won or
145     # the board is full.
146     # READER EXERCISE: YOU MUST
147     COMPLETE THIS FUNCTION
148     def minimax (player ,board ):
149         pass
150
151
152
```

```
153  class TicTacToe(tkinter.Frame):
154      def __init__(self, master=None):
155          super().__init__(master)
156          self.pack()
157          self.buildWindow()
158          self.paused = False
159          self.stop = False
160          self.running = False
161          self.turn = Human
162          self.locked = False
163
164      def buildWindow(self):
165
166          cv = ScrolledCanvas(self,600,600,600,600)
167          cv.pack(side = tkinter.LEFT)
168          t = RawTurtle(cv)
169          screen = t.getscreen()
170          screen.tracer(100000)
171
172          screen.setworldcoordinates(screenMin,screenMin,screenMax,screenMax)
173          screen.bgcolor("white")
174          t.ht()
175
176          frame = tkinter.Frame(self)
177          frame.pack(side = tkinter.RIGHT, fill=tkinter.BOTH)
178          board = Board(None, screen)
179
180          def drawGrid():
181              screen.clear()
182              screen.tracer(1000000)
183              screen.setworldcoordinates(screenMin,screenMin,screenMax,screenMax)
184              screen.bgcolor("white")
185              screen.tracer(0)
186              t = RawTurtle(cv)
187              t.ht()
188              t.pu()
189              t.width(10)
190              t.color("green")
191              for i in range(2):
192                  t.penup()
193                  t.goto(i*100+100,10)
194                  t.pendown()
195                  t.goto(i*100+100,290)
196                  t.penup()
197                  t.goto(10,i*100+100)
198                  t.pendown()
199                  t.goto(290,i*100+100)
200
201              screen.update()
202
203
204          def newGame():
205              #drawGrid()
206              self.turn = Human
207              board.reset()
208              self.locked =False
209              screen.update()
210
211
212          def startHandler():
213              newGame()
214
215          drawGrid()
216
217          startButton = tkinter.Button(frame, text = "New_Game", command=startHandler)
218          startButton.pack()
219
220
```

```
221         def quitHandler():
222             self.master.quit()
223
224         quitButton = tkinter.Button(frame, text = "Quit", command=quitHandler)
225         quitButton.pack()
226
227         def computerTurn():
228             # The locked variable prevents another event from being
229             # processed while the computer is making up its mind.
230             self.locked = True
231
232             # Call Minimax to find the best move to make.
233             # READER EXERCISE: YOU MUST COMPLETE THIS CODE
234             # After writing this code, the maxMove tuple should
235             # contain the best move for the computer. For instance,
236             # if the best move is in the first row and third column
237             # then maxMove would be (0,2).
238
239             row, col = maxMove
240             board[row][col] = X(cv)
241             self.locked = False
242
243
244         def mouseClick(x,y):
245             if not self.locked:
246                 row = int(y // 100)
247                 col = int(x // 100)
248
249                 board[row][col] = O(cv)
250
251                 self.turn = Computer
252
253                 board.drawXOs()
254
255                 if not board.full() and not abs(board.eval())==1:
256                     computerTurn()
257
258                     self.turn = Human
259
260                     board.drawXOs()
261                 else:
262                     self.locked = True
263
264                 if board.eval() == 1:
265                     tkinter.messagebox.showwarning("Game_Over","X_wins!!!")
266
267                 if board.eval() == -1:
268                     tkinter.messagebox.showwarning("Game_Over","O_wins._How_did_that_happen?")
269
270                 if board.full():
271                     tkinter.messagebox.showwarning("Game_Over","It_was_a_tie.")
272
273         screen.onclick(mouseClick)
274
275         screen.listen()
276
277 def main():
278     root = tkinter.Tk()
279     root.title("Tic_Tac_Toe")
280     application = TicTacToe(root)
281     application.mainloop()
282
283 if __name__ == "__main__":
284     main()
```

20.6   The Connect Four Front-End

This provides the GUI front-end to the connect four game presented in the last chapter of the text. This can serve as a front-end for a computer opponent back-end. This program can be downloaded from the text's website.

```
1   import turtle
2   import subprocess
3   import tkinter
4   import sys
5   import time
6
7   # The following program will play connect four. This
8   # program and a another program communicate through pipes (both input and output)
9   # according to this architecture. When a command is sent it is indicated
10  # with a right arrow indicating something is written to the other program's
11  # standard input. When the other program sends something to this Python Program
12  # it is indicated with a left arrow. That means it is written to the standard
13  # output of the other program.
14
15  # Python        Other
16  #   0 ————————>        # New Game is initiated by the Other Code
17  #   <———————— 0        # Other Code says OK.
18  #   2 M ——————>        # Human Move followed by Move Value M which is 0-6.
19  #                      # Move Value M will be on separate line.
20  #   <———————— 0        # Other Code says OK.
21  #   1 ————————>        # Computer Move is indicated to Other Code
22  #   <———————— 0 M      # Status OK and Move Value M which is 0-6.
23  #   3 ————————>        # Game Over?
24  #   <———————— Val      # Val is 0=Not Over, 1=Computer Won, 2=Human Won, 3=Tie.
25
26  # This architecture must be adhered to strictly for this program to work. Here
27  # is sample Lisp code that will handle this interaction. However, the other
28  # program may be written in any programming language, including Python.
29
30  #(defun play ()
31    #(let ((gameBoard (make-hash-table :size 10))
32          #(memo (make-hash-table :size 27 :test #'equalp))
33          #(lastMove nil))
34
35      #(do () (nil nil)
36        #;(printBoard gameBoard)
37        #(let ((msgId (read)))
38          #(cond ((equal msgId 2) ;; Human turn to call human turn function
39              #(setf lastMove (humanTurn gameBoard)))
40
41              #((equal msgId 0) ;; New Game message
42              #(progn
43                #(setf gameBoard (make-hash-table :size 10))
44                #(setf memo (make-hash-table :size 27 :test #'equalp))
45                #(format t "0~%")))
46                #;; Return a 0 to indicate the computer is ready
47
48              #((equal msgId 1) ;; Computer Turn message
49              #(setf lastMove (computerTurn gameBoard)))
50
51              #((equal msgId 3) ;; Get Game Status
52
53              #(cond ((equal (evalBoard gameBoard lastMove) 1) (format t "1~%"))
54                    #;; The Computer Won
55
56                    #((equal (evalBoard gameBoard lastMove) -1) (format t "2~%"))
57                    #;; The Human Won
58
59                    #((fullBoard gameBoard) (format t "3~%"))
```

```
60                          #;; It's a draw
61
62                          #(t (format t "0~%"))))
63                          #;; The game is not over yet.
64
65                    #(t (format t "-1~%")))))))
66
67   Computer = 1 Human = -1
68
69   class Tile(turtle.RawTurtle):
70       def __init__(self,canvas,row,col,app):
71           super().__init__(canvas)
72           self.val = 0
73           self.row = row
74           self.col = col
75           self.tttApplication = app
76           self.penup()
77           self.ht()
78           self.goto(col*100+50,row*100+50)
79
80       def setShape(self,horc,screen):
81           self.val = horc
82
83           if horc == Computer:
84               self.shape("blackchecker.gif")
85           else:
86               self.shape("redchecker.gif")
87
88           self.drop(screen)
89
90       def getOwner(self):
91           return self.val
92
93       def clicked(self):
94           print(self.row,self.col)
95
96       def drop(self,screen):
97           self.goto(self.col*100+50,0)
98           screen.tracer(1)
99           self.speed(5)
100          self.st()
101          self.goto(self.col*100+50,self.row*100+55)
102          self.goto(self.col*100+50,self.row*100+45)
103          self.goto(self.col*100+50,self.row*100+50)
104          screen.tracer(0)
105
106  class Connect4Application(tkinter.Frame):
107      def __init__(self, master=None):
108          super().__init__(master)
109          self.pack()
110          self.buildWindow()
111          self.running = False
112
113      def buildWindow(self):
114
115          self.master.title("Connect_Four")
116
117          bar = tkinter.Menu(self.master)
118          fileMenu = tkinter.Menu(bar,tearoff=0)
119
120          fileMenu.add_command(label="Exit",command=self.master.quit)
121
122          bar.add_cascade(label="File",menu=fileMenu)
123
124          self.master.config(menu=bar)
125
126
```

```
127            canvas = tkinter.Canvas(self,width=700,height=600)
128            canvas.pack(side=tkinter.LEFT)
129
130            theTurtle = turtle.RawTurtle(canvas)
131            theTurtle.ht()
132            screen = theTurtle.getscreen()
133            screen.setworldcoordinates(0,600,700,0)
134            screen.register_shape("blackchecker.gif")
135            screen.register_shape("redchecker.gif")
136            screen.tracer(0)
137            screen.bgcolor("yellow")
138
139            theTurtle.width(5)
140            for k in range(6):
141                theTurtle.penup()
142                theTurtle.goto(k*100+100,0)
143                theTurtle.pendown()
144                theTurtle.goto(k*100+100,600)
145
146            theTurtle.ht()
147
148            screen.update()
149
150            def checkStatus():
151                toOther.write("3\n")
152                toOther.flush()
153
154                status = int(fromOther.readline().strip())
155
156                if status == 1:
157                    tkinter.messagebox.showinfo("Game_Over", "I_Won!!!!!")
158                elif status == 2:
159                    tkinter.messagebox.showinfo("Game_Over", "You_Won!!!!!")
160                elif status == 3:
161                    tkinter.messagebox.showinfo("Game_Over", "It's_a_tie.")
162
163                #print("Status is", status)
164                return status
165
166            def ComputerTurn():
167                toOther.write("1\n")
168                toOther.flush()
169                status = int(fromOther.readline().strip())
170                #print("Computer Turn Other Status =", status)
171                if status == 0:
172                    move = int(fromOther.readline())
173                    #print("Move is", move)
174                    row = move // 7
175                    col = move % 7
176
177                    matrix[row][col].setShape(Computer,screen)
178                    screen.update()
179
180            def HumanTurn(x,y):
181                if self.running:
182                    return
183
184                #status = checkStatus()
185
186                #if status != 0:
187                    #return              .
188
189                self.running = True
190                col = int(x) // 100
191
192                row = 5
193                while row >= 0 and matrix[row][col].isvisible():
```

```
194                    row = row - 1
195
196              if row < 0:
197                  #Then we clicked in a column that was already full.
198                  self.running = True
199                  return
200
201              val = row * 7 + col
202
203              # Do the Human Turn
204              toOther.write("2\n")
205              toOther.flush()
206              toOther.write(str(val) + "\n")
207              toOther.flush()
208
209              status = fromOther.readline().strip()
210              #print("Status is", status)
211
212              matrix[row][col].setShape(Human, screen)
213              screen.update()
214
215              # Check the status of the game
216              status = checkStatus()
217
218              if status == 0:
219                  # Do a Computer Turn
220                  ComputerTurn()
221                  checkStatus()
222
223              self.running = False
224
225
226          matrix = []
227
228          for i in range(6):
229              row = []
230              for j in range(7):
231                  t = Tile(canvas, i, j, self)
232                  row.append(t)
233              matrix.append(row)
234
235          screen.update()
236          screen.onclick(HumanTurn)
237
238          sideBar = tkinter.Frame(self, padx=5, pady=5, relief=tkinter.RAISED, borderwidth="5pt")
239          sideBar.pack(side=tkinter.RIGHT, fill=tkinter.BOTH)
240
241          def NewGame():
242              toOther.write("0\n")
243              toOther.flush()
244              status = int(fromOther.readline().strip())
245
246              for row in matrix:
247                  for token in row:
248                      token.ht()
249
250              screen.update()
251
252          kb = tkinter.Button(sideBar, text="Pass", command=ComputerTurn)
253          kb.pack()
254
255          ng = tkinter.Button(sideBar, text="New_Game", command=NewGame)
256          ng.pack()
257
258
259          proc = subprocess.Popen(["clisp", "c4.fas"], stdout=subprocess.PIPE, \
260              stdin=subprocess.PIPE, universal_newlines=True)
```

```
261                fromOther = proc.stdout
262                toOther = proc.stdin
263
264                # To write to the other program you should use commands like this
265                # toOther.write(val+"\n")
266                # Don't forget to flush the buffer
267                # toOther.flush()
268
269                # To read from the other program you write
270                # line = fromOther.readline().strip()
271
272
273
274    def main():
275        root = tkinter.Tk()
276        animApp = Connect4Application(root)
277
278        animApp.mainloop()
279        print("Program_Execution_Completed.")
280
281    if __name__ == "__main__":
282        main()
```

Bibliography

1. Adelson-Veskii G, Landis EM (1962) An algorithm for the organization of information. Proc USSR Acad Sci 146:263–266
2. Carlis J, Maguire J (2000) Mastering data modeling: a user-driven approach. Addison-Wesley http://www.amazon.com/Mastering-Data-Modeling-User-Driven-Approach/dp/020170045X/ref=sr_1_1?s=books&ie=UTF8&qid=1404178333&sr=1-1
3. Coppin B (2004) Artificial intelligence illuminated. Jones and Bartlett, USA
4. Dijkstra EW (1959) A note on two problems in connexion with graphs. Nume Math 1:269–271
5. Kruskal JB (1956) On the shortest spanning tree of a graph and the traveling salesman problem. Proc Am Math Soc 7:48–50
6. Lutz M (2013) Learning Python. O'Reilly Media http://www.amazon.com/Learning-Python-Edition-Mark-Lutz/dp/1449355730/ref=sr_1_1?ie=UTF8&qid=1398871248&sr=8-1&keywords=learning+python+lutz
7. Tharp A (1988) File Organization and Processing. Wiley, New York
8. Wikipedia (2014) Bloom filter. Wikipedia.org http://en.wikipedia.org/wiki/Bloom_filter

© Springer International Publishing Switzerland 2015
K.D. Lee and S. Hubbard, *Data Structures and Algorithms with Python*,
Undergraduate Topics in Computer Science, DOI 10.1007/978-3-319-13072-9

Index

A
Algorithm, 1, 54–56
    recursive, 67, 68, 76
    sorting, 54, 56, 82, 100–102
Arithmetic
    modulo, 83, 206

B
Backtrack, 177, 179, 189, 192
Binary, 138, 143, 145, 166, 167
Bipartite, 204
Bloom filter, 205, 206
B-tree, 261

C
Canvas, 25–27, 115
Class, 3, 5, 6
Complexity, 41
    amortized, 58, 60, 62, 93
Computational complexity, 41, 50, 53, 54
Constructor, 6, 37, 93–95, 120

D
Database, 261, 263
Dict
    operators and methods, 309
Dictionary, 3, 4, 36, 38, 154–156, 159, 183, 237
    operators and methods, 309
    key, 4, 11, 27, 36, 38

E
Error
    run-time, 2
    syntax, 2, 168

Expression
    postfix, 166, 167, 169, 180

F
File, 3, 13–16
Float, 3–6, 8, 50
    operators, 301
Function, 2, 3, 10–13

G
Grammar, 33, 35, 168, 169
    tokens, 128, 129, 138, 168
Graph, 3, 11, 14, 15, 17, 20, 185
    bipartite, 204
    cycle, 187–189, 191
    dijkstra's algorithm, 185, 186, 197, 198
    edge, 186, 187
    kruskal's algorithm, 185, 186, 190, 191
    path, 185
    vertex, 186–189
    weighted, 188, 190, 197, 199

H
Hash, 56, 139, 144, 145
Hashtable
    map, 154–156, 159, 183, 237

© Springer International Publishing Switzerland 2015
K.D. Lee and S. Hubbard, *Data Structures and Algorithms with Python*,
Undergraduate Topics in Computer Science, DOI 10.1007/978-3-319-13072-9

Made in the USA
Lexington, KY
27 August 2015